TILL DEATH US DO PART

A True Murder Mystery

Also by Vincent Bugliosi

HELTER SKELTER:
  THE TRUE STORY OF THE MANSON MURDERS
      (*with Curt Gentry*)

Also by Ken Hurwitz:

MARCHING NOWHERE
THE LINE OF DAVID (*novel*)

TILL DEATH US DO PART

A True Murder Mystery

Vincent Bugliosi

with

Ken Hurwitz

 W·W·NORTON & COMPANY·INC

New York

With great appreciation to Jerry Cohen for all the help
he gave in the preparation of this book.

To my wife, Gail, and
my mother and father

The Los Angeles Police Department detectives did not know on December 11, 1966, the night of the first murder, that they would soon be drawn into a long, exhaustive pursuit that would lead them from the scene of a modest working-class neighborhood, circuitously but ever steadily into the fast, sporty lifestyles of Southern California, Baja, and Nevada. Nor did they know that it would take a series of unsolved, attempted murders and finally, a mysterious, terribly brutal second murder before the State of California would have what they believed to be sufficient evidence to commence a prosecution.

The job of that prosecution fell to me. Never before or since as a criminal lawyer have I been involved in a case that raised so many disturbing doubts as to what had actually happened.

Vincent T. Bugliosi
Los Angeles, California

Part I

1

LOS ANGELES IS a temptation. The chaise lounge, poolside life is everywhere. L.A. has its poverty and its struggles, but here perhaps more than any other place in the country, even the people near the bottom can, like the hired help in a mansion, reach out in almost any direction and touch a fantasy. From any one of the small stucco dwellings in Mar Vista a housewife can walk into her back yard and see the lights of twelve-room, split-level homes twinkling every night in the Hollywood Hills. Office clerks who live in hotter, smoggier Van Nuys drive to work in the city every morning over the eucalyptus shaded canyon roads of Beverly Hills. One cannot travel far on a freeway without passing a dozen Mercedes and maybe even a Bentley or two with a television personality sitting in the back seat. In Los Angeles, wealth can seem no more than a single business deal away. If you are young, you just have to hustle a little.

Hustling is everywhere. While, no doubt, the great majority of Angelenos live unpretentious, industrious lives, in a city of such magnitude there is still room for half a million on the make, people attaching themselves to fame and upward mobility by whatever means available. A liquor store owner displays glossy pictures of celebrity customers to attract those who want to buy their vodka where Dean Martin buys his. A thirteen year old girl announces proudly to a friend in a record store that her father sells John Denver his insurance. Nobody *feels* like a nobody.

Where there is not genuine prosperity there is often the façade of it. The movie industry's craft for creating illusion pervades. Apartment houses touted as "luxury" are slapped together almost faster than the bubble in a carpenter's level can settle. Although the Jacuzzi whirlpools they advertise may be roped off nearly every month for repairs, and the wallboard in the apartments may leak like papier-mâché with the first good winter rain, and though it may turn out that nearly all of the luxury budget was put into the building's fancily balustraded frontside, no one passing by on the street is the wiser and some even inside refuse to acknowledge the disappointments. It turns out the wet bars are extra, and half the Mercedes on those freeways are leased.

But somehow, the temptation never dims.

There is little wealth, real or pretended, in El Sereno, an old district on the east side of Los Angeles. The simple houses perched atop cement slabs do not vary. Their addresses belong to steeply inclined streets, narrow and winding. Many of the signs above the small grocery stores are lettered in Spanish. Milk is bought in the little half quarts.

In the early Sunday morning hours of December 11, 1966, Elbert Thompson, a post office clerk, the only black man in the Ballard Street neighborhood, was still not sleepy. He occupied himself with some late night reading. Shortly after 1:00 A.M., at last feeling drowsy, he inserted a marker rather than dog-ear the page of the library book, and after opening the bedroom window he joined his wife in bed. The air coming in from between the two closely built houses, his and the Stocktons', was crisp, freshly laundered by a fierce five day storm, and still smelled of rain and the sweet scent of vine and brush.

Above the scattered lights of the central city, only four miles distant, no one stirred in this hillside community.

But somewhere out in its darkness, someone watched. And waited.

At three in the morning, only one television set still flickered on Thompson's block. It was in the living room of the home next door. His neighbor, Henry Stockton, still up watching a late night movie, would not hear the door open slowly, nor would he pay attention to the small breeze which passed through his house.

At 3:30 A.M., Elbert Thompson awakened to a prickling sensation the residents of Southern California's thicketed hillsides never cease to dread. Lifting his head from the pillow, he saw, with horror, swirling flames a few feet outside his bedroom window. Throwing off the covers, Thompson pulled his still half-asleep wife from bed. Together they stumbled out into the cold night air to their tiny front yard where they had positioned a sprinkler and two hoses in case of just such a calamity. Each grabbed a hose, and in less than a minute they were pummeling their small house with water.

"It's not us!" Mrs. Thompson called through the smoke to her husband. She pointed to the Stockton house; it was the front bedroom of their neighbors' home that was ablaze.

Thompson turned his hose toward it and shouted over his shoulder to his wife to call the fire department. He edged closer to the flames and smoke. "Henry! Are you in there, Henry?" he yelled above the din of rushing hot air and hissing tar shingles. "Just give me a sign, and I'll come in!"

His heart sagged for Henry Stockton, that beefy, pleasant young man who looked so foolish on his tiny motor scooter, with his knees pointing out. The scooter could barely make it up the hill with the heavy fellow on it. He always asked the Thompsons if they needed anything at the store. Thompson had hardly ever seen Mrs. Stockton.

Within minutes, twisted overparked Ballard Street was a commotion of the red lights and sirens of Engine Company 16A. As the heavy hoses were wheeling off the trucks, Chester Willey, a seventeen-year veteran of the L.A. Fire Department, ran by himself up the front porch steps. Others rushed with axes to the side of the house, where most of the smoke was billowing. Willey found the screen on the front door closed but unlocked, and the door behind it ajar. The back door, other firemen were discovering, was closed but also unlocked.

Entering the house, Willey proceeded carefully into a living room filled with smoke, but still untouched by the flames. In the otherwise darkened room, a television set cast a diffuse glow, like headlights in a fog. Through the thick haze, Willey discerned a human form sitting eerily in front of the set. Drawing closer, he saw it to be a young, barrel-chested man, his head slumped to the side, blood trickling from his mouth. The television, Willey now observed, was merely crackling static, its screen snowy with a channel long since off the air.

Willey took hold of the man's legs—he was too heavy to lift—and began dragging him toward the front door. He was met at the porch by Captain Peter Pucio, and together they carried the victim onto the small front yard. The face they gazed down at on the scraggy grass had a look they had seen before. The mouth was agape; the eyelids were protuberant and purple with the blood collected behind them. There was no need to check for a pulse.

Squad cars from the Highland Park Division of the Los Angeles Police Department arrived. El Sereno is in their jurisdiction. As the sound of glass windows being shattered by firemen filtered down to the street, Sergeant Wayne Barone radioed for an ambulance. Waiting for its arrival, Barone climbed the slanted cement stairs that led to the pale yellow, one-story house. Pausing, he let his flashlight play across the body laid out on the front yard a few feet away. This was not a victim of fire. There were three holes in the left side of the head, blood matting the hair all around them. The victim's shirt unbuttoned, its flaps spread wide, Barone could also see that the man's entire upper torso was smeared with blood. A stream of it had run down and collected as a pool in the navel. And there were two more holes—in the chest. Sergeant Barone called homicide.

When the ambulance crew arrived, they pronounced the victim dead at the scene.

As the young paramedics performed that perfunctory task out on the front lawn, the fire fighters continued to pour water into the front bedroom, nearly all of which was charred. Departmental rules require that when the cause of fire is not "obviously accidental" the engine company captain is to call arson investigators. Captain Pucio did so, and just before 5:00 A.M., Merle Pugh, senior investigator for the L.A. Fire Department's Arson Investigation Section, arrived. By that time the fire had been "knocked down" but not entirely extinguished.

Pugh had investigated over five thousand fires. He moved quickly and efficiently. As he surveyed the damage inside the house, he estimated the fire had burned for approximately half an hour before detection.

On the floor of the front bedroom closet he found a pile of ashy clothing. It was not a random pile, spread out as when clothes fall off their separate hangers, but rather a compact one. A pile, Pugh's training dictated, that had possibly been constructed by human design. Directly above it, the metal pole where the clothes once hung was grotesquely warped by a particularly intense heat. Pugh believed he had found an origin of the fire.

Several of the drawers to the dresser were open. They had been open before the fire had started, Pugh was certain, because the varnish on their interiors was blistered by the heat. On the floor at the foot of the bed was another ashy pile of clothing. Inches above it, the bed's metal frame and springs were buckled up from the floor. Again, but less markedly, the result of a greater heat. Pugh looked back at the pile of clothing in the closet. Two independent origins of fire meant the crime of arson. Whether there had actually been two in this case, Merle Pugh could not be certain. In his report, he would merely term the fire "suspicious."

"Morning, George," Pugh said as he emerged from the house, flipping shut his notepad.

George Greene, coroner's investigator, nodded from where he knelt, yawned, and turned back to the body on the front lawn. The victim, now identified by his neighbor, Elbert Thompson, as Henry Stockton, was a Caucasian appearing to be in his late twenties. He was wearing a tan and white plaid shirt and khaki slacks, no underwear. In one pants pocket was a ring with fifteen keys on it and two sweepstake tickets. In the other a ten dollar bill.

Greene found five bullet wounds: one in the left temple, one just above the left tip of the nose, one near the left sideburn, and two in the upper right portion of the chest. One of those was directly into the breastbone, but the other was seemingly high and wide of its mark, near the collarbone.

Only around the head wounds was what is called "tattooing"—a pattern of small black dots caused by unburned gunpowder which, spraying out of a gun barrel, penetrates the skin around the wound. The confined (one to one and a half inches in diameter) as opposed to dispersed markings unmistakably indicated that the muzzle of the gun was nearly touching the victim's head when fired. Greene could not determine the sequence of the bullets. But from the absense of any signs of struggle in the living room and the presence of tattooing only around the head wounds, one could have speculated that the killer had come up on Henry Stockton, catching him unawares as he watched TV, fired three shots into the head, killing Stockton instantaneously, then stepped to the other side of the room and, as if taking target practice, pumped two more bullets into the slumped body. The first one was not very accurate, the second much better. There were, indeed, murderers of such mentality in this world; that sequence of events, although speculative, was grimly plausible.

At 5:30 A.M., Highland Park homicide detectives Joe F. Aguirre and R.J. Duretto made their way through the small crowd of policemen, firemen, and onlooking neighbors to the house at 2723 Ballard Street. Sergeant Aguirre, a man with dark luminous eyes, his black hair and mustache flecked with gray, stood with open notebook on the sagging front veranda, asking his questions of the firemen and police officers who were first to arrive at the scene. Because both the front and the back doors had been found unlocked and all the windows had been latched and unbroken, forcible entry appeared unlikely.

The critical step in police work—preserving the crime scene untouched for the experts (detectives, fingerprint specialists, blood analysts, etc.)—had been difficult in this case. Learning of the number of men who had already trudged through the house dragging hoses behind them, Aguirre jammed a second piece of gum in his mouth and shook his head.

While the police photographer he brought along snapped pictures of the body still out on the lawn, he went hunting for clues inside. On a flimsy TV tray next to the chair where the victim was found was an empty quart bottle of beer, no glass. It was a brand that Aguirre had never heard of—Old Timers Lager.

Also on the TV tray, ironically within reach of the victim, was Henry Stockton's own life insurance policy.

In the smaller back bedroom Aguirre found a disarray of toys and a small boy's clothing. In the living room, where the shooting had apparently taken place, the detective began taking detailed notes: the splatters of blood on the overstuffed chair Stockton had been sitting on, the streaks of it on the wall behind, a pair of woman's black gloves on the adjacent couch. On the floor was the strangest of the items: a white kitchen towel with a circle of blood on it—not a spot (i.e., filled in), but a *circle*.

Because there were no apparent signs of struggle, the LAPD neglected to take blood samples to determine if any belonged to someone other than the victim.

Rather oddly, there were five boxes of personal papers sitting on the dining room table. Aguirre rummaged through them and discovered two items of interest. One was a marriage certificate indicating Henry Stockton had married a Sandra Darcy Stockton on October 1, 1966, only ten weeks earlier. Because the last name on the certificate was the same, Aguirre assumed, correctly, that they had previously divorced and then remarried. The other item that caught Aguirre's eye was a receipt from Pachmayr Gun Works in Los Angeles. Receipt number: C886031. Type of weapon: Hi Standard .22 caliber Sentinel model revolver. Serial number: 757762. Description: blue

anodized, two-inch barrel; white grips. Date of sale: June 27, 1966.
Purchaser: Sandra Darcy Stockton.

Police officers who had seen the victim had all guessed his wounds
to have been made by .22 caliber bullets.

A quick, second look at Henry Stockton's insurance policy revealed that the beneficiary was also the wife, Sandra Stockton.

The widow's gun receipt in the dining room, the insurance policy
in the living room naming the widow as beneficiary—it was all too
pat. Someone, it would seem, had left an intentional trail that led sug-
gestively to the victim's spouse. But as Aguirre began mulling over
theories, his questions led him only to greater puzzlement. If Stockton's murderer had been trying to throw suspicion in the direction of
the wife, whose whereabouts this morning were still unknown, why
had he (or she) set the house on fire? That would only destroy the
very documents that directed the suspicion towards her.

On the other hand, the fire had been set in a bedroom, and the gun
receipt, insurance policy, and victim had been found in the living and
dining rooms, where the fire had not yet even touched. Was it then
not possible that the murderer had been even more subtle than
Aguirre had first considered? Had a clever killer set the fire only to
make it *appear* there had been no frame-up, gambling that the fire
would be extinguished before the flames consumed the house and the
documents with it?

Aguirre radioed his watch commander to send fingerprint experts.
After giving officers at the scene instructions to "seal" the house, he
loaded up the back seat of a squad car with the five boxes of papers
(along with the insurance policy), and took them down to Highland
Park headquarters.

It had been a year and a half since Vicky Stowe had last seen her
childhood friend, Sandra Stockton. Since that time, it had only been a
Christmas card from Sandra, not quite a year ago. With her own husband, a marine, having just shipped off to Vietnam, it was a pleasant
surprise for Vicky when her old friend telephoned her on December
2 and suggested they spend the following weekend together. Henry
had to work Saturday, December 10, Sandra had explained. How
would it be if she and Kyle, their four-year-old son, came out to
Twentynine Palms for the weekend? Twentynine Palms was only one
hundred and forty miles east of Los Angeles.

"Terrific," Vicky said. "Tell Kyle we'll take him horseback riding." There were stables for the enlisted men's families at the Marine base.

When the two women met Friday evening, Vicky was stunned by Sandra's new appearance. From having once looked like a matronly bookkeeper, the metamorphosis was almost total.

All her life Sandra had had a considerable weight problem, exacerbated as an adult by her taste for epicurean meals and her ability to cook them. Only five feet, two inches tall, she had bulged to a round, jointless looking two hundred pounds just after her first marriage to Henry. Now she was down to a plump but shapely 125 pounds. Health spas and singles bars were twenty-six-year-old Sandra's explanation, which she offered with a laugh.

Even more dramatically, her pilgrimishly simple, blue-eyed face had been made over with carefully brushed mascara and glistening pink lipstick, the heavy-rimmed glasses were gone and replaced by contacts, the once unremarkable teeth newly capped. Sandra's tumbleweed brown hair was now teased and dyed a striking blond—like that of a convent runaway having overdone her months of freedom as a cigarette girl.

It was astonishing, Vicky thought. If she had met Sandra under any situation other than this prearranged one, she probably would not have even recognized her. It was not the same person.

The good news this Christmas, Sandra told a staring Vicky, was that she and Henry were happily back together again.

Saturday, while Vicky's children and Kyle, a bouncy youngster with soft curly hair, played outside, Vicky and Sandra sat on the back porch steps and recalled their own school days with wistful laughter.

"Remember the first time you stayed overnight?" Sandra smiled kiddingly. "You couldn't believe mom read us *The Prophet* every night like it was the Bible. Wow, you gave me this look like, 'but they don't teach Kahlil Gibran in Sunday schools. Oh-oh, maybe this family's really a secret cult of some kind.'"

Vicky rocked her shoulder affectionately against Sandra's, accepting the needling.

Early Sunday morning, as Vicky fixed breakfast, the phone rang.

It was Sandra's father, Ted Bingham, asking to speak with his daughter. Vicky handed over the phone. In a moment, Sandra sank back against the refrigerator. She turned pale, and the hand holding the receiver began to tremble. In another minute she hung up and, in a restrained voice, managed to get out, "Henry's *dead.*"

Motioning Vicky away, she reeled toward the bathroom. For several minutes, Vicky, helpless, heard the sobbing. When Sandra emerged, she seemed in a daze. Vicky steered her to the living room couch and gave her a tranquilizer.

It was all very confusing, Sandra stammered. Her parents had received a call from Betty Stockton, Henry's mother. She had been so hysterical, the Binghams had barely been able to understand her sentences. The circumstances were still unclear, but one fact was not mistaken—Henry had been shot dead.

"How in God's name do I tell Kyle?" Sandra asked Vicky, pressing her fingertips to her eyes. They decided it would best be done at home.

"We better take him horseback riding like we promised," Sandra said.

She stared at the floor. "Yeah, that's what we'll do," she said, almost defiantly.

For twenty minutes, while Sandra stood by herself near the tack room, Vicky led her horse around the small track, first with her own children, then with Kyle.

Vicky insisted on driving Sandra and Kyle back to Los Angeles, and at 11:30 they all left in Sandra's red Rambler. Devil winds whipped the arid land. Even in winter the temperature in that stretch of California desert was in the eighties, and in the flat distance the sagebrush appeared to shimmer. The ride to Los Angeles passed in near total silence.

At noon that Sunday, detectives Aguirre and Duretto went to the County Coroner's Office in the drab fetid basement of the old Hall of Justice in the Civic Center near downtown Los Angeles. There they watched the autopsy on the body of Henry Stockton, which was being performed by Dr. Thomas Noguchi. The Japanese-born surgeon was then Deputy Medical Examiner and would soon become Coroner of Los Angeles County, an office that would bring him notoriety through such cases as the Robert Kennedy assassination, the Manson murders, and the so-called "SLA shoot-out."

Any one of the five bullet wounds, Noguchi advised the detectives, could have been, in and of itself, fatal. All five slugs, deformed from having hit bone, were recovered from the body, but the sequence of their firing could not be determined. There were no burns on Stockton's body and there was no evidence of smoke inhalation. The blood sample showed an alcohol content of .10 percent, what Noguchi would describe as "under the influence" but not "drunk." The detectives recalled that there had been nearly a dozen empty quart bottles of beer in the Stockton house. Had Henry Stockton drunk them all, sometime earlier perhaps? Or had someone else been there drinking with him?

Sandra, Kyle, and Vicky arrived at the Bingham residence in Downey, a suburb of Los Angeles, at 2:30 P.M. Sandra had fallen into her mother's arms at the doorway, weeping. By the time detectives Aguirre and Duretto sat down alone with Sandra a little after 3:00 P.M. in the living room, she had composed herself.

A common police practice during initial interviews is not to give out all the known facts at once. If the party has knowledge of certain facts which only a person involved in the crime could have, his relating these facts is evidence of guilt. But even if the party is innocent, investigators try to minimize the possibility of various pieces of information wending their way through office lunches and cocktail parties back to the culpable person. At the beginning of the conversation with Sandra, Aguirre made references to Henry's possibly "dying as a result of the fire." Later, he implied that suicide had not been ruled out. Eventually, out of simple decency, he related what they knew thus far about his death. Henry had been shot five times. Sandra cast her eyes to the floor and sucked in a deep breath.

Although needing a cigarette, Sandra answered the detectives' questions calmly, quietly.

Her marriage to Henry had been a troubled one in its early years, she explained, though it seemed recently that matters were improving. The problem had always been Henry's unassertiveness, his lack of ambition. A few years earlier, it had become too much for Sandra, and in April of 1965, after nearly five years of marriage, she had left him. The divorce decree (filed for in June of 1965) became final August 2, 1966, two months before their remarriage.

"I had yelled at him a lot," Sandra admitted, her voice soft and tired. "But he never argued back, not to me, not to anybody." She put out her cigarette, and looking at Aguirre a moment, she verbalized the detectives' problem simply: "Nobody would want to kill Henry."

Aguirre probed for the facts relevant to the previous few days.

What about the trip to Twentynine Palms? She had arrived there Friday evening, Sandra told him, having left directly from work at Harshaw Chemical in the City of Commerce that afternoon, stopping only to pick her son up from the babysitter. Because Henry had insisted on knowing that she arrived safely, she had called her mother from Twentynine Palms, and her mother relayed the message to Henry. As far as she knew, Henry had worked on Saturday and was planning on being home Sunday when she got back from her trip.

The sergeant asked Sandra for the names of Henry's friends. Jake Fields, she said, a Bobby someone, she gave them a few more. Most of them hung out at a bar called Lucky's. Aguirre asked Sandra if he might take her address book for a few days—perhaps there were other people she could not recall offhand who might know something. She dug a thick blue book out of her purse for them.

"We found a receipt in the house," Aguirre told Sandra, "indicating you bought a .22 caliber revolver last summer. Do you know where the gun is now, Mrs. Stockton?"

Sandra looked up, a little taken aback by the question. She explained that she had not really paid for the gun, but that it had been bought for her as a present by a man named Dick Scott. He was one of many fellows whom she had dated casually during her separation from Henry. She had met Dick Scott, she said, at a singles bar called the Stardust. They talked about going to the desert once to target shoot. Later she had discovered the gun did not work properly and she returned it to Scott, who promised to have it repaired. But she had not seen him or the gun since. When asked where Dick Scott could be located, Sandra could remember only that he sold insurance and lived somewhere in the San Fernando Valley. He was tall, on the handsome side, and he drove a blue Chrysler, 1965, she recalled vaguely.

The detectives thanked Sandra for her cooperation and asked if she would send her friend in for a few minutes.

"Are you Vicky Stowe?" Aguirre asked as the other woman came through the door.

"Yes, I am. I'm Sandra's alibi."

If that were an attempt at levity, Aguirre thought to himself, it was in bad taste.

He asked Vicky about the weekend visit, and her version corroborated what Sandra had told him. After the brief, ten-minute interview with Mrs. Stowe, Aguirre called Sandra in again and asked if she would be willing to take a lie detector test.

"Yes, of course," Sandra said with a puzzled look.

The test was not needed yet, Aguirre told her, and most likely it never would be. (Often detectives ask people if they will submit to a polygraph examination only to see what their reaction to the request will be.) Aguirre then asked Sandra to come down to the police station and give them an exemplar of her fingerprints. A normal procedure, he told her, in order to identify and separate hers from any others that might be found in the house. That same afternoon, Harold Tanney, a civilian fingerprint expert employed in the Latent Prints Section, Scientific Investigation Division (SID) of the LAPD, was back at the home on Ballard Street, photographing and "lifting" latent prints (i.e., dusting surfaces with a powder to "develop" the print, applying a transparent tape to the then visible print, and lifting the tape which bears the print onto a card with a contrasting background).

Sandra got her coat and accompanied the officers to the Downey Police station. Holding her arms tightly to her sides, her cheeks puffed slightly like a child who has been unjustly punished, Sandra became flustered as she looked around the station room.

"Does this mean I'm going to be arrested?" she asked.

"No, of course not," Aguirre assured her, gently guiding her to the table where there were ink pads and exemplar cards.

As one of the Downey policemen took Sandra's finger and began moving it down toward the ink pad, Sandra's eyes shot up toward the ceiling, out of focus. "Oh, my God," she muttered. Her knees sagged beneath her, and she began to fall backward. The officer at her side caught her and eased her down to a sitting position on the floor. Her eyes were closed, her mouth lolled open.

Aguirre knelt beside her and called for a glass of water. Sandra's eyes came open and looked directly at him, then over his shoulder and beyond him. Aguirre held her hand. Five minutes later, they finally took her prints.

2

POLICE WORK IS long unglamorous days sitting at a government-gray metal desk, dialing numbers until the fingers are sore. It is driving from community to community, interviewing estranged spouses, irate ex-landlords, observant gardeners, anyone who might know anything. Lunches are submarine sandwiches and coffee from styrofoam cups, wolfed down at the longer red lights.

Early Monday morning, December 12, the Highland Park detectives phoned the Provost Marshal's Office at the Twentynine Palms Marine base. A Sergeant Dugas there inspected the books and confirmed the fact that Sandra had checked into the base at 10:07 P.M. Friday night and had not checked out until 11:34 Sunday morning. The marine sergeant further stated that only if a resident of the base were accompanying, could a visitor leave the premises temporarily without signing in or out. Aguirre assumed either the rules were lax or the books were sloppy. Both Sandra and Vicky had said that Sandra had gone with Kyle to a gas station off the base early Sunday morning. The Provost Marshal's records showed no such excursion.

The officers went to the Sears store on East Olympic in Los Angeles. There they spoke with a William Gardner, Henry's supervisor. Henry had worked on the sixth floor as a stock clerk in the mail order department. He had been a good worker, never causing any trouble, never getting into arguments. Never.

Gardner directed the investigators to Bobby Sellers, who worked in the third floor repair department and was Henry's closest friend at the store. Sellers talked cooperatively with the police. The last time he had seen Henry, Sellers said, was late Friday night, when they had a few beers together at a neighborhood bar.

Bobby Sellers, in his late thirties and with a blond, '50s style duck-tail, lived with his mother and would be described in the police progress sheet as being "slightly effeminate" and having "become very upset when asked if Stockton might have homosexual tendencies."

While the interviews at Sears were being conducted, Officer K.E. Smith of the Highland Park Detectives and arson investigator Pugh were making an exhaustive search of the tangled ivy and surrounding grounds at the Ballard Street house for the murder weapon or any other physical evidence. There is always the possibility that a murderer will throw his weapon away at the first (perhaps even indiscriminate) opportunity, rather than chance being stopped leaving the scene with it still on his person. Borrowing a ladder from neighbors, Smith even went hunting on adjacent rooftops. The results of Smith's and Pugh's search, however, were negative.

The thoroughness of the job done the day before by Harold Tanney, the fingerprint expert, was questionable. Spending only one hour and fifteen minutes at the Stockton residence, of the sixteen readable latent prints he lifted, Tanney secured none from any surface other than beer bottles. Tanney determined that fourteen of those prints belonged to Henry Stockton. The identity of the other two was unknown. Shortly after making his findings, Tanney would, for reasons never ascertained, report to Sergeant Aguirre that all sixteen prints belonged to Henry Stockton, a contradiction that would eventually cause virtual chaos in the Stockton murder case.

Sergeant Aguirre and Officer Duretto journeyed to Lucky's Bar at 1214 South Boyle. It was a sorry little tavern that Henry and his friends had made their daily after-work haunt. The floor was dirty, the old wooden bar marred with carved initials and cigarette burns. The few booths toward the rear, with their high backs and wood cut-out designs, attempted without apology a Swiss chalet motif.

The proprietor, Charlie Parks, was the first person the officers talked with. His sentiments about Henry echoed everyone else's. Henry was a quiet polite fellow who could occupy himself for hours sipping beer or perhaps shooting pool with friends. Only once that he could remember had Henry pulled himself high on his barstool and ventured a meekly roguish remark about some new barmaid's figure. As to his best friends, Bobby Sellers and Jake Fields, "strictly fruits," Parks told Aguirre.

Sandra Stockton, Parks barely knew. No one at the bar, in fact, had even known Henry had been married until one day he brought Sandra and his son in with him and announced happily to his friends that they were soon to be a family again. All the Lucky's regulars—bus drivers, mechanics, welders—good-natured men after their hard work, with flannel shirts and an extra five dollar bill behind the lining flaps in their wallets—threw the couple a party.

During the course of the conversation with Parks, Jake Fields came into the bar and Aguirre proceeded to ask him a few questions in the privacy of Charlie Parks' office. Friday evening was the last Fields had seen of Henry. When the subject of sex came up, Fields could not speculate as to Henry's proclivities, but as for himself, "no bones about it, I go the line." Aguirre assumed the expression meant he was homosexual.

This first full day of investigation had turned up no clues and no leads. On this same Monday, in another part of town, Sandra Stockton called her very close friend, Audrey Scanlon. Audrey worked at the Automobile Club of Southern California in downtown Los Angeles where Sandra had also worked until just a half year earlier.

"How's everything, babe?" Audrey later recalled having asked. There was no answer, only a soft crying.

"What's wrong, Sandra? What's happened?"

Barely able to talk, Sandra told her. There was nothing Audrey could say to console her. After they hung up she took up a collection among Sandra's former co-workers. Men and women who worked at the Auto Club were not rich. They sent Sandra a large yellow bouquet.

Tuesday, December 13, police officers went once again to the house on Ballard Street in search of clues. They found nothing. Several more trips would be made there before the detectives finally gave up on the place.

While perusing Sandra's address book, Aguirre and Duretto came across the name "Scott" along with a phone number. They recalled that it was a "Dick Scott" who had bought the .22 caliber gun for Sandra. Their hopes for a break in the case rose. The man in her address book, however, turned out to be a Scott Jansen. The officers visited him Tuesday afternoon at his realty office in Bellflower.

Jansen had dated Sandra for several months during her separation and divorce from Henry, but no, he had certainly never bought her a pistol. He did know, however, that Sandra seemed interested in the hobby of target shooting. The detectives felt Jansen was not trying to conceal anything from them. They thanked him for his time and left.

Meanwhile, in downtown Los Angeles, a Sergeant Kenneth Beck went to Pachmyr Gun Works on Grand Avenue. Records there showed that the sale of the Hi Standard .22 to Sandra Stockton had been made by an employee named Mark Oberlin. Because the sale was in June and it was now December, Oberlin could not recall the circumstances surrounding the purchase, or even if it was a woman or a man who had come in to pick it up. Only one point of interest emerged from the interview with Oberlin. Sandra had stated to the police that when she gave the gun back to Dick Scott because it did not work properly, Scott had said he would take it back to be fixed. The records at Pachmyr revealed the gun had never been returned for repairs.

Aguirre and Duretto paid another visit to Sandra at her parents' home in Downey where she was now staying. Still in a nightgown at midday, her face was wan, her eyes pouched from lack of sleep. It had only been the night before that she had finally been able to bring herself to tell Kyle of his father's death, explaining to the boy that he would not see his daddy again. "He didn't leave because he didn't love you, honey,"—she had searched for the words, holding back her own tears—"he loved you very much."

The description she gave once more of the mysterious Dick Scott was only a bit more detailed. He was thirty years old, around six feet tall, two hundred pounds, and had dark brown hair. Still, however, she could not recall where he lived (except that it was in the San Fernando Valley, where over one and a half million other people lived), nor where he worked.

It was a glary, wintry sunlight that shone on Los Angeles on Wednesday, December 14, the day of Henry's funeral. Sandra sat moist-eyed next to her in-laws at the Downey Mortuary Chapel. Cremation followed the eulogies at 11:00, and Henry's ashes were taken to Rose Hills Cemetery in Whittier for interment.

Henry's parents, Hugh and Betty Stockton, later told police how perturbed they were about the bevy of men, none of whom they knew, who flocked around Sandra outside the chapel. One fellow, tall and broad-shouldered, took Sandra aside and told her how beautiful she looked. Minutes later, as family friends got into their cars, Sandra stood alone at the mortuary limousine. Her fair skin appeared flawless against the black mantilla she wore. With her lips perfectly shaded by lipstick but expressionless, and her faded blue eyes fixed vacantly on the stretches of lawn and family plots, she appeared like a lovely but abandoned play-doll. As if snapping out of a trance, she spotted Audrey Scanlon standing on the chapel steps. Sandra cried out her friend's name, and the two women ran into each other's arms.

By December 15, four days after the murder, thirty-one people had been interviewed. Aguirre and Duretto went back to reinterview a number of them. Elbert Thompson, the Stocktons' neighbor, had not heard any shots even though his bedroom window facing the Stockton house had been open. Because police had found a towel with a circle of Henry's blood on it in the living room, they theorized that perhaps the murderer had used the cloth as a partial silencer, wrapping it about the gun before putting the muzzle to Henry's head. Blood spurting from the side of Henry's head could have formed the circle on the towel. The center of the circle, where the gun barrel had been, would have remained clean.

Many policemen feel the chances of solving a case decrease geometrically with time. If a case does not break quickly, with a suspect identified or in custody within the first few days, the detectives are very likely to find themselves stranded—with the culprit, clues, and witnesses' memories washing farther and farther out to sea.

December 19, eight days after the murder, the Henry Stockton case was transferred from the Highland Park Division to LAPD Headquarters at Parker Center in downtown Los Angeles. Central Homicide assigned two veteran, top drawer detectives to head up the investigation: Sgt. Robert Guy and Officer John St. John. Guy, a slim, gaunt faced man around fifty years of age, was a plodder. He spoke slowly and precisely, and nodded at the floor when he listened to people's answers. He never had anyplace special to rush off to, and was always curious if the person he interviewed did. Talking to Guy, one got the feeling he had better fess up to having taken that piece of licorice back in the third grade if he expected to get out of the room before midnight.

St. John, known to television viewers as "Jigsaw John," a series based on his exploits, was a potbellied, balding charmer. He was the LAPD's most colorful homicide detective. Always dabbing with a handkerchief at the moisture that collected beneath his glass right eye, the profanities he muttered to himself were more endearing than offensive. St. John had lost his real eye when, as a green young cop, he had turned his back on an escape-bent youth in the county jail. He had not noticed that one of the metal legs had been unscrewed from a cot. The single blow to the face could just as easily have killed St. John. Now with one eye, Jigsaw John noticed everything. He told people he interviewed about his complaints with life before he asked them about theirs. People opened up to John St. John because they liked him. For St. John, tough cases became personal obsessions. St. John had an inkling he was now on what would become the toughest case of his long career.

He and Guy interviewed and reinterviewed the already known witnesses. Witnesses rarely tell whole lies or whole truths. It is all done in degrees. While Guy and St. John respected Aguirre and Duretto as cops, they wanted to judge the degrees for themselves. After reading the final Highland Park police follow-up report, they could not help focusing attention on the widow, Sandra Stockton. Although she had an ironclad alibi, because of the life insurance on Henry, she was also perhaps the only one to whom Henry's death would be a windfall.

For Sandra, the holiday season seemed to be an almost manic series of highs and lows. Christmas day she spent with Henry's parents, chattering away as though in desperate fear of silence. She had not considered expense in the gifts she brought with her.

When Audrey Scanlon called Sandra at home, Sandra's voice was somber, her words slurred.

"Babe, don't you think you're drinking a little too much?" Audrey asked.

Sandra could be heard whimpering. "Kyle asked me again today where his daddy was."

December 27, Guy and St. John called Sandra and asked if she would come down to Homicide Division the following day and give them a statement. Sandra consented. At 8:30 the next morning the detectives received a call from a Mr. Roy Marchetta, who identified himself as Sandra's attorney. His client had already given several statements to the police, he said. Why was another necessary? Bob Guy explained that he and his partner had just recently been assigned to the case, and that they would like a formal statement made directly to them. Marchetta wanted to know if Sandra would be advised of her constitutional rights. Guy gave full assurance that at this time Sandra was only a witness, but if the time came that she were considered a suspect, she would be properly advised of her rights. Marchetta relented, and at 10:30 A.M. Sandra arrived at Parker Center.

Transcribed, the interview ran over forty-five pages. Guy sat on the edge of his desk or walked slowly about the spare, fluorescent-lighted room. St. John sat in the corner, sucking Tums.

By Sergeant Guy:

Q. "And during this time (the separation), did you see Henry on occasion?"

A. "Yes. We saw each other frequently. It was just that we came to the decision that we couldn't live together. Even though we went to a marriage counselor for a year and a half, you couldn't build a fire under him—if you understand what I mean."

St. John raised his eyebrows but said nothing. He had just inspected the burned out ruins of the Ballard Street house two days earlier.

It was in April of 1965, Sandra said, that her mother-in-law had slapped her in the heat of an argument. Henry had not so much as raised his voice in Sandra's defense, and Sandra left him the next weekend.

Guy asked about Henry's sexuality. Having been away from Sandra for a year and a half, could he have had any homosexual affairs that might have eventually led to violence? Adamant that that could not have been the case, Sandra did admit their sexual life had once been a problem—a six-month drought included—but she insisted that after seeing the marriage counselor, matters had improved. Embarrassed by having to go into it, she mentioned in as few details as possible their enjoyment of intercourse and oral sex—on summer nights, even out in the back yard.

Guy asked about Henry's life insurance, and Sandra could not help smiling at what that question implied. She made no effort to conceal her knowledge of the details. She had, in fact, already been asked about the policies by her rather business-minded mother.

First, Sandra said, there was a group Metropolitan Life policy acquired by Henry nine years earlier as an employee at Sears. The face value was $15,000. Through Sears, Henry also had an Allstate fire insurance policy covering damage to the house, as well as several thousand dollars' worth of damage insurance on personal belongings. Sandra also expected to receive proceeds from the profit sharing program Sears offered its employees. Exactly how much, she did not know.

And then there was the National Life policy.

Q. "What was the amount of this policy?"

A. "Twenty."

Q. "Twenty thousand?"

A. "Yes."

Q. "Is there a double indemnity clause in this policy?"

A. "I understand there is."

Q. "So that would make it $40,000?"

Sandra looked directly into Guy's eyes and spoke evenly.

A. "That's what they tell me."

Sandra also cited a mortgage redemption policy which would, as a result of Henry's death, pay off the balance still owed on the home, a sum Sandra estimated to be around $18,000. Counting the profit sharing program, all proceeds came to somewhere between $75,000 and $100,000.

Q. "I talked to your lawyer this morning, a Mr. Marchetta. Is this the lawyer that got your divorce for you?"

A. "No."

Q. "How come you contacted a lawyer?"

A. "Because of the house. When we separated and got the divorce, I signed a quitclaim deed over to him (Henry), so the property is his and I am going to need a lawyer to clear this up. It will be given to my son. It will go into trusteeship. My mother is in real estate. She felt we should have an attorney."

Sandra's mother, the detectives had already learned from the people at Allstate, had been the one to phone in the fire damage claim on December 13, just two days after Henry's murder.

Toying with a strip of the Venetian blind as he stood at the window, Guy asked Sandra who might have been made jealous by Henry's remarriage. Sandra could think of no one; Henry had not even dated during their separation.

Q. "Did Henry have a gun?" Guy asked, pushing the blind down and letting it snap back up.

A. "Not to my knowledge."

Q. "You never saw one around the house?"

A. "No."

Q. "Do you have a gun?"

A. "No."

Q. "Did you ever have a gun?"

A. "Yes."

Q. "What kind?"

A. "I had a .22."

Q. "What, revolver?"

A. "Revolver."

Q. "Have you ever fired a gun?"

A. "Yes."

Q. "When did you have this gun?"

A. "Last summer some time."

Q. "Did you give it to someone, sell it, or what?"

A. "I gave it back to the person who bought it for me."

Q. "Who?"

Sandra retold the story of Dick Scott.

"He liked guns, and saw this one in an L.A. store and he said it would be just the thing for me. It had a white bone handle. It was definitely a lady's gun. He bought it and it was registered in my name. I think I had it almost a month, but I wasn't comfortable with it in the house. I asked him if he would meet me and take the gun back because I didn't want it, and he did."

In her December 11 statement, Sandra had said she had given it back because it did not work properly.

Wrapping up the interview, Guy asked Sandra to list the boyfriends she had dated before going back with Henry. While there had been many men from the singles bars she had seen occasionally, including the shadowy Dick Scott, there had only been three she had dated more than a couple of times: Scott Jansen, the Bellflower real estate broker, a Lonnie Rademacher, with whom she had discussed marriage, and a Bill Martin, an engineer at Rockwell International.

After the long interview had ended and Sandra had walked out the door, the two detectives did not speak right away. They only looked at each other and shook their heads.

Instinctual registers had rung up the same question in Guy and St. John. Had Sandra Stockton, whose feelings for her slain husband seemed to be more a simple regretful compassion than a grieving love, been—just perhaps—an unwitting pawn in someone else's opportunistic scheme? While there was every possibility that this widow had, in fact, helped plot her husband's murder from the very start, it was also conceivable that, for whatever her reasons, her role was now simply one of cover-up.

After Sandra had left Parker Center, St. John had the five slugs at the Coroner's Office sent over to Officer Dewayne Wolfer, Firearms and Explosives Unit at SID. Wolfer's findings were reported back that same afternoon. All five bullets were .22 caliber, fired from a revolver with rifling specifications of "six and six" with a right twist.

(The six and six referred to six "lands" and six "grooves"— grooves being the spiral indentations inside a gun barrel; lands, the ridges between the grooves. When a bullet passes through a barrel, the lands and grooves cut into the sides of it, giving it flight stability by causing it to begin twisting, like a well thrown football. But in the cutting process, the lands and grooves leave an identifiable imprint on the bullet called striations or markings. When a gun suspected to be the murder weapon is found, it is test fired to determine if the striations on the test fire bullets match up with those on the bullets recovered from the crime scene—this being a firearms identification test and not, as commonly thought, a ballistics test, which attempts only to determine the flight path of a bullet.)

Wolfer could not make a definitive finding as to the murder weapon's manufacturer. He could only say there was a good chance the revolver was made by Hi Standard.

The .22 caliber revolver Dick Scott had purchased for Sandra Stockton was also a Hi Standard.

Guy's and St. John's problem remained the same: They needed the murder weapon.

Bobby Sellers and Jake Fields consented to come to Homicide Division to take polygraph tests. Sergeant Henry Hernandez, who administered the tests, was thoroughly satisfied that neither man had any involvement in the murder. Ed Miner, a former acquaintance of Henry's who had recently taken to brandishing a gun, was located and, after lengthy questioning, he too was eliminated as a suspect.

On January 4, 1967, Guy and St. John drove to the City of Commerce to speak again with Sandra at the Harshaw Chemical Company where she worked as a receptionist-clerk. She greeted the detectives coolly, disturbed by what police interviews at work might look like to her employer and co-workers. After a short conversation, Guy asked if she would submit to a polygraph test. Yes, Sandra told them again, this time angrily. If it would clear this up once and for all, by all means, yes. Guy, however, did something Sergeant Aguirre before him had not done. He made the appointment definite—for the following day.

Sergeant Guy received a phone call at 8:00 A.M. the next morning from Sandra. She did not allow him a single word in the ten-second conversation.

"I have made all the statements regarding Henry's death to you I'm going to make," she said, seeming on the verge of tears. "You've already decided I'm involved in this somehow, and it's just not fair. If you have anything further to say to me, contact my lawyer, Mr. Marchetta. I'm not coming in for a polygraph examination, and I'm not going to talk to you any more about my husband's death." And with that she hung up.

Guy and St. John sat down for a little talk with Henry's parents at their home in South Gate. The Stocktons' reservoir of antipathy toward their daughter-in-law was bottomless. She had always been "bossy," they said, and ordering Henry about. Hold the chair for her, light her cigarette. Always buying clothes and having dinners out they could not afford.

After leaving the Stocktons' home that night, the detectives drove to the Downey Police station, where they rendezvoused with an Officer Gilbert of the vice squad. Gilbert accompanied them to the Stardust Bar at 7643 Firestone Blvd., the place Sandra had mentioned as her favorite "meeting spot" during her separation from Henry. Gilbert was acquainted with the Stardust's owner, Ray Ortiz.

The Stardust was like a thousand other swingers' places in the city —a dimly lit lounge with middle brand liquors and cozy booths. For any who preferred to sit on a stool and lean an elbow on the padded vinyl bar edge, there was the ubiquitous mirror where, after the third Scotch and tenth slightly forced, head-shaking laugh, one could check if the wave was still in place.

Ray Ortiz knew Sandra by description but not by name. She had come in many evenings, and as he recalled, she rarely had to buy her own second drink. With a tapering waist but thick legs, she was one of those who showed the men a smile and chatted the first hour from behind a booth table. On the name Dick Scott, the owner and his bartenders drew a blank. The description was familiar—too familiar. It fit a dozen of their male patrons.

As St. John led the way back out of the lounge—tinkling glasses, laughter, and mellow guitar music lingering behind him—he could not help thinking of the contrast between Sandra's nights as a single woman and the life Henry had asked her to come back to—the prosaic little house on Ballard Street, the grimy tavern called Lucky's.

The name Dick Scott (and variations thereof—Richard, Rick, etc.) was fed into both the California Department of Motor Vehicles and the California State Bureau of Criminal Identification and Investigation (CII). A number of men by that name were found, but none fit the description Sandra had given.

On the morning of January 17, Guy and St. John visited Dr. John Hoffman, Sandra's and Henry's psychologist and marriage counselor in Monterey Park. During late 1964 and early 1965, Sandra and Henry had engaged in both individual and group therapy.

Hoffman described Henry as a man who was essentially introverted and underachieving, with a surprisingly high I.Q. Sandra, the psychologist said, was far less intelligent than Henry, and was quite aggressive—a woman who was still resenting a domineering mother. But violent? No. Sandra had shown no tendencies toward violence, and Hoffman firmly believed she was incapable of murder.

Exactly one month after they had taken over the Henry Stockton case, Guy and St. John received a call from Mr. Carl Jackson of the National Life Insurance Company. Jackson's office had received a request from Sandra Stockton for payment on her husband's policy. Because it was a case of murder and the policy had been in effect for so short a time, and because the sum in question was considerable, $40,000, Jackson's company wanted to investigate before making payment. The detectives could only advise Jackson that the police investigation was continuing, and that as of yet there were no formal suspects.

Because of Sandra's refusal to cooperate any further with the detectives, they decided to initiate a surveillance of her. Her refusal to take a lie detector test, although not uncommon once someone is represented by a lawyer, had nonetheless made the police wonder even more whether Sandra was hiding *something*. Making her life a bit uncomfortable was perhaps the only way to get her to talk. The surveillance began on February 7 and continued for two weeks. Wherever Sandra went, a squad car followed, the officers making no effort to conceal the fact they were following her.

Sandra's nerves soon began to fray. If she visited her friend Audrey Scanlon at her home, the police car was waiting at the curb when she came out. If she went into a restaurant for lunch, the policemen relaxed with their own sandwiches outside. Sandra began calling Betty Stockton, Henry's mother, for solace. She complained of not being able to sleep, of one time waking in the middle of the night having dreamt she had seen Henry standing at the foot of the bed. Though the elder Stocktons had suspicions of their own, they held their tongues if only to not cut themselves off from their grandson Kyle.

The entries Sandra made in her diary revealed her anxiety: "To Stardust for drink, met fellow for coffee and to his home—talked and fell asleep, wanted to go home late—didn't. He was L.A. cop—I didn't think anything of it at first . . . looking back, feel it was a set up."

The fellow she met was, in fact, just a cop out for a good time. He had no connection with the investigation.

Toward the middle of the month, Sandra wrote in her log: "Really began to fall apart, and discussed it with the boss—it was decided I should resign. Did resign the following day to be effective 17th of Feb."

Sandra was in a position to quit. On February 16, she received a check from Metropolitan Life for $15,000.

That same day, John St. John drove to the Auto Club in downtown L.A. where Sandra had worked for over six years. There he interviewed half a dozen of her former co-workers. No one was unwilling to talk with the grandfatherly detective. Office gossip was that Sandra had once had an affair with a guy across the hall named Alan Palliko. St. John went over to talk with Palliko, who was still working in the Auto Club's Metro Unit.

St. John's one good eye was quite sufficient to see that Palliko—tall, muscular, with dark brown hair and eyes—bore a curious resemblance to the mysterious Dick Scott. St. John spoke with Alan Palliko a good deal longer than he had talked with the other employees. Palliko was congenial, pulling up a more comfortable chair for the older man and offering him a cup of coffee. Palliko had been a Los Angeles policeman, too, once. He still appeared as fit as a rookie cop beneath his sportcoat, with a rugged, cement eagle face that looked like it would chip before it would bleed. Palliko joked easily about the life policemen go through. He threw his head back and laughed at hearing how the office secretaries were gossiping about his love life. Yes, he had gone out five or six times with Sandra in January and February of the previous year while she was separated from her husband. It was nearly a year since he had last seen her, he said.

When Sandra had been asked to list the men she had dated, she had given the police three names. None was Alan Palliko.

St. John talked a bit more with Palliko, and as he rose to leave, asked him about the kind of car he drove. St. John explained that with all the descriptions they were getting of various men who used to come by Sandra's apartment, they were just trying to keep all of her past beaus straight. The car Alan was presently leasing was not the one St. John was looking for, the mid-sixties blue Chrysler Dick Scott drove, according to Sandra.

"How about the one before that?" the detective asked.

"Last month? That was my Continental. Only had it a couple of weeks."

"Before that?"

"Oh, let's see . . . last fall? A Mustang Fastback. New model, '67. Four on the floor."

"You like fast cars?"

Alan smiled.

"How about last summer, Alan? Were you leasing a car then?"

Alan thought hard. Remembering, he filliped his bronze horse paperweight.

"How could I forget my favorite? Had it almost half a year. A Chrysler 300, 1966. The blue'd knock your eye out."

The following day, February 17, Guy and St. John wrote in their progress report that an investigation of Alan Palliko would be initiated immediately, and that if Sandra Stockton were again questioned, she would be advised of her constitutional rights.

3

WHEN ALAN PALLIKO was twelve years old he sneaked out of his parents' large, gabled Tudor home in Forest Hills, New York, and caught a bus for El Paso, Texas, where he had decided he would become a cowboy. A horse and a gun were all a young man needed in this world, he told his friends. And land, wide open stretches where people would not crowd him. Two thousand miles on a bus gave Alan time to plan out just how he would start building his ranch empire. Money and mental superiority—that was what his father taught him ruled the world. The note Alan left his parents said he felt he was a disappointment to them, and that he was sorry. They would someday be proud of him, he promised.

Alan was not on the sun-baked streets of El Paso for more than a few hours before he had given nearly all of his life's savings, $200, to a pleasant stranger who promised to get him a horse, saddle, and rifle at a bargain price. Alan, of course, never saw the man again.

He called home.

"You're so smart getting yourself down there," his father boomed, "you can just figure out a way to get home."

"I . . . I don't have any money," Alan sputtered, his half-adult voice cracking.

After a long silence on the phone, Sid Palliko, his own voice a little shaken, said, "Thank God you're all right."

That afternoon he caught a plane for Texas to bring his son back. Once home, Alan agreed to see a Manhattan psychiatrist.

Alan was an April Fool's baby, born the first of the month in 1937 in Beth Israel Hospital in Newark, New Jersey. He was never like the other kids in the neighborhood. He was a loner, he was rebellious. His alert, little brown eyes watched for things coming up from behind. He did not like surprises.

When he was five years old, Alan became allergic to an array of foods. His system did not even tolerate cake; his mother baked oatmeal cookies for him instead. He came out of those few years of sickliness as unaccountably as he had entered them and grew to be a good-sized sturdy kid. While his mother, Miriam, doted over him in their Forest Hills home, his father, Sid, was seldom there. He was off doing what Alan was taught a man was supposed to do—building his own business. First a fleet of taxis in Manhattan, then a large Chrysler dealership in Flushing. The man with the deep gravelly voice who had scraped his way up from poverty was the household's disciplinarian.

Alan resented discipline of every form. He resented being sent to orthodox Jewish religious school most of all. Even as a ten-year-old, Alan was not about to be told when to wear a hat. Hats were reserved for gangsters, men who knew how to get what they wanted. No one liked Jews anyway, Alan thought. Alan had heard the story about the Jew who told a kid to jump from a fiery window, vowing he would catch him, then stepped aside to watch the child fall to his death. You can't trust anyone in this world. Alan's uncle had the idea; he let everyone in business think he was gentile.

As a compromise with his parents, Alan attended classes in a reform synagogue. At thirteen he forced himself through the motions of a bar mitzvah.

Academically, Alan was always a laggard. While his classmates, many of them Jewish and from close-knit families, talked about becoming brain surgeons and lawyers, Alan doodled or looked out the window and fantasized about strong-legged palominos and long-barreled .22s. His father had done just fine without a college degree. Alan wanted desperately to please his father. As a teenager Alan shoveled snow from neighbors' sidewalks, he grabbed off tips delivering groceries, he got up early Sunday mornings to wipe off counters and sweep the floor at a nearby drugstore. He was a newspaper boy, he was a soda jerk. What difference did it make that he could not manage good grades? He would show his father he understood what really made the world go 'round.

Alan would tell friends in later life that while he wished his father had been home more, he despised his mother for nagging his father about the very same thing. She was weak, Alan thought, a drain on his father. Alan loved his father, he respected him, he hated him. Mostly, it was all just a painful confusion for him.

Alan had no brothers or sisters. His happiest times were by himself, riding horses. It was when his father tried to teach him a lesson in thrift and refused to give him an advance on his allowance to go riding that he stole away to Texas. The next summer his parents sent him to a dude ranch.

Alan would, in the years ahead, win friends easily with a ready charm, then drive them away, every one of them, with his unrelenting suspicions. By the time he was eighteen he was cocky and swaggering. A little over six feet, one inch, strong-shouldered and looking good in his Saks Fifth Avenue sweaters, he sensed girls' attraction to him. Though brick-jawed as the Jewish prizefighters of the '30s, his smile was not that of an old neighborhood pug, but broad and assuring, his nicely rowed teeth polished with suburban care. Were it not for too jutting a nose, one might have called him handsome.

He always kept his dark brown hair trim, like a young man at the country club waiting to take over his father's business. His hands, too powerful and indelicate to ever have been a surgeon's anyway, gestured with open pride whenever he spoke of his father's success.

Alan began to use lies to fill the holes in his own life, the moments of failure he chose not to acknowledge. They were fanciful lies that impressed many people, but only for a while. Long after the others had seen through their airy substance, Alan was left the only one believing in them. He played the easy mark to his own shill. Half of what Alan Palliko pretended to be, he became; the other half he continued to cart around with him like a vaudevillian's suitcase of stale tricks, only forgetting over the years they were just tricks.

After graduating in January of 1955 from Forest Hills High School, Alan went off to college the next fall at West Virginia Wesleyan. Alan had little trouble repeating to others what his mother said, that he wanted to attend a small school, when in reality he simply could not get in anywhere else. During his one year at Wesleyan, Alan, a poker playing kid from New York marking time in the rolling green hills of West Virginia, did not have to strain himself terribly to collect his respectable Bs. His major was psychology.

During Easter vacation of his freshman year Alan flew out to Los Angeles to visit his parents, who were looking into a real estate investment there. Alan's meeting up with sunny California was as inevitable as driftwood washing up on a beach. Drinks at poolside, sleek convertibles traveling along sprawling, foliage-banked freeways, stables for thoroughbreds, sport-shirted entrepreneurs with tawny young women on their arms—you did not have to be an egghead to make it in California, Alan thought. The irreverent beach kids whom Alan hung around with during that Easter vacation, their hands dripping with ice water from the beer cooler, forever planning next Friday night, seemed to do just fine with half an effort.

The Pallikos decided to move permanently to Los Angeles, Alan's father having entered into the property venture he had been considering. With his mother's promise of a new Jaguar as an incentive, Alan made plans to transfer to a southern California school. Whenever his father caught wind of Miriam Palliko's promises to their son, however, the spoiling of Alan would be abruptly reduced by half. When Alan arrived, the new Jag turned out to be a Ford convertible. Feeling betrayed, Alan drove the car into the ground within a matter of months.

In September of '56, Alan enrolled at the University of Southern California, a traditionally reddish bricked private university for superfleet halfbacks and a goodly number of sons and daughters of the affluent with unjeweled high school transcripts. Alan's major at USC was commerce, with a stated interest in "industrial psychology, motivational research." But if what motivated people in business interested Alan, what motivated them in school certainly did not. He spent most of his time at his fraternity house, playing cards with the rest of the fellows of Tau Delta Phi and arranging for beer suppers with girls from the sororities. These were Alan's salad days, and he was not about to mix them with anything so dry as term papers. His first semester Alan received two C's, two D's, and an F, and was immediately placed on probation.

With a certain instinct for playing catch-up, Alan sprang off the probation list with solid grades, only to settle back too comfortably again. Four semesters and scores of parties later, the bottom of Alan's transcript read: "Disqualified."

On September 19, 1958, Alan was drafted into the army. He was sent to Fort Ord, California, for his basic training—two months after another young man by the name of Henry Stockton had finished his training at the same installation. After Ord, Alan went to Ford Hood, Texas, for six months of tank training, and thereafter was assigned to the U.S. Army's 2nd Tank Corps for eighteen months of active duty just outside Nuremberg, Germany.

Like his academic career, Alan's history in the army was a checkered one. Twice he was promoted to sergeant, and twice he was busted back to private. Cold German mornings found him dousing his breakfast corn flakes with vodka, and it was in a Nuremberg barroom brawl that an airborne barstool separated his shoulder and landed him in a hospital for three weeks—demoted. He would tell friends later with a disarming smile and wink, "I didn't think a worldly man of twenty needed permission to get a drink." Women he dated back in the States would hear of the injury as a war game maneuvers tank accident.

In letters home to his parents the only complaints Alan expressed about army life concerned the fact that his height made sleep in a tank unpleasant, and his growing animosity for the blacks with whom he had to serve. It was a black sergeant in particular who nettled Alan, the young defiant man who did not cotton to taking orders from anyone. What began back there in the service as a festering racial prejudice would over the years grow into a malignant hatred that would take more than one ironic turn in Alan Palliko's life.

In November of 1960, Alan returned to Los Angeles with his honorable discharge. Once home, he was adrift again. He was insouciant and developing a midnight snack paunch. His bed was his castle until noon. Knowing the names of a few French wines and some trendy European watering holes, he thought he had his start on an image of worldliness. He dabbled in a few liberal arts courses at L.A. City College, but without any objective in mind. Though he was no longer enrolled at USC, he spent most of his afternoons at his old frat house, playing poker and seemingly attempting to retrieve the years that were past him. When he sauntered through the kitchen, freshmen pledges stepped aside and gave him room. There was a certain presence about Alan that told others he did not want to be crowded. Younger fraternity brothers whispered their fear of him. It was odd, indefinable. No one had actually ever seen Alan lose his temper, yet they all sensed a pent-up volatility. If anyone ever returned one of Alan's many joking barbs and directed it at him personally, he would not pick a fight. Disappearing from the card game, he would later be seen sitting by himself in another room, rolling a pin between his fingers, looking hurt and brooding.

Alan became sweet on a girl, a sister of one of his fraternity brothers. Though she was already engaged to another man, Alan continued to pursue her, with his sense of humor more winsome with every phone call.

"I promise to put you under a pedestal," he told her, deadpan.

Alan even proposed marriage. When the girl's brother finally told him it was useless, that she was indeed going to marry someone else, Alan conducted a private investigation of the other fellow until he was satisfied with the man's social and financial standing. As Alan told her brother, "She deserves the best."

Eventually, Alan took a job.

It was a job without much glory. Junior salesman. For use of a company car and $500 a month, Alan went begrudgingly to work for Western Carloading, a large freight concern in the Los Angeles area. Additional money for a few luxuries came from his father. Much of the acrimony between the two men was submerged for the time being. To both friends and family, Alan sneered at his job with Western and said it was beneath him. He would make his big move in life soon enough, he promised. That was one of the first things he told to a young pretty woman he met in June of 1961.

It was on a blind date.

Katherine Drummond came from an unadorned, middle America home. For thirty-nine years her father was a gear setter at the Ford plant in Dearborn, Michigan. Her mother kept the family active in the Church of God. The Drummonds—Katherine, her parents, and two brothers—weathered financial struggles together. At age fifteen, Katherine (friends called her Katy) helped out by working after school as a receptionist for a portrait photographer.

A year after graduating from high school, Katherine, although ambivalent, made her first attempt at independence and moved to Los Angeles.

Finely featured and attractive, but in a prim, scrubbed working-girl fashion, Katherine found her romantic life in California sparse and disappointing. Sometimes she wondered if she might not have been happier if she had agreed to marry the high school football captain she had gone steady with back in Michigan. In four years of being a teletype operator for Pacific Telephone she met only one man with whom she felt any bond, but that never quite worked out, either. Now the phone company had him down in San Diego for six months of every year. Katherine was lonely.

When the married woman in the apartment next door suggested she knew a man who might be interesting, Katherine hesitated only a moment before agreeing to go out with him.

Preparation for the blind date was rushed. This man named Alan had been caught uncharacteristically without a date for a fraternity brother's barbecue, and would be over within the hour. While Katherine showered and ran a brush through her pixied hair, her neighbor pressed her amber, shirtwaist summer dress for her. Katherine was nervous; she had never gone out with a "college boy" before.

Her case of jitters turned out to be fully justified. She felt like a hayseed accidentally blown over the stone wall at the palatial Pasadena home where the barbecue was held. The other young people there, all college kids, smiled politely and looked around for another drink after hearing Katherine's first sentence about her job. But Alan, like a gentleman, stayed close-by and danced with her often. He seemed to like dancing quite a bit, and Katherine could only wonder why. He was thoroughly uncoordinated. During one of the numbers he kissed her lightly on the forehead, and it brought Katherine a flush of good feeling.

They stopped for coffee on the way home. Alan talked animatedly about his army experiences and rolled up his sweater sleeve to show her the tattoo of an eagle with his name in the middle. Well . . . he was younger then, he said, seeing her reaction. Looking down at his tattoo with a frown, he asked, "What did you expect, a signed and numbered Picasso?"

Alan loved to laugh, and his natural smile put Katherine at ease. But if she were becoming slightly infatuated with this fellow, a constant weight on that feeling was Alan's overfed sense of self-importance, like a childhood egocentrism that had somehow never been shed. Where others would have stopped after the fifth army story, Alan went on and on, full of energy and enthusiasm, oblivious to the possibility that Katherine might have wanted to get a word in.

Nevertheless, later on at the doorstep when Alan asked her for a second date, Katherine blurted out "Yes!" so fast she embarrassed herself. And with that began a six-year relationship—a relationship sometimes full of love and closeness, but more lastingly full of threats, recriminations, and terror.

Their dates were to the movies. Alan seemed to live his days just for the nights when he could sit in front of the big screen and watch anything from slapstick comedy to James Bond cleverly placing a strand of hair across the lock of his attache case so he would know if it had been disturbed. The spy and detective thrillers were the favorites he dragged Katherine to. Men were supposed to be strong, worldly, and enigmatic, women fragile and naive. The first time Katherine uttered a mild profanity in front of him, Alan, who prided himself on never using vulgar language, peered a long stern moment at her.

Katherine's taste in music was classical, and while she was once able to get Alan to attend a Van Cliburn concert with her, his pleasure was standards and rock-'n'-roll, reverberatingly loud as if to always have the feeling of a party around him.

What caused the greatest amount of strife in their relationship was Alan's two-timing. Often they double-dated with one of Alan's old fraternity brothers and his girlfriend, Maggie, a rich breezy coed from USC. More than once Katherine detected Alan and Maggie playing "kneesies" beneath the table. Much later, Katherine learned that Alan had run a Dun & Bradstreet financial check on Maggie's parents.

Alan was always a little nervous—flexing his steepled hands, or cracking his knuckles, or rolling between his fingers a straight-pin he carried with him. He rarely went anyplace without his German shepherd watchdog, Ponza, named after his old army tank.

Katherine did not like Alan's attitude toward blacks. Half conceding his feelings were irrational, Alan told her of incidents from childhood such as when he brought a black friend home for cookies, and his mother said he was never to do that again. Whatever unpleasant trait he might have, Alan insisted it was traceable to his parents, and that it would take time for him to work some things out. He confided to Katherine about the psychiatrist.

Glumly, his eyes darting across the floor, Alan began to tell her more twisted stories. Katherine wondered how many of the stories were real and how many imagined. Like Alan's telling her that when he was eleven his parents were constantly trying to purposefully humiliate him by making him hold his arms up so they could inspect for hair. Or the time he was home sick from school, and Alan claimed his mother crawled into bed with him and played with him sexually, and made him touch her as well. Or when he was only a small boy, and Alan said his father stood him on the dresser and told him to jump. He had started to bawl, went Alan's story, and his father promised to catch him. When he jumped, his father let him fall to the floor and instructed with a wagging finger that no one in the world could be trusted, not even one's own father.

Katherine wondered if she had not heard that story somewhere before; it sounded vaguely similar to an antisemitic story she had overheard Alan tell someone else—something about a kid and a fiery window.

In November, 1961, Alan stopped working at Western Carloading. He claimed he had quit, though Katherine suspected he had been fired for padding his expense account. For a few months he became a cashier at a savings and loan company, and for a short while worked for an auto parts manufacturing company, where his father was on the board of directors. One afternoon he came over to Katherine's apartment and, patting Ponza, who lay at his feet, he proclaimed: "I've decided what I want to do with my life, Katy. You can't just be parasitic about society, you have to give something back. I've decided to become a police officer."

Alan was in for an unpleasant surprise. After taking his physical he was informed he had to lose weight. He was carrying too much of the rich kid's pudge on his frame to be a cop. That unexpected and humbling comment on his physique Alan answered with a fanatical commitment. He went on a crash diet, rose early every morning to jog, and hour upon hour exercised in gymnasiums. He stopped drinking, he gulped vitamins by the handful. He became a health freak. The weight came off, and his chest and arms and legs built themselves up into rigid muscle. For over a month people barely saw him; they only knew at which gym he could be phoned in case of an emergency. If nothing else, Alan Palliko was a motivated man, and he passed his second physical with a vengeance.

On February 5, 1962, he entered the Training Academy of the Los Angeles Police Department, set in the grassy and tranquil (except when the crowds are roaring at nearby Dodger Stadium) hills of Elysian Park. April 27, at the age of 25, he graduated. But mediocrity would not cease haunting his illusions of greatness. His final rank was exactly mid-class. Still, he was a Los Angeles police officer, and to Alan, it was the first important accomplishment of his life.

Alan loved being a cop, working harder and longer and volunteering for more assignments than most other rookies. He intended to make the department his career and had designs on rising high. When his long days ended he spent his nights moonlighting as a private investigator for lawyer Roy Marchetta. The day he pulled an old fraternity brother over for speeding, Alan chatted amiably for forty-five minutes with his friend, then still with a pleasant smile on his face, handed him his ticket.

His superior at the police department, Sgt. Jack Herron, described Alan as "a good officer, a gung ho guy with real promise." What his superiors did not know was that Alan broke regulations every time he stepped into his patrol car. The one, authorized .38 service revolver was not enough weaponry for Alan. Surreptitiously he took along several other guns of his own. Only his patrol partners were aware of it, and none of them dared betray him.

Alan started off in the Hollywood Division of the Los Angeles Police Department, then shifted to West L.A., later to the 77th Division (an area which would come under fire during the 1965 Watts riot), and eventually ended up working undercover on the vice squad in the mid-Wilshire District, an older area of Los Angeles rife with hustlers working only blocks away from stately brick homes and high-priced apartments. Working vice was what Alan loved most. Dressed up in red shirt and tight pants, he set up busts of pushers, pimps, and prostitutes, many of them black.

"Hey, man," Alan tossed his hands in the air as he stood on the corner, "don't tell me about no sweet smelling nickel bags of weed. You got something to *show* me, okay. You just looking for a loan, you go see the dudes at First National, all right?"

Alan loved being an actor, pretending he was something he was not, until that delicious moment when he could flip out his badge.

Police work brought out traits in Alan that pulled Katherine tight inside. It was during this time that his attitude toward blacks grew from one of mild disdain to that of vicious retribution. He bragged to friends about how he could make some of his busts by planting pills on them. He told his parents about halting a stolen car and giving foot chase to a lanky black youth who hopped out. Alan reached for his gun, took aim, and was about to fire when the suspect turned around and surrendered. He was thirteen.

"It's a good thing he stopped when he did," Alan told the story solemnly. "I would have had to shoot him, you know."

If Katherine were to come over to his apartment and it was quiet, she knew she was likely to find Alan lying on the bed reading his favorite novelist, the politically ultra-conservative Ayn Rand. Katherine, a moderate Republican, watched Alan's politics pass her by like a runaway train—from a Kennedy Democrat to a Goldwater supporter to membership in the John Birch Society to receiving literature from the Minutemen. Over dinner at a restaurant he told her why he loved police work so. He said it with a faint smile. "It's like . . . like being God."

How or why Katherine stayed with Alan Palliko remained a mystery to many of her friends, including her visiting brother, whose dislike for Alan's inflated ways was instantaneous. But somewhere within the filaments of her religious and forgiving nature, Katherine believed he desperately needed her.

Not often, but just often enough, she saw glimpses of compassion in him, moments when he was not afraid to show at least her, if no one else, that he was vulnerable. When his dog Ponza died, he cried. He was saddened and quiet for weeks.

And what was most difficult for Katherine to dismiss, as it perhaps is for any human being, was that there was now someone who told her he loved her.

Just before Christmas Alan proposed, and Katherine accepted. They picked out a ring together and spent a cheery Christmas day with some of Katherine's old friends visiting from Dearborn. The following afternoon, Alan phoned and called the engagement off.

"Marriage is sacred," he told her earnestly. "I'm just not ready to commit myself." In the same conversation he also broke their date for New Year's Eve.

During the first part of 1963, hurt yet also oddly relieved, Katherine saw little of Alan. Feeling good about herself, she went her own way and dated other fellows.

As summer waned, Alan began coming around again. With mixed emotions, she allowed it to continue. Alan took her to meet his parents, and Katherine was as ill at ease as on their first date to the Pasadena barbecue. The Pallikos lived in a plush home in Beverly Hills, and it was all Katherine could do to figure out which of the exquisite, gold-leafed furniture she was allowed to sit on. There was little warmth in the household, no family joking. Mrs. Palliko acted strangely the entire visit, and on the way out to the car Alan mumbled something about a breakdown and a hospital. It was only upon meeting his parents that Katherine learned that Mr. Palliko, like Mrs. Palliko, was Jewish, not Italian as Alan had told her.

"I was ashamed to tell you I was Jewish," Alan said later, his eyes skittering away from Katherine's. "Let's let it go at that, okay?"

His failures Alan invariably attributed to strokes of bad luck. But what happened to him during the summer of 1963 was, in fact, an instance of genuine ill fate.

Alan was rooming with another police officer named Freddy, who was separated from his wife and sharing his bed with his girlfriend, Linda. In a short time, Linda became pregnant and was in the market for an abortion.

In those days abortions were a felony. Alan was reluctant to become involved, but wanting to be a good guy, he contacted another officer in the department who had some connections, and within a few days Alan was able to give his roommate a slip of paper with a doctor's name on it. The melodrama turning one more notch, Freddy and Linda moved into a house together in Los Angeles' Silver Lake District and decided to cancel the abortion.

That Labor Day weekend, Freddy's wife, her resentment having smoldered over a long loveless summer, tracked down the address where her husband and Linda were living, broke into Freddy's car and grabbed his .45. Entering the house through a window, she found the couple in bed together. Freddy lunged, managed to wrestle the gun away, and his wife went running from the house to the nearest phone booth to call the police.

The call that Alan received on Labor Day from his superior, Sgt. Herron, was vague but ominous. Alan was to report Tuesday morning to the Internal Affairs Office at Parker Center. Monday night, Alan phoned his parents in Las Vegas, where they were vacationing.

"Something terrible has happened," he told them in a shaky voice. "I've been called down to headquarters. I don't know what's going on."

The Pallikos caught a plane back to Los Angeles the next day, but by then all that remained for them was to try to cheer their son up. That morning, Sergeant Herron, while empathizing, had not minced words. Alan's attempt to arrange an abortion was cause for dismissal. His chances before the LAPD's Board of Rights were nil. Herron advised that he resign. At first Alan sat stunned, not seeming to fully comprehend. By the end of the morning-long conversation, his head was in his hands and he was openly choked up. Herron would later say he had to respect Alan for his mulish refusal to divulge the name of the third officer involved in obtaining the name of the abortionist.

Over the next several months, Alan filed applications with a number of suburban police departments. He should have known better. It took only a phone call by any of those departments to ascertain the reason behind Alan's resignation from the LAPD.

"Biggest setback of Allie's life," his mother lamented over the phone to a relative back east.

Alan began to attend more nighttime meetings of the John Birch Society. For emotional comfort, he turned to Katherine, and ever sympathetic, she would not refuse his need to have talks that lasted long into the night. At the same time, his behavior began to frighten her more than ever. Law enforcement agencies began to slip into the same category as black people, the enemy, the ones Alan would have to get before they got him. Sometimes when she visited Alan at his apartment she found him sitting by himself, staring absently out the window at the sky.

In time, Alan's brooding began to subside. He had become a private investigator for the Kaplan Investigation Agency and, with the long hours he willingly put in, was making upward of $1200 a month. Conversation between Katherine and him again turned to marriage. In March of 1964, they became engaged for the second time; the wedding was set for June.

In April the engagement was broken for the second time, this time by Katherine.

"I love you," she told him in a timorous voice over the phone, "but . . . I can't explain it . . . I'm afraid of you. I'm physically afraid of you, Alan."

Alan begged, he pleaded, he vowed he would never harm her. Katherine remained resolute; her instincts about this man thrummed in her head too loudly.

But if words and vows cannot drown out instincts, fits of despair can. Over the next months Katherine dated other men, but every relationship left her at a dead end. Every man she met was out for the quick make. If there were no sexual relations on the second date, Katherine knew better than to hope for a third. It seemed her religious traditionalism was by 1964 something of am amusing oddity to big city livers. At least with Alan that had not been a problem; sex was one of the last things on his mind.

A warm July night Katherine came to her decision. The man she was with must have said, "Let's just go in the other room awhile," at least four times. Home by midnight, Katherine called Alan. She was crying.

"Do you still love me?" she asked.

"Yes. Of course."

"Do you still want to marry me?"

"Yes."

They set a date—August 14. After hanging up she lay in bed awake. In a darkened bedroom the young bride-to-be's face was ridged with anxiety.

Alan was out to be a success, and Katherine could only be delighted by his spirit. His first decision after their engagement was to enter law school. Because his long hours at the Kaplan Investigation Agency precluded time for anything else, Alan quit and took a forty-hour-a-week job at the Automobile Club of Southern California. His position was in the Auto Club's Metro Unit as a claims investigator for bodily injuries; his starting salary was $490 a month. Alan's nights were spent either attending classes at Southwestern Law School in downtown L.A., home studying, or at Marcy's Gym where it was said he could bench press 255 pounds.

While taking his evening law classes Alan became friendly with another student by the name of Jack Dodd. Jack was in his early thirties, married, and with two small boys.

"He's good people," Alan used to say of Jack. Alan's friendship with Jack Dodd astonished Katherine. Jack was a black man.

Jack Dodd respected Alan's strong will and confidence, and almost believed Alan's prediction he would make his first million by the age of thirty-five.

Alan and Katherine, and Jack and his wife, Dianne, spent many Sunday brunches together. With full heads of steam, Alan and Jack jousted politically, but never with any personal enmity. Jack was a calm and articulate man who listened patiently to Alan's conservative positions on race, then pointed out his own opposing views with an unflagging good nature. Alan relished the intellectual combat and looked forward more than any of them to their Sunday morning omelet and bacon colloquies. Katherine was elated.

The people Alan avoided, at times with open, adolescent cruelty, were his parents. A week before their wedding, Alan brought Katherine over to see them for only the second time. Sid and Miriam

Palliko were sincerely trying their best, Katherine thought. They brought out champagne and presented the bride with a lovely pink gown and peignoir. But still it was all miserably awkward. Mr. Palliko fumbled for his words.

"As far as I'm concerned, Katy," he said, "you are now our daughter. Not our daughter-in-law. Please call me dad. Or father. Or whatever you want to do."

The day Alan and Katherine drove to the Civic Center for their marriage license, the building was closed and swarming with firemen who were putting out a blaze there. Alan strode up the front steps, buttonholed a fireman and a city bureaucrat and explained the situation to them. One hand fondly on the bureaucrat's shoulder, Alan motioned with curled finger for Katherine to get out of the car and join them. The marriage bureau was reopening that day for one last charming groom.

The small wedding was held on the evening of Friday, August 14, 1964, at the South Hollywood Presbyterian Church where Katherine was a member and sang in the choir. Her minister and very good friend, the Reverend Hank Vigeveno, presided. Katherine wore a long-sleeved white gown, Alan a plain black suit. At first amazed that Alan chose his father as best man, Katherine sadly realized, upon reflection, that although Alan had a great number of casual friends, he really had no one friend he could have asked to stand up for him without appearing embarrassingly desperate.

According to Alan, his parents were to have given a reception afterwards; according to them, their son had never even broached the subject.

"Never gave me one lousy birthday party as a kid," Alan cursed them as he and Katherine drove away from the church. "People never change," he lectured his bride, gunning his newly leased Jaguar from lane to lane. "They . . . just . . . don't . . . change."

The Pacific Ocean sparkling off to their right, the couple drove down the coast highway toward San Diego. Champagne and the honeymoon were awaiting them in a Shelter Island motor hotel room Alan had reserved. Once out on the highway, Alan did not feel like talking. For the entire trip down he listened to the radio talk show of Joe Pyne, the southern California superpatriot.

Early married life brought out a solicitous side of Alan that was a pleasant surprise for Katherine. Despite his full work weeks at the

Auto Club and evenings of law classes and study, he made genuine efforts to be a responsible and attentive husband. On the days he arrived home earlier than Katherine, he got the dinners started, and while his cooking was smoky and expedient as a scoutmaster's, his willing spirit was endearing. Saturday mornings he insisted Katherine sleep late while he went out to do the laundry and go grocery shopping.

His efforts in law school, too, seemed sincere. His grades were passing, and in one course, Legal Method, he scored a 90.

They shared times of closeness. At the end of long weary days they held each other, and like all young enamored couples, found unabashed delight in baby talk. Alan and Katherine came to call it "chipmunk talk." Her nickname for him was Herb. He called her Wurf.

Alan was not averse to laughing a little at himself. Sometimes. Even at his continued fanatical exercising and the satisfied gazes at his body in the mirror. Katherine felt free to make playful fun of his narcissism.

Making ends meet was not easy. A day Katherine was out of cigarettes and did not have even a nickel in her purse, she asked Alan for a dollar. When he handed it to her she saw he had written on it in red felt pen: "I love you."

Alan's growing obsession with money, however, began to scratch away at Katherine's normal equanimity. He insisted on foregoing the smallest pleasures in order to save, but usually it was only those luxuries which they both enjoyed that suffered. There was always suddenly enough money around whenever Alan wanted to lease a newer, faster car or to buy himself expensive sweaters. For a while, Katherine thought she could learn to live with a self-indulgent man.

Alan was fastidious, almost to the point of compulsion, about his dress. Pants and shirts had to hang in the closet in the order he would wear them the next week. He checked on them regularly to see they had not been moved.

The weekend afternoons that Alan was not lifting weights at the gym he drove to the desert for target shooting. Sometimes he went with friends, sometimes only with his Great Dane, the dog that had replaced his German shepherd Ponza. He boasted that his Great Dane was a killer that would attack anyone who touched it without his permission. In the Marcy's Gym parking lot, Jim Gates, the gym's manager, grasped it by the neck, jostling it, and the dog slobbered all over

Jim's arm with affection. The next day Alan sold it and bought a Doberman.

Alan's zealous machismo left Katherine mildly amused; his fascination with guns left her cold. She knew only that his collection of weapons was considerable and growing.

As the months wore on, new facets of Alan Palliko began to emerge. He was a miasma of contradictions. One moment he was full of fun and clowning with his put-on, cartoon voices, or calling Katherine "mommy"; the next moment he was quiet and sulky. He told Katherine that the only person who understood or cared for him was the psychiatrist back in New York with whom he still corresponded. Rarely could Alan sleep for more than four hours at a time. He got up in the middle of the night and gulped vitamins. Sometimes he woke up screaming. Katherine tried to comfort him, but all Alan wanted was to know if she had been able to make out any of the words he had uttered during his sleep.

"What did I say? Tell me what I said," he demanded. He was relieved if she had not been able to understand anything he said.

Their sex life, while at first frequent enough, was never satisfying for Katherine. Love-making seemed to be a methodical obligation for Alan. His caresses of her breasts were more an awkward pawing that hurt Katherine. Their first time in bed, she suggested he be more gentle.

With an incongruously innocent look on his face, Alan said, "I thought women *liked* to be handled rough."

Katherine urged him to read sex manuals with her, but he never would. Her forthrightness only stirred a prudish reluctance in him to discuss the details of sex. Eventually, Alan began to let her go to sleep by herself while he stayed up to watch a late night movie or the news. She could see him through the open bedroom door, sitting in front of the television with his back against a chair, polishing a gun or rifle while he watched a mystery—one star or four, it did not much matter. If it were the news he was watching, it would invariably be that given by the most conservative of the local commentators. Often Alan would blurt out, "That's right!" in enthusiastic agreement.

What remained the greatest source of stress in their marriage was Alan's need to flirt, his need to know he was attractive to any and all females. Walking down the street with Katherine, he turned his head back to women who had just passed, to see if they were looking at him.

It was during the Christmas holiday season that he teased Katherine about an office flirtation of his down at the Auto Club.

"Yeah? I'd like to hear about it," Katherine said.

"I'm just getting your goat, Wurf. You know me. I'm straight arrow."

"Well, what's she like?"

"Oh, she's short and blond, and *very* shapely. And she has a little boy. I'm trying to give her moral support with her dieting. She has big legs. You know how I love big strong legs on a woman," Alan smiled.

Katherine did not return the smile. "What's her name?"

Alan laughed his snorting laugh. "Oh, what does it matter?" he said, and left for the gym, keeping the name a secret.

4

EXACTLY WHEN AUTO CLUB employees Alan Palliko and Sandra Stockton caught each other's eye, no one at the office remembers. By early 1965, though, several months before Sandra walked out of the Ballard Street house from Henry and filed for divorce, it was clear to all the Auto Club secretaries that Alan and Sandra were friends, though it would be a year before they began dating. Lunching together often, Alan became something of a mentor in Sandra's determined plan to diet and exercise and at long last become one of L.A.'s beautiful people. To be sure, Alan's flattering ways, shown to many women routinely and accepted by most of them as merely an idle part of the man's nature, were to Sandra quite new, their impact dizzying.

Sandra was three years younger than Alan, born in August of 1940. Her parents lived at that time in South Gate, a Los Angeles community that even then was beginning to choke with industry. Its residents worked hard just to keep their heads at the smoggy surface line of middle class. The neighborhood blocks formed rows of similarly boxy, pastel houses. Sandra's father was a supervisor at the 7-Up bottling plant. Her mother's ambitions to be a stage star had been abandoned for selling real estate, getting married, and having a family.

Harriet Bingham had never gone beyond small parts in the San Diego Civic Light Opera or as a faceless extra in a few B movies. Like her first daughter, Sandra, she was overweight. But ambitions run high in a city like Los Angeles; for some, children can provide a second audition. Harriet Bingham passed a chatty gregariousness on to Sandra. She saw to it her daughter took dance lessons and learned all the social amenities. Sandra's knack for drawing was nurtured.

Sandra was a chubby, giggly little girl. She never lacked for friends and was always a ready joiner, active in the Brownies, and afterward the Girl Scouts until as late as eighteen. But Sandra was never truly confident. Her Scout leader was always troubled by the little girl's refusal to attempt new skills. Invariably, Sandra begged off with a pouting, "I can't do that. I'm too dumb."

Sandra was a daddy's girl. She lived for each afternoon when her father would come home from work and she could sit on his lap like a queen. When Sandra was only five, Ted Bingham was drafted. The effect on the child was devastating. She became rueful and withdrawn, believing her father had left because she had done something wrong and that he no longer loved her. Harriet Bingham recognized that her daughter needed a more trained eye to help combat the situation, and along with Sandra, she began visiting a psychologist. The advice was simple—lavish affection upon the child in the father's absence. Mrs. Bingham did just that, and the results were marked. Sandra returned to her outgoing ways, and no one had reason to suspect any emotional scar would remain.

Two years after Sandra was born, Mrs. Bingham gave birth to twins, Tracy and Pat. Though the mother did her best to keep all the children close and show no favoritism, it became clear to everyone that Sandra was gradually being left out. Not by her parents, but by her sisters. The twins often played together without Sandra, and as they all grew older, Tracy and Pat, both of them slim and fetching, went out on dates together while Sandra stayed home. Somehow the twins did everything right, and Sandra did not. Where they learned responsibility and thrift, Sandra squandered her allowances. The profligacy was concentrated on clothes that could never quite hide the fact she simply was not like her lithe younger sisters. But those who knew Sandra said if she harbored resentment, she never showed it.

When Sandra was fifteen, the family took a trip to Snow Valley, a winter resort area in the mountains east of Los Angeles. On an early morning toboggan slide, with all three sisters aboard, Sandra saw that they were swerving toward a boulder, and it was Sandra who put her leg out in an attempt to avoid the accident.

Suffering sixteen fractures in the heel and ankle, and requiring several operations for metal pins to be inserted, Sandra remained in a wheelchair for over fourteen months. Her overweight turned to obesity.

After graduating from high school in 1958, Sandra worked part-time as a salesclerk at Bullocks, a downtown department store. For a year and a half she took art classes at East L.A. City College. Thoughts of becoming a fashion designer did not go unencouraged by her mother. Living at home, Sandra led an almost nonexistent social life.

Her sister Pat was dating a man named Tim Barnes, whom she would eventually marry. Tim had a friend from high school and the army named Henry Stockton. In December of 1958, Henry and Sandra went out on a blind date to the County Fair. Henry was a husky, shy fellow with a dollar-seventy-five haircut, and below the short clipped brown hanks, a face helpful and common as a Nebraska drugstore clerk's. The relationship that resulted from the blind date was never one of torrid passion, but it was steady, and it was reliable. Sandra had something new in her life—a boyfriend.

Nearly every evening when Henry came home from work, he found Sandra waiting for him on the front porch steps of his parents' home where he was still living. Some nights she kept him company in the chilly, floodlighted garage while he tuned and polished his new Plymouth. Dates out were sandwich dinners in South Gate, or long slow drives—their reserved conversation quiet and regardful of each other.

Henry and Sandra, no longer school kids, did not fool themselves about the circumstances of their lives. Henry, the round-faced stock clerk, and Sandra, unable to shed her curseful weight, still going to sleep every night in the bedroom she had as a child, now walked into friends' parties together, glanced over at each other often during the evening—and were appreciative.

Despite both families' lack of enthusiasm, Sandra and Henry were wed July 16, 1960. Their honeymoon was a one-day trip to Newport Beach.

To be sure, there were good times in the marriage, but one suspected they were better for Henry than for Sandra. On camping trips to Lake Cachuma he enjoyed teaching her how to fish. Sandra's pleasures—dinners out, shopping for new clothes, and her still unfulfilled desire for a sporty car—cost more than their combined incomes could afford. They were nearly always in debt. Grating at Sandra were her parents' clumsily disguised reminders of the material good fortune the twins had found in their own marriages.

Inevitably, Sandra's and Henry's marriage began to falter. The baby Sandra thought would save it did not help, nor did buying the little home on Ballard Street. Henry worked on the house on weekends, painting and fixing it up, but by then Sandra's eyes were already peering at a different lifestyle. While Henry was satisfied to spend nights home, Sandra began to spend more and more evenings out—some at the League of Women Voters, more at Weight Watchers, and most just with nightlife friends. Losing weight and dyeing her hair blond, she suddenly found she was becoming attractive to men. Not all, but more every day. Sandra's five-year-old marriage to Henry Stockton was near collapse by the time she became friendly with Alan Palliko.

Alan's sleepless nights did not improve. They got worse. Often Katherine was awakened in the early morning hours to the sound of her husband moaning, "No . . . no." Alan drove himself ragged with his long days at work and nights at law school. Even his oddly shuffling, head-bobbing walk became faster, his forward lean greater, as if he were walking into a wind. By the summer of 1965, he had to enter a hospital for treatment of a duodenal ulcer. Convalescing in bed at home, he railed at Katherine for not showing him enough sympathy.

Even before the ulcer, their sex life had diminished to a cipher. Katherine tried to talk to him about it, but the subject aroused anger. Once, she suggested they were perhaps not meant for each other.

"I'd kill you before I'd give you a divorce," was Alan's answer, his neck muscles tightened and red.

At first Katherine regarded that kind of language as just part of Alan's blustering ways. It was just an expression with him. But she began to wonder. Words like that came so easily to him. "Somebody should kill my mother," he would say. "She's a drain on dad." Sitting in front of the late night news, polishing his guns, he muttered to himself at hearing the riots in Watts: "They should all be shot."

Katherine visited her minister, Reverend Vigeveno, and by those visits summoned the courage to tell Alan that their marriage would soon be in jeopardy if the psychological and sexual problems Alan wrestled with could not somehow be faced and beaten.

Alan only responded with two more stories from his childhood. A day after a terrible argument between his parents, he said, he sat nervously in class, waiting for an exam to begin and unconsciously rubbing his legs together. It was there in class, he said, that for the first time—and accidentally—he had masturbated.

He also told her something of a corollary, his voice anguished in the telling. As a boy he had once gone to visit a friend. His friend was not home, but the boy's sister was. The girl was taken with Alan, but Alan was not interested in her. She was skinny and shapeless. At one point in the afternoon the sister invited a girlfriend over, and the girlfriend, curvaceous and sexy, quickly won Alan's attentions. When an argument ensued, the skinny sister threw the other girl to the floor, ripped off her clothes and proceeded to beat her. Alan did nothing. He sat and watched as the girl got beaten up. Even today, he would fantasize two women physically fighting, and derive sexual stimulation from it.

Now as an adult, Alan told Katherine, he would frequently masturbate when he sat before violent movies on television. His habit of rolling a pin between his fingers, his psychiatrist had told him, was another form of masturbating. The long slow confession to his wife seemed to bring Alan a sense of relief. On her part, Katherine could not keep her heart from going out to what she was beginning to consider a seriously disturbed man. Alan promised that with her help he would work things out. Nothing came of his promise.

Alan spent more and more evenings away from home, and Katherine could not help questioning whether all that time was really being devoted to study at the law library.

As Katherine sat home by herself one humid summer night, the phone rang.

"Is Alan there?" a woman's voice asked.

"No, he's not," Katherine said. "Can I say who's calling?"

"Mamie."

"Who?" Katherine asked.

"Mamie Van Doren." The woman began to giggle, then broke the connection.

Friday, August 13, 1965, was the day before Alan's and Katherine's first anniversary. As Katherine drove home for lunch that day, she wondered how they would celebrate the occasion the following evening. Alan had not mentioned anything. For all of his rigid habits,

Alan still liked to think of himself capable of some spontaneity when it came to the night life; his reputation among friends was for being where the action was. Despite his constant grumblings about money, he relished their evenings in a good restaurant—wine and a New York strip. He played the *bon vivant,* snapping his fingers for service and leaving enough of a tip to have his name remembered.

Katherine put her VW in the carport that Friday noon and started up the sidewalk toward their apartment's front door. The roar of a car engine made her stop and turn her head. All she saw was the glint of sunlight off a metal grille, and her own shriek was the last noise she heard as the car leaped the curb and slammed into her body. She tumbled over and over along the sidewalk, her head and arms and legs smacking against the cement. She rolled to a stop, and was alive.

Neighbors heard Katherine's cries and called for help. It was only a matter of minutes before she was bundled into an ambulance and rushed to Central Receiving Hospital. All things considered, the limited extent of her injuries was miraculous. Katherine suffered a severe concussion, numerous head cuts, a gash on her right leg, a broken big toe, and what doctors would later diagnose as partial amnesia. She was transferred to Mount Sinai Hospital, where she remained for three weeks.

When Alan arrived later that afternoon his knees were buckling so, he had to grab hold of her bed rail and sit down. There were tears in his eyes.

"Please don't cry, Herbie, or I'll start too," Katherine mumbled through the cotton swabs in her mouth.

When Katherine was released from the hospital, Alan took her to his parents' place where she remained for another week. Alan did not want her to be alone during the day. Around dinner time he came over to help nurse her and get whatever she needed before putting his law books under his arm and leaving for the evening. It seemed it had taken a hit and run driver to jolt their marriage into working again.

When she signed over the $5,000 insurance check to him which she had received for pain and suffering above and beyond medical expenses, he told her with a grin meant to cheer her up, "Well, Wurf, at least you got us out of debt for a while."

Back in their own apartment, however, Alan gave Katherine a disquieting piece of news. The accident had so upset him, he said, he had dropped out of law school. Finding that hard to believe, Katherine phoned the administrators at Southwestern and learned that

Alan had in fact dropped out of school, but some weeks before the accident.

That, of course, explained why they had not had Sunday brunch with Jack Dodd and his wife for over three months. What it did not explain was where Alan had been spending all of his evenings.

Alan Palliko was not the only man Sandra Stockton, who had filed for divorce from Henry a half year earlier, was seeing by the beginning of 1966. Almost indefatigable, she took her new shapely body out on the town every night after dinner like a kid who had been the last on her block to get a bicycle. The evenings generally began at the Stardust Bar. In her diary, which she kept up only sporadically, she wrote: "Met and dated many fellows—names and faces I don't remember. Only a few did I date more than once. Met a restaurant owner named Mark and dated him for a while—said he'd give me a hostess job. Never came about. Dated two fellows from the Auto Club. It's so hard to remember dates and places in retrospect. With my new figure, I'm tasting more of life than I ever have & I like it."

Los Angeles is a sprawling collage of lifestyles. It is vibrant as only mixture and experimentation can be. It is the melting pot of a nation that is a melting pot. For a woman who had seldom ventured farther than South Gate and Downey, a place like West Hollywood could seem as exotic as Istanbul. Wide-eyed Sandra lapped up the drinks and stories men offered her. On weekends she took whirlwind trips with some of the men to San Francisco. The elder Stocktons were more than happy to babysit for their grandson.

Lonnie Rademacher, a short sandy-haired fellow from New England, was a kind and gentle man who rekindled the warm and stable side of Sandra. It was the side of her that had taken care of a friend's children and house for several weeks while the friend was hospitalized for a serious operation. It was the side of Sandra that loaned money to friends and never asked for it back, indeed loaned them more when they again needed it. It was the Sandra who had been raised by her parents to be caring and thoughtful, who fell for Lonnie Rademacher.

But in February of 1966, the relationship ended. Lonnie was in night school in addition to working his full-time job at Cushman Motor Sales. He had neither the time nor the money to entertain Sandra the way she was beginning to expect from a man. Lonnie lost

Sandra to someone whose influence upon her was growing by the week.

Though Katherine had known Alan Palliko for four and a half years and had been his wife for over one year, he had become no less a mystery to her. If anything, the cloudiness about his entire existence had only thickened. His moods of euphoria and depression were more intense, his plans for the future more vacillatory, his reasons for unexpected actions more suspicious. Once a month he departed with one of his rifles in a case for a weekend of "hunting," yet never once returned with any bagged game.

On a Friday afternoon he called Katherine at work to tell her about a sale on mink coats he had seen advertised. Together they went down to the store to look at them. One stole that was regularly $1,200 and on sale for $800 caught Katherine's eye. As she stood before the mirror in it, Alan walked in circles around her, nodding with a smile.

"Stunning, Katy. Downright stunning."

Over the weekend they talked about how they could arrange for the financing.

"Maybe I'll just go out and get hit by a car again," Katherine laughed.

"Don't ever joke like that!" Alan snapped. "Ever!"

Conversing with Alan Palliko was like rolling dice.

The following Tuesday, it was just after 5:00 P.M. when Katherine walked hurriedly through the parking lot at work toward her car, thinking of the luxurious fur coat Alan and she would go down and purchase that evening. Her heart sailed high as a schoolgirl's. She had the key in the lock and her hand on the car door when she once again heard the sound of an engine roaring and tires squealing. What she had just a half a moment to see was a sharp featured man in a beige Valiant heading directly for her. Crying out, she threw herself against her little VW, hugging it desperately. In another moment she heard the crash of glass and metal. Smashed against her own car, she crumpled to the ground as if part of the debris. As she lay on her side, with an arm and leg twisted beneath her, she picked her head up from the pavement. Only semi-conscious, she saw the car slow up. The stranger looked back at her in the rear view mirror, then sped away.

It was the second time in five months that Katherine was rushed to

Central Receiving Hospital. Her legs were cut, her pelvic bone broken. This time, though, her husband was like a stranger to her. He paced her hospital room, rolling his straight-pin in his fingers, interrogating her as if he were the police.

"You didn't see anything?" he asked her over and over again. "You can't give me *any* kind of a description?"

Katherine repeated her hazy recollections, and if Alan's stony features seemed to relax any, she chose not to see it. The idea that Alan would have had anything to do with these accidents was wild, incomprehensible. Had he not been in tears the first time? Still, she began to sink into doubts.

Katherine had only two choices. One was to leave Alan and seek a divorce. But on what grounds? Not legal grounds (those were easy enough to come by in divorce proceedings), but on what personal grounds could she make sense of it to herself? She was twice a victim of a hit and run, and therefore Alan must be behind it?! It was too fantastic, paranoid. Her other choice was to do nothing, to live with the waves of fear until they subsided and she would see how silly she had been. Alan Palliko was eccentric, but not a murderer. Could a man hold her in his arms and sing her to sleep the way he did—"Button up your overcoat/when the wind is free/take good care of yourself/you belong to me"—and at the same time be considering how best to do away with her? A fantasy of hers, she tried to assure herself. But if true, it was nightmarish.

Once home, Katherine signed over another $5,000 insurance check to Alan without a peep. She went about her days as quietly as possible.

February brought Katherine the deepest depression of her life. Alan showed no concern for the pain she was still suffering from her second accident, and a friend from the Auto Club told her that everyone down at the office knew about another employee there being "Alan's woman." Katherine asked Alan about it. She told him about the Mamie Van Doren phone call as well. Alan appeared genuinely hurt that she would accuse him of infidelity.

"Anything else you'd like to run me through tonight? Don't worry about me," he sulked, "everyone knows I have no human feelings." He handed her the phone as he dialed the Auto Club and had her listen to several of the secretaries' voices.

"There, are you satisfied?" he asked when she did not recognize any of the voices.

"Yeah . . . I guess," Katherine lied.

That was one of Alan's problems, one of the cracks in what he considered to be his impenetrable wall of superior intelligence. He thought most people were stupid.

In March, Katherine phoned her friend in San Diego, the man she had dated before meeting Alan. They had a long confiding talk. Giving her the name of a lawyer in town, David Marcus, he told her if she would get a divorce, he would marry her. Once in April and again in June, Katherine went to see Marcus. Both times she brought herself to the brink of filing for divorce, and both times she could not follow through. A lawyer could get her her divorce, but no one, not even the police, could protect her. Every night she crawled into bed, her heart quickened with a rushing fear of the man who lay next to her under the covers.

The weekend of June 18, Katherine told Alan that as long as he was going hunting, she would drive down to San Diego to visit a girlfriend. Alan waited for her car to disappear around the corner that Saturday morning, then hopped into his own Chrysler 300. His rifle and scope were in the back seat.

Alan followed her onto the freeway, and for the two and a half hour drive managed to remain far enough back to be out of her sight. When she pulled into a San Diego motel, Alan waited a few moments, then parked his car across the street. As a man came out of one of the motel rooms and helped Katherine with her bags, Alan began loading his rifle. Calmly, not in any haste, he adjusted the scope. Alan was always meticulous.

He rolled down the window and waited. When the couple emerged just a few minutes later, they were holding hands and laughing. They paused at the doorway to embrace. Alan smiled to himself at how easy they had made it for him. One shot would do it—clear through her back and into the man's chest. Alan leveled his rifle and brought the middle of his wife's torso into the sight's cross hairs. His finger tightened slowly on the trigger.

He never fired. Perhaps at the last instant he considered how ill conceived the crime was, how likely he was to be caught. That thinking appears odd, however, in light of what happened the next week— for the following week Alan did make up his mind to kill Katherine, but in the most haphazard manner of all.

The days following Katherine's return from San Diego, Alan was quieter than ever, at times forbidding. He puttered endlessly around the den with his gun collection. More than once Katherine looked up from a magazine to catch him staring at her. Sometimes he smiled—faintly, almost derisively.

Katherine thought it was perhaps her imagination, her own feelings of guilt. Her self-condemnation was relieved only slightly by the fact that, as it turned out, her friend in San Diego had been impotent that Saturday night. To be sure, Katherine had been prepared to have sex with the man, and for Katherine, the willingness to commit adultery could not be easily rationalized.

The evening of June 24, a Friday, Katherine left their apartment for one of her Eastern Star meetings (the organization for female relatives of Masons). The night was sultry, and rather than changing as she customarily did into a long gown and the new mink she had finally bought, she left wearing the clothes she had worn that day to the office. Alan decided she was bound for another tryst.

Following in his own car, he lost her in traffic and went on to the place where the Eastern Star met. Bolting out of the car, his eyes swept across the parking lot for Katherine's VW. Not finding it, he got back behind the wheel, his temples throbbing, and tore away for home. Perhaps he had looked over the parking lot too cursorily, perhaps something inside him had not wanted to see his wife's car—for it had been there. Back home, Alan opened up a new bottle of bourbon and sat by himself in the living room, drinking. No one could be trusted in this world. He had more respect for the pink-booted hookers on the Strip than the high-button phony Wasps like Katherine. Worse, it was people like Katherine who kept him from succeeding, who squandered money on mink coats instead of helping him build toward that business empire, people who kept dragging him, Alan Palliko, back down into failure. One shotglass after another, Alan kept pouring the drinks down. By midnight he had finished off the bottle. He went outside and began walking the streets.

Katherine knew the hour was getting late, but not wanting to be rude, she accepted the invitation from Mr. and Mrs. Donald Johnson, her Eastern Star "worthy patron" and "conductress," to stop for a drink. She excused herself when she could, but by then it was after one o'clock.

A block and a half from home, Katherine saw a man, shirttail out, step off the curb into the street. Frightened, she braked. Her headlights revealed the man to be Alan. He walked over to the car and got in.

"You startled me," Katherine said.

"Hmm?"

"I said you startled me, Alan."

Alan pulled the car door shut and looked down at the floorboard. The rest happened so fast, Katherine did not even see his right fist come across as he turned toward her. The impact sent her head back against the driver's window pane. One blow after another stormed down upon her, in the face, in the stomach, in the face again.

"What are you doing!" she screamed. "What are you doing!"

She tried to get out her door, but the seatbelt held her where she was. Alan's fists slammed at her without stop, cracking against her right cheek and jaw. As she cried out for help, he unfastened her seatbelt and pulled her by the shoulders across to the passenger's side. Putting his knees on the edge of the seat, his back to the windshield, he wrapped his hands about her neck, and with his thumbs and all the weight he could bring to bear, pressed down into the middle of her throat. When Katherine, struggling, had a chance to gasp and scream for help again, he punched her in the face. Katherine started to choke on her own blood which began filling into her mouth.

Suddenly Alan released her and yanked open the passenger door. He got out and stood for a moment beside the little VW. He grabbed his moaning wife again, pulled her from the car, and flung her to the pavement. He fell upon her, his knees in her belly. His breathing was labored, but his voice was even.

"I'm going to kill you," he said.

He put her head between the vise of his two hands, and methodically began pounding her skull back against the pavement. Katherine lapsed in and out of consciousness.

She felt Alan drag her to her feet again. He tried to force her back into the car. With consciousness, the pain returned. With all the strength left in her she grabbed hold of the doorframe and resisted. 'I'll die,' she thought. 'If he gets me in the car again I'll die. I don't want to die.' It would at that moment have taken five men to pry her hand from the doorframe.

Again Alan took her head in his two hands, and beat it against the car metal. Then he stepped back and gazed at her for a moment.

"Oh, my God," he mumbled, and walked off into the darkness.

A small crowd had gathered—neighbors on front porches, a few passers-by. Through the blood streaming down past her eyes Katherine spotted a man on the corner, standing with his arms folded.

"Help me . . ." Katherine gasped.

The man studied her for a moment, a perplexed look on his face. His mouth opened, as if to say something. Then he turned and walked quickly away.

A woman in a Mustang pulled up alongside Katherine's car that was still in the middle of the street.

"What happened?" she demanded. "What's going on here?"

Katherine could not talk.

"Get in," the woman said.

Katherine tottered toward the car and collapsed in the back seat. As the woman pulled away, she asked Katherine where the nearest hospital was. From the back seat Katherine could only be made out to murmur, "Police station . . . police . . ."

The woman drove along Colorado Boulevard in Glendale until she spotted a squad car outside Bob's Big Boy. Inside the restaurant she found Officer D.J. Wheeler of the Glendale Police Department, who radioed for an ambulance to take Katherine to Glendale Memorial Hospital. She was examined in the emergency room by a Dr. Maatz. It was believed her neck was fractured.

Doctors attended to the multiple lacerations and contusions over Katherine's face and scalp while two male nurses needed a file to cut the wedding ring off her swollen finger. A bruise one inch in diameter was found at the base of the neck, but X-rays revealed there was no actual break in the cervical spine. Only her zygomatic (facial) bone was broken—that in three places. Once fully conscious again, Katherine managed to tell police who was responsible. With her less injured right hand she was able to sign the criminal complaint. An hour later, Alan was apprehended.

He had still been wandering the streets. His green pants and brown shirt were bloodied. He made no effort to resist arrest. The charge was wife beating; he paid the fifty dollar premium on a five hundred dollar bail bond, and was released immediately.

When Alan called Katherine at the hospital he was crying. Katherine hung up at the sound of his voice. He called again.

"Please don't hang up, Katy. I know about San Diego," he said quickly.

Katherine did not hang up. Alan pleaded for a chance to see her, and she relented.

To have won Katherine back in any meaningful way would have been impossible; to get her to drop charges against him, Alan was quite able to manage. His appearance before her at the hospital was nothing less than pitiful. He sat like a little boy, hang-dog, his feet drawing nervous patterns on the floor. There was something inside him that was wrong, he confessed, mixed up like the rest of his family. He confided to Katherine his constant fear of dying. What would he do in this world, he asked, if Katherine were to leave him?

He swore he would make up for the harm he had caused her. She did not even have to love him in return, only give him another chance. He admitted he had had her in the cross hairs of his riflesight down in San Diego, and that the previous night he had not just been trying to injure her, but had indeed been trying to kill her, to snap her neck. His mind had been addled by liquor; he vowed to never drink again.

The importance of the next thing he said to her would not be fully realized by Katherine or anyone else for another two years.

"I love you," Alan said, then thinking, added, "as much as I'm capable of loving a woman."

The police were aghast when Katherine told them she was dropping charges. They did all they could to change her mind, and left her hospital room shaking their heads.

"I just couldn't be the one to send Alan to jail," Katherine later told a friend.

She could not send him to jail, but she also knew that she had to get away from this man as quickly and as delicately as possible, without incurring Alan's wrath. From a hospital bed a simple girl from Dearborn, Michigan, who had never really wanted much more than things like a back yard with a pomegranate tree in it and one address for a long enough time to know the mailman's name, could now see it all with total clarity. Alan Palliko was virtually impelled through life by the energy of revenge. Whatever love there was in him was so repressed as to be unrecognizable. Human beings were like currency to Alan, to be exchanged at the best rate possible. Whether it was renting apartments or leasing cars he could not afford, his mission was always singular—to convince people he was more than he was. It always came down to money—money and women. If his victories were not conspicuous, they were not victories.

How and when Katherine would make the break, she did not know. She believed she would have some time to find her opportunity.

June 27, just two days after the beating and Alan's hospital room begging, Sandra Stockton and a man allegedly named Dick Scott walked into Pachmyr Gun Works and purchased a Hi Standard .22 caliber revolver.

On one of the last nights in June, Sandra Stockton went out on a date with Lonnie Rademacher. Since she had broken up with Lonnie in February, the evening was really just for old times' sake. They first dined at a Chinese restaurant, then went to a drive-in double feature. The story Sandra began telling over dinner, she finished as they walked around during the movies' intermission. Lonnie could barely believe what he was hearing. It was as if Sandra were reading lines from a play, or repeating rumors about someone else's life, certainly not hers.

"I picked him up in his own car," Sandra said, "after he ran her over with the stolen one. She didn't know it was him. It didn't work, anyway. All she did was get banged up a little. Don't you even want to know the man's name?"

"No," Lonnie answered her flatly. "I don't want to know anything more about this."

Sandra continued. "I have a gun in the house now, and I know how to use it, too. He's going to take her target shooting with him— somewhere up in the mountains. But I'm going to be waiting there, and I'm going to kill her. I don't even want any of the insurance."

A long silence passed.

"Well?" Sandra asked. "What do you think?"

"I think you have very serious problems, Sandra. You need help, don't you see that?" Lonnie could feel the tightness in his chest. "You'd kill another human being—just like that?"

Sandra met Lonnie's eyes and said, unflinching, "I want to know if I actually have the guts to pull the trigger. Anyway, haven't you ever just wanted to get away with something?" she asked.

5

KATHERINE REMAINED IN the hospital for a week, and had to return the following week for reconstructive facial surgery. Afterward, she convalesced, as she had two times previously, in the care of Alan's parents. By this time the Pallikos were living in an elegant apartment in the mid-Wilshire district of Los Angeles. Eventually Katherine decided she would be more relaxed and comfortable recuperating at her own family's place in Michigan.

With Katherine gone, Alan's nights out on the town began costing him more money than he had. Striding into his bank, he tried to cash Katherine's last paycheck from the phone company as well as her few shares of AT & T. He failed, both transactions having required Katherine's signature.

His wife out of the way for the month, Alan's womanizing became flagrant. The seventeen year old girl he brought up to the apartment would have stayed had she not seen Katherine's nightgown hanging in the bathroom. The girl did not believe Alan's story of being an abused, abandoned husband, and slipped out the door the first time Alan left the room. Even a woman visiting an apartment house neighbor did not get past Alan in the hallway without being asked for a date. Once informed by the neighbor of Alan's marital status, the woman called back to cancel.

Alan found female companionship elsewhere. Four-year-old Kyle Stockton told his grandmother in August about the fun he was having going on picnics with his mother and a man named Alan. Cathy Smith and Linda Jones, women who lived in the same Downey complex where Sandra had just rented a new apartment, wondered if it was

Sandra's ex-husband who kept coming over during that month of August. He was tall, mildly handsome in a rough-hewn way, and on several occasions carried up the stairs what appeared to be a rifle case.

Late in August, while still in Michigan, Katherine received a phone call from Alan. Alan's father had been shot. It was a head wound but only a graze, and Sid Palliko was expected to recover without complication. Over the phone it seemed to Katherine that Alan was more upset by the fact it had happened while his parents were vacationing at a hotel Alan had recommended. Shortly after leaving their hotel in Ensenada, Mexico (on the Baja peninsula), the Pallikos had been followed out onto the highway by a car that kept moving from behind them to in front of them to in back of them again. The driver was a woman, the passenger a man. One shot had been fired before the car sped away. The police had no leads.

"Just as long as your father's okay," Katherine said.

Alan's anxiety over the phone did not diminish.

"But I was the one who told them what hotel to stay at," he repeated.

The following day Alan retold the incident to his closest friend at the Auto Club, Michael Brockington. Alan was not anxious about the matter at all anymore. He was quite cavalier, massaging his wrists as if uninterested in his own story.

"Shame the guy was a lousy shot," Alan muttered from the side of his mouth, and left Michael sitting at his desk in a chill.

The morning after Katherine returned from Michigan, Alan asked if she would join him on a trip to the mountains where he wanted to do a little target shooting.

"You know I don't like that kind of stuff," Katherine said with a puzzled smile. "You go ahead."

Alan became insistent, saying he did not want to go alone. Sighing, Katherine picked up her purse and went out to the car.

During the long ride Alan was unusually silent. He appeared nervous, gripping the wheel tightly with both hands. Katherine was just as happy to not have to converse. Alan took one of the winding roads into the San Gabriel mountains and parked in a secluded area of thick green boscage. Katherine sat on a blanket near a tree while her husband paced off a distance for his shooting.

Lifting her hair off her neck, Katherine leaned back against the tree and breathed in the licorice-scented wild fennel. Except for some birds in the distance, all was as quiet as dew burning off in the morning sun. Suddenly, twigs began snapping above and behind her. Alan whipped his head in Katherine's direction, his half-open mouth in a freeze, as if holding his breath.

"Cute little fellas," Katherine laughed, looking up at the two squirrels scampering along the branches overhead, one with an acorn in its mouth.

Alan smiled weakly.

Something was amiss, Katherine thought. Alan appeared to be wasting time more than anything else. He looked about skittishly between each round he fired. At times he just stood still, arms akimbo, as if disgusted.

After firing only several rounds of ammunition, Alan suggested they go back home. Katherine shrugged and got back into the car. She did not give the incident much thought, but passed it off as merely another display of Alan Palliko's moodiness.

For Henry Stockton, the period of separation from Sandra was a wretched time. For the most part, he grieved alone in the dismal solitude of their lifeless little El Sereno cottage. When parching loneliness overtook him, he sought relief in the sad sawdusty oasis, Lucky's Bar.

By the end of August, 1966, however, shortly after their divorce had become final, Sandra and Henry began seeing each other again regularly. Sandra had quit her job at the Auto Club in April and had taken a similar clerk-typist position at the Alcoa Company in Vernon, which she held until August. Often at Sandra's suggestion that summer, Henry and she took their son Kyle down to the Marina, where they watched how the other half lived, with their sixty-foot sloops and triple-decked yachts.

Sandra agreed to remarry Henry. In September they took an apartment together in Downey and began efforts to rent out their little house on Ballard Street.

September 19, Katherine opened the August telephone bill at home and saw that while she had been back in Michigan, Alan had made toll calls at all hours of the day and night to a number she did not recognize. Having worked for the telephone company for six years, Katherine knew how to trace the number. She discovered the unpublished listing to have belonged until just recently to a woman by the name of Sandra Stockton.

A week later, Alan went on one of his supposed hunting trips. Katherine was by that time quite convinced that her husband had been cheating on her. Although snooping on her spouse had always been repugnant to her, she stole a look that weekend at Alan's appointment book. The name Sandra was scribbled throughout, and going as far back as January 8, 1966.

At long last, Katherine screwed up the courage to see her lawyer again, and to tell Alan that he had left her no choice but to file for divorce, making it clear it was she, not he, who had been rejected. To her surprise, Alan did not become angry. He took the news calmly, even admitting to having had sexual relations with Sandra as far back as the previous December. Alan agreed not to contest the divorce with one stipulation. The grounds cited were not to be adultery; there was to be no mention of the name Sandra Stockton. Katherine consented.

Neither one having enough money to move out immediately, the couple spent the next two weeks living under the same roof with a begrudging politeness. Katherine suggested they ask Alan's father for a loan so she might be able to move to her own place. Once again on the outs with his father, Alan sent Katherine over to make the request.

When she arrived at the Palliko's apartment, Mr. Palliko was in a robe, still taking it easy from the shooting incident in Mexico. Mrs. Palliko, he explained, was back east visiting her family. He finished the drink he had and proceeded to pour himself another. Each time Katherine brought up the loan, Alan's father turned the conversation to another subject.

"You know the first time Alan ever brought you over," he said, "all I could think of was what a lovely young woman you were. Did you know that, Katy?"

Katherine did not answer, and began moving uneasily in her chair. Alan's father pressed on as he drank.

"What would you think of taking a trip to Hawaii with me?" he asked. "I bet you could use a vacation right about now, am I right? I don't know what good an old man like me could do you, but I'd do my best and if you . . ."

Looking into his glass, Mr. Palliko did not see that Katherine was already at the door with her coat and purse. She had never believed

Alan's stories before—the ones about fixing his father up with coeds when Alan was still a student at Southern Cal. Katherine did not even wait for the elevator. She ran down the apartment house stairs. All that raced through her mind was, 'They're crazy, all of them, they're all crazy, the whole family, they're crazy, they're . . .'

Katherine told Alan what had happened. He only laughed, wishing he had been there to see his father's advances rejected.

Having remarried Henry on October 1, Sandra picked Audrey Scanlon up at the Auto Club for lunch that week to tell her the good news. Sandra did not linger in her old work place, Audrey later recalled, not even to stop by her old friend Alan Palliko's desk to say hello.

Katherine scraped together what money she could from friends, and moved to her own apartment on November 5. The last day with Alan, she gave him back a dollar bill—the one on which he had written in red felt pen: "I love you."

Michael Brockington had always liked being around Alan more than he had ever really liked Alan. Believing most of the stories about an abused childhood, Michael pitied Alan Palliko. He believed he could someday penetrate Alan's shell of aloofness.

Michael was a claims adjuster at the Auto Club, a position that put him above Alan Palliko, who was only a claims investigator. But if Michael had a more comfortable desk job while Alan was out in the field, in every social sense Alan was the boss.

Five years younger than Alan, Michael was also going through a divorce, his wife having custody of their two small children. He was always quieter than Alan and more serious-minded. Alan's flair for creating action and parties and good times was attractive to Michael. Somehow, Alan always had the ability to get Michael to loosen up.

Michael was tall and broad chested, although a little flabby around the middle. His fleshy, office-white face was gentle but not handsome, almost middle-aged in its earnestness, with heavy brows as furrowed as those of a scientist over his microscope. Women were flocking to the newly separated Alan, and Michael soon learned he could get in on some of the overflow if he would only stay at Alan's side. Girlfriends of Alan's eventually sat down with Michael at parties. He was a teddy bear. The women saw the kindness in his close-set hazel eyes. His sensitivity to the unhappiness of his own divorce made an appealing contrast to the callousness of his friend Alan. Many of Alan's girlfriends, tired of being part of a harem and lied to, in time gravitated toward Michael. The consoling friendship they found with him sometimes slipped into romance.

In November of 1966, separated from Katherine, Alan began frequenting a steakhouse-bar in Glendale called the Round Robin. Sometimes Michael tagged along. Alan made friends with little Joe Cavatelli, the five-foot-five bartender, as well as dozens of the Round Robin regulars. Two of Alan's friends there were Del and Gloria Cook, operators of the Yours and Mine Beauty Shop. Del cut the men's hair, his wife coiffed the women's.

Del Cook was a stocky man in his forties. He wore tight pants and shirts, and even in 1966 kept his hair in a crewcut, indifferent to fashion or the fact that his ears stuck out like radar screens. His nickname was "Cookie." Everyone at the Round Robin knew Del was not all there mentally, and had in fact once been institutionalized. His stories were humorous and never totally coherent. Alan kept him around as a kind of court jester. Michael Brockington never considered himself blameless for sitting there and watching it happen.

Del's wife, Gloria, was a slim blonde, getting on into middle age, but tan as a beachgirl. The heavy make-up she wore gave her a brittle jaded look. The first time Alan met her he made an obvious pass. Gloria sloughed it off with some nasty remarks, while her husband, sitting right there, remained oblivious to the entire incident.

One can eventually use people like Cookie to his advantage, Alan told Michael. He would bide his time.

"The only important person to me is me," Alan said, his brown eyes narrowing. "If you don't feel the same way, you're a fool. Money and mental superiority rule this world."

Alan's cynicism repulsed Michael, but at the same time he remained glued to Alan. Like an exemplary schoolboy intrigued by the class troublemaker, the one who always seemed to get away with it, Michael remained loyal and did Alan's bidding against his better judgment. Living out his own fantasies of daredevilness through Alan, he hung on Alan's words of approval.

"Start deciding which of our friends you want to invite for New Year's Eve," Alan told him in late November of 1966. "I'm landing a lot of bucks soon. Think I'll throw myself a coming out party."

Michael was curious to know how much money he was coming into.

"Let's just say a low six figures," Alan replied with his best titillating wink.

The strident ring of a phone woke Sgt. Joe Aguirre in the middle of the night on December 11. A man in El Sereno by the name of Henry Stockton had been murdered.

Alan moved to a new luxury apartment building in Glendale. He took his Mustang back to the leasing agency and outfitted himself with a Lincoln Continental. While the rest of the country lay in the dead of winter, Alan sat out by the pool every weekend, sipping bourbon and making up lists of guests, food, and champagne.

On December 28, Alan received the loan he had been after his father for—$3,000.

A suite at the fashionable Biltmore Hotel in downtown Los Angeles was none too good for Alan's New Year's Eve "coming out" party. Michael and he began calling friends to invite them. Alan said he would take care of the Las Vegas and New York crowd, old "connections," he called them.

Alan also invited Katherine and her date. She declined when she realized the only reason he wanted her there was to serve as a hostess.

Alan had the Biltmore cater the affair with fine buffet hors d'oeuvres and their top brands of liquor.

Natalie Post, a five-foot-eleven, freckled, strawberry-blonde, was Alan's date. He had met her at an exercise spa. For a good part of the afternoon Alan stood in the Cooks' beauty salon, fussing over how Natalie's hairdo was coming out.

Natalie was not the only woman Alan invited. There were several others who had been given the distinct impression they would be Alan's date. Alan sent Michael on a long car ride into the San Fernando Valley to pick up and escort one of them.

While only fifty people had been invited, twice that number eventually passed through for at least a drink and a few canapes. Among the uninvited, all of whom were made to feel welcome, were several members of the Purdue football team, in town for the next day's Rose Bowl. Alan, flushed with bourbon and pride, took them around to meet his friends.

It was a rowdy, at times tasteless party. Two girls passed out.

As the night wore on, Alan got drunk. Sometime after midnight Michael heard him getting vociferous with a man in the middle of the room. Suddenly, Alan's fist came out in a swing. It was a bona fide lifter, sending the man sailing over the coffee table. The fellow landed with his back against the couch, raised his head, lay back, and the party went on.

It went on until four in the morning. Early the next day, Alan called Del Cook, who could barely see the phone through his hangover. Alan had the sure cure. At noon, he picked Del up in his new Lincoln and took him down to the gymnasium. For two hours, Cookie sat on a bench, feeling sick. With disbelief he watched Alan run, jump rope, and lift weights.

The next evening Alan was explaining to Michael why, disappointingly, most of his "tight friends," the New York crowd, had not been able to make it. He boasted about how the party had run him five C-notes. What he did not tell Michael was that when the hotel's bill came, he simply ignored it. It would be over a year before the Biltmore would finally sue Alan and recoup part of its money.

January 16, 1967, Alan took his Lincoln Continental back to Harger-Haldeman Auto Leasing after having it for only three weeks, and traded it in for a new, mist-green Buick Riviera.

By early February, however, Alan was not so jovial and free spending. Michael detected a more than usual nervousness in him.

Alan's gun collection was quickly becoming a full-fledged arsenal. He rarely went anyplace without either his old beat-up .45 or his new PPK Walther automatic. When Alan and Michael went to the Round Robin, Alan placed his gun in a bag and checked it with the manager until they left. He often talked about the racial upheaval he believed was coming, a civil war, the way Alan painted it.

"Every citizen and his sister is going to be packing a gun," he told his friend with a grave nod. "On the street, in a holster."

His birthday gift to Natalie Post, his New Year's Eve date, was a .22 caliber revolver.

What Alan complained to Michael mostly about in February, though, was the money he was waiting for—money from some house sale he alluded to in passing.

Katherine, too, noticed how jumpy Alan was on the few occasions they saw each other in late January and early February. In the middle of a conversation, he would fling himself to the floor and do thirty quick push-ups, then sitting up and breathing deeply, would appear more relaxed. Alan insisted he was still planning on paying, as he had promised back in mid-December, for her Christmas bills, but that the money was taking longer than expected.

By the middle of February, Detectives Guy and St. John were keeping an eye on Sandra Stockton's every move, her every financial transaction. February 16, 1967, she deposited her $15,000 beneficiary check from Metropolitan Life at Security First National Bank on Firestone Boulevard in Downey. $5,000 went into her existing checking account, $10,000 into a savings account. The following day, February 17, she went to another Downey branch of Security First National, the one on South Lakewood Boulevard, and wrote a check for cash in the amount of $3,030. This she used to purchase $3,000 worth of American Express traveler's checks: fifty $20 checks, ten $50 checks and fifteen $100 checks. Returning then to her branch bank on Firestone, she withdrew $3,500 in cash from her savings account—$3,000 in hundred-dollar bills, $500 in twenties.

Guy and St. John obtained the serial numbers of the American Express checks, put "flags" on them, sat back, and waited for them to begin clearing.

During the last week of February, Alan invited Katherine over to his apartment to give her her Christmas money. When she arrived, there was an open suitcase full of cash on the bed. Another suitcase was still packed with Alan's clothes. Alan told her he had been out of town.

When Alan handed her $200, Katherine could not resist asking where all the money came from.

"Don't ask,"Alan cut her off.

Lightheartedly, Katherine persisted.

"I really don't want to be asked," Alan said, then turning to the window and the slow, cold drizzle outside, he tucked his hands beneath his armpits for a sense of snugness, and added somberly, "It was a horrible thing I had to do."

Katherine did not ask again. No longer having to live with Alan, she found his sense of drama and storytelling an eccentricity she did not have to bother with anymore.

A few days later, Alan took her out for dinner in Beverly Hills and paid for the meal with a hundred-dollar bill. Afterward they went to the Melody Room on the Sunset Strip, where Alan ordered two bottles of champagne. Then it was to the Scam, also on Sunset, where they capped their long evening with still more champagne—Dom Perignon.

Katherine could not be sure whether Alan had come into an inheritance or merely had wangled the loan from his father, but she was pleased he was at least making an effort to apologize in his own fashion for the years gone by—even if a second, unadmitted reason were to make himself in her eyes the bigshot he had always said he would become.

Guy and St. John were aware of Sandra's expenditures—her new apartment on Verdugo Road in an L.A. neighborhood adjacent to Glendale, her trading in her old Rambler for a late model Buick Wildcat, her large purchases of expensive clothes. What they were not aware of, however, was the toll the investigation was exacting from Sandra's nerves. Her diary continued to be the patient ear to her problems. In February she wrote in it: "Tail always there. I felt I had to get away. Did. Finally left house at 2 A.M. Sat. morning—went to a motel, flew to Lancaster for 2 wk. stay at health resort for much needed rest."

The health spa Sandra stayed at was the Bermuda Inn in the Antelope Valley just northeast of Los Angeles. She had not only been losing rest, but her hard won glamour had been vanishing as well. Since her husband's death she had gained back forty pounds.

Ever since St. John had gone down to the Auto Club and interviewed Alan Palliko, the detectives were keeping track of Alan's activities as well. They checked every written record of his they could find—bank transactions, phone bills, messages taken by his answering service.

Royce Straub, installment officer at Valley National Bank, informed the detectives that on February 23, Alan Palliko deposited $2,500 in his account. Straub had personally watched Alan thumb the bills off a thick roll of hundreds. The remaining wad of money that he held, practically undented, Alan had put back into his pocket. His balance before the deposit had been $34.45.

With the assistance of a Sergeant Stewart of the Glendale Police Department, Robbery Division, it was learned from Alan's answering service that a Miss Walther (sometimes, but less frequently, *Mrs.* Walther) was calling him almost daily. Though the lady was leaving a myriad of call-back numbers with the answering service, one of the numbers, 247-2692, appeared more often than the others. LAPD Intelligence Division informed Guy and St. John that the number was an unpublished listing belonging to Sandra Stockton. On only three occasions did "Miss Walther" leave a message for Alan in addition to just leaving her name: on March 3—"Secretary will call after 6:00 P.M."; on March 21—"Your secretary called"; and on March 9, far more significantly—"Definite word on policy tomorrow."

Guy and St. John sent Alan's fingerprint exemplar (taken when he was with the LAPD) over to fingerprint expert Harold Tanney for comparison with the latent prints found at the Ballard Street house. Tanney reported back that same day: Alan Palliko's prints were not among those found at the murder scene.

"Like I told Aguirre," Tanney said, "all of the prints belong to the victim."

Forgotten in his second to bottom desk drawer remained Tanney's written log of his actual findings made two months earlier: two of the prints found at the murder scene had *not* been matched up with the victim's. Their identity remained unknown.

Michael Brockington could always tell by Alan's tone of voice when he was on the phone with a woman. From the living room he could only catch snatches of conversation with the one who kept calling Alan at his apartment that spring of 1967.

"Okay, Tiger, okay," he heard Alan say patiently. "Just calm down, Tiger, all right?"

On one of the calls, Alan dropped the affectionate term and, working himself up, fumed, "Listen to me, will you! The police can't prove a thing. I've gone too far to let you blow it now."

Quite naturally, Michael began to assume that Alan had, in fact, involved himself in something illegal, but by the look on Alan's florid face when he returned to the living room, Michael knew better than to ask about it.

Keeping in touch with the people at National Life, Guy and St. John learned that Sandra had filed a Superior Court lawsuit against that company for the $40,000 on Henry's double indemnity policy. If Sandra were actually guilty of her husband's murder, the detectives asked themselves, why would she force yet an added, close examination of the facts at this time, when the police were still actively investigating her for the murder?

By the middle of March, all of Sandra's American Express traveler's checks had cleared. They had all been cashed on February 20—$1,750 at the Stardust Hotel, Las Vegas, Nevada; $600 at the Thunderbird Hotel, Las Vegas; $400 at the Desert Inn, Las Vegas; and $250 at various clothing stores, all in Las Vegas.

On March 21, St. John, with snapshots of Alan and Sandra in his pocket, caught a plane for Las Vegas.

As a matter of routine procedure, St. John began with the car rental agencies at the city's airport, McCarran Field. He did not have to go beyond Hertz. Ellen Bendas, a clerk at Hertz, found rental agreement No. 1807212 that was issued to Alan J. Palliko on Saturday, February 18, at 7:45 A.M. Alan had charged it to his Diner's Club Card—No. 518548516. Miss Bendas, who had been the clerk on duty that day, identified Alan as the man in the picture St. John showed her. St. John asked how she could be so positive about the man's face more than a month later. The clerk's answer was twofold. First, it was rather rare to rent a car that early on a Saturday morning; and secondly, because it was so early, she had had to make Alan wait at the counter for fifteen minutes while the car he wanted was being gassed up and readied.

She also identified a picture of Sandra as Alan's female companion that morning, and even went as far as to remember that Sandra had worn a coat over either a suit or a dress, and that the coat was a darker color than whatever was underneath.

The car Alan rented was a 1967 Ford Mustang with Nevada license C82541. On the rental application, Alan stated he would be staying at the El Morocco Hotel.

St. John talked to the El Morocco's co-owner and manager, Edward Doumanni. Together they went through the registration records for February 18. They found no card with the name Alan Palliko, but they did find a guest who had listed as his car a Hertz '67 Mustang, license C82541. The name on the card was hand printed: Jerry Pace—home address, 1321 J. Street, Bakersfield, California. Though a Helga Jordan had been the desk clerk that day, Doumanni had also been present to see the man print out both names—Jerry Pace on one card, S. Stockton on the other. Sandra's home address was given as 2723 Ballard St., Los Angeles. Doumanni made a positive identification of both Alan and Sandra from the pictures St. John showed him.

For the nights of February 18 and 19, Alan occupied room 238. Sandra stayed in 239 across the hall.

St. John's next stop was the Shoehorn on Las Vegas Boulevard.

One of Sandra's American Express checks had been cashed there. The Shoehorn's owner, Lawrence Mushkin, found in his records that Sandra had bought two pairs of shoes and a handbag. He was able to identify both Sandra and Alan from the photos quite easily because he had personally delivered the apparel to their hotel. Sandra had requested the delivery because she had more shopping to do that day and did not want to be loaded down with boxes. Around 6:30 that evening Mushkin had taken the packages to room 239 of the El Morocco Hotel. Alan was in Sandra's room at the time. They appeared to be getting ready to go out to dinner, Mushkin said.

St. John continued his interviews around the city. Frank Wilcox, cashier at the Desert Inn, had cashed $400 of Sandra's traveler's checks. He remembered Alan because he had cashed a number of his personal checks over the years.

The cashier at the Stardust, where Sandra had cashed $1,750 of her American Express checks, was intransigent. Unless forced by subpoena, he would not talk to the police about any of the casino's patrons.

The people at the Thunderbird Hotel St. John found more helpful. Sal Bel Angelo, pit boss at the casino's twenty-one game, remembered Alan quite well. As Bel Angelo explained, it was his job to "watch customers as they come to the tables, what change they make, what change they buy, what change they get from dealers, and their ordinary play"—in short, to try to miss nothing and remember everything.

Alan and he had even struck up a conversation while Alan was trying his luck at twenty-one, the game commonly called blackjack. Alan had volunteered that he was staying at a nearby hotel with his sister. Only once did Bel Angelo see Alan talking with the "sister" as she stood at the slot machines. Because her back was to him, he could only recall she was "short and a little on the stocky side."

Alan was a considerable winner his first night at the twenty-one tables, ending up on the plus side in the vicinity of eleven or twelve hundred dollars. The next day he presented Bel Angelo with a gift of a dozen golf balls, Bel Angelo's name engraved on them. He also gave the pit boss his business card. The card identified Alan as a private investigator and indicated he had offices in San Diego and Las Vegas as well as in Los Angeles.

The second night at the tables, Alan made himself an example of why every year new hotel-casinos are built and not one comes down.

He lost his previous day's winnings and then some. Bel Angelo could not remember the exact amount, but knew it was a large enough sum to prompt Gerald Tassone, the Thunderbird's shift manager, to introduce himself to Alan and give him a blanket invitation to return anytime as the hotel's "guest." Casino operators have antennae for spotting the type that will jump at such invitations—the type that like being known as regulars and feel like VIP's when they are given accommodations on the house and first row tables at the hotel's nightclub acts, the seats Buddy Hackett refers to in his routine as "the schmuck tables."

Alan Palliko did return. While the Hertz records showed that Alan brought the rented car back to McCarran Field on February 20, presumably to catch a flight back to L.A., the Thunderbird Hotel's ledger revealed that Alan had apparently turned right around and come back to Las Vegas the very next day. February 21, Alan returned to the Thunderbird with three friends in tow, all assuming they, too, would be the hotel's "guests." Gerald Tassone accommodated them.

For the nights of February 21 and 22, Alan stayed in room 4144. "Mrs. Palliko," described by hotel employees as a tall good-looking redhead, stayed across the hall in 4141. St. John, trying to piece together the personality he was investigating, began to discern in Alan a man who was more concerned about having a woman at his side than in his bed. The other two friends, Mr. Joe Cavatelli (the Round Robin bartender) and his wife, took 4145. An investigation of Cavatelli revealed no known criminal history.

On this second trip to Las Vegas, Alan, no longer in Sandra's presence, registered under his real name and gave as his address P.O. Box 6126, Glendale, California. This in fact was Alan's correct P.O. Box.

Alan, Tassone recounted, gambled only one night in the Thunderbird casino during his second stay. He dropped two thousand dollars.

St. John returned to Los Angeles with a briefcase full of evidence. It was all very circumstantial, but it all pointed toward a conspiratorial sharing of insurance money. Working backward from the information he had, St. John soon learned that on Alan's trip to Las Vegas with Sandra, he had also made his flight reservation under the alias Jerry Pace. The names on the plane tickets were Mr. J. Pace and *Mr.* B. Johnson. St. John assumed Sandra was Mr. B. Johnson.

Jerry Pace and Mr. B. Johnson had taken Western Airline flight

26, departing Los Angeles International at 6:30 A.M. and arriving at McCarran Field at 7:10, about twenty minutes before the man named Alan Palliko registered at Hertz.

From Nevada police records, St. John discovered that Alan had bought a Colt 357 Magnum for $82 at Las Vegas' Gunsmoke Shop. He had purchased it on February 20 and had picked it up on his second trip on the twenty-third. In California, gun stores must wait fifteen days for a police background registration check before releasing a gun to the purchaser. In Nevada, the delay is only three days.

A check by St. John with CII gun registration records revealed that while Alan's collection varied from month to month, at any given time he was the owner of approximately thirty handguns and rifles.

Guy and St. John visited Katherine at her small Glendale apartment on March 28. The detectives had by that date discovered Alan's single arrest record, and that Katherine had dropped the charges of wife beating. She told Guy and St. John of the two hit-and-run accidents. While married to Alan, she had carried a life insurance policy for only $12,000 through her employers, Pacific Telephone. Alan was the beneficiary. She related to the officers that her reason for divorce had been Alan's admitted affair with Sandra Stockton. Her interlocutory decree had come through just the previous January 12.

Katherine went with the detectives to Parker Center, where she made an official statement of the same information she gave at her apartment. She also promised them she would not tell Alan she had been interviewed.

Katherine had never been a good liar. When Alan next visited her and told her of how the police were investigating him for the murder of Sandra's husband (though he would not tell her how he had learned this), he could see just by her one quick glance away to a coffeepot that was not brewing that she had already been contacted. Katherine could not deny it.

Alan swore his innocence to her. He may have been a difficult, at times impossible man, but a murderer? No, he was not a murderer. He knew how the police worked. They used circumstantial evidence to distort.

"Please don't talk to them again," he asked of her. "You could hang me without realizing it."

In the course of interviewing Sandra's former boyfriends, the police made contact with Lonnie Rademacher on April 4, almost four months after Henry's murder. Though Lonnie apparently still had feelings for Sandra, under firm prodding he delivered the kind of information the detectives had been waiting for. He told in entirety Sandra's story of her dating a married man, of a hit-and-run of the man's wife, and of their plan to shoot the woman in the mountains.

Lonnie agreed to try and revive his relationship with Sandra and find out what he could for the police. Deciding it would come under the heading of helping to further the interests of justice, Guy smilingly told Lonnie he would take care of a speeding ticket Lonnie had just received, to free up more funds for the "nightlife mission."

That evening, Lonnie contacted Sandra by phone and informed her of his agreement with the police, but said that he could not go through with it. If she had been involved in the murder of her husband, he told her, he believed she should be punished, but that he did not have it within him to be the one to put her in the gas chamber. Sandra insisted she was innocent. They agreed it would be best not to see each other—at least for a while.

The police felt they were closing in on Alan and Sandra, but still there was no solid evidence connecting either of them to the murder of Henry Stockton: no match-up of bullets with the murder weapon, which was yet to be found, no fingerprints at the Ballard Street house, no telltale article belonging to the murderer left behind at the scene of the crime. Moreover, Sandra had an airtight alibi for the night of the murder, and Alan no longer needed one. It had been four months since the murder, and no one could really be expected to remember where he had been on a given date after that period of time. If Alan were to say he could only assume he had been alone in bed the early morning hours of that Sunday in December, a prosecutor would hardly be able to suggest his story was unlikely.

During the month of April, the police continued to keep close tab of Alan's and Sandra's financial transactions. On April 5, the detectives asked for and received records of all charges Alan had made so far that year on his Carte Blanche and Bank Americard. As their progress report noted, Alan spent "considerable time and money" at the Round Robin Restaurant. If Alan were aware of the police looking over his shoulder, he clearly was not intimidated by it. On April

17, he turned in his Buick Riviera and took out a lease on a new, blue hardtop Corvette.

On April 25, Guy and St. John conferred at length with their supervisor of investigations, Lt. R.C. Madlock, and with Captain Hugh Brown. All officers at the meeting agreed that, while no one piece of evidence was by itself damning, the sum and weight of all the pieces surely was. What they still sought, however, was one or more pieces of *physical* evidence. The time to move in that direction, they felt, was now. The move was swift and well coordinated.

At 7:30 P.M. on April 26, a separate team of officers knocked on the doors of three apartments—Alan's, Sandra's, and Alan's parents'. The head of each team carried a copy of the search warrant issued to them that day. The evidence sought, and carefully listed on the warrant, was: "a .22 caliber handgun, the type used to murder Henry Stockton, any written communications and photographs showing contact and association between Alan Palliko and Sandra Stockton, and any canceled checks indicating the exchange of money between the two above persons."

Mr. and Mrs. Sid Palliko were cooperative. The police explained that their apartment had to be searched only because Alan had listed their mid-Wilshire residence as his home address on several of his gun registrations. None of the evidence sought was found there. The parents were so shaken by the ordeal that after the police left, they burned the copy of the search warrant just to rid themselves of it. They called their son and left a message with his answering service for him to call back, no matter what time of day or night. It would be after midnight before Alan returned their call and told them he did not know what any of this was about.

No evidence was found in Sandra's apartment. In Alan's apartment, St. John noted the number 247–2692 in Alan's telephone-address book. It was the number the Intelligence Division had previously established to be Sandra's unpublished listing. St. John also observed fifteen to twenty handguns and rifles, all fully loaded and all with accompanying boxfuls of ammunition—but none was the weapon sought. After their apartments and cars (which were included in the warrant) had been searched in their presence, Alan and Sandra were placed under arrest for murder and brought to Parker Center for interrogation.

After being advised of her constitutional rights, Sandra refused to make any statement. Alan, too, was advised of his rights and, without a hint of lost confidence, talked with Guy and St. John in room 318 of Parker Center for approximately two hours. He provided only the most general information, and when pressed for details proved nimble at deflecting their questions. His blend of cooperativeness and arrogance frustrated and infuriated the detectives.

As Guy and St. John were not at all sure that the District Attorney's office would file a murder charge against Alan and Sandra, they decided not to book them. Just after midnight, the two were released without bail being set or posted.

The next day, Captain Hugh Brown, Sergeant Guy, and Officer St. John went to the Hall of Justice, headquarters for the Los Angeles County District Attorney's Office, with some 430 prosecutors at the time. There they met with Deputy District Attorney James Shea, head of the Complaints Division. They sought a first degree murder complaint from Shea against suspects Palliko and Stockton for the murder of Henry Stockton.

For several months, Shea had been kept abreast of the investigation through the police progress reports. The previous day's arrest, however, had been a decision taken by the police alone, without the benefit of Shea's consultation. As the deputy district attorney looked over the final follow-up report, dated April 25, his feeling was that, while there might be enough circumstantial evidence to get past a preliminary hearing, there was not nearly enough to convict. When one separated the facts from the speculation, virtually the whole case against Alan and Sandra was that they had shared in the proceeds from Henry's death, and in a suspicious looking fashion. *That* was not a crime.

Not only was the evidence insufficient to establish guilt, but there were too many possible interpretations of what might have actually occurred. Had Alan and Sandra conspired from the very beginning to murder Henry as the police believed, or was it not just as possible that Sandra had hired someone else to murder Henry, and Alan had subsequently blackmailed her? Perhaps Sandra had even asked Alan originally to do the job for her, Alan had refused, and that was how he knew she was behind the murder. Another possibility was that Alan was merely Sandra's gigolo, ready to take her money when she came into it. That setup could just as easily have accounted for the use of aliases in Las Vegas. Perhaps, too, Alan could have murdered Henry on his own, knowing that with his emotional hold on Sandra he would eventually be sharing in the insurance money, maybe even as Sandra's new husband.

The problem with circumstantial evidence before a jury was that, like an abstract painting, it could have as many interpretations as viewers.

The biggest hole in the case was that nothing directly tied Alan Palliko into the crime itself. And if nothing tied Palliko to the murder, Sandra Stockton's association with him was almost meaningless in terms of establishing *her* guilt.

Jim Shea did not know that Alan Palliko had told his ex-wife Katherine that he had had to do a "horrible thing" to get his sudden new source of money. But even when this information and a great deal more like it would ultimately find its way into law enforcement files, it would do little to peel away the layers of mystery surrounding Alan Palliko. The problem with Alan's seemingly incriminating statements was basic. Alan Palliko was a storyteller, a Los Angeles bullslinger. Killings he would later boast of, all evidence indicated he had simply never committed.

Jim Shea knew that if they were to prosecute now and lose, the case was over. Alan Palliko and Sandra Stockton could never be brought to trial again for the murder of Henry Stockton. The law of double jeopardy made no exceptions, no matter how conclusive a subsequently found piece of evidence might be.

Even if a jury did look on the body of evidence the same way as did the police—that Palliko and Stockton sure as hell *seemed* guilty— "seemed" was not enough. To put a man and woman in prison for life, or possibly in the San Quentin gas chamber, a juror had to believe in their guilt "beyond a reasonable doubt and to a moral certainty."

For two days, Jim Shea agonized over his decision. Investigations were like ballgames, their final outcomes predicated partly on psychological momentum. What would happen to this investigation if he now told the detectives, who had worked for four months on the case, that their success had been only partial? Other cases were piling up on these men's desks.

Jim Shea made his decision alone. On April 28, he officially rejected the case on the grounds of insufficiency of evidence.

On May 3, Bob Guy received a phone call from Alan Palliko. Indignantly, Alan reprimanded the sergeant for having interviewed his ex-wife Katherine and demanded he not do so again. Guy remained noncommittal, and at the conversation's end suggested Alan come downtown voluntarily and submit to a polygraph test. Alan said he would consult with his attorney and call back. He never called back.

To Katherine it appeared that Alan had for once been telling the truth. The case had been rejected. Just as Alan told her, shaking his head, "They had the wrong guy. Dumb cops. How could I have ever wanted to be one?"

6

ALAN BEGAN TO wear hats. No one in Los Angeles wears hats. Alan's were wide brimmed fedoras, the kind that New York gangsters were supposed to wear. He began to buy tailored silk suits as well. His deep tan was from the weekends at his apartment's poolside and from periodic trips down to Baja. To his numerous girlfriends he dropped suggestions about working on the side for the "organization." His appearance lent some credibility to his new pose of syndicate operative, just returned from a business-pleasure trip to Costa Rica.

Memorial Day, Michael Brockington tagged along to a "lease breaking party" given by one of Alan's neighbors. Alan had recently moved into a new apartment, even larger and swankier than the last one. Alan brought a woman named Debbi Simmons to the party. Though Alan and she had been dating since early March, Michael had never met her. Almost all of Alan's girlfriends were striking, but Debbi was extraordinary. A complexion out of a Swedish travel brochure and flowing blond hair halfway down to a bottom that would make burlap cling—one hundred and twenty-five pounds so impeccably distributed on a five-foot, seven-inch frame, no one at the party could take his eyes off her. No one except Alan, who left her on the couch and gadded about from group to group.

As often happened, Michael found himself sitting next to just one more of Alan's surplus women. All of them, excepting only Katherine, whom Michael had met just once quite briefly, were attracted to the physicalness of an Alan Palliko. Michael sometimes thought of telling some of these women they were only courting trouble by hanging around Alan, but then of course they could have said the same thing to him.

Michael drank nearly the whole bottle of Canadian Club he had brought, and over the entire afternoon listened woozily to Debbi's story: the marriage at seventeen in her home town of Centralia, Illinois; the divorce and working as a model in Chicago; being supported as a mistress, who could type a little, by a wealthy grey-haired businessman; the trips to Europe with him; and coming out to Los Angeles (dreams of becoming an actress kept to herself) to take up with her benefactor in the meandering house off Mulholland with the intoxicating view.

But amidst all the luxury and escorted trips was loneliness. Some women moved to the heart of men's lives. Debbi never got off the arm.

Then came Alan. He told her he loved her, and promised to marry her when his divorce became final. She left for another trip to Europe and was to stay there with her rich friend for several weeks. Alan wrote her almost every day. He told her twenty-four dollars for a phone call to her in Rome meant nothing, and the thirty-three dollars to hear her voice again just three days later when she was in Paris was worth every penny. Debbi cut her trip short and came home a week early. At Alan's insistence, she happily broke off her relationship with her sugar daddy.

Alan would be a success, too, someday, she told Michael at the party. And how could you not love his sense of humor? He called his Corvette "Max." Debbi liked the way Alan lived—the snazzy apartment, the parties, the cars. Michael learned for the first time that Alan had even bought a quarter horse that he kept out at the Hildebrand Stables in the San Fernando Valley. Often Alan took Debbi along when he went out to ride the horse or to help the stable hands groom it. It had a sand-colored mark on one shoulder and that, Debbi bubbled to Michael enthusiastically, was why Alan had named it Sandy.

In May, in the company of her father and Mr. Thomas Nixon of the Santa Barbara Savings and Loan, Sandra inspected the house on Ballard Street. The home had been vandalized. Furniture was overturned, walls were dirtied, beer cans were strewn all about. Holding a nub of cheek between her teeth, Sandra listened to Mr. Nixon's news that the fire insurance money for the house would go only to Santa

Barbara Savings and Loan, the first trust deed holder, not to her. Nixon also informed her that Henry had, before his death, allowed his mortgage redemption policy to lapse, thus still leaving Sandra with the unpaid mortgage. If Sandra were wondering how any one man's incompetence could live so long after him, she kept it to herself. She ignored the $109 monthly payments, and lost the home in foreclosure.

The police reinstituted their surveillance of Sandra. Wherever she went that early summer, a squad car, in her clear sight, trailed behind. If either suspect were to break, they believed it would be she. While they were following her and her mother on an afternoon of shopping, Sandra came over to the police car and suggested flippantly, "Why don't you come in with us and have lunch? It's a lot cooler." The officers, sweltering in their unairconditioned car, declined. Coming back out from lunch, Mrs. Bingham was quite polite, ingenuously so, to the policemen. She explained she would have to make a sharp left to get back into traffic, but that she was not trying to shake them. Sandra and she were going to the Broadway to do some shopping.

"All you have to do," one of the officers called to Mrs. Bingham's daughter, "is come down and talk to us, and all of this will be over."

The police were bluffing. They had no new source of leverage. Sandra watched herself carefully, especially her spending. In June she took a job with Allied Pacific Manufacturing. That same month she moved in with her sister Tracy, who was in the process of getting a divorce. The sisters split the $120 rent.

The ardor of the detectives involved in the case began to languish. In a progress report they wrote: "From the period of May 23, 1967 to August 3, 1967, officers periodically received other information relative to this case and continued the investigation. No new significant facts were learned."

By autumn, nearly a year after Henry's murder, the investigation had come to a near standstill.

"They know me here," Alan told Debbi, pulling on the brim of his hat the first time he ushered her through the door of the Round Robin.

In addition to Joe Cavatelli, Alan was also friendly with Bob, the Italian drummer in the band. Alan told Debbie that being Italian himself, he liked to stay close with the "clan."

"Big Dude," Alan called himself. He protected his women. Debbi was girlishly enamored of Alan's toughness, his guns, his stories. She did whatever he asked, even allowed him to take pictures of her in the nude.

It was only his submachine gun that made her nervous. She saw it around the apartment several times. Rolling a straight-pin between his fingers, he said it was for when the next riots came.

In telling Debbi of doing "jobs" for some sort of organization while he continued to work for the Auto Club, Alan made slanted references to "dead" guns—guns that were broken down and reassembled with different parts so as to be untraceable.

Sometimes late at night, as if wearied of being tough, Alan let Debbi mother him. She was moved by a man whose mind was sometimes so sadly distant and roiled with inner turmoil. Alan showed her his letters to his psychiatrist in New York and told her, as he had told others, that the doctor was the only person in the world who cared about him. Debbi would later say that the letters were mind-boggling, they were such a chronicle of a persecution complex.

It was grossly unjust, Alan told her, that he had been dismissed from the police force. What he had done, went the story, had been in self-defense. Having come home to find his wife in bed with another man, Alan said, he had grappled with the man and in the course of the fight had thrown him out the window, killing him. Everyone had agreed it was self-defense, and yet they had still seen fit to dismiss Alan from the department. Debbi found the story a clear explanation of why Alan sometimes woke in the middle of the night in a cold sweat, having just suffered his recurrent nightmare of killing a man.

When Alan and Debbi made love—for Debbi, an unnervingly infrequent event—it was, Debbi told a friend without elaborating, "weird . . . awfully weird."

On June 13, Debbi was involved in a car accident—not a hit-and-run. An elderly woman ran a stop sign and struck Debbi's VW broadside. Her son, Timothy, was unscathed, but Debbi received a number of lacerations that put her in the hospital for four days. Alan insisted that he handle the insurance matter for her. The money would be used for a down payment on a bar, their bar. When their business together was flourishing, they would be married. Though an accident had apparently been needed as a love catalyst, Debbi was ecstatic.

Alan also arranged for Debbi to meet a friend of his who was an actors' agent. The agent did not care whether Debbi could act or not

—he liked her looks and was eager to sign her. Acting lessons could be arranged. Alan began talking excitedly about becoming Debbi's business manager.

Later that month Alan telephoned Katherine, asking her for a Mexican divorce. He needed to be free to marry a "wealthy woman." Katherine refused, telling him they would wait for the final Los Angeles decree like respectable people.

While Debbi waited at home for Alan's calls, Alan roved the city's after-dark spots for still other women.

Drinking his bourbon straight and puffing on dark little Shermans, he struck up a conversation with Marjorie Huebner, a slender, small breasted young woman with the laugh of a good sport, and big deer-brown eyes, who was working toward her B.A. in cosmetology at UCLA. Looking casual that night, like a Sierra Club member in her jeans and tennis shoes, and oversized sweater, Marjorie listened with interest as Alan told her he had to leave town to be in an auto race, but that he would call her when he returned.

A few days later, claiming he had just gotten back from the race, Alan took Marjorie to the Playboy Club on the Sunset Strip. It was a hundred dollar evening. Dinner and champagne, a batch of pictures from the table hopping photographer, a Playboy necklace for Marjorie, a Playboy wallet for himself—the works.

Later that night, perhaps sensing Marjorie's critical though unspoken appraisal of him on the dance floor, Alan suddenly grabbed his leg and hobbled back to the table. He cursed about some sort of old football injury—he had played, he said, at Southern Cal until the bad knee had forced him to quit. Every time Marjorie saw him over the next several weeks he had a cane.

On their third date, in the middle of dinner, Alan said, "Let's go to Las Vegas."

"I'm not much of a gambler," Marjorie replied.

"No," Alan said, "I mean to get married."

Marjorie laughed and returned to her plate. When she looked up, Alan raised his eyebrows quizzically. Marjorie put her fork down.

"Alan, I'm not stupid," she said.

Alan shrugged, looking hurt, and Marjorie realized that he had not been putting her on.

"Alan, I don't know you," she exclaimed. "You don't know me!"

Alan smiled and nodded, and Marjorie put her hand lightly on his, saying sweetly, "Sorry."

Alan would not give up on Marjorie that easily. For her birthday he gave her a gold cigarette lighter with a card that read: "Would you like something that is utterly useless, completely impractical, and just a little bit wicked? Me? My love is with you. Alan."

There was, of course, the usual delay in obtaining the insurance check for Debbi's accident. Each time Alan brought the subject up in July, Debbi used the opportunity to bring up the subject of marriage, but Alan remained elusive—and single. He was looking to buy a bar called the Honeybucket, he insisted, but so far was unsuccessful in securing a loan from a friend of his in the car business, someone he had met at one of the gyms.

In mid-July, Debbi and her son Timothy flew to Illinois for a visit home. The next weekend, Alan joined them. On the airplane back to California he said he had not wanted to spoil her last two days at home, and thus had waited to tell her that his horse was dead. A piece of food had become lodged in Sandy's throat and the horse had choked to death. Graphically, Alan described how it had been to sit there and watch as the horse kicked spasmodically against its stall. At last, on its side, with the front and hind legs that lay on the ground thrust out stiffly, the legs on its other side shot into the air and froze there. The animal was dead. Ever so slowly, the legs in the air descended, like a box lid closing on an air cushion hinge, until they came to rest against the other legs in the bed of hay. Death was horrifying, Alan said.

Alan had come to a decision over the weekend. He suggested Debbi move in with him. It was what Debbi had been waiting almost five months to hear. The week after they arrived back in Los Angeles, she packed her belongings and took up residence with Alan. Michael Brockington helped her move.

Neither Alan nor Debbi liked crowds. They spent countless hours in Alan's Corvette, driving the winding canyon and beach roads. North of Malibu where traffic was sparse, Alan let the car "run," taking the coast highway's curves at tire squealing speeds. Time and again he was pulled over by the police. Alan scoffed at the tickets, saying he could beat them in court.

During the first week of living together, Debbi answered a phone call from a woman asking to speak to Alan. Alan took the phone in the other room and closed the door behind him. Debbi could hear him getting progressively angrier, cursing the person at the other end to whom he referred alternately as Sandra and Tiger. After hanging up, he emerged from the room and shouted at no one in particular, "No woman is going to threaten me! Not a woman!"

Debbi listened quietly, fearfully, as Alan in time told her more specifically about his role with the organization. He had already, he said, "nine hits" to his credit. There was always a front man, he told her, who assembled the maps and necessary facts about each intended victim. Both times Alan went out of town, Debbi believed it was for another hit. Both times he packed a dismantled rifle and scope in his little carrying case. It was the one rifle he never kept around the apartment.

Debbi thought she could always tell when Alan was on the phone with one of the organization bosses. It always ended up in rancor. Now they wanted Alan to take care of some woman, he told her, and Alan would not do it, not even for the $25,000 fee.

"I could never kill a woman," he told Debbi.

But the organization would not let him go so easily, he complained. Alan was always going off at night to "meetings." They were held in the hills, he said, where the rich cats lived. His top bosses were in Detroit. Before each meeting he told Debbi he would once and for all lay down the law with them, but each time he returned he could not sleep because "they got their way, they won't let me go."

The police were hounding him for a murder he did not commit, and the organization would not let him go. Everyone was against Alan, and closing in.

"You better think twice about marrying me," he told Debbi soberly one night. "Anyone who marries me better take out plenty of insurance."

In late July, Alan and Debbi took a weekend vacation to Rosarita Beach on the Baja Peninsula. The trip was to help settle Alan's nerves.

While sitting in their hotel's bar, Alan's face went slack; Sandra Stockton and her son Kyle had just walked in. Flustered, Alan made the awkward introductions, and had no choice but to invite Sandra to join them. After putting her son to bed, Sandra returned to their table. Alan was on edge the entire evening. Debbi could see that he was constantly fingering the handgun in his right coat pocket. Sandra had sat down on that side of him.

Later that night a group of noisy party revelers came into the bar, led by a bulbous nosed old man with white wild hair who called himself Captain El Rosco. The "Captain" invited the three of them to join in their partying and dancing. Alan and Debbi did not move from their seats, but Sandra gladfully got up to frug with the Captain. Suddenly, after several dances, Sandra collapsed in the middle of the floor. A doctor was called but could find no clear reason for Sandra's fainting. After resting for about twenty minutes she was back on her feet, although shaky. In the confusion, the Captain had disappeared.

The next morning, Debbi was awakened by Alan's ranting as he paced around their hotel room. He was tossing clothes everywhere, looking for his gun. Someone had taken it, he said.

"Sandra, do you think?" Debbi asked.

"No . . . no," Alan dismissed the notion unconvincingly. "Down here, could have been anyone."

The couple packed hurriedly and headed back to Los Angeles.

August 3, Debbi received her car accident insurance check. It was for $4,750. Agreeing that it would be spent as a down payment on a mutually owned bar, she handed the full amount over to Alan. The next day, he deposited $2,725 to his checking account and used the balance as a down payment on $4,500 worth of furniture.

When the furniture arrived, Debbi, flurried, followed Alan throughout the apartment, demanding an explanation. Alan ignored her as he instructed the delivery men where to put it all. Over the next several weeks almost everything he did appeared calculated to drive her away from him. He spent more nights then ever playing cards at the legalized poker halls of Gardena. When home, he carped about her changing her mind and turning down the acting agent's offer just because it would have meant being out of town with stock companies much of the time.

"I want to be here in Los Angeles with you!" she yelled at him. "I want to marry you!"

Disgusted, Alan just shook his head.

The more shabbily he treated her, the more Debbi hung onto him, though she feared she was getting close to the hole in the ice with Alan. When she noticed one night at the Round Robin that Bob, the drummer, was no longer there, Alan told her with a glint of warning in his eyes that Bob had crossed him in a money deal. He had no choice but to break the drummer's fingers.

On a weekend of target shooting with Marjorie at her uncle's cabin near Mount Palomar, Alan told her about Debbi and that he was having trouble getting her out of his apartment.

"Just gonna have to lean on her a little more, I guess," he said, blasting off a row of tin cans with a submachine gun.

Marjorie later told a friend that that weekend Alan had "brought enough weapons to start a war."

It would be two months before Marjorie would hear from Alan again.

On August 8, Sandra's attorney, Roy Marchetta, arrived at a settlement with John Morrow, attorney for National Life Insurance, on the $40,000 Superior Court suit. Having successfully resisted only the claim on the double indemnity clause, Morrow handed Marchetta a check for $20,000.

On August 15, Alan convinced Debbi to move to her own apartment.

Michael Brockington was over his head with Alan Palliko. Although never actively taking part in what seemed to be illegal operations, he still did Alan favors, nervously aware of his flirtation with a life that did not come naturally to him.

The lunch hour at the Auto Club that Alan asked to borrow his driver's license, Michael gave it to him. When Alan returned to the office after lunch, he gave Michael back his driver's license and said with a smile, "If you only knew how much money you had, friend. Safe-deposit boxes under false names are definitely the thing for hiding money."

Michael could not bring himself to renege on the favor and ask Alan to go back to the bank and cancel the box.

Alan also asked Michael if he would pick up some money for him. He described how the money would be in the trunk of a car, and that the keys to the trunk would be in the car's ignition. Michael politely declined.

A couple of days later, Alan requested only that Michael accompany him on a ride. To that, Michael said yes.

They drove in Alan's Corvette with Alan behind the wheel. It was insufferably hot and smoggy in Los Angeles that day. Street tar was going soft and the horizon was brown as tobacco. As they drove east on the Santa Ana Freeway, refrigerated air blasting up at them from the air conditioner, Michael smoked a cigarette, flicking the ashes out the windwing, and not asking any questions. Alan was tense and continually referring to the local Thomas Guide next to him for directions.

"Close that windwing and use the ashtray," he barked. Michael obeyed.

After getting off the freeway, they took a series of streets, the names of which Michael did not pay attention to. He knew only that they were in the city of Santa Fe Springs, an industrial area. Alan drove to the end of a street, turned around and parked next to a fire hydrant. Leaving the motor running, he got out, walked up a driveway and disappeared behind a building a hundred feet up the block. In a few minutes he came back out from behind the building, a Manila envelope in his hands. He walked to the curb and motioned for Michael to pick him up. Michael went around to the driver's seat and pulled forward. When Alan got in all he said was, "Drive."

As Michael drove along the freeway back to the Auto Club, Alan opened the envelope and dumped what appeared to be thousands of dollars onto his lap. No bills in the rubber banded stacks were less than fifties or hundreds. After a few minutes of sorting, Alan put the money back and crowed, "Well, it appears to be all there."

The remainder of the trip back into L.A., Alan was silent.

There is a premium on good looks in Los Angeles. There are no bundled winter clothes in which to hide one's body, and the sunshine is too bright to excuse a bad complexion. Many in the city think of Easterners as skinny bookworms taking refuge in dreary libraries. Teenage boys and girls in Los Angeles have reading skills below the U.S. average. They are outside setting national pole vault records instead.

Even when the weather is inclement, libraries are not the sanctuaries in L.A. Health spas are—spas by the score where the water is turquoise clean, the air is filtered, the exercise healthful and strenuous. The names of some of the spas are pretentious.

The Aristocratic Spa was on Brand Boulevard, the main business thoroughfare of Glendale. Off the small but plush lobby glittered a pool. A bluish haze of sunlight filtered down on it through the glass skylight. Fluted plastic columns at one end of the pool, reflected in the water, gave the interior expanse a surrealistic, Byzantine ambience. To the other side of the lobby was a large workout room with muscle toning equipment reared from the floor and projected from the walls. Pulleys, weights, sit-up boards. All were doubled by mirrors.

Judy Davis, a long, coltish-legged twenty-one-year-old with soft auburn hair, was a new instructor at the Aristocratic Spa. Judy was a friendly chatty east coast transplant whom all the customers liked. When she smiled, her cool graceful beauty turned more to cuteness, her rounded cheeks pushing up like a chipmunk's. A few thought Judy a little too cocksure of herself. When she was not in her leotards at work, around town she sometimes wore hip-huggers and tie-top blouses, coquettishly teasing men with her tan flat abdomen.

Judy told Helen Porter, one of the spa members with whom she had become friends, about meeting up with a "smart aleck" at the spa named Alan. Lifting weights by himself, not wanting to take part in the exercise class that Judy instructed, Alan had made "an ungentlemanly comment" to her. Later in the evening, Judy—more indifferent than intentional—let a door close behind her, catching Alan's fingers. When she reopened the door Alan just stared at her, frozen with anger and disbelief.

A week later their eyes caught each other's across the room. Animosity passed between them, but something else as well—a feral attraction, a gut-deep understanding. Alan's glare seeped slowly into a smile, ever so faint.

One of the last times Debbi saw Alan, he was pensive. He gazed out his apartment window, rolling a pin between his fingers.

"I have a plan," he said, "that's gonna leave me either set for life or dead."

As long as Debbi had known Alan, he had talked about how one correct plan was enough to leave someone set for life.

"It's going to happen next March . . . maybe April," he said. Then laughing, almost at himself, "You might even read about me in the paper."

7

JUDITH LYNN DAVIS was born November 16, 1945, in Brooklyn. Judy, as she preferred to be called, had always been an independent strong-willed girl. She often borrowed the family car to go fishing by herself off Montauk Point in New York. Once as a teenager she sat the entire night with rod and bobber on a pier in Jamaica Bay, and did not come home until after dawn. The Davises were always hesitant to discipline her. Judy, after all, never got into trouble. She was never intentionally defiant, but only driven by an irrepressible spirit. From childhood on, the girl's greater strengths, her beauty, her ability to succeed at most things she tried, her moods that seemed to psychically anticipate good and bad news by a day or two, had somehow reduced her own parents and older sister to respectful, almost intimidated observers.

For thirty-seven years Judy's father, Franklin, was a mail carrier in their Cypress Hills neighborhood. The Davises were stay-at-home people; Judy was an adventurer. At age five, she insisted her mother enroll her in the "Little Fishes" swimming program at the YMCA. When she was older she earned a Green Belt in judo at the Y, and later taught the sport. She was a tomboy, physically strong and agile. As she grew older, she developed sides more traditionally feminine. She taught herself cooking and sewing. She spent hours in her room singing love ballads, and when she drove off by herself on Sundays— no one knew where—she took her guitar. Any boy in her class would have gone with her. Judy was a knockout.

Judy was never studious, but had a facility for foreign languages, able to speak French and Spanish fluently. After high school, she worked for six months as a varitype operator and graphics artist at the United Nations and there picked up a smattering of three more languages. She learned German from one of her few serious boy-friends, Felix Zimmer, a quiet, endlessly pleasant man. Felix was an immigrant.

They met the day Judy, having stepped in front of Felix's car, bawled him out for not watching where he was going. They had argued, Felix in his broken English, Judy gesticulating and poking her finger into Felix's chest. Within a month they fell in love. To Felix's surprise, and at times dismay, it would be half a year before Judy would sleep with him.

Felix always sensed that no single relationship could hold Judy. A free spirit, she was too much woman for any one man. Eventually she began to see others. One was a David Boin whom she met at a beach in Rockaway. But their month of romance did not last. David was Jewish, Judy was Methodist, and for him more than her the difference was an insurmountable one. After David had returned to California, Judy repeated a complaint to her mother she had once made as a small child: "Why *shouldn't* all my friends be Jewish? I want to be Jewish, too."

When Franklin Davis retired, his wife, Ethel, convinced him they should move to California. She had visited there in 1936, and her memory of Los Angeles was one of broad, lightly traveled streets where cars parked on an angle, and of a sprawling San Fernando Valley dotted with a few houses between the orange and walnut groves. Surely that could not all have been spoiled, she persuaded her husband. Not all of it. In June of 1967 they bought a new station wagon and, not needing to say much to convince their two daughters to come with them, drove west.

If Ethel Davis was perhaps a little disappointed that not even a scrap of idyllic farmland had been left unpaved, modern L.A. made Judy tingle with warmth. The zig-zag of freeways and curving Pacific Coast Highway were a playground for a girl who loved sporty cars. The beach sand was draped with tan brawny men. Judy could see herself lying in her bikini with her eyes closed, never tiring of the sound of volleyball leather slapping on athletic skin, young people shouting from the water, the popping of beer cans. There would be no more winters in her life. In the middle of the first day of driving around the city by herself, she stopped back home for a snack and exclaimed to her mother, "Mom, this is the grooviest place in the world!"

In August, Judy answered an ad in the paper for an instructor at the Aristocratic Spa. She walked into the place confidently and that afternoon convinced the owners she was exactly the kind of lithesome, athletic woman they were looking for. Within a short period of working there, she was made assistant manager and offered the manager's position at another branch. Judy declined. She was content for the time being where she was.

By early September, Helen Porter noticed Judy dawdling by the pool with the man named Alan, the one Judy had termed a "smartaleck."

Katherine sensed Alan wanted her back. Although he never explicitly proposed to her that September, he discussed his ability to marry again, now that he was on his way to financial success. He had just recently purchased a place in Burbank called the Grand Duke Bar.

Leaning back in his chair, he had tossed out his figures to the bar's owner as though flicking lint from his jacket: "Look, I'll take just one shot at you and save us both some time. Sixteen thousand for the whole shebang, four thousand down. If you think that kind of money can do you some good, wonderful. If not," Alan said, shrugging, "let's shake hands and part friends."

The transaction went into escrow September 15.

"My father's not the only businessman in the family, you know," Alan would tell Katherine later that month.

After Alan had broken off all communication with Debbi on August 29, she had turned to Michael for moral support. Michael could no longer hide his infatuation with Debbi, and sprang at the opportunity to be of help. The two of them began going out together. Having just been jettisoned by Alan Palliko, dating Michael Brockington was like being tossed up by a moody angry sea onto solid, though flat land. No guns, no fast cars. Michael's favorite activity was indoor ice skating together. Often he figure skated in community ice shows. Sometimes he took Debbi golfing. He did everything he could to show her that although he was a friend of Alan's, he was not of Alan's stripe.

When Debbi asked Michael to help her get her car accident insurance money back from Alan, they drove together to Alan's new apartment on North Central Street in Glendale and waited him out. Michael was the only person to whom Alan had given his new address.

Michael and Debbi had to wait until midnight before Alan came home.

Alan sat down behind his desk in the den and began polishing his Walther P-38 automatic. Michael and Debbi took chairs across the desk from him.

"She gave me the money of her own volition," Alan said. "What's the problem here?"

Michael spoke for Debbi. "The problem is that she thought you were going to marry her. The fact is, Alan, she needs the money. In another eight months or so she's going to have your baby."

That was a lie, a ruse Michael and Debbi had cooked up.

"I see." Alan spoke matter-of-factly, not looking at them. Meticulously, he worked a chamois cloth around the trigger and barrel of his Walther. "Cover your ears for a second, baby, will you. There's something I have to discuss with your new boyfriend."

Subserviently, Debbi put her hands over her ears. Alan just stared at Michael for a moment, then, still polishing the gun, raised its barrel until it was pointing directly into Michael's face.

"You know, I feel like blowing your head off," he said.

"Talk big with other people, not me," Michael said. Pure bluff—Michael's heart was heaving. Very slowly, Alan smiled and lowered the gun. He leaned forward and spoke very quietly. "I'll tell you, I think you brought a suicide case up here."

Michael did not understand.

"What I'm saying," Alan continued beneath his breath, "is I feel like loading her up with pills and dumping her over the balcony."

"Right," Michael said. "Now what about the money?"

Alan studied Michael for a moment, then threw his head back and snorted a laugh. He motioned for Debbi to remove her hands from her ears.

"What do you say I give you $500 now and then a few hundred every month? Mikey, I'm counting on you to remind me—the fifteenth of every month, okay?" With Debbi listening, Alan was nothing but genial. He gave them the $500 and, shaking Michael's hand at the doorway, said, "Nothing reasonable people can't solve."

Over the next several months, Michael would have to argue, cajole, and flatter to get every payment out of Alan. At one point Alan threatened to send the nude pictures he had taken of Debbi back to her parents.

One night, Alan told Michael to open up a sealed envelope Alan had entrusted to him a half year earlier with the caveat: "Only if I'm in trouble does this get opened. Right, Mikey?" The envelope, it turned out, contained Debbi's and her son Timothy's passports. As Michael stood there looking blankly at the passports, Alan confided that he had once had in mind a contingency plan of shipping Debbi and her son out of the country without their papers. Michael could not fathom what that had to do with the possibility of Alan being "in trouble," and in any event, what such an action could possibly accomplish. People lost their passports every day of the week, and certainly they managed to return to the U.S. It was as if Alan's mind had short-circuited over an excessive energy for intrigue—as if he had seen some clever scheme in a spy movie, had then thought up a makeshift variation on it, and if only for the sake of drama, had given Michael a sealed envelope.

What a character, Michael thought.

Alan would later insist on meeting personally with Debbi at a restaurant in Van Nuys to see for himself whether she was pregnant. Michael helped her pack her dress convincingly with a small pillow. Alan fell for it. When he dribbled out his last payment, however, he still owed her over $1,000.

A month after the Davis family had arrived in California, Felix Zimmer followed them out in his battered Pontiac. Judy helped him pick out a bachelor apartment just a few blocks from where the Davises lived, but it soon became apparent to both of them that their moment had been lost.

Although a crush of men had already begun to lavish Judy with attention, she complained to her sister Lisa that the man named Alan at the spa, the one she found interesting, had not so much as called her for a date.

October 1, Alan proudly took ownership of the Grand Duke Bar. Alan, for the first time, was now an entrepreneur. The Grand Duke, at 1623 North San Fernando Road in Burbank, was a modest sized, dune colored structure with its name, written in old English script, hanging on a placard out front. The Grand Duke was just a beer bar;

no hard liquor was sold, but from the way Alan carried himself all that week, one would have thought he had just purchased the Waldorf.

Surprisingly, Alan did not seem to bear a grudge against Michael over the money dispute with Debbi, and offered his friend a part-time job at the bar. Michael, kept off balance like everyone else who associated with Alan, was happy to accept. He needed the extra money for his alimony and child support payments.

On Alan's part, the need was for Michael's business savvy, which Alan himself did not possess. Michael had a sense of how to keep a proper cash flow, how much items like bar stools and neon signs should cost; periodically, he straightened out the muddle Alan would make of the books.

Still, however, Michael let Alan dominate him and make him into a virtual errand boy. As a demanding person, both of others and of himself, Alan handed out compliments only sparingly, but by their very rareness they bore a curiously splendid value. His moments of unfeigned warmth and gratitude, like a single balmy day in the middle of harsh winter, had an uplifting power to them.

"You did a really terrific job, Mikey," Alan said as he surveyed the carpentry work done on the Grand Duke, which Michael had supervised. "Thank you." He put his strong arm on Michael's shoulder, giving the back of his neck a little squeeze of friendship.

Michael took Alan's clothes to the laundry for him, he had his car washed for him, sometimes he even did Alan's grocery shopping. Like a press secretary, he made Alan's apologies for him—to vendors and friends when Alan often failed to make meetings. When Alan was not prepared to see someone, whether it was Katherine, or Debbi, or the fire inspector, or the loan officer from the bank, he simply would not show up for the appointment. Like a kid, he thought certain problems would just evaporate.

But Alan was determined to make a success of the Grand Duke. After putting in his days at the Auto Club, he worked another full eight hours at the bar—from 6:00 P.M. until the 2:00 A.M. closing time. The thought of failing in his first business venture awakened him more than once with nightmares. Sometimes he asked Michael to stay over with him. Alan took Seconal to get to sleep and uppers to keep him awake during the day. As with any new business, it was slow going in the beginning, but Alan could not believe it would ever turn around. He raced around the city double-checking on the smallest of matters, used up unnecessary time and energy with his own franticness, and at times was nothing less than manic. The pills made him moodier than ever, guffawing almost uncontrollably at a piece of good news and lashing out at a barmaid the next moment for a minor slip-up. At home he could not fall asleep unless the radio was on, and at the Grand Duke he needed to gulp Cokes that were spiked with Jim Beam. The weariness began to show in his red, at times unfocusing eyes. Michael worried he was headed for a nervous breakdown.

Alan trusted no one—not the barmaids he hired, not the bartenders, nor even Michael completely. The people he distrusted the most were the banks. Relaxing over at Alan's apartment one afternoon, Michael looked up from the copy of *Field and Stream* he was thumbing through, incredulous at what he was witnessing.

The Grand Duke's personalized checks from Valley National Bank were a little late in coming, and Alan was on the phone with one of the bank clerks, screaming into the receiver as he paced.

"A week! That's how long!" Alan yelled. "It doesn't matter to you if the Grand Duke goes under, does it? Does it!"

Alan carried the phone into the living room as he raged, then back into the kitchen and back again into the living room. When he hung up he stared at the phone, trying to catch his breath. Then, rearing back, he hurled the phone against the wall. He sat down in the middle of the living room floor, and putting his head in his hands, he began to weep.

Business did pick up. Indeed, it began to boom. Before Alan took over, the Grand Duke had had a reputation as a "rowdy's bar." Alan intended to clean it up. The first two months, he kept a clutch of beefy friends from the gymnasium around, including one sumo wrestler, and when a fight broke out, the fight's instigator would be taken out back, where Alan's friends impressed upon him—only with talk if at all possible—the need to remain civil inside the Grand Duke. When Michael asked Alan what his chief bouncer, Gus Pilich, had done before then for a living, Alan just made his hand into a gun and, with a wink, hammered down his thumb.

Infrequent patrons of the Grand Duke began to become regulars. As business improved and Alan started to relax, his consumption of pills and alcohol slackening markedly, the Palliko charm again began to emerge. He cultivated customers like a slick maitre d', making them feel at home with his personal attention and keeping up daily running conversations with all of them. How their kids were, their work, horses to watch at Santa Anita.

"I'm Italian too," he told Gilda Vent, who always came in after her work. "We've got a hell of a lot to be proud of." Whenever she walked in, Alan gave her a thumbs-up.

Marjorie Huebner's home number was once again up on Alan's corkboard. He had found a way of fitting her right into his new scheme of things. Because Marjorie was a pretty fair pool player, and being the tight-jeaned attraction she was, Alan encouraged her to come into the Grand Duke every evening and play a little eight-ball with the men. She never played for money and she never accepted dates from the fellows, but it was clear to anyone she did not hurt the bar's business. That Alan might have looked at her as just another capital asset, like a new pinball machine, never bothered Marjorie, at least not at the beginning. Often Alan took her out to dinner beforehand, and an evening of playing pool while she nursed a beer was really a bit of fun for her. Where Alan's emotions lay in the relationship, she had stopped trying to figure.

For a second time, he proposed marriage, and for a second time she turned him down. The second proposal made no more sense to her than did the first. It was not exactly love that Alan exhibited toward her. Every night that he drove her home after closing time, all she received from him on the doorstep was a kiss on the forehead. Usually having to fight men off, Marjorie, a strict Catholic, at first felt respected and flattered. As time wore on, she began to feel less Catholic and only twenty-five years old and frustrated.

An evening Alan left her alone in his apartment to study for her exams at UCLA, Marjorie saw bundles of cash in a partly open desk drawer. That night Alan told her simply, without emotion, "I always test people."

During the autumn months of 1967, employees of the Grand Duke Bar saw a short blond woman come in on a number of occasions to see Alan. Often the two of them left the bar together for dinner. Only Michael Brockington knew the woman by name; he remembered Sandra Stockton from the Auto Club. She was the one whose husband had been murdered.

Alan had been making comments lately about wanting to get married again, and Michael wondered if Alan had Sandra Stockton in mind. He knew that Alan and Sandra had always been close friends when they had worked together at the Auto Club. "She's good people," Alan had always said of her.

Michael recalled how Alan had spoken privately to that LAPD detective down at the Auto Club about Henry Stockton's murder. Being an ex-policeman, Alan seemed to have a special interest in crime solving. And in the motivations behind crime. He was often tossing out those crazy hypotheticals of his—like the one Alan had once posed to Michael in his apartment: if two people got together to kill someone, and if one of the killers were becoming frightened and weak, should the partner do away with him or her?

Alan was, if nothing else, an interesting fellow given to entertaining conversation. Sandra Stockton could do a lot worse, Michael thought to himself as he saw Alan usher her out the Grand Duke's door for dinner.

After almost ten years with Pacific Telephone, Katherine quit her job in October of 1967. She needed something more stimulating, but mostly she first needed a rest. Without income, she began to accept favors from Alan, who had started to call her regularly that month. Often they went out to dinner, and on almost every occasion Alan brought up the subject of marriage. Why could they not give it another go, he asked. Katherine reached across to put her hand on his, and rounding her lips as if to give the answer before she uttered it, she said in one gentle but drawnout syllable, "Nooo."

On November 7, Katherine received a phone call from home. Her father had suffered a heart attack. Alan rushed to her aid, sending Michael over the next day with a round-trip ticket to Detroit plus a hundred dollars spending money for her. Michael by then lived in the same apartment building as Katherine, and although Katherine believed he had been put there by Alan to spy on her, Michael had in fact picked the building simply because of Alan's recommendation of the place.

Katherine accepted the ticket and money from Michael with a cold and wary thank you.

That night, Alan called her. "Let me come with you to your folks' place. You may need a shoulder to lean on—okay, Wurf?" he said softly.

"Okay," Katherine said, old unwanted emotions lumping up in her throat. Alan was like the two faces of the same clown on a flat wooden spoon you could get as a kid. Twirl it with a rubber band and you get a smile and a frown and a smile and a frown and a . . .

In order to make the trip, Alan called in sick to the Auto Club, an excuse his office had become familiar with since the Grand Duke had opened.

While sitting in the front room of her parents' house in Michigan with a friend, Katherine felt like shriveling up and disappearing as Alan carried on a phone conversation with someone back in California. Whatever he was discussing, it did not sound legal. When he hung up he turned to Katherine and said, even in the presence of Katherine's friend, "I beat the cops. I can beat the FBI, too."

Michael could not wipe off the bar counter or work on the books without having to pause and respectfully listen to Alan's mad little, vindictive scenarios.

As soon as Alan had learned his bosses at the Auto Club were unhappy with his many absences and were thinking of firing him, he had begun planning his revenge against them. Borrowing Katherine's VW and ramming it into a pole without getting hurt had been easy enough, he told Michael. His chiropractor friend was willing to burn the old X-rays—which showed that Alan had been born with a reverse curvature in the spine—take new ones, and testify that the defect was caused by the accident. Would those Auto Club suckers pay through the nose, Alan laughed. On an evening of quiet business, Michael saw Alan slip two customers each a twenty-dollar bill for having "witnessed" the mishap.

But even that was not enough to satisfy Alan. He began negotiating with a two-bit hoodlum who frequented the Grand Duke to "steal" Alan's Corvette, drive it down to Mexico, disassemble it there and sell the parts, once again putting Alan in a position to collect insurance.

Just as he had been anticipating, his Auto Club superiors called Alan onto the carpet, wanting to know the reasons for his absences from work. They also wanted to know about his two recent insurance claims. Alan launched into a minor melodrama about his recent illnesses and car problems, and called on Michael to back him up. Michael had no choice but to nod his corroboration, but after Alan had left, Michael lingered in the boss's office. Out of loyalty to a company that had treated him fairly for a number of years, Michael told his superiors that Alan's two auto claims were fraudulent. They thanked him for his candor, and the following day Alan was fired. The company resisted Alan's two insurance claims, and eventually Alan dropped the matter.

Del Cook, the slow-witted barber, was having marital problems. His wife Gloria was threatening to divorce him. When Cookie called Alan for advice later that December, Alan's suggestion was simple.

"Does she have much insurance?" he asked. "If she were my wife, baby, I'd shoot her."

"Thanks anyway, Alan," Cookie said. "I love her, so maybe I'll figure out something else."

On Christmas day Barbara Gutman, a casual patron of the Grand Duke, went out on a first date with Alan Palliko. A couple of days later they went out again. It was then, while they were driving in the car, that Alan proposed marriage. Barbara's mouth hung open in a dumb slot. When she recovered, all she thought to answer was, "Oh, for Christ's sake, Alan!"

When an old fraternity brother passed Alan on the sidewalk that December, Alan was attired in a tweed jacket, a British trilby with a little feather atop his head, and carried a silver-headed walking stick. Alan tipped his hat like a landed gentry squire, and walked on.

Michael could only wonder how Alan managed to juggle his half dozen girlfriends. Ruth, Marjorie, Paula, Susan, Theresa, Barbara . . . the list went on. He also wondered what Alan intended to do with all of them during the big New Year's Eve party he was planning. The party was to start at the Grand Duke; afterwards, "selected guests" were to go on to Alan's showy new apartment on North Central. Michael knew Alan had already invited Marjorie, and that Barbara, too, was under the impression she would be Alan's date. And then there was the other one, a stunning sensuous girl who had been coming into the bar for brief chats of late. Alan had invited her, too. All Michael knew of her was that she worked at the Aristocratic Spa, and that her name was Judy.

8

MICHAEL HAD NEVER seen a barroom as crowded as the Grand Duke on New Year's Eve. To get from one end to the other he had to put his hands in front like a snowplow and wedge his way through. Lots of laughter, lots of body heat, lots of booze. Alan kept Michael circulating, asking the patrons to keep their bottles of hard liquor inside their coats or below the tables in case the people from the A.B.C. (Alcoholic Beverage Control) stopped by.

Although when women were around, Alan usually wore sport shirts that accentuated his rock-hard biceps, he chose to wear a grey, vested herringbone suit that New Year's Eve. Michael wondered if Alan were not contemplating a change in public image, to that of a respected prosperous businessman. Having heard the clang of the cash register and worked on the books, Michael knew Alan came to the new image rightfully. The Grand Duke, approaching only its fourth month under Alan's management, was grossing $4,500 a month and netting over $2,000.

With handshakes and smiles, Alan kept moving from table to table the entire evening. Everyone was kept happy—everyone except three confused women.

Barbara Gutman sat at a corner table, simmering as she watched Alan parcel out his personality with almost stopwatch equality. Every hour or so she rated the same few seconds as everyone else.

"Lookin' great, Barbara. Just great. Everything okay at this table?" Then striding off and calling, "Hey, Cookie! I *said* it was five, three and even that you and that gorgeous wife would make it here tonight. Now, no lovers' quarrels. How are ya, Gloria? . . ."

Unlike Barbara, Judy Davis remained outwardly unruffled. She sat in her silver lamé dress at a table with two male friends of hers from the spa, trying to enjoy the spectacle.

From the instant she walked through the door, Marjorie knew she should not have accepted the invitation. Alan barely acknowledged her. Early in the evening, he told Michael, "You'll look after Marjorie for me tonight, okay? I knew I could count on you."

On her way to the restroom, Marjorie saw Alan sitting by himself in the back office, slowly shuffling through some papers. She paused at the doorway.

"I don't understand what it is you're trying to do, Alan," she said.

Alan looked up from his papers a moment, then looked back down.

"When you have garbage on your feet, you can never get it off," he said resignedly. "You were right when you turned me down. I'm no good for you, Marjorie. I'm sorry."

Two bedrooms, two fireplaces, a sprawling living room, and a den—the place on North Central was Alan Palliko's fourth apartment in nine months. The party that began at 2 A.M. was raucous. Music was loud, jokes had to be louder. Cocktail shakers rattled with ice. People wandered aimlessly through the spacious rooms. The two fireplaces were alight—L.A. fireplaces, gas flames licking in an unaltering pattern at synthetic logs.

As the New Year grew older, Barbara and Judy began competing for Alan's attention. Barbara stalked after Michael, demanding to know what the story was. Was she or was she not Alan's date? Judy began taking empty glasses into the kitchen for Alan and wiping off coffee tables.

In the living room, Alan was gathering the men around a table for his favorite game—"liar's poker." Stacks of chips were being passed out. Just a few feet away, Barbara began pushing for a scene, eventually ranting at Judy who just stood there, embarrassed. With a sidelong glance toward the two women who appeared to be on the verge of physically fighting, Alan dealt out the first hand with an excited flourish.

Escorting Marjorie home at her request, Michael put his arm around her just outside the door and said, "You don't know how lucky you are to be done with it all."

Judy Davis kept a daily calendar book. The entries were made in small, slanted, exquisitely feminine script. Beginning with New Year's Eve, Alan's name began appearing in her 1968 calendar alongside notations such as "Drinks," "Dinner," "Movies," "Dance." Alan called Judy New Year's day for a date, and continued to call almost every day thereafter. Flowers arrived at the Davis apartment weekly.

Early in the romance, Judy told her sister Lisa, "He doesn't have as much polish as I'd like in a man, but I guess it just comes from his profession. He lives a different life than we do."

Alan told Judy he had been involved with mobsters, but now, he promised her, that was all behind him. The names of other men were interspersed with Alan's in the first two weeks of Judy's January calendar sheet, but by the middle of the month she was dating Alan exclusively.

Judy's mother Ethel Davis never liked Alan. She did not like the way he kept her daughter out at all hours when Judy had to get up for work the next day, nor did she like his talk of marriage that came so prematurely. The whole romance was too much of a whirlwind, she thought. She did not much care for the wide-brimmed hats Alan wore that made him look like a gangster, either.

"Ethel? Al Palliko calling," he would fire out his name on phone calls to the Davis' apartment.

Told by Judy of her mother's reservations about him, Alan diligently set about to improve the impression he had made in the Davis household. He would arrive early for dates and, while Judy got ready, would sip coffee with Ethel or have a drink with Franklin, speaking nostalgically with them about being raised in an Italian home and his determination to provide a close, secure family life for Judy.

Judy told her sister Lisa that although she did not quite know why, she felt she might be falling in love with Alan. Believing it was something less than love, but keeping the thought to herself, Lisa observed a powerlessness in Judy she had never seen in her before. The attraction to Alan, she sensed, was that Judy had for the first time met someone stronger than she.

In late January, Alan called Katherine to ask her one last time if she would remarry him. Katherine, by then happily in her new job as secretary to an anesthesiologist, said no—flat out, absolutely, positively no.

"Okay then," Alan said. "I'm going to have to do something again I don't want to do. I guess I just got in with the wrong kind of people. You'll probably be reading about me in the papers." He chuckled —morosely—and hung up.

In order to live closer to the Grand Duke Bar, Alan moved to a smart, fifty-four-unit apartment complex called the Castillian at 2021 Grismer Avenue in Burbank. He told the resident managers, John and Evelyn Miller, that he was a bachelor. Because he would be living alone, he was given ten dollars off the rent. A few days later, the Millers saw him with a woman, and unmindfully, Alan introduced her as his fiancée. Evelyn Miller promptly taped a three-day notice on his door. Alan strolled down to the managers' office, turned on some charm, and the Millers relented. His fiancée, the Millers decided, had seemed rather pleasant, after all. John Miller would later recall that she was short, blond, and would have been quite attractive were she only to lose some weight.

Whether or not Alan seriously intended to marry Sandra Stockton, no one knew. He never discussed Sandra with friends.

Judy Davis wrote in her calendar on January 30: "Alan, Gun, 2:00 P.M. Dinner." The handgun Alan insisted she accept as a present and keep in her purse at all times was a .32 caliber B/S Llama automatic. On one side just below the barrel was engraved the word "Love." On the other side, "Alan."

January 31, Judy wrote in her little book: "Alan. Dinner—10:00 P.M." Then in another color ink, written after returning home from dinner that night, was another word: "Engagement."

Information that had been dribbling into Guy's and St. John's office had done little to rekindle an active pursuit of the Stockton murder case. Then, beginning in late January of 1968, events began rapidly unfolding that forced the homicide detectives to sit up and take notice. They were events that put them right back onto Alan Palliko's trail.

It was not until six days after Sergeant J.R. Ide of the Van Nuys Detectives had received a phone call from Alan Palliko that Ide in turn called Guy and St. John at Parker Center. The date was January 30. On January 24, Alan had phoned the Van Nuys Division of the LAPD to, in his own words, "aid law enforcement" by turning in two men who had the day before committed a local residential robbery, pistol-whipping the owner of the residence, Herman Siegel, in the process. The men Alan identified were Jason Simcoe and Donald Whalen, both male Caucasians in their mid-twenties. The men came to the Grand Duke Bar the day after the robbery, Alan said, in an attempt to use Alan as a fence for their stolen goods. Alan told Sgt. Ide he did not want that kind of activity going on at the Grand Duke. Simcoe and Whalen were subsequently picked up and charged with the armed robbery (which involved the theft of $20,000 worth of jewelry and a .25 caliber automatic handgun) and assault with a deadly weapon.

The detectives who had studied Alan's background for the better part of a year were puzzled by his motivation in taking such action. The only logical conclusion they were able to reach was that perhaps Alan, believing he was still being actively investigated for the Stockton murder, had suspected Simcoe and Whalen to be cops working undercover. If, after giving his tip to the Van Nuys police, Alan learned that Simcoe and Whalen were not arrested and tried, then his suspicions would be proven correct. If Alan's hunch were wrong, he would have made himself two enemies, but they would be enemies who would be sitting in jail for a good long time.

John St. John interviewed Simcoe and Whalen in the County Jail on February 2. He talked with them separately and told each at the outset that he only wanted to question them about Alan in regard to the Stockton murder, and that they need not discuss or give information concerning the charges on which they were being held. Both men were cooperative.

They had been told by both the police and their assigned public defender that Alan had turned them in. Although they certainly had cause to seek revenge against Alan, both denied to St. John that Alan had ever told them of having had any role in the murder of Henry Stockton. They did, however, state that Alan was involved in fencing stolen goods as well as providing "clean guns" for robberies. They also both told St. John of a plan Alan had offered them. A relative of Alan's, who would be carrying approximately $70,000 on him, was to be arriving from the east at L.A. International. Alan suggested Simcoe and Whalen meet the man at the airport, kidnap him, rob him, and what they did with him after that was "strictly up to them." The money would be split three ways. Simcoe and Whalen declined the offer.

"That kind of stuff's too heavy for us, man," Jay Simcoe told St. John.

Both Simcoe and Whalen indicated they had additional important information they would reveal only if they were given some help from the courts, should they be found guilty at their forthcoming trial. St. John advised them that no such deal would be made; at least at this point, all information had to be voluntary.

On February 7, Guy and St. John were told by Lieutenant Killeby, Commander, Highland Park Detectives, that their bureau had received information to the effect that Alan Palliko was about to commit a murder for $5,000. That information was not quite accurate, but it was not thoroughly inaccurate either. The problem was that it had come from a man who was somewhat mixed up mentally, Alan's barber friend, Cookie.

The story Cook gave his good friend and customer, I. Kasper, a Highland Park detective, was that on January 26, he was served divorce papers by his wife Gloria. Cook went for advice to another man whose hair he cut, his other good knowledgeable friend, Alan Palliko. Del was still in love with his wife and when he called Alan on the twenty-seventh, he was crying.

Alan's advice was the same as it had been earlier: "Kill her."

When Del said he could never consider such a thing, Alan suggested that he at least protect whatever savings he had during the divorce proceedings. To that, Del was willing to listen. Alan had a plan whereby he could conceal Cook's money in a way that Gloria would not get any of it: Cook would give Alan the money in question for safekeeping until the divorce was over, and in return, Alan would give Cook, in addition to an I.O.U. for the money, a "Paid in full" false promissory note for divorce court purposes, indicating that Cook had used the money to pay off a loan from Alan. Alan would take care of the arrangements and charge a $500 fee for his services.

Del blubbered some more, saying that it was wrong and that he was scared. Again Alan calmed him down.

"But I don't want you discussing this with any lawyers," Alan said. "There are some things you can tell lawyers and some things you can't. Do you understand what I'm saying, Cookie?"

When Del began to have second thoughts, he went back to see Alan at his apartment.

"Why don't we just step into my office," Alan said, and showed

Del to the desk he kept in the second bedroom. On top of it was a little American flag.

Alan again suggested killing Gloria for her insurance.

Del laughed nervously. "You are crazy, Alan. You are nuts."

Alan smiled and went on to the phony loan plan, and Del agreed to it.

The following evening, January 29, Del and Alan met over a drink in Eagle Rock. They sat at the bar and when Alan told him to, Del passed him fifty one-hundred-dollar bills below the bar. They finished their drinks and shook hands. Del told Alan it was all right to give him the I.O.U. and false promissory note later.

The next morning, a log must have rolled over in his mind, for Del saw his mistake in not having demanded the papers immediately. He called the Grand Duke Bar, but was told Alan was "not available." Del continued to phone, hoping to get either Alan's I.O.U. or his money back, but to no avail. The following Saturday morning, Alan called and said he was coming to Del's barber shop. Alan brought a friend. The friend was six feet, five inches tall, his face hammer-marked from acne. The T-shirt beneath his unzipped jacket stretched tautly across his chest. Politely, Alan asked Del to excuse himself from his customer and have a word with him outside.

"You got taken, Cookie," Alan told him out on the sidewalk. "No use crying over it now. It's better that I have the money than Gloria. You look out for yourself in this life, 'cause no one looks out for you. I don't want you ever calling my bar again. Right?"

His eyes cast to the sidewalk, Del nodded.

"Now if you want me to blow up your barber shop," Alan continued, "I will. Got insurance on it? I can take care of Gloria, too."

Del looked at Alan a moment, shook his head, and walked back into his shop.

Stepping to the doorway, Alan's last words to Del were: "Use that old noggin now, Cookie. Remember—you've got a daughter."

Tuesday, February 6: "Alan—3:00 P.M., blood test."

Thursday, February 8: "Alan—Mom & Dad for cocktails. Engagement ring."

Tuesday, February 13: "Alan—Travel agent, Hawaii."

Judy's calendar book looked much like that of any young woman who was about to be married.

On the evening of Sunday, February 11, Franklin and Ethel Davis, resigned to their daughter's decision, gave the couple a sumptuous engagement dinner at the Davises' apartment. Wanting to please Alan, Ethel Davis prepared an all Italian meal of antipasto and chicken cacciatore. Alan brought a long-stemmed bottle of chianti.

Many of Judy's aunts and uncles were invited. The only person Alan brought was Michael Brockington. Well-mannered, respectable Michael was just the kind of friend Alan knew to call on to be at his side for "meeting family."

Michael could see from the looks Alan and Judy were giving each other the entire night that they had been squabbling. At one point during the dinner, they excused themselves to have a word with each other. Later in the evening Michael heard Judy say to Alan quietly, from the side of her mouth, "I did not. I said I *wanted* to be Jewish."

Because Judy had seemed so distressed, Felix Zimmer broke a date in order to have dinner with her on Saturday, February 17. They met at the Ruben E. Lee, a popular restaurant on Newport Bay.

She told Felix Alan's story of having killed his ex-wife's suitor.

"Where did you pick up this bum?" Felix asked in his clipped German accent.

"No, no, it was in self-defense," Judy insisted.

Felix questioned her as to why the wedding had to be March 1, why they could not wait a little longer.

Judy quoted him Alan's answer when she herself had asked that: "It will be March 1, or it won't be at all."

What Judy wanted to know from Felix was whether he would take her back if the marriage did not work out.

"It depends," Felix said. He took a long careful look at Judy as she drew patterns with her fingernail through the beads of condensation on her water glass. Felix still loved her. "It depends," he sighed.

Six days later, because Alan would not take no for an answer, Judy moved into Alan's apartment. Also at his insistence, she quit her job at the Aristocratic Spa.

"No wife of mine is ever going to have to punch a clock," he told her.

Michael's and Alan's friendship was beginning to show strain. The tug of war over Debbi's money had not helped. Still, Michael was the one man Alan went to when he was feeling low.

On a cool overcast day in February, Alan was in one of his deep funks. As it grew dark outside, the slow, five o'clock traffic on San Fernando Road streaking the bar's front windows with the red of taillights, Alan asked Michael to leave the Grand Duke with him for a few minutes and join him for a drink, something stronger than beer. They walked across the street to the Marlindo Bowling Alley. Who but Alan, Michael thought, a man who needed to have a radio on to fall asleep, would find the day's relaxing cocktail hour more secure surrounded by the clatter of bowling pins?

They took a small table in a corner of the bowling lanes' lounge. Michael ordered Drambuie on the rocks. Alan had his usual, Jim Beam with a water chaser. Alan seemed preoccupied, every few minutes tossing out a piece of small talk as if only to hear his own voice. Then out of nowhere he asked Michael, "Do you have any idea where I get all my money?"

"No," Michael answered casually, concealing his interest.

"You may as well know the whole story," Alan went on quietly. "Do you remember Sandra Stockton?"

Michael nodded. "Yeah. The woman from the Auto Club."

"I killed her husband."

Michael glanced nervously away. A fat lady in tights was almost falling over the scratch line, trying to give her bowling ball some body English. The impact of Alan's words finally struck Michael, delayed like the pain that comes a half moment after cracking one's shin. He turned back.

A single tear was slowly rolling down Alan's cheek. Alan wiped it away. Neither of them spoke. The two finished their drinks and walked back to the Grand Duke.

During the lulls in bar business that night, Michael studied Alan's face. He half expected Alan to break into peals of laughter at any moment and nudge him in the ribs. But Alan did not laugh or smile the entire night.

The next week, as they stood on a streetcorner, Michael saw a policeman nearby. "Here is Alan," Michael thought, "and there is a policeman. All I have to do is . . ."

"They'll question him, release him, and he'll blow my head off," was the next thought. Like Katherine a year and a half before, Michael realized he had to get away from this man as discreetly as possible.

When Katherine went to her carport she noticed the door of her storage locker was ajar. The padlock on it had been opened, not broken. Her Tourister luggage and crystal punchbowl set were missing. Only one other person had a key to that locker.

The first thing Katherine did when she phoned Alan was to remind him that he had given her the luggage and crystal set as a wedding present. Alan responded only by saying, "I just wanted you to know, Katy, that I'm still around."

"Fine," Katherine replied crisply. "So you'll return my things."

"Fair enough," Alan said, and the two hung up.

He did not return the items. He gave them to Judy as wedding presents.

The wedding was set for Friday, March 1. There was a twenty-ninth of February in 1968, as if the Fates, Franklin Davis joked joylessly to his wife, had given their daughter Judy one extra day to change her mind. She did not. On that last day of the month, Judy's parents gave her a wedding gift of $500, a sizable sum for people of modest means.

When she gave the check to Alan that afternoon he was too busy to call his in-laws-to-be and thank them. He used the money that very day as a down payment on a beer bar in Sunland that he had been dickering for. The establishment had operated with limited success under such names as Dogpatch and The Kitten. Alan hired painters to put up a new sign: "Judy's Grand Duchess."

March 1 was sunny and smogless. The entire Los Angeles basin was fresh with a smack of ocean air. Ethel Davis was aghast when she got out of the car in Burbank and had her first look at the "Historic Wedding Chapel" that was attached to what was dubbed the Home and Family Life Museum. The sign outside with black, two-foot-high letters (illuminated at night) announced: "Weddings. Receptions. Banquets." Weddings went for twenty-five bucks a throw. Las Vegas quickie style. The place was run by Pierina E. Lo Piccolo and her husband, Sam. Attached to the chapel and museum was "Lo Piccolo's Unique Restaurant."

Alan, who had made all of the wedding arrangements on his own, had not yet arrived. Judy stood on the sidewalk in her white satin wedding sheath, her jaw slung low. Ethel Davis seethed.

"I'll kill that man," she said. "I swear it."

The unmitigated tastelessness of where they were to be married merely capped an altogether miserable week. First, Alan refused to invite his parents to the wedding. When Ethel Davis unleashed her fury over this, Alan agreed to at least invite them to the reception. "Just you see," he muttered. "The only thing they'll bring is their feet."

Alan further alienated Judy's mother when he had insisted that Judy move into his new Burbank apartment the weekend before the wedding. Even the morning of the wedding day itself, Alan had Judy driving around town doing errands—buying her own bridal bouquet and paying one of Alan's traffic tickets.

Not wanting to anger Alan, Michael honored his request to be best man. The two of them were fifteen minutes late in getting to the chapel, and the Davises had no choice but to let Pierina Lo Piccolo, a bubbly little woman, show them around the place. Inside the Family Museum were California and Western memorabilia—cowbells, horseshoes, and glass encased scenes of toy Indians and buffalo. On a plaque was the homily: "Homes Measure the Nation's Strength." A faded yellowed poster on the patio advertised the coming performances of a locally staged opera from thirty years ago, starring Pierina Lo Piccolo.

When Alan finally arrived, it was all Ethel Davis could do to say hello. The ceremony was short, ten minutes, performed by a Unitarian minister who was provided by the Lo Piccolos. No one could say, however, that Alan and Judy did not make a physically beautiful couple—Judy in her high-waisted gown with a bolero top, Alan in a handsome mohair suit. After the ceremony, Mrs. Lo Piccolo invited the wedding party to stay for a glass of champagne. It came with.

About sixty people attended the reception at Nick Tagli's Hearthside Inn, a garish, tropically motifed place with little loin-clothed figures perched around a center room fountain, like natives at a waterfall. Most of the guests were Alan's friends from the bar. They were an uncouth crew of men. Judy's sister Lisa found herself spending the better part of the afternoon fending off their various insults and propositions.

Alan went over to shake Franklin Davis' hand, and said sheep-ishly, "I think I ought to thank you for the money."

Franklin, the mellow dispositioned, retired mailman, leaned back in his chair. "Better late than never, Alan," he said with a smile.

Alan's parents came late. Judy introduced her mother to Mrs. Palliko. The two had never met.

"Nice to meet you," Mrs. Palliko slurred. "Don't mind me. I'm drunk."

Ethel Davis tried to take up slack in the awkward pause. "Well . . . special occasions and all . . ."

"Yes," Mrs. Palliko giggled, "but we'd been drinking before we got here."

The Pallikos left after half an hour.

The liquor flowed and at least Alan's friends had a rollicking good time that afternoon. Telegrams were read. One came from the movie director Stanley Kubrick, a relative by marriage of Mrs. Palliko's.

Late in the day, Ethel Davis noticed a newcomer standing off in the corner by herself. She was a short young woman, heavy around the hips. Her blond hair was elaborately teased and coiffed. Her face was quite pretty, almost angelic. Ethel went over to introduce herself, but the young woman disappeared into the crowd. Later Ethel saw her in an animated conversation with Alan. When Judy walked up to them, the three began talking. Judy's mother edged closer. Alan in-troduced the young woman to his bride as Shelly Scott. At one point in the conversation, Judy reached up to kiss Alan on the cheek, and a look of disdain, almost horror, shot across Miss Scott's face.

"Oh no, why did you have to go and do that?" she said, wheeling about on her high heels and walking away. Before Judy could ask her husband what that was all about, they were surrounded by more well-wishers.

A Frank Glendon struck up a conversation with Shelly Scott at the reception. She told him she was a mother of two, and living in Long Beach. Glendon took her out to dinner that night and afterward Miss Scott gave him her phone number. Glendon never called her, but if he had, he might have wondered while dialing why a woman living in Long Beach would have a Downey exchange.

Michael Brockington drove the newlyweds to the International Hotel at the airport that night. The next morning the couple left for

Hawaii. They stayed at the Outrigger Hotel on Waikiki Beach and returned to Los Angeles the following Thursday. The first day back, Alan accused Michael, who had been left in charge of the Grand Duke, with having stolen $200. The books had been altered, Alan charged.

"You think it over," Alan said, "and tomorrow you'll let me know if you care to admit the truth. When you hand over the two hundred bucks we'll forget the whole thing."

The next morning, Michael, denying any wrongdoing, suggested they shake hands and go their separate ways. The two never associated with each other again.

When Katherine learned of Alan's marriage, she wasted no time contacting Sergeant Guy, urging that the police tell the new wife of Alan's history. Fearing Alan, she did not think she could go to Judy Davis about it herself. Despite the other information about Alan that had been recently coming into police headquarters, Guy's response to Katherine's suggestion was a shrug.

"He wouldn't be that stupid to try it again," the detective told her.

Like girls in junior high school, Judy and Lisa could chat away a sisterly afternoon, confiding and advising on the matters of love. Judy's days and nights as a wife were not going well at all.

Not only had Alan not made love to her on her wedding night because he was too "tired," she told her older sister, but they had not had sex even on their week-long honeymoon. The first day in Hawaii, Alan slogged in from the surf, claiming to have suffered a slipped disc. Toward the end of the week his reason for abstention was sunburn. The night they got back to Los Angeles, Alan arranged a party at their apartment with several other couples. The party turned out to be a marathon night of poker for the men while the women were expected to sit by and watch. After everyone had gone home Alan made love to Judy—or rather at her.

"He treated me like a whore," Judy told Lisa. "Afterward I felt . . . dirty."

For Judy, who had the boundless pep and enthusiasm for exploring life's sidestreets, the harness of marriage would be sprung, she had determined, by making domestic life into the new frontier. Always an eye towards accomplishment, she would turn running a household into an art.

But Alan did not let her begin. He did not even let her launder his shirts because he wanted them sent out and done just so. Judy had fantasized they would spend some evenings alone together—a bottle of Beaujolais blanc and her sole Véronique, the kind of softly lit intimacy she had been so sure her marriage would be full of. It did not work out that way. Every evening Alan would stop by the apartment on his way from one of his bars to the other and grab a TV dinner. Promises to begin relaxing a little in his business and to take his bride out to some special, out of the way restaurants were forgotten.

Never did Alan get home before 2:00 A.M., his beer bars' closing time.

"Go back to sleep," he would whisper as he undressed. "I don't want to disturb you." Within minutes, he was under the covers on his side of the bed and asleep. In the mornings, he woke up early. His brief routine was unvarying. Popping out of bed, he would fix Judy a cup of tea and before she had finished it, he was out the door.

Judy became a percolator of maddening energy. She began to take pills—pills to go to sleep, and inevitably, pills to keep her awake the next day. John and Evelyn Miller, the managers of the Castillian Apartments, often saw her through her living room window, puttering about, seeming to be searching for something to do. Judy was never one to keep the drapes closed. She was always chicly dressed, as if about to go out somewhere, but she never left the apartment much at all. The Millers saw her strumming her guitar every day as she sat on the ledge by the living room window. Often, she paused to wave at another tenant or a passerby. A few times on the weekend they saw Alan in the apartment. He was always striding through the living room, a white towel around his neck, its ends tucked into the collar of his sweatshirt. Alan was one of the few tenants to get his money's worth out of the exercise room next to the pool.

Alan gave Judy a walkie-talkie and insisted she take it with her whenever she went out. Several times a day he buzzed her from the bar to ask if she was all right. Ethel Davis did not mind telling her daughter point blank she thought Alan's only reason for the device was to keep track of Judy, to see to it she did not have too long a conversation any afternoon with another man. Judy poo-pooed the idea. It was everything else that was going on that made her a jangle of nerves.

"I can't keep living like this," she told both her sister and her mother.

Her marriage was one month old.

When she broached the subject of children, Alan dismissed the matter out of hand.

"Can you imagine another little me?!" he joked.

When Judy got him to discuss the matter seriously, Alan became somber, almost depressed. His grandfather had died insane, he told her, and he feared his mother would end up the same. Having children? No, it was simply an impossibility.

Judy finally realized that the only way for her to see her husband was by planting herself at the newly acquired beer bar, Judy's Grand Duchess. The bar was at 7855 Foothill Boulevard in Sunland, a San Fernando Valley community about fifteen miles northwest of downtown Los Angeles. The area was known for its incongruous collection of horse ranches, stables, and because of its dry air, homes for the arthritic. While a friend of Alan's, Pete Morris, oversaw the activity at the Grand Duke Bar in Burbank, Alan spent most of his time at Judy's Grand Duchess in Sunland. He had no choice. Business there was failing.

The Grand Duchess was housed in a low building of knotty pine exterior. Inside, the walls were a rather tasteful dark wood paneling. There were the usual pool table, jukebox, and game machines. Toward the rear was a small cluttered office room. The barmaids often saw Judy in the office or sitting at the end of the bar by herself. She seldom had a drink. Always she was with pencil in hand, working on the books for Alan. Whenever Alan had to step out, he told whoever was the bouncer that night, Gary Deaton or Gus Pilich, "Look after Judy while I'm gone." Alan had given Pilich a .45 caliber automatic.

It seemed to the barmaids that Alan and Judy were happy during their hours together at the bar. The only moment they came close to an argument in public was the day Martin Luther King was assassinated. When the news came over the barroom TV, Alan made the next round of drinks on the house. Utterly appalled, Judy walked out of the bar.

The city's pink oleander were blossoming, and there was an April-wet, fertile smell in the air. Like any newlywed, Judy was swept up in spring fever, and one morning insisted Alan come home for an elaborate dinner she wanted to prepare. Late that afternoon, she set the table with candles and wriggled into an Hawaiian dress she had bought on her honeymoon. She sat down on the couch in the living room to touch up her nails.

An eerie feeling came over Judy that she was being watched. When she looked up she saw a woman standing just outside the living room window, looking in at her and smiling. Believing she did not know the woman, a short overweight blonde, Judy assumed she was just admiring the apartment. Smiling back, Judy returned to her nails. The sensation did not go away. Judy looked up again. The woman was still there—she was no longer smiling. She was staring at Judy. Thinking she would ask the stranger if she wanted anything, Judy went to the front door, but by the time she opened it the woman had vanished.

9

WHEN ALAN GOT home that night, Judy told him about the woman in the window. Alan brought out old pictures of Katherine and asked Judy if it were she. Shaking her head, Judy said there was no resemblance at all.

"No," Alan agreed, "I didn't think Katy would do something like that."

April 18, Alan kept a promise he had made to Judy. He leased for her a sleek, new, yellow Jaguar XKE convertible. The next day, a Friday, Judy phoned Lisa and suggested her sister come over on Saturday and spend the day with her at the pool. They had not seen each other in a while and had a lot of catching up to do. Judy arranged to pick Lisa up in the new Jaguar the next morning—"just to show off a little, sis,"—and bring her back to the apartment.

When the day turned out to be overcast, they decided to forget the pool and instead drive out to the mall at Topanga Canyon for some shopping.

It was a typical April day in Southern California, warm and moist. A white sky, thick as unspun cotton, hung low over Los Angeles. Judy and Lisa rode with the top down, the wind flapping their blouse sleeves. Before going to the mall, they detoured a bit and drove out to Malibu for some lunch.

Lisa could not figure her sister out as they drove around together that afternoon. She thought Judy would be an unstemmable flow of talk about married life, but instead Judy's mind seemed far away. Lisa tried to start conversations and Judy gave one word answers. Her brow was tight, her lips anxiously pressed. Lisa soon fell silent as

well. She was a little afraid to pry. She had always believed her sister
was clairvoyant.

A buzz on the walkie-talkie from Alan did not lighten Judy's dark
mood. He was more concerned about the condition of the Jaguar than
how Judy was feeling.

On the way home, Judy stopped for a couple of errands. She
picked up a pair of Alan's shoes that were being resoled, and afterward stopped at the stationery store to pick up his personalized
memo pads.

When she dropped Lisa back at the Davises' apartment around
four o'clock, Judy for the first time that day became her animated
self again. The two daughters and their parents got into a lively conversation about marijuana. Judy had tried it a couple of times a few
years ago, she said, and was adamant that "the police should just
leave those people alone." After half an hour of good-natured debate, Judy suddenly grew quiet again. She excused herself, saying she
had to go home and change and then meet Alan for dinner.

Susan Peters arrived for work at the Grand Duchess at 7:00 P.M.
that Saturday night, April 20. Theresa Condi was the other barmaid
on duty that night. Also there when Susan arrived were Gary Deaton,
the bouncer, and Gus Pilich, who had been elevated from the Grand
Duke's bouncer to the manager of the Grand Duchess.

Alan tramped into the bar around 7:30. Susan tried to stay out of
his way. Alan had not been himself the last two weeks, much testier
with his employees than usual.

When Judy arrived about forty-five minutes later, Alan and she
left to go out to dinner. They came back an hour and a half later, and
what they saw was a sorry sight for bar owners. It was 10:00 P.M. on
a Saturday night and the place was nearly empty. With little to do,
Susan Peters was sitting on a barstool.

"Can I get you anything, Susan?" Alan asked sarcastically as he
passed to go behind the bar. "A glass of water? A beer maybe?"

Susan shrugged, got up from her stool and circulated among the
few scattered customers at tables, asking if anyone needed a refill.
Getting no takers, she sat back down next to Judy at the end of the
bar.

"What's gotten into Alan lately?" she asked beneath her breath.

Judy shook her head. "I don't know. I've almost been tempted to
go back and live with my folks."

She sighed. "But you want to know something? I love the guy."

A little after 10:30 P.M., Alan turned to his wife and told her with a curt nod, "It's time for you to go home now, Judy."

Obediently, Judy slipped her belted, houndstooth coat over her sleeveless dress and tied a white silk scarf over her head. Susan had always been envious of Judy's long, rich auburn hair. She wore it in a ponytail that night, augmented by a fall. Taking Alan's arm, Judy and he walked out to her car.

Susan Peters would later say Alan came back into the bar ten to fifteen minutes later, and that about five minutes after that, as he played a game of pool with bouncer Gary Deaton, the pay phone behind the bar rang. Susan answered and called over to Alan that he was wanted. Alan spoke on the phone for only a couple of minutes and returned to his pool game.

Acording to Susan Peters, the caller was a woman.

A young man named Robert Jenner was the weekend night attendant at the Standard Station at 8700 Foothill Boulevard on April 20. Shortly before 11:00 P.M., Judy drove in for gas. Jenner would later recall having a pleasant conversation about cars with her. Jenner drove a Dodge Charger and so did Judy's husband, she told him.

Judy was still wearing her scarf, Jenner later recalled, and had a blanket across her legs. The young station attendant wondered why she had the car top down. The day's cloud cover had lifted, and the night air was sharp.

When she pulled away, Robert Jenner did not see anyone following her.

Driving home, Judy would have had to continue along another stretch of Foothill past the Sunland Playground with its picnic tables and Little League fields, its wooden bandstand painted chalky white as if only to stamp the behinds of kids who sit on it—like the old sagging bandstand that Judy, as a little girl, used to climb around and sit on when her mother and father took Lisa and her to the park on warm summer afternoons.

At the junction where Foothill becomes California Highway 118, the road climbs off into the rolling hills. At that junction, the road sign reads: San Fernando 8 Miles; Sun Valley 5 Miles; Burbank 9 Miles. Judy would necessarily have had to swing left at that intersection and drive down Sunland Boulevard to either the Golden State

Freeway or to broad, easily traveled Glenoaks Boulevard. Judy usually took the freeway.

As she listened to soothing FM music on the car radio, someone was inserting copper-coated lead bullets, each a sixth of an ounce in weight, into the magazine clip of a .25 caliber automatic.

Alone in her car, and wanting to get home, Judy accelerated.

It was around 11:15 P.M. when Judy pulled into the parking lot of Nick Tagli's Hearthside Inn across the street from her and Alan's apartment. Her reason for stopping at Nick Tagli's was to tell their restaurateur friend that Alan and she would be in Monday to pay the $250 tab for their wedding reception.

"No sweat," Nick assured her.

Although Judy did not order a drink, she continued to chat with Nick inside the restaurant for ten minutes or so. Karen, a waitress, thought Judy appeared on edge, glancing about as she sat on a barstool. After saying goodnight, Judy walked back out to her Jaguar and drove the short hop across the street to her apartment's assigned car stall, number 17.

Donald and Margaret Benn, tenants in apartment 2 of the Castillian, had just come in from the carport and were waiting for an 11:30 television show to come on when they heard shots.

Margaret Pruitt, in apartment 11, first heard a loud "thump," then shots, three of them. And then a wailing, a terrible wailing like that of a wounded animal.

In apartment 38, Marion Wood, Jr., his wife, and another couple were also waiting for an 11:30 TV show to come on when they all heard three distinct shots. They commented to each other about it, but hearing nothing more, they did not look out the window.

Larry Beauregard was in bed with his wife in apartment 12 when the three sharp reports echoed up from the driveway. Having been in the army, Beauregard had spent enough time on rifle ranges to know the difference between a car backfiring and the sound of gunshots.

"Did you hear that?" he asked his wife. "It sounded like a twenty-two."

"Mm," she replied sleepily.

Because of a couple of recent carport thefts, the Castillian manager, John Miller, had made a practice of checking the parking area each night before turning in. Thinking that Miller might now be in trouble, Larry Beauregard slipped on a pair of Bermuda shorts and went outside.

All was quiet in the carport area. The overhead lights creaked from their chains, their arcs swaying slowly on the asphalt pavement. A prowler, Beauregard thought, might still be hiding in the darkened pool and patio area or, even more likely, might be fleeing down the street. Beauregard ran out to Grismer Avenue. He saw only parked cars, no people. Surveying the scene for only a moment, he began walking back toward the pool and patio.

As he did so, Judy Palliko sat in her car, unconscious and gasping, blood spilling from her breast and from the side of her head.

Shortly before 11:30 P.M., John and Evelyn Miller came back from their Saturday night out. The couple they were with dropped them off in the carport area. As John Miller got out of his friends' car, he was seized by a moment of fear as he saw a man peering over the gate to the pool and patio. The man whirled around. It was Larry Beauregard. Miller relaxed and waved to him.

Beauregard waved back, and convinced now that the night's peace had been shattered probably by just some mischievous kids, he went back to his apartment.

In walking to his own manager's living quarters, John Miller passed the yellow Jaguar that was parked in stall 17. The car's motor was running, its headlights on. The radio was playing softly. As he walked past the rear of the car, it appeared to Miller that no one, strangely, was inside it. Miller continued toward the pool and patio area to see if perhaps one of the Pallikos was there. Everything on the other side of the locked gate was dark and quiet. As he walked back toward the Jaguar, he heard a terrible sound, a low and guttural moan.

Miller ran to the side of the car and found Judy. She was sitting upright in the driver's seat, her head thrown back. Her right hand was still on the gear shift, her left hand in her lap. Judy's eyes were closed, her mouth open. She was gulping for air. There was so much blood running from the left side of her head, Miller did not see the blood flowing from her breast as well.

Miller shouted to his wife to call an ambulance and the police. He turned off the car's engine and radio, but not the headlights, and for some reason he could not later explain, he looked at his watch. It was exactly 11:30 P.M.

Miller ran to Larry Beauregard's apartment, panting, "Come and help. The girl in seventeen has been beaten up real bad."

As they raced out of his apartment, Beauregard corrected Miller: "You mean she's been shot."

It was 11:37 when Officer George Wood of the Burbank Police Department received the radio message to proceed to 2021 Grismer Avenue to meet an ambulance that was already en route. While Miller and Beauregard waited for their arrival, and while other tenants who had heard the commotion outside began venturing out of their apartments, Evelyn Miller called the Grand Duke Bar in an attempt to reach Alan. Pete Morris, the Grand Duke's manager, answered and told Mrs. Miller that Alan was at the bar in Sunland.

"Have him call me at the Castillian right away," she said frantically. "His wife's been in an accident."

When Officer Wood first arrived and was led back to the carport by John Miller, he saw that Judy was bleeding profusely from two bullet wounds in the head, one above her left ear, the other just to the side of her left eye. The streams of blood that ran down her face were already thickening in the cold night air. Wood held a compress to the wounds until the ambulance arrived at 11:44. Judy was still unconscious and gasping. The ambulance attendants worked hurriedly to get her onto a stretcher and hooked up for a plasma transfusion.

While Mrs. Miller waited for Alan to call back, she learned that Judy had in fact been shot and that they would be taking her to Burbank Community Hospital. She could hear the siren of the departing ambulance as she talked on the phone with Alan.

"What's happened?" Alan asked. "Judy was in a car accident? What happened?"

Mrs. Miller told him that Judy was shot and what little more she knew. Alan said he would leave immediately for the hospital.

Patrolman Wood questioned the various tenants who had seen or heard anything. While his partner, Officer Phillips, insured that the crime scene was not disturbed until the arrival of an investigating officer, Wood searched the pool area and grounds for a gun or other evidence. Nothing was found.

Robert Wells, a Burbank Patrol Division investigator, arrived at 12:17 A.M. It was now Sunday, April 21.

The yellow Jaguar sat in stall 17, its headlights still burning. It was a stark picture of life halted in midmotion. Wells observed a bloodied woman's hairpiece overturned on the console between the driver's and passenger's seats. Fallen inside the hairpiece were Judy's

Chevron credit card and the gasoline receipt from an hour earlier. Also on the console was a green leather wallet with approximately $35 in it. On the passenger's seat was an open purse. Inside it was a .32 caliber Llama automatic pistol. The gun was loaded with five rounds in the clip and one in the chamber. The hammer was on half cock, the safety in the "on" position. While it was conceivable the purse had been open during the car ride home, if it had not, it appeared Judy Palliko had perhaps been desperately trying to reach that gun when she finally succumbed to her attacker.

Also on the passenger's seat was a white blanket as well as a white scarf. The scarf was so drenched with blood it was stuck to the purse.

The carport to the right of the Jaguar was empty. A tenant's 1967 four door Oldsmobile was in the carport to the left.

In and around the Jaguar were three spent .25 caliber shell casings and two unfired .25 caliber live rounds (cartridges). One of the spent shells was on the floor behind the passenger's seat. A second was on the pavement of the empty car stall next over, four feet, nine inches from the Jaguar's right rear tire. The third shell was in the same area, eleven feet, one inch from the Jag's right rear tire. It appeared odd to Wells, in that the description given to him of the victim indicated she had been shot from the left side, and yet the spent shells were well to the right of the car. The presence of empty shell casings at the scene indicated that the murder weapon was not a revolver but an automatic, which ejects its shells.

Of the two *un*fired rounds—even more curious at the scene of a shooting—one was behind the passenger's seat and the other was atop the Jaguar's trunk. Investigator Wells collected and tagged them as evidence along with the spent shells.

Even after the police had departed, bystanders lingered, speaking in hushed voices as they gazed at the sports car and its bloody, black leather interior. None stepped forth to turn off the car's headlights.

When the Snyder Ambulance team arrived at Burbank Community Hospital, a Dr. Compher gave Judy a fast looking-over and, shaking his head, ordered that she be immediately transported to L.A. County General Hospital. He called ahead to have a neurosurgeon stand by.

Alan arrived at the Burbank hospital just after Judy had been transferred, and was directed to L.A. General. There he was told by nurse Kathleen Egan, "I'm sorry, Mr. Palliko, but your wife isn't expected to live."

"No . . . no, that can't be," Alan said, dropping his hand to his side.

He paced the waiting lounge, speaking to no one.

Judy died at 1:35 A.M. She was being prepared for surgery by Drs. Haravey and Cohen at the time. Nurse Egan and a young intern were present when one of the surgeons informed Alan of his wife's death. Alan nodded and looked at the floor. When friends of his who had heard the news of the shooting arrived a few minutes later, Alan slammed his fist down on the coffee table in front of him and shouted, "I know who did it! I swear I know who did it!"

The friends, Paula Boudreau and her husband, Thomas, offered to drive Alan home. Alan refused, and drove home by himself.

Burbank detectives were called in: Lt. Ernest Vandergrift, Lt. Warren King, Sgt. William Nylander, and Detective Harry Strickland. When they arrived at L.A. General, they were informed that the attempted murder case they had been called in on at 12:35 A.M. was now a case of murder.

The detectives viewed the body. Besides two gunshot wounds to the head and a slash across the left breast, they also observed the damage done by what comes under the police catch-all "a blunt instrument." On the top and back of Judy's head were seven long gashes—seven ugly, half-inch-deep rents in the skull.

It was one of the most vicious murders the officers had ever seen. Two bullets in the head had not satisfied the perpetrator of this crime. Seven times the murderer had brought something—perhaps the butt of a gun—smashing down into Judy's skull. As the detectives left the hospital, unable to get that battered, sickening picture out of their minds, they thought they knew a little more about the person they were seeking. He (she) was no slick professional. But was the excessiveness of the murder the result only of inefficiency—or hatred as well?

The team of men split up. Vandergrift and King went to the Grand Duke Bar in Burbank and there interviewed Pete Morris, who told them of getting the call from Mrs. Miller and of relaying the message to Alan at the bar in Sunland. A half hour later, he said, Alan called back, asking Morris to close the bar for him at the end of the night and adding that he had asked Gus Pilich to do the same at the Grand Duchess.

At 2:00 A.M., Sergeant Nylander and Detective Strickland found Alan at his apartment. He was quiet, seemingly numbed. The questioning went along standard lines. Alan told them what he knew of Judy's activities that day, and that he had given her a $50 bill that morning for shopping. Robbery had already been tentatively ruled out as a motive in that money was found in her purse, and Judy was still wearing her wristwatch as well as her diamond engagement and wedding rings when she was found. Judy sometimes parked in the carport, but sometimes she parked on the street, Alan said. Concerning the blanket, Alan explained that it was always kept in the car because they had not received their tonneau snap cover yet and therefore used the blanket to cover the seats at night.

When asked about possible suspects, Alan did not draw a blank. "That German fellow" Judy had dated and who lived a few blocks from the Davises was Alan's guess. Another possibility, he said, was Tod Glenn. A big strapping Texan recently paroled from the Oregon state prison, Glenn and his girlfriend Sissa Kolovik had caused a commotion in the Grand Duke the night before and Alan had had to call the Burbank Police to cool him off. Glenn, the detectives would later discover, was the friend who had accompanied Alan to Del Cook's barber shop.

Nylander and Strickland looked over Alan's collection of guns and rifles, and found among them a .25 caliber Colt Junior B/S semi-automatic. They asked if they could take it with them and Alan offered no objection. They told him that if he wished, he could come to Burbank P.D. headquarters the next morning and accompany them to the Davises to tell them of Judy's death. In the meantime, they suggested Alan try and get some sleep.

For their part, Nylander and Strickland did not go home and sleep. Upon returning to headquarters around 3:00 A.M., they ran a routine check on the victim's spouse with the LAPD and found that he was a suspect in the Stockton murder case, a wifebeater, and possibly involved in hit-and-runs. At eight o'clock in the morning, the Burbank detectives were again on the phone in a back office with the people at Parker Center, while Lt. Warren King kept Alan occupied in the Burbank headquarters' waiting room. For about fifteen minutes, King made small talk with Alan, all the while looking for clues in his demeanor. Alan was stoic, looking around the waiting room or back down at the floor whenever his and King's eyes met. By the time Nylander and Strickland emerged from their phone conversations with the LAPD to take Alan over to the Davises' apartment, they knew a great deal about Alan Palliko.

Franklin Davis, a picture of retirement, was sitting out on the front steps fixing a broken chair leg that Sunday morning. As Alan walked over to him, Nylander and Strickland remained in the car.

"I have terrible news," Alan said. "Judy was shot last night."

The frail wispy-haired man looked up for a moment, hesitating, and touched a trembling hand to his brow.

"Is my daughter dead?"

Alan nodded.

Staring at the pavement, Franklin asked, "How? . . . How?"

"Out in the carport. Nobody knows."

Franklin Davis sat paralyzed. Slowly, he stood up. With barely any voice in him, he said, "You better wait here while I tell the girls."

His hand shaking on the railing, he moved with slow steps, head bowed, up the front porch to his apartment.

"Where's that old boyfriend, Felix?" Alan called after him.

As if he had not even heard Alan, Franklin Davis continued inside his apartment. After a few minutes, he came to the doorway and motioned for Alan and the detectives to come in.

Ethel and Lisa sat on the living room couch, Lisa's face buried in the folds of her mother's arms. "Oh God, no. Please, no," she sobbed.

Alan sat down on the couch next to Judy's mother, and asked Mr. Davis if he could have a drink. Franklin brought him a bottle. At one point Ethel Davis, her knees only inches from Alan's, looked her son-in-law in the eye and said, "You wouldn't know how this could have happened, would you, Alan?"

Their eyes locked in a long cold stare before Alan shook his head and looked back into his glass.

Ethel Davis informed the detectives that Felix Zimmer could have had nothing to do with Judy's murder. At eight o'clock the previous night, Felix had walked over to the Davises' apartment and asked if he could tag along to a Moose Lodge party the family was planning to attend. All three of the Davises—Ethel, Franklin, and Lisa—could verify that Felix Zimmer was in their presence until approximately 2:45 A.M.

Ethel Davis mentioned a former boyfriend of Judy's by the name of Prescott Nelson. Nelson, she said, had written Judy many letters trying to convince her to return to New York. As a nosy mother she had intercepted the letters and had torn them up. As far as she knew, Nelson still lived in Flushing, N.Y.

Even in front of Alan, Ethel did not mind telling the police she never could understand why Judy had had to carry a gun. Judy, she said, had told her it was because Alan now and again had to throw some rough people out of the bar that he insisted his wife be armed. Listening to his mother-in-law's version of it, Alan nodded.

Franklin Davis put his head in his hands and began to cry. Nylander and Strickland excused themselves after only twenty minutes of interview. They dropped Alan back at his apartment and proceeded to the Orange Street apartment of Alan's former wife Katherine. They arrived there at 10:00 A.M.

Katherine quite literally shook at hearing the news. She could not get her hands to be steady. It was as if a two-thousand-pound crate had fallen out of a window and had landed three feet from her. Katherine was convinced she had come that close to being the one. She told the Burbank detectives the whole history—the hit-and-runs, the beating, the threats, in sum, her life with Alan Palliko. Although Nylander and Strickland hardly assessed Katherine to be the kind of woman to seek revenge against Alan's second wife, they asked her for her whereabouts the previous night as a matter of formality. She related that her boyfriend, Steven Arbogast, and she had gone to the Roxy Theater for a show that had started at 10:00 P.M. and not let out until 12:45 A.M. Afterward, they went for a drink and then retired to Katherine's apartment. Steven Arbogast, who was still at the apartment when the police arrived, produced the ticket stubs.

If Franklin and Lisa Davis found it difficult to talk to the police that Sunday morning, Ethel Davis did not. Detective Strickland received a phone call from her when he returned to Burbank headquarters at 11:30 that morning. There were things she wanted to tell them she had not been able to say in Alan's presence.

Alan, she related, was a strange and secretive man. He had recently even hired a mammoth friend of his named Tod to "watch over Judy," Alan claiming she needed protection. Ethel Davis told Strickland that the man who knew the most about Alan's backdoor life, perhaps the only person Alan had ever trusted—the man they should interview without delay—was Michael Brockington.

Bitter accusation in her voice, Mrs. Davis went on to tell Strickland that although she had known Alan had taken out a life insurance policy on Judy before they were married, naming Judy's father Franklin as the beneficiary, it was only recently she had learned that on March 20, Alan had Judy change the beneficiary—from Franklin to himself.

The Burbank detectives had already begun to suspect that Alan Palliko was involved in his wife's murder. The evidence that would emerge, however, in the long months ahead would melt into an amalgam of contradictions. A mystery, if you will, as dark as the criminal mind.

10

JUDY'S YELLOW JAGUAR was towed to a garage that Sunday and inspected for evidence. "Fair quality" latent fingerprints were lifted from the exterior and preserved for future comparison. A .25 caliber bullet was found embedded in the console between the two front seats. The next day the car was returned to Alan. How well the police inspected that Jaguar is open to question. Gary Deaton, the Grand Duke's bouncer, would later tell detectives that when Alan asked him to clean the car up for him he was not able to finish the job. He had become physically ill because of all the blood and "that piece of skin."

That Sunday morning, neighbors saw Alan walking up and down the street outside their apartment building, a mug of coffee in his hand. Up and down the sidewalk he shambled, pausing, scratching his head, inspecting.

A week later, he called Lisa Davis to say he wanted her to have the Jaguar.

"Oh, Alan," Lisa sighed with disgust, "you know that car is leased."

Monday, April 22.

In the morning, King, Nylander, and Strickland met with Lt. Robert Helder at Parker Center. Helder was Bob Guy's and John St. John's direct superior. He furnished the Burbank detectives with copies of all reports on the Henry Stockton murder, and the men from the two police forces promised to stay in close contact.

The one statement in the Stockton reports that snared the Burbank detectives' attention was Alan Palliko's quote to Katherine Drummond, which she had repeated for Guy and St. John when they interviewed her a second time on March 6: "I'm going to have to do something again that I don't want to do, but I have no choice. I got myself in with the wrong kind of people."

The Burbank P.D. not having its own crime lab, the three spent shell casings, the two live rounds, and three expended bullets (two recovered from Judy's body and the one found embedded in the car's console) were all taken to the crime lab of the L.A. Sheriff's Office and examined by Deputy Sheriff James Warner, an expert in firearms identification. All were determined to have been fired or ejected from a .25 caliber automatic. The murder weapon had probably been a Colt, or possibly one of several Spanish imitations of the Colt. Warner test fired the Colt Junior semi-automatic Alan had relinquished to the police during their first interview with him, and ruled it out as the murder weapon.

Of the shell casings and live rounds, three were stamped by the manufacturer "WW" (Winchester Western) and two were stamped "WRA" (Winchester Repeating Arms). This knowledge was helpful to the police in that the Winchester Company had been manufacturing its "WW" ammunition only since October of 1967, less than seven months before the murder, thus greatly narrowing the time span during which that ammunition could have been bought.

After leaving Warner at the crime lab, Nylander and Strickland went on to the Coroner's Office where they interviewed Dr. John Holloway, the Deputy Medical Examiner who had performed the Sunday afternoon autopsy. Holloway advised that the two bullets recovered from Judy's body, one of which had entered just above the left ear, the other above the outer corner of the left eye, were found "floating free" in the cranial cavity. There was tatooing around both wounds. Dr. Holloway was certain that the slash across Judy's left breast was also caused by a bullet. That bullet, police assumed, was the one found embedded in the Jaguar's console. During the two hours Judy had survived, she had lost a great deal of blood. The spleen was found to be reduced in size, and the lungs were light-colored, nearly bloodless. Dr. Holloway did not know what the blunt instrument was that caused the seven deep rents in Judy's skull. His educated guess was that it was the butt of a gun.

Alan Palliko called Burbank headquarters that Monday afternoon to advise he would be putting up a reward for any information about the case. The manager of the Grand Duchess, Gus Pilich, would later tell a friend that Alan spent the better part of Monday on the bar's office phone calling people in New York and Detroit and "various places" in Texas, trying to "get to the bottom of things."

When the police re-interviewed Alan back at his apartment later in the day, he suggested another possible suspect, telling the detectives about being recently threatened in a San Diego federal courtroom by a Jeffrey Gatz. Gatz, Alan said, had stolen his Corvette and had been caught trying to sell it in Tijuana. Because the alleged crime violated the federal Dyer Act, the case was being handled by an agent McNulty of the FBI.

When detectives interviewed Theresa Condi, one of the two barmaids at the Grand Duchess on the night of the murder, she was tense and notably reticent. She stated only that she knew a phone call came for Alan about a half hour after Judy left the bar, and that soon after the call Alan left, leaving Gus Pilich in charge.

Shortly after that Monday interview, Theresa Condi disappeared without a trace from the Los Angeles area.

At 7:15 P.M. that Monday, investigators received an anonymous phone call. The male voice told them of Alan's father once being mysteriously shot near Rosarito Beach on the Baja Peninsula. The caller said there was bad blood between the father and son because of money owed the father. After that tidbit, the caller hung up.

Tuesday, April 23.

Detectives conferred with agent McNulty of the FBI. McNulty advised that Jeffrey Gatz was out on bail and was believed to be staying in Connecticut until his trial. The FBI brought Gatz back to California a few days later and he produced the airline ticket showing he had left California just prior to Judy's murder. After questioning by the Burbank detectives, he was eliminated as a suspect.

Franklin, Ethel, and Lisa Davis were again interviewed. Ethel did most of the talking. As far as she knew, a pendant Alan had given Judy had come out of Alan's divorce settlement with his former wife. Judy had used the two diamonds in that pendant (one diamond, a carat; the other, a quarter carat) for her engagement and wedding rings, the engagement ring having the much larger stone. She had designed both settings herself. A pendant of the exact same description the Davises gave the detectives had been part of the take, the police already knew, in the robbery committed by Jason Simcoe and Donald

Whalen. The pendant was one of the pieces of jewelry that had yet to be recovered.

Wednesday, April 24.

Interviewed in the morning, Tod Glenn said he was home watching TV with his girlfriend Sissa Kolovik at the time of Judy's murder. Sissa Kolovik corroborated the story. For the time being, the police let it go at that.

The detectives used Judy's calendar book to help compile a list of the men she had dated in California before Alan. Eventually, all were located and eliminated as suspects.

Marjorie Huebner, interviewed at her mother's home in Glendale, where she still lived, told Nylander and Strickland of Alan's two proposals of marriage to her; his remark, "when you have garbage on your feet, you can never get it off"; that Alan had once told her he had "taken care" of people who "had to be taken care of"; and that the people around the Grand Duke had told her Judy was bisexual.

The name that continually came up in the interview was Michael Brockington. Marjorie said it was Michael who told her that women who went out with Alan always "ended up paying somehow." He had also confided to her once about Alan's keeping a diamond pendant and other jewelry from someone else's robbery. Michael told her as well about accompanying Alan to a place in what Marjorie recalled to be Covina, where Alan went into a building and came out with a large case of money.

Michael, Michael, Michael.

Why Michael Brockington, as it turned out, would be virtually the last of Alan Palliko's associates to be interviewed, some ten days after Judy's murder, would never be quite explained.

Thursday, April 25.

Forest Lawn, Hollywood Hills Memorial Park. The lambent beauty of the spring morning only sharpened the pain of the Davis family, who had come to bury their daughter Judy, twenty-two years old.

Over seventy people attended the funeral. Among them were Lieutenants Vandergrift and King, and Sergeant Nylander. While two of the officers copied down license plates, the third recorded the names of those who had signed the guest book. After the ceremony in the chapel, the detectives questioned the mortician, a Mr. Mispagel. Alan

Palliko, he said, had given him his wife's wedding ring, requesting that she be buried with it on her finger. Before the hearse conveyed Judy's body to the burial spot, Mr. Mispagel opened the casket for the detectives and showed them the ring. Noticing the small diamond on the ring, the detectives suspected it was the quarter carat stone from the stolen pendant. The larger, one carat stone Alan apparently had not wanted buried.

The funeral arrangements, Mr. Mispagel stated, had been made through a friend of Alan's who was now one of the pallbearers. He was also Alan's insurance agent. His was the only black face at the funeral. His name was Jack Dodd.

Friday, April 26.

Mrs. Davis was again interviewed, this time by Lieutenant Vandergrift. Ethel Davis related to Vandergrift the tense, rather awkward ride she had had with Alan in the funeral limousine. At one point, Alan had looked her straight on and said, "You think I killed Judy, don't you?" Not giving Mrs. Davis a chance to answer, he went on about the reward he was planning to put up.

Ethel told Alan quite frankly that Judy would not have needed a gun if Alan had not left her alone all the time.

"When she saw that woman in the window, you didn't even care."

"Your daughter had some peculiar fantasies," Alan mumbled.

After a long grudgeful silence in the limousine, Ethel told Alan she thought it was "lousy" he had not asked his parents to come to the funeral. Alan suddenly became emotional and told the Davises they were the only family he had. He asked if he could still see them and perhaps come over for dinner now and again.

Ethel forced a nod.

Burbank investigators contacted Nadine Camp, operations officer of the Valley National Bank. Camp checked bank records and found that Alan and Judy Palliko had opened a new checking account for the Grand Duke Bar on February 2, 1968, and that on February 5, they had opened a personal checking account. Between the dates of 2/28/68 and 3/27/68, Alan had deposited into those accounts a total of $12,218.84. Of that, $2,200 was from bank transfers. According to Alan's own financial statement, his bar grossed approximately $4,500 that month. Adding in the $500 wedding gift from Franklin Davis, that still left $5,018.84 whose source was unknown.

Monday, April 29.

Nylander and Strickland went to see Sergeant Ide at the Van Nuys police headquarters. The Burbank detectives listened to a tape recording of statements made by robbery suspects Simcoe and Whalen. Both men disclosed that Alan Palliko (aka Big Dude) had bought some of the stolen jewelry from them.

There was no mention on that tape of a .25 caliber automatic that the robbery victim, Herman Siegel, had also listed as missing.

Tuesday, April 30.

In the morning, Tod Glenn was reinterviewed at the Burbank police station. Glenn denied that Alan had ever hired him to be Judy's "bodyguard." He was at one time, he said, only a weekend bouncer at the Grand Duke. Alan paid him $10 a night. Once, on a Saturday morning, he had accompanied Alan to a barber shop on Verdugo Road. Alan and the barber had discussed their business outside on the sidewalk, and according to Glenn, Alan never did tell him the reason for the trip there or why he wanted Glenn along.

Glenn agreed to take a polygraph in connection with the murder of Judy Palliko. Police had the feeling he was telling them all he knew.

Glenn's fingerprint exemplar, along with Alan Palliko's and those of all of his close acquaintances, were compared by an Officer Ralph Posten, Burbank Police Department, with the latent prints lifted from the Jaguar. The results were negative.

Just after lunch, Nylander and King sat down with Michael Brockington, who had at last been summoned to the Burbank police station. The interview commenced at 12:35 P.M.

Michael Brockington impressed the detectives as a sensitive man. "I knew Judy," Michael said at the outset, "and I'll tell you, when I heard about it, I just got absolutely sick. Just, you know, mentally and physically sick."

But Brockington also struck his questioners as a man who was not telling them everything he knew. He was denying just too many facts the police were already aware of.

Q. BY LIEUTENANT KING: "Did you ever go out to Covina with Alan, Mike?" (Marjorie Huebner had quoted Michael incorrectly when she told the police the trip had been to Covina. It had been to Santa Fe Springs.)

A. "No, not that I can remember."

Q. "Ever recall going out to Covina with Alan? Picking up any money? Have no recollection of that?"

A. "No."

Q. "Do you know anything about a robbery that took place in Van Nuys this year?"

A. "Not that I remember, no."

It was clear Michael was protecting Alan, Warren King thought.

When King shifted to the subject of Judy Palliko's murder, Michael told King that Alan loved Judy and would never have murdered her.

Brockington's ability to reconstruct his own whereabouts the entire night of Judy's murder, some ten days earlier, including his watching the movie "Man of a Thousand Faces" alone at home at 11:30 when Judy was shot, had the detectives trading glances. Brockington, however, was also able to review every night of the past week in the same uncanny, detailed fashion.

Eventually, King stopped playing games with him.

Q. "Here's the thing, Mike—look, we don't want to get you involved, and I know you don't want to get involved. Obviously, we're concerned with one thing and that's who killed Judy. A young girl has been murdered, brutally murdered. If you're not involved in that, fine, but please don't lie to us about these other things. We've just got too much information that you can't overlook."

Michael took a deep breath, and looking around the room, he finally capitulated.

A. "Well . . . okay. If I can go off the record . . . we're not being bugged or anything, are we?"

Q. "We'll go off the record. We're not being bugged, no," King told him, as the reels of a tape recorder in an adjoining room continued to turn. "Are you scared of Alan?"

A. "You're darn right I am."

After Michael's fears of personal harm were allayed, he came clean of everything he had heard and seen: Alan's acceptance of the stolen jewelry from Simcoe and Whalen; his faking of the accident with Katherine's VW; Alan's expropriation of Debbi Simmons' $4,700; the plan to have his Corvette "stolen"; the theft of $5,000 from the barber, Del Cook. Michael also told of the trip to Santa Fe Springs and the pick-up of the envelope full of money. Although he could not remember street names, Michael described the place in detail and promised that if they would drive out to the area, he could find the exact spot again.

The police suspected that the envelope of money was from the Stockton insurance proceeds. And it was on that subject that the great revelation of the afternoon came.

Q. "Now, let me ask you this question. Do you know Sandra Stockton?"

A. "If it's the same one who used to work at the Auto Club."

Q. "Right. Do you know her?"

A. "Oh, I worked with her for—it had to be the better part of three or four months while she was working down there."

Q. "She isn't working there now?"

A. "No."

Q. "Do you know anything about her relationship with Alan?"

A. "Uh-huh, yes, he told me about it."

Q. "Well? What's the story?"

A. "The only thing I know for sure, and he said it in a very weak moment—was in a bar, which was in fact the Marlindo Lanes—it was just like three or four words and nothing else was ever said. I guess it was in a mood . . . ah . . . I don't know what it really was for, but he was feeling real bad. He made the remark that quote, 'I killed her husband.'"

At 5:20 P.M. that afternoon, Michael Brockington sat down in Room 318 of Parker Center and made a formal statement to Sergeant Bob Guy of the LAPD. Although the police saw this as *the* break in the case, they also knew that juries are instructed to view unwritten, unrecorded self-incriminating statements of a defendant "with caution." And of all such statements, they were well aware that those made in a barroom are the least apt to hold up in court.

Moreover, there was a crucial question that had not been asked out in Burbank. Guy asked it now.

Q. "Was anyone else present when Palliko told you this?"

A. "No."

Q. "Any chance someone might have overheard it?"

Brockington shook his head.

A. "No. We were all by ourselves."

Embarrassed and ashamed that he had ever managed to fall in with Alan Palliko, Michael told the police: "Don't ask me why I continued working for him. I still can't give you a logical explanation of why I did it."

At 6:45 P.M., four officers armed with shotguns walked into the Grand Duke Bar and placed Alan Palliko under arrest for the murder of Henry Stockton and Judy Palliko. Alan, in desert boots and a gold turtleneck sweater, threw his just lit Sherman on the floor and ground it out with disgust when he saw the policemen come through the door.

"You guys never give up, do you?" he said.

Alan was booked at the Los Angeles County Jail.

Another team of police went to Downey, looking for Sandra. At 1:50 A.M., they finally caught up with her at the apartment she shared with her sister, Tracy, as she was returning from a date. She was arrested for the murder of her husband Henry and booked at Sybil Brand Institute, the county jail for women in east Los Angeles. Both Alan and Sandra, on the advice of attorney Roy Marchetta, refused to make any statements. As this was a capital case, they were denied bail.

The very morning that Sandra was arrested, her mother was able to retain the services of famed trial lawyer Melvin Belli. Mrs. Bingham had seen Belli on a talk show along with F. Lee Bailey and Percy Foreman just the night before. That morning, Belli told a battery of newsmen there was "not one speck of evidence" against his client in the "macabre" murder of her husband.

Belli's fee was $20,000, paid by Sandra's parents. Friends contributed $2,300 toward Sandra's defense.

The morning edition of the L.A. *Times* frontpaged the case with photographs of Alan, Sandra, Henry, Judy, and Katherine. "The Late Show Comes To Life," U.P.I. would headline their own story. "One of the most memorable movie dramas ever made was an oldie called *Double Indemnity*," U.P.I. said. The article went on to point out the curious similarities between the Palliko-Stockton case and the fictional movie in which a Los Angeles insurance agent conspires with his lover, a "sexy, bored wife," to murder her husband for double indemnity insurance, the man doing the actual killing and trying to make it look like an accident. "The Palliko-Stockton case," the U.P.I. story added, "goes *Double Indemnity* one better." Here there were two victims, not one.

The same day, May 1, Sgt. Bob Guy and a Sgt. E.H. Henderson drove Michael Brockington out to Santa Fe Springs. Moving slowly up one street after another, Michael finally pinpointed the place where Alan had picked up his envelope of cash sometime in August of 1967. The building located there was that of Allied Pacific Manufacturing Company. Back at headquarters, Bob Guy phoned Allied's personnel department and learned that Sandra Stockton had worked at Allied from June, 1967, until January, 1968.

At 9:00 A.M. Thursday, May 2, Sergeant Guy and Lieutenant King met with Assistant District Attorney Bill Ritzi at the Hall of Justice. From there they walked down the hallway and appeared at the doorway of my office. Having to be in court in a few minutes, I was finishing a cup of coffee with one hand and riffling through the morning sports page with the other. My name is Vince Bugliosi.

Part II

1

WHEN A BIG, complex capital case comes down, it becomes your life.

The Palliko-Stockton case's drama, which like a magician's box revealed new sides from each angle, immediately captured the interest of people in Los Angeles. More spectators would line up each morning outside our courtroom, Dept. 110, than they would down the hallway where Sirhan Sirhan was concurrently being tried for the assassination of Senator Robert F. Kennedy. Sirhan Sirhan was admitting killing Kennedy; dozens of people were eyewitnesses. The reason for the spectator attention in our case was simple: it had all the ingredients of a fictional murder mystery—only it was true.

Contrary to what is depicted in movies and on television, in real life most murders are relatively open and shut cases. An irate husband is found two blocks from the murder scene, the bloodstained knife he used to kill his wife still in his pocket. At a party, friends get into an argument. Shots are fired and someone is killed. During the course of a robbery, the robber shoots and kills the proprietor of the liquor store. Witnesses nearby identify the robber from the witness stand.

The murders of Henry Stockton and Judy Palliko were extremely well planned and executed. One of the defendants being an ex-policeman, this did not surprise me. We went into the case with no eyewitnesses, no "smoking gun," no fingerprints, no bullet match-ups, no physical evidence connecting the defendants with the crime. If ever there was a classic, textbook case of circumstantial evidence, this was it. We went in with assumptions. It would take a very long murder trial for a jury to arrive at their own conclusions about those assumptions.

At the time I was assigned the Palliko-Stockton case, I had been out of law school (UCLA) and with the Los Angeles DA's office just under four years.

Some call me "expansive" in a courtroom. Although I do have an instinct for the dramatic, I am just basically of an Italian nature. I raise my voice when I am in full rhetorical flight, I gesture with energy. During direct examination of my own witnesses, I sit in place at the counsel table, doggedly trying to get into the trial record the facts and evidence upon which my case is based. On cross-examination and final summation to the jury, however, I am apt to roam every inch of the courtroom floor. This is just my natural, unconscious style. But style is only a small part of trying a case. Much more important is *thoroughness*—infinite, yes, exquisite preparation for which I almost have an obsession. "The readiness," as Hamlet says, "is all." Just during the thirteen-week trial itself of the Palliko-Stockton case, I would put in over four hundred hours of overtime.

My wife, Gail, has often wondered how I can have such an affinity for details in a case, and yet manage to hit my head at least once a month, without fail, on the swag lamp which I am told hangs from our den ceiling.

After reviewing the police reports that Thursday morning, May 2, I issued the formal complaints charging Alan and Sandra with the murder of Henry Stockton, and charging Alan alone with the murder of Judy Palliko and the attempted murder (the beating) of Katherine Drummond. That afternoon at 2:00 P.M., Alan and Sandra appeared before Judge Joan Dempsey Klein for arraignment. Both pleaded not guilty.

Every defendant has a constitutional right to a speedy trial. Because of that, the prosecution often finds itself racing against time to collect all the facts it needs. In early May, however, I was not thinking ahead to the trial as much as I was anticipating the Grand Jury hearing, where it would be determined if there was enough evidence to even take the case to trial. In most crimes, it is usually a magistrate at a preliminary hearing who passes on the question of whether there is sufficient evidence to require the defendant to stand trial, but crimes of this magnitude are frequently taken to the Grand Jury. The

Grand Jury hearing for Alan and Sandra was set for May 14, less than two weeks away.

Although I did not charge Sandra then nor do I now in this book accuse her of Judy Palliko's murder, there were facts the detectives and I could not avoid thinking about. We thought about the woman who was staring at Judy through the living room window only a week before Judy's death, a woman Judy had described to her sister Lisa as a "short, chubby blonde." We wondered about the "short, stocky blonde" at Alan's and Judy's wedding reception, the one who said, "Oh no, why did you have to go and do that?" and walked away when Judy kissed Alan on the cheek. (She would later be positively identified by several people who were there as Sandra Stockton.)

We were also curious about the short phone call Alan had received from a woman just five minutes after he returned from walking Judy out of the bar the Saturday night of her murder. Other facts would come to my attention only after the Grand Jury had already handed down the indictment.

First, while on a search of Alan's apartment, Lieutenant King found a crumpled sheet of Alan's notepad in the wastebasket. In the top corner of the sheet was a penciled-in date, "4/28." In the middle of the sheet was written: "Sandra. 1:00 P.M. Tony's. Monday." Off to the side were the words: "Gun shop. Pasadena. Carbine clips. Ammo. Enforcer stock."

Secondly, Phillip Weatherwax, a tenant at the Castillian Apartments, told the investigators that at 4:15 P.M., Monday, April 22, the day after Judy's death, he saw a short blond woman coming out of apartment 17, the Pallikos' apartment. Weatherwax was able to positively identify that woman, from pictures, as Sandra Stockton.

And finally, there were the phone calls between Alan and Sandra. The only local calls that are traceable in Los Angeles are ones made from one "toll area" to another. The charges for the "message units" are listed on each monthly bill. I had asked the detectives to get Alan's and Sandra's past bills from the phone company. Those bills revealed that Alan (in Burbank) and Sandra (in Downey) had maintained weekly, sometimes daily contact during the weeks just before and after Judy's murder. Moreover, we discovered the following:

At 5:22 P.M. on April 20, just hours before Judy was murdered, a call was made from Alan's apartment to 869–8389, the Downey number listed to Sandra's divorced sister, Tracy, with whom Sandra was then living. That conversation lasted only one minute. Then immediately thereafter, at 5:24 P.M., another call was placed from Alan's apartment, this one to 923–2073, Sandra's private number, which was also located at her sister's apartment. That second conversation lasted twelve minutes. One might speculate that Sandra, during the first phone call, told Alan to call right back on her private line, the one in the shared apartment where she would have some privacy. What was said in the following twelve-minute call we will never know. All we do know is that the conversation took place and that it took place less than six hours before Judy Palliko was shot.

If in return for Alan's killing her husband, Sandra did in fact agree to and then kill Alan's wife, we had a murder conspiracy the likes of which I had never heard of.

To be sure, the facts and their possible inferences certainly were not enough to warrant an indictment, much less a conviction, against Sandra for the murder of Judy Palliko.

We are a society of due process. Sandra Stockton was never indicted nor even accused of Judy's murder. If the term "innocent until proven guilty" means anything at all to us, Sandra did *not* commit that murder. Period. The day I stepped into the case, it was clear to me we would have trouble indicting even Alan for that murder.

My first chore after the arraignment was to assemble in my office the investigators on the two cases, and to begin coordinating their future activities. They came from two separate police forces: Helder, Guy, and St. John of the Los Angeles P.D.; and King, Vandergrift, Nylander, and Strickland of the Burbank P.D. Keeping communication flowing between the two police departments was vital. A small fact that might appear irrelevant to, say, the Burbank officers investigating Judy's murder could very well be of great significance to Guy and St. John, who were working on the Henry Stockton case. It was part of my job to keep all of us a single team for the next ten months.

My practice was to write down questions and things to be done on a yellow legal notepad, and whenever I had collected thirty or forty of them I would call a meeting. In between the meetings I became heavily involved in the investigation myself, tracking down leads, interviewing witnesses, etc. Although it is not the traditional role of a prosecutor to be an investigator, that being left up to the police, I have always found that I can be much more effective in court when I have had a hand in putting the case together.

The first day the officers gathered in my office they were followed through the door by a battery of TV news reporters and cameramen. The very next morning, Detective St. John found a note left in his box by the night watch. It was written by an Officer Brown of the Metro Division. A friend of Brown's, Dave King, had heard about the Palliko-Stockton case over television. Having sold Alan Palliko a .25 caliber automatic the previous July, King felt an obligation to come and talk to the police about it.

Dave King told the detectives he had sold Alan a gun he had obtained from a girlfriend in a small town in Louisiana. As far as he knew, it had never been registered. When King met Alan at a party in Van Nuys, they got to talking about guns, and King arranged to show his .25 caliber automatic to Alan at a later date. On July 8, 1967, King sold Alan the gun for $30. It was nickel plated, with a simulated white pearl handle. King was "almost positive" the manufacturer was Colt. We already knew, of course, that the gun used to kill Judy Palliko was either a Colt or a Spanish imitation of a Colt.

Debbi Simmons (since having married and become Debbi Fox), interviewed at her apartment in Van Nuys, reluctantly related to the detectives many of Alan Palliko's stories to her. To hear gullible Debbi tell them, one would believe Alan had been in a high-hedged Long Island home to kiss a Godfather's hand more than once.

Valuable information did emerge from the interview, however: Alan's March or April "plan" that would leave him either "rich or dead"; the name of the gun store (Strade's Gun Shop in Glendale) Debbi said Alan took his guns to for "dismantling"; and the phone conversation Debbi overheard in which Alan referred to the caller as Sandra and "Tiger."

The police now had an important link. Michael Brockington had told them of the phone conversation between Alan and "Tiger," in which Alan had said, among other things, "Calm down. The police can't prove anything."

The detectives wanted to know more about the incident down in Rosarita Beach when Sandra had shown up unexpectedly, and the following morning Alan's gun was missing. Debbi could provide no explanation for the very bizarre and mysterious hijinks of that night—and no one else would ever be able to, either.

The afternoon of May 3, the same day the Grand Duchess closed due to a lack of business, I prepared a search warrant. It allowed us to search Alan's apartment for a .25 caliber automatic, a .22 caliber revolver (the kind used to kill Henry Stockton), and a copy of Judy's life insurance policy—but it would allow us to seize nothing else. Warrants must be carefully worded, and the wording must be scrupulously followed. I decided to take part in the search to help make sure no procedural slip-up would occur.

By the time I rounded up the officers who were to conduct the search, however, it was well into the evening. Being a Friday, the Hall of Justice was practically deserted, and no matter how many judges' chambers I poked my head into, I could not find a judge anywhere to sign the warrant. I did not want to wait out the weekend. Just the day before, John Miller, the Castillian Apartments manager, had called to say he had found a man about to enter Alan's apartment. The man had had a key. We advised Miller to change the lock, which he was allowed to do, in that Alan's rent was now overdue. The man who had wanted to get into the apartment, we discovered later, was Gus Pilich, manager of the Grand Duchess.

It was not until close to eleven o'clock that I found Judge Leo Freund to review our warrant. He was at home in robe and slippers, watching the last inning of a Dodgers-Reds game on television. Between glances up at the pitchers' duel going on that night, he read over the warrant and signed it.

A half hour later at the Castillian, before going into Alan's apartment, I asked Mrs. Miller, the apartment manager's wife, to describe for me Alan's reaction over the phone when she informed him that Judy had been shot. She told me he had not sounded shocked, but to the contrary, quite calm. I turned to Nylander and asked him to make a point of finding out who informed Alan at General Hospital of Judy's death, and to interview that person. Initial reaction to such news is something juries are always interested in.

Inside of Alan's apartment it appeared as if the young couple who lived there had just stepped out for a minute. Everywhere were the signs of daily life—a record on the stereo turntable, food in the refrigerator, a warm and touching love note that Judy had written and taped to the lamp on Alan's desk. But of course there was also the arsenal of firearms, all of them immaculately polished, some of them in glass cases. The whole scene gave me a shiver.

Although rifles and guns were everywhere, including a loaded .38 beneath Alan's pillow, we found no .25 caliber automatic. We did find a copy of Judy's insurance policy. It was in a metal box in the bedroom closet. I looked at the amount of the policy—$25,000—for a

long moment, struggling to comprehend this man Alan Palliko. It was
very obvious that what Alan Palliko wanted above all else from these
murders was money. But outside of Henry Stockton's death, I wondered about the relatively small amounts involved—the moderate sum
of $25,000 on Judy, and the paltry $12,000 on Katherine to be
gained from the hit-and-runs had Katherine been killed. Could it be,
I thought, that even if for some reason he ended up getting no money
from a murder, for Alan Palliko, he was not coming away empty-
handed? That the satisfaction of extinguishing a human life was still
some recompense?

Also in the bedroom closet was a nine-inch by six-inch sealed
wooden box. Because it could have contained a gun, the officers pried
it open. Inside were ashes and very fine bone fragments. Not allowed
to seize it, we only made note of it as possible evidence to be taken
under a subsequent search warrant. Other possible evidence we saw
and listed for incorporation in a second warrant were: a partially full
box of .25 caliber ammunition (type WW); a notepad ("From the
Desk of Alan Palliko") containing the name "Sandra"; an appointment book containing the name "Sandra" on several pages; and two
safe deposit keys.

It was just after 2:00 A.M. when we concluded the search. We left
a copy of the search warrant and a list of the property seized (this
time around only the insurance policy) on the desk in Alan's study.
At home, my wife Gail had an apology coming. Another Friday night
lost. Sometimes I wonder why she puts up with me. Perhaps she loves
me as much as I love her, that dark-haired, no-nonsense woman.

I requested Detective Strickland to make timed car runs on a Saturday evening around 11:30 P.M. along the fastest routes between
the Castillian Apartments and the Grand Duchess. The question was:
did Alan have time to shoot Judy (the estimated time of the shooting
being between 11:27 and 11:28 P.M.) and then get back to the bar
and speak with Evelyn Miller when he did? Strickland reported to me
that taking either the quickest city street route (a distance of 8.4
miles), which he traveled at speeds up to 50 m.p.h., or the Golden
State Freeway (a distance of 9.4 miles), which he drove at speeds up
to 65 m.p.h., the time consumed in both cases was *twelve minutes*.

Evelyn Miller had been unable to tell the police precisely when
Alan Palliko returned her call, but from what the police could gather,
Alan had called Mrs. Miller within *ten* to *fifteen* minutes after the

shooting. Based on Strickland's timed car runs, they concluded that although physically possible, it was highly improbable that Alan was the actual killer. The consensus of the investigating officers remained what it had always been—that Alan had had someone kill Judy for him.

Janet Turnbull, one of Alan's barmaids, called to tell the police that whoever Judy's killer was, he was still on the loose. On the morning of May 2, she said, she had received a call at the bar in Burbank. The voice sounded familiar, but she could not place it. "Who is this?" she had asked. The male voice, she claimed, stated: "I'm the one who's going to come and get you."

"All right then," Janet said she replied. "I'll find out when you get here." No one ever showed, or followed up the threat in any other way.

Gus Pilich told the police he had received a similar threatening call just the day before. "You're next, Gus," Pilich claimed the caller had said. The detectives listened to the new information, which would suggest Alan's innocence, a bit doubtfully. Gus Pilich, after all, had been the one to state in an earlier interview that Alan was "like a father" to him.

When Phil Kennon of Harger-Haldeman Leasing came to pick up Alan's cars a few days after Alan's arrest and incarceration, we asked him to make an inventory of any items that might still be in the cars. On the floor behind the driver's seat of the Dodge Charger, Kennon found a 14-inch, rolled steel bar. Kennon knew the steel bar belonged to Alan because he had seen him place it in the Charger's trunk at an earlier date. We had the bar sent to the crime lab. Results were negative: no blood, no tissue, no fingerprints. If the bar had been the "blunt instrument" used to so grotesquely batter Judy's skull, it had subsequently been carefully wiped clean.

Personally, I did not believe it had been one of the weapons used. If the murderer, probably crouched in the shadows of the carport as he waited for Judy, had a gun in hand, why would he feel a need to have a metal bar in the other hand? It conjured up pictures of a gladiator about to do battle, distrustful of any single primitive weapon to do the job. Guns are not primitive; they do the job. No, I agreed with Dr. Holloway who believed, in coroner's terms, that the "blunt instrument injuries—multiple" were caused by the butt of a gun.

Officers Nylander and Strickland went to speak with Mr. Roland Strade, owner of Strade's Gun Shop, the place Debbi Fox said Alan patronized. Strade was no more helpful to the detectives than was absolutely required of him. He stated he knew Alan, but only as a customer. A check of sales records for the previous seven months revealed that the only gun Alan had bought was a .38 caliber revolver. Strade said he had made a number of repairs for Alan, but that he could not recall what any of those repairs involved. The books showed only the types of guns brought in and the dates: 7/27/67—a Ruger .44 magnum carbine; 7/28/67—a .22 magnum lever action rifle with Weaver scope; and 8/29/67—a Remington 12-gauge shotgun.

Strade recalled selling Alan a .32 caliber Llama with engraving on the barrel (presumably the gun he gave Judy), but no receipt or dealer's record of sale had been written up. Strade said he did not make out a receipt because, "I knew Alan was an ex-policeman and a private investigator."

Hearing that not all sales were recorded properly in his books, the officers asked to see all loose receipts from January 1, 1968, to April 20, 1968, the period just prior to Judy's murder. A receipt was found, dated March 16, 1968, showing Alan had purchased a .25 caliber Colt automatic. The serial number, however, corresponded to that of the .25 caliber Colt Alan had surrendered to Sergeant Nylander the night of Judy's murder. That gun had already been ruled out as the murder weapon.

Under persistent questioning, Strade further recollected that Alan had come in about a month earlier and had bought a box of ammunition, which Strade "believed" was .25 caliber.

Tuesday, May 7, I prepared a second search warrant which would allow us to seize the various items of possible evidence we had observed in Alan's apartment our first time in. Judge Joan Dempsey Klein reviewed and signed the warrant, and that afternoon Guy and St. John and Burbank detectives King and Strickland went to Alan's apartment.

The officers brought back with them the notepad and appointment book with Sandra's name in them, the partially empty box of .25 caliber ammunition, the safe deposit keys, and the small wooden box containing the ashes and bone fragments. When we sent the ashes over to the crime lab at the Sheriff's Office, we were told they could not determine their origin. We got the same response from the Coroner's Office and still the same response when we even sent the box to the County Museum for analysis. It was only when I mentioned the box in a later conversation with Katherine that we got our answer. Alan had been so grieved by the death of his German shepherd, Ponza, he had had the dog cremated and for those half dozen years had kept the remains in his bedroom closet.

A week after Alan's and Sandra's arrest, Michael called to say he had just been phoned by a man named Bob Dancer, a private investigator working for Alan's attorney, Roy Marchetta. It was "urgent," Dancer had said, that he speak with Michael. We directed Michael to set up a meeting in his apartment for 7:30 P.M. the next evening. On the possibility that either a threat or a bribe was in the offing, we received Michael's permission to hide microphones in his apartment. The installations were made by a Sergeant Rydell and Officer Dasenzi of SID. Then getting the consent of Katherine, who still lived in the same building, we set up the listening devices in her apartment. Because of his past association with Alan, she did not trust Michael, but she did trust us.

The police waited around in Katherine's apartment until 9:30 P.M. Bob Dancer never showed. We later learned that because of a disagreement between Dancer and attorney Marchetta, Dancer had abruptly withdrawn from the case.

Frank Batten, vice president of Valley National Bank (where Alan did most of his banking), was being very helpful, calling us whenever he came across a piece of information he thought we could use. The day before we were to go to the bank to examine the records of Alan's activities there, Batten phoned to remind us that if we came across any safe deposit keys (which we had), they probably belonged to the box Alan rented at Valley National. I immediately prepared a search warrant for the safe deposit box. When King and St. John opened the box up, however, all they found were old leases between Alan and former landlords, Alan's discharge from the army, and other miscellaneous papers.

The next day, Batten phoned again to say that one of the bank's employees was going around telling fellow workers she had dated Alan Palliko some time ago and that in February of 1967, he had given her a .22 caliber revolver as a gift. That was two months after Henry Stockton had been shot dead by a .22 caliber revolver. The employee turned out to be Natalie Post, the five-foot-ten strawberry blonde whom Alan had taken to his first big New Year's Eve bash at the Biltmore. Officers Guy and St. John called Miss Post and arranged to meet her at her apartment that evening. When the detectives arrived, however, they found her sitting in her living room with the lawyer she had just retained. The detectives explained that Miss Post was in no way a suspect and asked to interview her in private. Her attorney, a Mr. George Conway, did not budge from the couch and added that his client would talk only if they subpoenaed her as a witness. Promising they would do so, the detectives showed themselves out.

The following morning, I subpoenaed Miss Post to testify before the Grand Jury. Rather than waiting for the hearing, she came to my office accompanied by her attorney. Mostly, she was just frightened. After a bit of talk between us, she surrendered the .22 that Alan had given her back in February of 1967. I had the gun test fired and it was determined that it was not the weapon that had killed Henry Stockton. One has to explore every possibility, but I was beginning to get that feeling of wasted motion, that sense of futility that can make you start to feel foolish. You can almost begin to hear the man behind the bars laughing at you. Alan Palliko, I felt, was intelligent enough to make sure we never would find those two murder weapons.

In my first interview with Michael Brockington, he told me that Alan had used his own money for the down payment on the Grand Duke Bar, but had convinced a friend of his in the auto business, a Howard Koebrick, to accept a falsified promissory note from Alan indicating that Koebrick had loaned Alan $5,000 for the bar's down payment.

Koebrick, owner of Koebrick Pontiac in North Hollywood, was interviewed by Nylander and Strickland. Realizing the cat was already out of the bag and scratching at his own front door, Koebrick admitted to his complicity in the scheme. He first met Alan, he said, at Marcy's Gym in the early part of 1967. Everyone at the gym liked Alan, Koebrick told the detectives, because he was such a "personable gentleman." Alan told them he "dabbled in investments and securities," but also said he was interested in going into the bar business, and asked Koebrick if he would invest some money in the venture. Koebrick declined. Then, during the first week of September, Alan again approached Koebrick, telling him he himself now had the $5,000 for a down payment. But the Alcoholic Beverage Control, Alan said, was not inclined to grant a license to an ex-policeman who had been dismissed from the force, and for that reason he wanted it to appear he was being backed by a respected businessman.

Koebrick claimed he believed Alan's story about the A.B.C. and agreed to the false loan. On September 14, Alan handed him $5,000 in cash and they went to the Bank of America in Toluca Lake, where Koebrick purchased a $5,000 cashier's check in favor of Alan Palliko. Alan then had Koebrick write "Paid in full" on the reverse side of Alan's promissory note to him. Alan, apparently, had been wise enough to make sure Koebrick would not someday double-cross him and claim that Alan still owed him the $5,000. Alan kept the note and sent a copy of *only* its front side to the A.B.C., along with a copy of the check and an accompanying reference letter from Howard Koebrick.

It was clear to all of us that Alan merely wanted to hide the fact from the A.B.C. (and any other interested agencies, namely the police) that he himself suddenly had a ready $5,000. It was little surprise that in February or March, probably just after Alan's gambling losses in Las Vegas, Alan wanted Koebrick to invest some money, but by the first week of September Alan had the money himself. According to Michael Brockington, it was just a couple of weeks earlier, in late August, that Alan had picked up his envelope of cash in Santa Fe Springs.

So far, Michael Brockington appeared to be reliable. It was of course all-important that my star witness, the one to whom Alan had allegedly admitted the murder of Henry Stockton, was credible. If the defense could succeed in depicting Brockington as a witness unworthy of belief, as they undoubtedly would attempt to do, our whole case would most likely be destroyed in the process.

It was impossible at that time for me to foresee that Brockington would give testimony so damaging to his own credibility, I would almost be able to feel the rejoicing in the air at the defense table.

Our theory being that Alan and Sandra committed the first murder and Alan the second murder for the purpose of collecting insurance, it was crucial that we knew all the details surrounding the purchases of those insurance policies. Although the prosecution bears no legal burden to prove motive, from a practical standpoint, in the eyes of the jury, just as the presence of motive is circumstantial evidence of guilt, the absence of motive is even stronger circumstantial evidence of innocence. And in a case of circumstantial evidence, a prosecutor walking into court with a briefcase full of evidence but no motive is like striding onto a tennis court with a ping-pong paddle under your arm.

As to Henry's insurance, the policy he held through his employers at Sears showed neither more nor less than what met the eye. It was insurance that came with the job, and Henry had held that policy for the entire nine years he had worked at Sears.

It was the larger policy, the double indemnity insurance with National Life, that posed a problem for us. I was looking for proof that it was Sandra, not Henry, who had been the active force in obtaining that policy. I asked the detectives to find out who the insurance agent was who sold the policy. They learned that the National Life agent was a man by the name of Bernard Croucher, but it seemed that Croucher had moved from the state. Neither those friends of his we were able to contact nor his old employers had a clue as to his whereabouts. All I could tell Guy and St. John was to keep trying.

It was with respect to Judy's insurance that the prosecution's case opened up beneath our feet. The Equitable Life agent who sold Alan that policy was Jack Dodd, Alan's old law school friend.

Jack Dodd's statement to the Burbank detectives was essentially this:

It had been some time since Dodd had seen Alan when the two ran into each other in the fall of 1967. Dodd had just sold some insurance to a Dwight "Butch" Rolapp (who, unbeknownst to Dodd, was Alan's car mechanic and close friend), and after the transaction Dodd and Rolapp went to a nearby bar for a glass of beer. The bar was the Grand Duke Bar, and it came as quite a surprise to Dodd to find Alan there as the owner. The two reminisced about their times together at Southwestern Law School, and in the course of conversation Alan suggested he could use some liability insurance for the bar and its employees. A few weeks later, Dodd sold him the coverage he wanted.

Dodd also tried to sell Alan a personal life insurance policy. Although reluctant, Alan did finally agree to make application for such a policy, but declined the insurance because the company had "rated" him (i.e., quoted him a higher than normal premium) due to Alan's bad back. Dodd did not give up, and called Alan a number of times that autumn trying to make the sale, but with no success.

Then in February of 1968, Alan called Dodd, saying he was about to get married and that he wanted to talk again about a personal life insurance policy. On February 22, Dodd went to Alan's and Judy's apartment and sold Alan a $20,000 policy. It was at that time, according to Jack Dodd, that he, not Alan, broached the subject of Alan's buying a policy on Judy's life as well. Alan, Dodd told the police, absolutely refused the idea. According to Dodd, however, he was not about to take no for an answer. He remained at the apartment for a couple of hours, and while Judy sat quietly by, argued with Alan over his resisting a sensible idea. It was only because of his insistence, verging on pestiness, Dodd swore to the police, that Alan finally backed down and told Dodd to write the policy up.

Jack Dodd pointed out to the police that Alan took out the absolute minimum amount on Judy (minimum, that is, for a term policy with Equitable—$25,000), and that the policy he chose did not even come with a double indemnity clause.

Needless to say, I was dumfounded when the detectives reported back with that account of the transaction. It was evidence which was diametrically opposed to the whole thrust of my case.

I had no reason, really, to believe that Jack Dodd would lie for Alan about the circumstances surrounding the sale of Judy's insurance. Just the same, I sent the Burbank detectives back for a second interview. Perhaps Dodd had just been mistaken in his recollection. His story, however, did not change the second time around.

When the police asked him for a written statement, Dodd courteously refused. He said that his lawyer had advised him against it, and that if they wanted his information in writing they could look at the memo he had already given to his superiors at Equitable Life. He seemed to believe the police were pursuing his friend, Alan Palliko, unjustly.

That "friendship" was a genuine curiosity to me. Alan and Jack Dodd had had no social contact with each other since their days together in law school, and yet immediately after Judy's death, I learned, Alan had sought out Jack Dodd for apparent "comforting." Alan spent a good part of that Sunday, April 21, with Dodd, and it was Dodd whom Alan asked to accompany him to the Coroner's Office to view Judy's body. He also asked Dodd to help him with the funeral arrangements and to be one of the pallbearers. Had Alan, I wondered, simply and cleverly been laying the foundation for a friendship he knew he might soon have to call upon? Or was something else going on here that I, as of yet, could not see?

Dodd's statement put a gaping hole in our theory of the second murder, but with the Grand Jury hearing upon us I had to proceed with what we had. The hearing (always held behind closed doors) lasted two days, May 14 and 15. I called thirty-three witnesses for the prosecution. At 2:00 P.M., May 15, the Grand Jury handed down the indictment we had sought against Alan and Sandra. My relief was minimal. To secure a Grand Jury indictment, the prosecution does not bear the burden of proving guilt beyond a reasonable doubt, which *is* their burden at the trial, but rather has the far lesser burden of proving only that there is "probable cause to believe" that the defendant committed the crime. Translated, this means that a reasonable man need only have a strong suspicion of guilt, enough suspicion to justify sending the case to trial.

Alan and Sandra were arraigned on the Grand Jury indictment May 16. Having obtained the indictment, I proceeded to have the original complaint dismissed, which we would have used only if we had moved forward by way of a preliminary hearing before a magistrate. Alan's and Sandra's pleas to the indictment were put over until May 24.

The lion's share of work was ahead of us. Between the time of the Grand Jury hearing and the actual trial, some six months later, I would build my list of prosecution witnesses from thirty-three to eighty-nine.

As in all my cases, I had already begun working on my final summation, it not being uncommon for me to prepare at least half of my argument before the first witness at a trial has even been called. As soon as I learn the strengths and weaknesses of my case, I begin almost immediately to work on how I am going to argue these strengths and what I am going to say in response to defense attacks on the weaknesses. Getting an early start on the summation, and continuing to expand and modify it during the trial, gives me up to weeks and sometimes even months to develop arguments and articulations.

The detectives thought our chances for conviction on Henry's murder were slightly better than fifty-fifty. I felt our chances were higher. As to the charge against Alan for the murder of Judy, it appeared we were about to learn if there was any philosophical value in confronting futility. Six tired cops and a disgruntled deputy DA— hardly the kind of guys to sit around and discuss existentialism.

What we did discuss was the very real and very frightening possibility that Sandra Stockton was going to walk out of that courtroom free and that Alan Palliko, after serving a few months for only aggravated assault against Katherine, would soon join her.

Juries are intrinsically unpredictable.

My office decided we would seek the death penalty against Alan and Sandra. The people of California had expressed through their state legislators their belief in the propriety of that ultimate punishment, but the guidelines for imposing it were not defined. It was left up to the total discretion of the jury to decide what was or was not a "proper case" for the imposition of the death penalty.

I had just recently prosecuted two other capital cases. In the first, a man by the name of Wallace Clarke had been accused of killing his wife's paramour, and was found guilty of first degree murder. Nevertheless, to the consternation of my office, which wanted me to seek the death penalty, I argued to the jury that they instead sentence him to life imprisonment. Even though two weeks had passed between the time Clarke learned of his wife's affair and the time he murdered her lover, it was in a sense, I believed, still a crime of passion with extenuating circumstances. I could not in good conscience, therefore, argue for the death penalty, and the jury, after long deliberation, returned a verdict of life imprisonment.

Shortly thereafter I prosecuted a second murder case, this time, however, making what I later felt to be a serious mistake.

In 1966, there had been a record 367 bus robberies in Los Angeles. Finally, a seventy-one-year-old driver who was due to retire within a month was murdered when he resisted the robbery of his bus, surprisingly the first homicide in the history of Los Angeles' Rapid Transit District bus line. My office decided to seek the death penalty against the non-trigger man as well as the trigger man, and I agreed.

The defendants, two twenty-year-old youths, were convicted of first degree murder (first degree being the charge for killings perpetrated during the course of a robbery, even if there is no premeditation). In the penalty trial, I sought, and the jury returned, verdicts of death against both defendants.

It was only months later, after a searching reconsideration of the *non*-trigger man's culpability—his age, background, the fact that the killing apparently had been spontaneous and unpremeditated, and that he had not done the actual shooting—and particularly after observing other cases in the office in which far more heinous killers had received life imprisonment, that I came to believe the death penalty for the non-trigger man in my case was wrong.

Distressed, I contacted the defendant's new lawyer, a professor at UCLA Law School who was taking the case up on appeal, and informed him that if the matter of execution ever actually reached the governor's desk, I would intervene and ask for clemency. Although the lawyer felt that such an unusual intervention by the prosecutor would have heavy influence on a governor, I knew, of course, that there could be no assurance of this.

(It turned out I did not have to face that eventuality. As a result of a subsequent decision by the United States Supreme Court, the death penalty for both defendants was commuted to life imprisonment.)

But what of the Palliko-Stockton case, I now asked myself, giving long and deep thought to the question. It was, as Damon Runyon once said, "murder in the worst degree." Cold-blooded murder had been committed—not because of uncontrollable passion or years of intolerable cruelty, not because of a zealot's vision of changing the world politically. Nor was it a situation, like the bus driver case, involving a spontaneous killing where the accomplice, in all probability, had never expected a murder to take place. No, but as a result of greed and a long, thought out plan. With less compunction than a hunter would have in shooting quail, Alan Palliko walked up to Henry Stockton and sent three bullets tearing through his brain, then put two more slugs into the dead body from the front for good measure. To Alan Palliko, slick sports cars and a pocketful of money were, if my theory on the second murder was correct, worth arranging to have his bride of seven weeks shot and battered to death. To Sandra Stockton, dinners out and closets full of new clothes were worth seeing her four-year-old son grow up fatherless.

Previously, I had prosecuted eleven murder cases, but in none of them had the motive been as reprehensible as in this case. I was born and raised in a place called Hibbing, Minnesota. My father worked hard to feed his family of seven, first as a grocery store owner, and later as a conductor on the railroad. The people in Hibbing are hesitant to use even a credit card to acquire the luxuries of life. But to *murder* for them?

If this were not a "proper case" for the imposition of the death penalty, I did not know of one that would be. The final decision would rest with twelve of Alan's and Sandra's peers.

2

MAY 20, JASON SIMCOE and Donald Whalen, the robbers Alan had informed on, told their jailers they wanted to speak to St. John again. (Earlier, when they realized they were not going to get any leniency for the additional "important information" they told St. John they had back in February, they had pleaded guilty to the armed robbery charge against them, the assault charge being dropped as a result of plea bargaining.) Although they no longer had anything to gain by it on their own cases, they came forth with their information concerning Alan anyway. May 20 and 21, St. John conducted separate interviews with them.

Both told St. John essentially the same story. They said they went to the Grand Duke Bar the day after pulling the Siegel robbery, to fence the goods. Alan, they said, bought a diamond pendant (consisting of two diamonds, a quarter carat and a one carat), a man's diamond ring, and a .25 caliber automatic, all for $160. He gave them $100 then and promised the other $60, which he never made good on.

Simcoe and Alan had just recently run into each other in the County Jail infirmary. Their conversation, needless to say, was less than friendly. Alan did, however, make a few comments about his wife's murder, and one of those comments, Simcoe alleged, was: "The police haven't found the gun and they never will, so I ain't worried." The rest of the conversation, Simcoe said, had just been typical prisoner-to-prisoner grumblings about doing time in the "state joint." The next day Donald Whalen would claim to St. John that Alan had repeated to him the comment about the police never finding the gun, adding to the statement, "That's a hole (loophole, according to Whalen) to stand in, man."

Simcoe believed, but was not sure, that the manufacturer's name on the gun he sold Alan was German. He said that while driving away from the robbery on the Ventura Freeway, they had fired it out the car window to see if it was operational. They found the gun would jam unless loaded manually. The car they had fired it from was a '59 Cadillac, owned by a friend. They could not say whether any of the spent shells might still be in the car.

From the bullets and shells recovered after Judy's murder, we had three categories of identifying marks with which to connect or eliminate any gun as the murder weapon. The bullets recovered from Judy's body and the Jaguar's console had the identifying striations imprinted on them by the barrel. Secondly, the spent shells found had "ejector marks," the marks an automatic leaves on the sides of the shells when it ejects them after firing. And thirdly, the live rounds of ammunition as well as the spent shells that were found had "extractor marks," the very slight nicks made on the rim of the shell when the round is loaded into or unloaded from the firing chamber, regardless of whether it is fired.

What we wanted, of course, was Herman Siegel's gun. But even without the gun, if we could just find one round of ammunition that had gone into the gun, fired or unfired, and match up its striations or marks with those found on the bullets and shells recovered from the murder scene, we would have our concrete, physical evidence that the weapon used to kill Judy Palliko was, at least at one time, owned by Alan Palliko.

The story of Siegel's gun jamming had the Burbank detectives convinced it was the murder weapon. It explained the two live, unexpended rounds of ammunition found at the murder scene. The detectives theorized that the murder had occurred as follows:

When the killer rushed up to the car, Judy instinctively swung her left arm out, deflecting the gun. The first shot fired grazed her left breast, the bullet embedding itself in the console between the seats, the empty shell ejecting to the ground. When the killer tried to shoot Judy again, the gun jammed. It was very likely that the killer then brought the butt of the gun down on Judy's head, knocking her unconscious. It was improbable that the killer struck her more than once at that time, for all of the Castillian tenants who heard the shots said they came in fairly rapid succession. He (she) then operated the slide mechanism manually, ejecting a live round in the process. A second shot was then fired, point-blank into Judy's head. The gun again failed to reload automatically, jamming. The killer operated the slide manually for a second time, and for a second time ejected a live round. A third shot was then fired, again into Judy's head and probably also from skin contact range.

As Judy sat upright but unconscious, dying, the murderer brought the butt of the gun down six more vicious times onto the top and back of her head.

I asked Dewayne Wolfer, the firearms expert from SID, to visit Jay Simcoe in jail, and go page by page with him through "Smith's Pistols and Revolvers." From the catalogue, Simcoe picked out a .25 caliber automatic made by Waffenfabrick.

There was one major problem. The barrels of all five German manufacturers of .25 caliber automatics (Waffenfabrick, Suhl, Mauser, C.G. Haenel, and Schmuser) impart a *right* (clockwise) twist to the bullet. The bullets that killed Judy came from a barrel with a "6 *left* twist." That was the "rifling specification" that had made firearms expert James Warner quite certain that the murder weapon was a Colt or a Spanish imitation of the Colt. We had, however, a possible explanation. Debbi Fox had said Alan was always having his guns dismantled and reassembled with other parts. Given that, it was quite possible it was a German gun but with a Colt (or Spanish imitation) barrel that was used to murder Judy.

The Cadillac the gun had been fired from was eventually located and searched for spent shells, but to no avail. Inasmuch as Herman Siegel said that he had never fired the gun (and thus had no empty shells himself), we had lost all chance to match up ejector markings. The only hope left was to match up the extractor markings.

Siegel, however, could not recall ever having even loaded the gun. He had accepted it years earlier from a customer (whose name he very unfortunately could not remember) who had given it in exchange for some clothing he had purchased at Siegel's store. We brought Siegel down to the crime lab to look through gun catalogues.

Siegel's recollections were foggy at best. Paging through the catalogues, he picked out *twelve* dissimilar guns that he said looked like his. We thanked him for his time.

Weeks later, something must have refreshed Siegel's memory, for he called my office and stated he had, in fact, once put a round in the gun chamber and had immediately taken it out. That round was presently in a box of .25 caliber ammunition somewhere in a back closet of his apartment. Excited, I called Detective Strickland and asked him to pick it up. Dewayne Wolfer examined the rim marks on the round, but they were so scant, no match-up could be made to the live rounds found at the murder scene.

It was not many days afterward that Dewayne Wolfer and James Warner trudged into my office, and each wanting the other to spit it out, advised me they had just discovered that the barrels on all German .25 caliber automatics cannot be replaced by any other barrels. If Simcoe were right about the Siegel gun being a German make, it could not have been the murder weapon. But I was not at all sure Simcoe was right.

Without the Siegel gun, we were left only with the Colt that Dave King had sold to Alan back in July of 1967. We had no bullets or spent shells from that gun whatsoever for purposes of comparison. As to finding the murder weapon itself (whether it had been King's or yet a third gun we did not know about), I took Alan Palliko at his word when he allegedly told Jay Simcoe in the County Jail infirmary: "The police haven't found the gun and they never will."

On May 24, Sandra's plea to the Grand Jury indictment was continued to June 3, and Alan's plea to June 5. As expected, both pleaded not guilty.

June 24, Melvin Belli argued a 995 motion before Judge James Tante. Under Section 995 of the California Penal Code, a Superior Court judge may set aside a Grand Jury indictment if it was not based on sufficient evidence.

Belli argued: "May it please Your Honor, on December 11, 1966, there was the death by criminal means of the defendant's husband in El Sereno, an area which is about one hundred miles distance from Twentynine Palms, where the defendant whom I represent was on that day and on that weekend. The only way that she can be connected to this crime is by means of aiding and abetting or by means of some conspiracy.

"The witness at whose home Sandra was visiting when she received the phone call from her father said: 'Well, I thought she was going to faint. She became very white and pale.' And then she had difficulty, apparently, in catching her breath. In other words, when Sandra got the news of her husband's death she acted distraught, and this came from my good friend Mr. Bugliosi's own witness at the time."

Belli continued later on in his argument, "Now, we do find that Mr. Palliko knew the defendant, but the two knowing each other and having worked together cannot of itself be ominous and sinister. And whether we like it or not, whether it squares with our morality, there might have even been at one time an illicit relationship between the parties. Mr. Palliko and Sandra took a trip to Las Vegas together . . . she gave this other defendant some money. We could look at those facts and I would say that she had some feeling toward this fellow.

"With respect to Mr. Palliko's alleged statement that he killed Henry Stockton, even assuming it to be correct, there is still no connection between Palliko and Sandra in this crime . . . he may have had some hold over her, that she having this money gave him that money. I cannot see how that would raise a suspicion and parlay that into probative evidence showing a conspiracy some months before."

Belli concluded his address by saying: "Here is the practical matter, Your Honor. One of the best police departments and one of the best district attorney's offices in the United States have been running Sandra down since December 11th of 1966, and have come up with nothing. There is nothing such as a fingerprint. There is nothing such as a note. There is nothing.

"I respectfully submit that our motion for dismissal be granted."

In response, I briefly summarized the incriminating evidence against Sandra. I then observed: "Mr. Belli did not examine the evidence at the Grand Jury in its totality. Rather, he segregated each particle of evidence and examined it alone." I pointed out to Judge Tante that in a case such as this, one had to look at the entire landscape, the complete set of circumstances.

I concluded: "I don't think there's any doubt that a reasonable man would at least entertain a strong suspicion of Sandra Stockton's guilt. Whether or not a reasonable man would believe that she is guilty beyond a reasonable doubt, is not a question before this court at this time."

Judge Tante denied Belli's 995 motion.

A word about Melvin Belli. I have never been a strong believer in reputations. From my experience, I have found that if many prominent lawyers met their reputations out on the street, they would not recognize each other. But Belli unquestionably is one of the most accomplished trial lawyers of our day, particularly in the area of tort law, where he has sown new ground. With his drifts of snow white hair, fashionably unshoveled, and his rotund vested frame, he frequently intimidates the opposition before he ever opens his mouth. When he does speak, he is convincing. Most important of all, he does his homework; he comes into the courtroom prepared.

Having always believed that in a close case, final summation is the most important part of the trial, I photostated copies of many of Belli's closing arguments from trial transcripts on file at the state Attorney General's office down the street from my office, and studied them nightly. I looked for holes in his methodology, in the logic he was accustomed to employing. I could not let Sandra Stockton walk just because she had a good lawyer.

The better part of the summer was spent answering Belli's motions and briefs with my own counterbriefs. One of Belli's motions was for separate trials for Alan and Sandra. That motion would be denied all the way up through the California Supreme Court.

Alan promptly relieved his first lawyer, Roy Marchetta, and hired Leonard Stein, an attorney who had a good reputation doing appellate work. Soon dissatisfied with Stein—Alan never seemed to believe *anyone* was really on his side—Alan made a motion to relieve Stein and substitute himself as the attorney of record. The legal term for being one's own attorney is "in propria persona," commonly called "pro per." On September 4, Alan made his pro per motion before Judge George M. Dell in Department 100.

THE COURT: "I believe I am required under law to follow your request. Not in the case of every defendant, but in your case, in view of your education and experience."

Alan, dressed in a dark conservative suit and tie, smiled faintly. His fingers played along the top of the attaché case next to his chair as though it were a hunting hound. He answered Judge Dell's questions confidently, stating his familiarity with the basic books on California Criminal Law, such as those by Witkin, and Fricke and Alarcon.

Judge Dell lectured Alan briefly on the wisdom of being represented by an attorney in a case as extremely serious and complex as this one.

THE COURT: "As you know, Mr. Palliko, your very life is at stake. Is this a decision you are sure is the right decision?"

DEFENDANT PALLIKO: "Yes, sir. I have retained, since my incarceration, two attorneys and have spent considerable sums of money on them, and I have felt they have not been defending me or operating in a manner beneficial to my best interests. I have retained the firm of Goldin & Towne for the purpose of assisting me, whereby I will still be able to utilize their knowledge and services as far as specific points I miss."

Shaking his head to himself, Judge Dell signed the court order giving Alan his pro per status.

In a courtroom, most pro pers, even intelligent ones, are like wrecking balls on a chessboard. No judge or prosecutor relishes a case where the defendant is pro per. Alan was overestimating his own ability, but then again, he would not have been facing the present charges had that not been a lifelong habit of his.

During one of the pretrial motions, Belli and I were discussing a trial date, and we agreed to ask for as early a date as possible. When Mel asked me how long I anticipated the trial would last, I estimated two to two and a half months. Mel frowned. He wanted to try the case himself, but a previous commitment which could not be set aside would be intervening toward the end of our trial.

Mel first handed the case over to Fred Cone in his office. Eventually, the representation would fall to one of the top trial lawyers in Belli's firm, a slender, darkly complected man by the name of Terry Callas. Terry, a classmate of mine at UCLA Law School, had worked for a few years in the L.A. Public Defender's office before joining Belli. Sandra Stockton had a fine attorney in Terry Callas, but it did get back to me she was angered by Belli's not trying the case himself.

Sandra had frequent visitors during those summer months she was in Sybil Brand Institute. Her parents and sisters remained supportive. Her friend from the Auto Club, Audrey Scanlon, could not help crying when she first saw Sandra behind the thick glass window and had to talk with her through ear phones. Sandra told her friend she had "loaned" Alan money for his bar business—somewhere in the vicinity of $25,000.

"I guess I should have asked for I.O.U.'s," Sandra said, "but that just doesn't occur to you when you're sleeping with a guy."

She added that at one point before the arrest, Alan had called her and warned that the police could fabricate a case against anyone, telling her: "They finally think they've got something on us. Better pack and get out of there (her sister Tracy's apartment). Split."

"No, I haven't done anything wrong," Sandra told Audrey she had responded. "Why should I run? If they want to arrest me, fine. I'm sick of it."

Sandra also talked to Audrey about politics. She told Audrey she was terribly upset by the assassinations of Martin Luther King and Robert Kennedy. Her choice for president was Eugene McCarthy, the man who said he would bring peace to Vietnam.

I wondered to myself how Sandra, a liberal Democrat, and Alan, the John Bircher, had ever managed to even get together for lunch, let alone murder.

The case was transferred to Judge Pierce Young in Department 110. Young, a former California assemblyman who attended Oxford University on a Fulbright scholarship, set the trial for November 18, 1968.

On October 24, Alan, apparently realizing finally that he had made a mistake, made a formal motion to have attorney David Goldin be his "associate counsel," with Goldin, an able attorney, actually conducting the courtroom proceedings. A defendant, Judge Young pointed out to Alan, may represent himself in court *or* have an attorney represent him, but he cannot have both. He must make an election. Alan promptly moved to have Goldin substituted as his attorney of record, and thereby lost his pro per status.

I suggested to Dave Goldin that while Alan had decided to give up his pro per *status,* he should be allowed to keep his pro per *privileges* —i.e., daily access to a law library, three telephone calls a day, a "runner," a typewriter and supplies, etc. I felt that Alan was the kind of person who could help with his own defense. Although pro per privileges are normally forfeited along with pro per status, I thought an exception should be made here. This man, after all, was fighting for his life. Goldin of course agreed, and we talked it over with Judge Young in chambers. In that I had no objection, Judge Young permitted Alan to maintain all of his pro per privileges throughout the lengthy trial.

During all of the pretrial motions, the corridor outside the courtroom was clogged with television cameras. Sandra seemed to shy away from the publicity, dropping her eyes to the floor as she walked past the cameras into the courtroom. Alan, predictably, found a little warmth in the floodlights. He knew as well as anyone that his smile had some charm to it.

On November 1, Judge Pierce Young, a cultured and relaxed man whose long, lank brown hair often hung youthfully to the side, read the following statement from the bench:

"It appears to the Court that the within case is one of considerable public interest and may result in substantial publicity . . . that may interfere with a fair trial . . ." Young went on to issue a so-called "gag order," prohibiting participants in the trial from discussing the case with the news media.

Neither of the defense counsel, Goldin and Callas, nor I had any objection to Judge Young's ruling.

Mel Belli, still working on the case with Callas, made a motion for a court trial (judge only) rather than a jury trial. Goldin joined in the motion. Belli stated that his client wanted to "waive her constitutional right to a trial by jury." But while defendants indeed have a constitutional right to a jury trial, they have no constitutional right to a court trial, which requires the consent of the prosecution. I did not join in a jury waiver, and Judge Young denied the defense's motion.

Normally, when the defense waives jury, the prosecutor joins in the waiver. Although court trials are invariably shorter and far less demanding of the lawyers in the case, I almost always ask for a jury trial. While I must admit I enjoy the drama of presenting a case to a jury, there is a more substantive reason for my position.

When the criminal charges are serious, I am reluctant to permit one person to decide whether the defendant is guilty or not guilty. Two people in this case had been brutally murdered. I was going to be asking for the death penalty for both Alan and Sandra. The right of a society to pass judgment on those members who are accused of crime is a right of enormous social meaning. Given the choice to allow that judgment to be made by a judge or by twelve average men and women—a "community in microcosm," usually with over five hundred years of collective human experience—I will usually choose the latter. Although it is far from perfect, no one, in my opinion, has yet devised a better way than the jury system to determine the fate of one's fellow man.

There were no more motions for the court to rule on. In two days the trial would begin.

Because the Palliko-Stockton case was comprised not just primarily but solely of circumstantial evidence, the reader's understanding of the important distinctions between direct and circumstantial evidence is necessary.

Direct evidence is evidence which, if true, proves a fact in issue without the necessity of drawing any inference. Almost by definition, direct evidence can only be given by the testimony of a witness who purports to have actual knowledge of that fact. The most common type of direct evidence is eyewitness testimony.

Circumstantial evidence, on the other hand, is evidence which only *tends* to prove a fact in issue by proving a secondary fact. From this secondary fact, an inference can then be drawn that the fact in issue exists. For example, from the secondary fact of seeing a stolen television set in the defendant's home, *one* reasonable inference is that it was he who stole the set, the identity of the thief being the fact in issue.

The same evidence can be direct evidence as to one fact, but circumstantial evidence as to another. The witness who testifies to seeing the television set in the defendant's home is furnishing direct evidence of that specific fact, but only circumstantial evidence that it may have been the defendant who stole the set.

Actually, all evidence, even eyewitness testimony, requires that *some* inference be drawn. When a witness to a robbery testifies he saw the defendant rob the victim, from the secondary fact of the witness' observation (including the distance, lighting, obstructions, etc.), the jury must still draw the inference that the witness was correct, i.e., that it is not a case of mistaken identity, a not uncommon occurrence.

Arguably, then, it could be said there is no such thing as direct evidence. But if the only inference sought is that the fact testified to is true (as opposed to circumstantial evidence, where the inference sought is that some *other* fact is true), then the evidence is still deemed to be direct evidence.

As to facts in issue, the Palliko-Stockton case was, by anyone's definition, a case of purely circumstantial evidence, the added difficulty being that most of the circumstantial evidence was not once, but several times removed from the issue of guilt.

3

THE CASE OF *People v. Palliko and Stockton* commenced the morning of November 18, 1968, in Department 110 of the Los Angeles Superior Court. Sandra walked into the courtroom appearing disoriented and nervous, unsure whether to remain standing or to sit, until Terry Callas held her chair for her and nodded. When I looked over at her, her blue eyes darted from mine. Quite often during the trial I would glance over at Sandra to see how she was reacting to whatever was being said from the witness stand, and every time she avoided my look. Not once during the thirteen-week trial did she allow our eyes to meet.

Sandra's jailers thought she was an icy, dyed-blonde Jezebel. I do not doubt that a cold calculation was a part of Sandra Stockton, but during the course of the trial I saw another side of her as well. Every morning when she and Alan were brought in and seated at the counsel table, all of this before the jury entered the courtroom, Sandra would lean over the railing to embrace her mother. Harriet Bingham did not miss a day of the trial; Sandra's father, Ted, could rarely come because of work. Mrs. Bingham often handed Sandra changes of clothing over the railing, and almost always the first words from Sandra's mouth were: "How's my Kyle?"

She often gave letters to her mother to take to her son. One of the first was just a short note: "I am from grandma. You are from me. And we are like a circle. You and me and grandma."

One of the most difficult parts of being a prosecutor is, without doubt, witnessing the suffering that a defendant's family must go through. It is the one part of the job I never quite learned to live with.

When Alan walked into the courtroom, he was a picture of self-assuredness. With his charcoal grey suit and tie and his attaché case, he had the air of a man who was being inconvenienced. In the "holding tank" behind the courtroom, other prisoners sat literally at his feet while he expounded on the law.

Throughout the trial, Alan was seen smiling and winking at the attractive women in the gallery. That was all, of course, before the jury filed in. As soon as they did, Alan turned back to the front of the courtroom and assumed his expression of earnestness.

Alan's parents came to court every day of the trial. Whenever they began to wave at their son, they had to let their half-raised hands fall back to their sides, for nearly every time, Alan turned his head away, refusing to acknowledge them. It was sad.

Young attorneys fresh out of law school are quickly disabused of the notion they can pick jurors who will be favorable to their clients just by noting the prospective jurors' outward appearance, their manner of speech, or even by the answers they give during *voir dire* (the questioning of prospective jurors by the court and counsel to determine their competence and impartiality). Although still the common subject for joking back in chambers is that prosecutors are always looking for crewcut Nordics, defense lawyers for long haired fellows with wide red ties, most trial lawyers realize that the greatly limited scope of allowable questions on voir dire reduces jury selection to one third art and skill and two thirds guesswork. Even in the area of art and skill, however, I have never felt particularly adequate, having never been a terribly good judge of people early on.

I was rather unhappy with the panel of seventy-five prospective jurors called for the Palliko-Stockton case. It was the first time either Judge Young or I could recall a totally "virgin" panel. Not one of the prospective jurors had any previous jury experience in a criminal case.

Prosecutors generally prefer jurors who have had some prior jury experience, partly because of their ability to sort through complicated evidence, and partly because virgin jurors have the misconceived notion that guilt must be proven "beyond a shadow of a doubt," i.e., not just beyond a reasonable doubt, but beyond *all* doubt. If that were so, very few defendants would ever be convicted of any crime.

In California, when the prosecution is asking for the death penalty, we have what is known as a "bifurcated" trial. If the jury finds the defendant(s) guilty of first degree murder, those same jury members remain for a second, generally much shorter trial called the penalty trial, at which the issue for them to decide is whether the defendant(s) should receive life imprisonment or the death penalty.

In the Palliko-Stockton case, a heavy part of the voir dire questions concerned the prospective jurors' views on the death penalty, and I ended up facing a jury whose majority of members stated that, although they had a conscientious objection to the death penalty, they could bring themselves to vote for it if the circumstances of the case were sufficiently aggravated.

One could have anticipated many of the other questions asked during the jury selection: Would you be likely to give more or less weight to the testimony of a police officer simply because he was a police officer? (The answer should be neither more nor less); could you vote a first degree murder conviction even if there were no eyewitnesses? (I hardly need mention who asked that question); would you be "prejudiced" against a defendant who you learned to be adulterous? (Nor need I point out which side asked that question.)

Although both sides seek to excuse jurors who have prejudices which will work against their side, ironically, to ask a juror that very question, i.e., if he is prejudiced against something, is almost pointless, as a juror will rarely admit he is "prejudiced" against *anything*. Phrases like "lean towards," "preference for," or even "like" or "dislike" have to be employed in related but indirect questions to expose the bias.

David Goldin, a young attorney with a premature paunch and the constantly amused smile of an observer of humanity, asked a good line of questions of one of the prospective jurors.

Q. "Have you ever watched the Perry Mason program?"

A. "Yes, I have."

Q. "Something always happens in Perry Mason that I have never seen happen in court, and that is usually when somebody is on the stand in the middle of cross-examination, somebody will stand up—usually in the audience—and say, 'Yes. I confess; I did it. I couldn't help myself.'"

I sat back and smiled.

"Do you then get a good feeling from the program," Dave went on, "because not only was the person charged found not guilty, but you also found out who did it? Do you have the feeling in this trial that we have to *solve* the crime?"

A. "No, I don't."

Q. "You don't feel you will have a tendency to say, 'Well, if they didn't do it, who did? I want an answer to that question before I will find them not guilty.'?"

A. "No."

Invariably, jurors sit wooden in the jury box during a trial, believing they are never supposed to change their expressions, as though participants in a black-tie poker game. This extreme decorum on their part while amidst a completely foreign atmosphere of officialdom starts with voir dire, making them hesitant to speak their mind. Urging them to relax, I tell them that if they disagree with any of the rules of law I refer to, it is important they speak up then, not back in the jury room at the end of the trial. If they do not disagree, I get a commitment under oath from each juror (which I remind all of them of during my summation) that they will faithfully apply the law of the case during their deliberations.

Perhaps the most important question I asked the prospective jurors pertained to the "vicarious liability" rule of conspiracy. In nonlegalese, this rule provides that when people conspire to commit a crime, the criminal act of one is the act of all (unless, of course, the act had nothing to do with carrying out the objective of the conspiracy). In this case, even though we were not alleging that Sandra killed Henry or was even present at the scene, if, as we *did* allege, she and Alan conspired to murder Henry, and Alan subsequently did the actual killing, Sandra would be equally guilty of the murder.

Likewise, with respect to Judy's murder, if Alan, as we believed, had someone kill Judy for him, by definition, he had to have conspired with that person. And under the law, even if the identity of this other party were never ascertained, Alan would be equally guilty of the murder.

It has been my experience from questioning jurors that some people are disinclined to assign equal guilt and/or punishment to the conspirator who does not actually perpetrate the crime. With this in mind, I asked each juror if he or she understood the rule of vicarious liability, and if they would unhesitatingly apply this rule if they found a conspiracy existed.

At the end of six and a half days, we had our jury, five women and seven men: four housewives, a machinist, an advertising director, an electrician, a forklift operator, a social worker, a furniture craftsman, a production control manager, and an engineer. An unremarkable, black and white picture of a city that is usually thought of in Technicolor. The three alternates, often referred to by trial lawyers as "spare tires," were a civil engineer, a housewife, and a phone company maintenance worker.

After the jury and alternates were sworn in, Judge Young recessed the court until after lunch. At 1:45 P.M. the prosecution and defense would give their opening statements (a lawyer's preview to the jury of the highlights of the case he intends to present), and I would begin my case by calling my first witness to the stand.

Although I usually waive opening statement, feeling that, among other things, it takes the edge off my witnesses' testimony when the jury has already heard the story from me, the evidence in this case was so fragmented and scattered in its times, places, and events, that I made a brief, fifteen-minute statement to the jury to enable them to better follow the evidence as it came from the witness stand.

On the subject of the second murder charge, I stated: "We intend to prove by very strong circumstantial evidence that Alan Palliko was responsible for the murder of his wife, Judy." The flexible word *responsible*, I had chosen carefully since I knew very well I was not prepared to prove that Alan had actually pulled the trigger himself, but at the same time I did not want to box myself in by saying that Alan had definitely had someone else kill Judy for him. While the trial was going on, the investigation was continuing, and new evidence might emerge that Alan did, in fact, kill Judy himself. Thus, the word "responsible." Lawyers have to be careful in their opening statement so they do not have to contradict themselves or retract by trial's end.

At the conclusion of my remarks, I asked that all the jurors take as detailed notes as possible during the trial. When they deliberated on their verdict some three months hence, they would be grateful they had, I told them.

Terry Callas waived opening statement. Dave Goldin gave one of the shortest opening statements I have ever heard—and also one of the most startling.

MR. GOLDIN: "Your Honor, Mr. Callas, Mr. Bugliosi, ladies and gentlemen of the jury. I will be even more brief than Mr. Bugliosi.

"I expect—I have very high hopes—that the evidence, all of the evi-

dence offered, will show the identity of the person who did kill Judy
Palliko and Henry Stockton.

"It was not Alan Palliko.

"Thank you."

I gazed hard at Dave. Had I heard correctly? Goldin was telling
the jury that not only was I unjustly prosecuting his client, but that
he thought he knew who the actual killer was. Dave sat down non-
chalantly, as if not even hearing the sudden rustling throughout the
courtroom.

If Goldin had evidence to support his claim, as much as I wanted
it, he had no legal obligation to furnish me with it. Under the law of
"discovery," although the prosecution has to permit the defense to
examine and/or copy virtually all of the evidence the prosecution has
gathered, the defense does not have to reciprocate. The rationale for
requiring discovery from the prosecution is the defendant's constitutional right to a fair trial. The courts have held that the prosecution
should not be permitted to sandbag the defendant by the surprise tactic of introducing evidence at the trial which the defense had no prior
knowledge of and against which it had no reasonable opportunity to
prepare a response. The reason the defense does not have to reciprocate and turn over its evidence to the prosecution is that the defendant
might then be furnishing evidence which the prosecution could use
against him. Such a forced disclosure would violate the defendant's
right against self-incrimination under the Fifth Amendment to the
U.S. Constitution.

The one bit of discovery I was able to get from the defense was a
list of the witnesses they had subpoenaed. Not what they were going
to testify to, just their identity. But even this was valuable. I immediately attempted to have every defense witness interviewed. If they
gave a statement to us, I could use it as a basis for impeachment at
the trial if their testimony was in conflict with the statement they gave
us. Even if they were unwilling to give us a statement, this too could
work to our advantage. On cross-examination, this refusal to give a
statement can be brought out to show the bias of the defense witness.

More than anyone else in the courtroom, I wanted to know just
who Dave Goldin was intending to prove was the true murderer of
Henry Stockton and Judy Palliko.

My first witness was Elbert Thompson, the Stocktons' next door
neighbor, who testified to discovering the fire and to his wife's calling
the fire department. On cross-examination, Goldin asked Thompson

if he had noticed whether Henry Stockton had any visitors over that night. Thompson had not.

When Merle Pugh, Senior Investigator for the L.A. Fire Department's Arson Investigation Section, took the stand, he could only say there was a "possibility" that the fire was a result of arson.

Terry Callas cross-examined:

Q. "You do not have an opinion as to the cause of the fire, do you?"

A. "I have classified it as suspicious, sir."

Q. "Which, as an arson investigator, is really no opinion at all, right? In other words, you can't eliminate factors or say that one cause is more probable than another in this case?"

A. "That's correct, sir."

I did not bother belaboring the question of arson on redirect examination. It was obvious to anyone that it would have taken an extremely bizarre coincidence for a fire to have started accidentally in the bedroom around the very same time Henry was shot five times in the head and chest in the living room.

Sgt. Joe Aguirre testified to his observations when he arrived at 5:35 A.M. that Sunday morning—the gunshot wounds to the body that still lay out on the front lawn, the splattered blood on the living room chair and the wall behind it, the absence of any signs of forcible entry (I would later argue to the jury that Sandra had probably furnished Alan with a key), et cetera. I intended to recall Aguirre to the stand the next day to testify to his interview with Sandra upon her arrival back from Twentynine Palms, but before I could introduce that testimony of Aguirre's, I anticipated a tussle with defense counsel in the judge's chambers over its admissibility.

This first, abbreviated day of testimony concluded, the judge left the courtroom and then the jury filed out. When it was time for the defendants to leave, the bailiff, Gary Booker, put his hand on Alan's shoulder from behind. Alan's body jerked as if touched by an electric wire.

"Don't ever touch me!" he snarled at Booker. "Tell me what to do, but don't ever . . . *ever* touch me."

4

On the second day of testimony, I called Dr. Noguchi to the stand to state his autopsy findings that the cause of Henry Stockton's death was "gunshot wounds to the head with massive hemorrhage." I then asked Dr. Noguchi about the number and nature of the wounds, the trajectory of the bullets, etc. Dave Goldin objected to any such line of questioning. Upon approaching the bench, where lawyers argue their objections to the judge outside the earshot of the jury, we got into a short but heated dispute. It set a pattern for the entire trial. Although Dave and I are friends, we apparently rubbed each other wrong in our first courtroom experience with one another. It is only natural that opposing lawyers spar with each other, but the arguments between Dave and me during this trial sometimes became regrettably personal.

MR. GOLDIN: "Your Honor, I would object to the further amplification by the doctor. It is just dwelling on something that can have absolutely no value except to take the Court's time and, possibly, I think the District Attorney feels hopefully, inflame the minds of the jury."

MR. BUGLIOSI: "No, I think the jury is entitled to know where those bullet entries were. They are the trier of fact."

MR. GOLDIN: "For what relevance? For what relevance?"

I argued to Judge Young that it is always relevant to know exactly how a killer committed his crime—where he shoots his victim, how many times, from what range. If for no other reason to want the evidence in, I had the burden of proving a specific intent to kill, a necessary element of the crime charged. Shooting someone three times in the head and twice in the chest (as opposed to, say, five times in the foot or leg) shows just such an intent.

We submitted the matter for ruling, and Judge Young denied Goldin's objection.

As Dr. Noguchi went over his autopsy findings and described the wounds in detail, Sandra bowed her head and winced at the floor. Perhaps she was putting on an act for the jury. Perhaps she was really giving some thought to the horrible and violent death Henry had suffered.

The second witness I called that day, Harold Tanney, the civilian fingerprints expert from the LAPD, was a disaster. Tanney's unexpected testimony virtually handed Alan and Sandra the kind of key they were looking for to walk out of the courtroom acquitted of the first murder count.

Though his actual conclusion had been that there were two unidentified prints at the murder scene, for some reason Tanney had informed Aguirre, Guy, St. John, and me that *all* the readable latent fingerprints he had found belonged to the victim, Henry Stockton.

"Latent" fingerprints (as opposed to a fingerprint "exemplar," which is the model for comparison taken in ink at the police station) is merely the technical term for fingerprints left on everyday objects. The prints are transmitted by a residue of oil naturally secreted from the body. Contrary to popular belief, the perspiration from one's fingers and palms contains no such oily substance. The fingers and palms acquire that residue of oil when they come into contact with parts of the body that do have such secretions, e.g., the hair, face, etc.

There has been no reported case of two people having the same fingerprints. Desperate attempts by criminals to destroy or alter their fingerprints by burning or filing the skin have proven unsuccessful. The original patterns reappear with the healing of the epidermis. Only skin grafts have worked.

It has always been my practice, although an unusual one, to call a fingerprints expert to the stand even when no latent prints are found at the crime scene that match up with the exemplar card of the defendant. I present what I call "negative fingerprint testimony," a tactic I have found to be very successful.

Defense counsel like to argue that because their clients' prints were not found at the scene, this is conclusive evidence they were not there and hence, is proof of innocence. My negative fingerprint testimony gives a jury some perspective on that claim by citing for them some rather surprising statistics from the LAPD. Those statistics show that in approximately only 30 percent of the times fingerprint experts are dispatched to the scene of a crime are they able to secure clear, readable latent prints belonging to *anyone*. In most cases the prints found are just too fragmentary, smudged, or superimposed with other prints to be used for comparison purposes. Furthermore, of the cases where readable prints *are* secured, only 10 percent of the time do those prints match up to those of the defendant. The rest belong either to the victim or to some third party. A simple equation: 10% of 30% = 3%. Hence, in only 3 percent of the times that fingerprint experts go to a crime scene are they able to secure the latent prints of the *accused*. Ninety-seven percent of the time the experts are unsuccessful. This is a powerful statistical rebuttal to the defense argument that since the defendant's prints were not found at the scene, he was never there.

It was for this "negative fingerprint testimony" that I had called Harold Tanney to the stand. But Tanney, a gangly man with a brown knit tie as short and narrow as a ruler, had testimony of his own to give.

Q. BY MR. BUGLIOSI: "Were you able to get any clear, readable, identifiable fingerprints other than those belonging to the victim, Henry Stockton?"

A. "Yes, two."

Inside my mind I was screaming, 'What?!' The best thing a trial lawyer can do when he is shocked by a witness' testimony is to proceed as calmly as possible, and try not to reveal his shock to the jury.

Q. "Where did you find these prints?"

A. "One was found on the side of a beer bottle that was in the wastebasket in the kitchen. The other was found on the neck of a beer bottle beneath the dining room table."

Q. "Did you compare these two prints with the prints of any other people?"

A. "Yes, I compared them with several other people at the time. I also compared them with the defendants'."

Q. "You did not find Alan Palliko's fingerprints nor Sandra Stockton's fingerprints; is that correct?"

A. "That is correct."

Q. "But you have indicated you found two prints *other* than Henry Stockton's?"

A. "That did *not* belong to Henry Stockton, yes, sir."

Q. "Did you ever ascertain to whom these two fingerprints belonged?"

A. "No, sir."

I proceeded perfunctorily to elicit from Tanney the negative fingerprint testimony for which I had called him, but by that point that information had paled almost to insignificance. The obvious question going through the jurors' minds now was: if the prints did not belong to Henry and if they did not belong to Sandra or Alan, to whom *did* they belong? The true murderer?

At the recess, I hurriedly caught up with Tanney on a stairway outside the courtroom.

"Why the hell didn't you tell me you found prints that weren't the victim's?" I asked him.

Tanney gave me a long, quizzical look. "I did."

"No—no, you didn't. You must have this case confused with one of your other cases."

"No, sir," he said, rapping the stairway bannister. "You're confused about this case."

"I'm confused?! I've been *living* with this case!"

Tanney's face bunched up. "Now that I think about it, I don't recall you ever asking me."

"Just yesterday! In the hallway. I asked you yesterday and also a couple weeks ago and both times you told me that only Henry Stockton's prints were found."

Tanney could not remember ever having told me that he had found no readable prints other than Henry's, nor could he remember telling that to Aguirre, Guy, and St. John.

If Tanney had found a third party's prints on anything other than beer bottles, the prosecution's case would not have been nearly so damaged. Fingerprints have sometimes been known to remain on objects inside a house for as long as six months; if a third party's prints had been found on, say, a coffee table or a magazine, it would have had minimal significance. They could have belonged to friends who had been in the house days or even weeks beforehand. Beer bottles, however, are generally thrown out on a daily basis. A strong inference, then, was that someone other than Alan Palliko had been drinking beer with Henry on the night of his murder, and that person very likely was his murderer. It would, no doubt, be the defense's argument, and there was not too much I could do to rebut it. With that kind of reasonable doubt injected into the case, a not guilty verdict could be expected.

I immediately started to work on arguments I would use in my final summation to convince the jury that the person whose prints were on the bottles was not Henry's killer. I felt too sure of Alan Palliko's guilt in this murder to believe otherwise. I thought of five distinct arguments, the strongest of which was that it just was not reasonable to believe that Henry and a friend, the killer, were drinking beer and engaging in a friendly conversation, when suddenly they had an argument, and without a struggle (none of the furniture or lamps being damaged or tipped over), Henry's friend, who just *happened* to have a loaded .22 caliber revolver on him, drew his gun and shot Henry five times (the shots not being heard by neighbors because the gun had very likely been carefully wrapped in a towel which served as a silencer), and that the friend then had the presence of mind to set the house on fire.

It was not a bad argument, but hardly an indestructible one. The defense could argue that an acquaintance of Henry's had, in fact, planned out all of his actions and had merely engaged Henry in some "friendly" beer drinking to lull him into the trap. I did not kid myself for a moment; I was in trouble in this case.

The next day, Gail, my parents and I, and my two children—Wendy, four, and Vince, Jr., two, ("my baby birds," I call them)—had Thanksgiving dinner at the home of my sister, Adeline. My sister is a doll, but attempts to get me into the holiday conversation were hopeless. My mind was back in the courtroom while plates of white meat and stuffing and silver gravy boats were shuttling back and forth in front of my nose. When I got home I spent a long evening in the study writing down new assignments for the detectives concerning those fingerprints.

The following morning I assembled all of the investigators in my office, including Bill Pratt from the District Attorney's Bureau of Investigation. The air was close and thick with half a dozen different shaving lotions in that office, a sparse little room with only a couple of straight back chairs and an army surplus cot I used for noontime cat naps during long trials. Leaning against the window sill, I told the investigators what I needed to have done.

I wanted fingerprint exemplars of every single fireman and policeman and anyone else who entered the Stockton house on the morning of December 11. Bill Pratt was to coordinate that effort. We also needed exemplars of all acquaintances of Henry's or Sandra's who had been to the house on the day of the murder or even several days earlier. In addition, I asked the detectives to find out who the local distributor was for Old Timers Lager beer. That was the label on all ten empty quart bottles found at the Stockton residence. It was an uncommon beer in Los Angeles; none of the investigators had ever heard of it. If we could locate the local distributor, we could find out what stores in Henry's vicinity sold it. A large supermarket with the usual quick turnover of employees would not be as promising as a "Ma and Pa" type grocery store, where the prints just might be traceable to the proprietors or whoever placed those bottles in Henry's shopping bag.

The investigators immediately went to work, and over the weekend were able to secure most (but not all) of the fingerprint exemplars we needed from the firemen and police officers who had entered the Ballard Street house. None matched the two latent prints in question. By Monday, Pratt had also learned that Old Timers Lager beer was bottled in West Bend, Wisconsin, but he had not yet ascertained the names of the local outlets for the beer.

While Pratt and the other investigators continued their work, I pursued another avenue. I recalled Dr. Noguchi to the stand. I needed medical testimony from which I could draw the inference that, based on Henry's blood count, it was not impossible for Henry to have drunk all ten quart bottles of beer himself—i.e., that the person whose prints were on two of the bottles was not drinking beer with Henry prior to the murder, but had placed his prints on the bottles at some previous time. Noguchi had already testified that a toxicology examination had revealed Henry's blood alcohol content at the time of his death to be 10 percent. Based on the fact that Henry was 72 inches tall and weighed 220 pounds, Noguchi now testified that to get a blood alcohol content of ten percent, Henry would have had to ingest approximately five one-ounce shots of 100 proof whiskey or five to six 16-ounce cans of beer. We already knew (even from Sandra's own statements to the police) that Henry drank only beer, no hard liquor. Five or six 16-ounce cans of beer, however, was equivalent to only about three one-quart bottles. Who drank the other seven bottles?

I elicited from Dr. Noguchi the fact that alcohol in the blood is absorbed (i.e., wears off) at the rate of .02 percent per hour, although the absorption ceases at death.

Q. "Would it be true, then, that if Henry Stockton had continued to live, about one-fifth of the alcoholic content in his blood would have worn off with each succeeding hour?"

A. "It is simple mathematics: .10 percent was found in his blood, and one eliminates at the rate of .02 percent per hour, so it is mathematically one-fifth."

Q. "I take it that it would be *equally true then,* Dr. Noguchi, that Henry Stockton could have drunk quite a few bottles of beer earlier in the day *before* his demise, and because of the absorption rate to which you have just testified, the alcohol from these bottles of beer would *not* be reflected in his blood at the time of his death?"

A. "It could. That's—yes."

Not only could Henry have drunk those extra seven bottles earlier that day, but he could have drunk them the day before. It was not inconceivable that the empties would still be lying around the house at least for a day or so. Henry, after all, was having himself a bachelor's weekend while his wife visited a friend out of town.

Dr. Noguchi's testimony helped, but it certainly did not eliminate the major, nagging question. I had proved that Henry *could* have drunk all the bottles, but it was only a possibility. I certainly had not conclusively established that no other person was drinking beer with Henry just before the murder. It still came down to the fingerprints.

It was well after 1:00 A.M., Tuesday morning, and I was in my study at home, jotting down on my yellow legal pad the things I wanted done the next day. Item 11 on my pad read: "Call fingerprint section and have them *recheck* the latents."

When you begin to begin all over again, it is time for bed.

The following morning I called Sergeant Dean Bergman, who was in charge of the Latent Prints Section, and asked him to look at the fingerprint cards himself. Bergman had twenty-one years of experience in the field. He called back in two hours and, with his news, brought me to the front edge of my desk chair. The latent print on the bottle found beneath the dining room table *did* belong to Henry Stockton. It was from Henry's right ring and right index fingers. Bergman was positive of his conclusion in that he had found ten points of similarity (ridges, whorls, forked lines, etc.) between the latent and the exemplar. Anything short of ten points of similarity can lead a print expert to an "opinion," but ten full points of similarity is considered a sufficient number by most American law enforcement agencies, including the LAPD, to warrant an unqualified conclusion (in Europe, the minimum requirements range from eight in West Germany all the way to sixteen at Scotland Yard).

As to the print on the bottle found in the kitchen wastebasket, Bergman determined it was not a fingerprint at all, but rather a palm print. Comparing it to Henry's palm print exemplar yielded inconclusive results. Because of rigor mortis, a victim's palm skin is usually surgically removed before it is used to make a print exemplar. For some unexplained reason, this had not been done in Henry Stockton's case, and the palm exemplar that resulted was sketchy and inadequate for purposes of comparison.

Although Bergman was able to find only four points of similarity between the latent and the exemplar, he found no points of clear *dis*-similarity that would have ruled out the latent belonging to Henry. The palm print, therefore, simply fell into that large majority category of fingerprints whose identity is unknown. It might have been Henry's, and it might not have been. That was all I needed, however, to eliminate the defense's argument that a third party was definitely drinking beer with Henry that night. If Bergman's findings were accurate, the prosecution was back from the hospital.

I asked Sergeant Bergman to have Harold Tanney examine the prints again, but to scrupulously avoid indicating to him beforehand what his (Bergman's) findings had been. After studying the print cards, Tanney went back to Bergman to tell him he had made a mistake. His new conclusions were precisely the same as Bergman's. I did not want to take a chance this time around, and requested Sergeant Elmer Smith of the LAPD's Latent Print Section to also examine the prints. Smith had fifteen years of experience in the field. His findings confirmed those of Bergman's and Tanney's—the fingerprints on the one bottle belonged to Henry Stockton, and the palm print on the second bottle *might* have belonged to Henry Stockton.

The next day, I recalled Tanney to the stand.

Q. BY MR. BUGLIOSI: "Are you testifying then, Mr. Tanney, that your original opinion with respect to that latent fingerprint was an error on your part?"

A. "It was an *oversight* on my part, yes, sir."

For the remainder of his testimony, I tried to remember to refer to his blunder as his "oversight."

Q. "Now, with respect to the second print, the palm print, I believe

it was your previous testimony that that partial palm print did not belong to Henry Stockton; is that correct?"

A. "That was my testimony, yes, sir."

Q. "When you testified to that effect, did you mean to convey the
impression that the palm print belonged to some other human
being?"

A. "No, sir, I did not mean that."

Q. "Will you admit, Mr. Tanney, that the statement, 'The print
does not belong to Henry Stockton,' compels the inference that it
does belong to another human being? Will you admit that?"

A. "Yes, possibly that inference could have been misconstrued."

Misconstrued? I did not dwell on the point. Tanney acknowledged
that upon rechecking the palm print, he now determined it "could
have" belonged to Henry.

Harold Tanney had a diploma from the University of Kansas in
standard criminal investigation, a diploma from the FBI in advanced
fingerprint training, and twelve years of experience in the field. What
his problem was, I do not know. During cross-examination by Dave
Goldin, Tanney kept referring to "byafaction" until Goldin corrected
him, realizing the word Tanney was trying to pronounce was "bifur-
cation" (in fingerprinting, meaning a forked line).

After Tanney's testimony, I called Sergeants Bergman and Smith
to the stand for their corroborating conclusions, and the point I
needed was made.

I suggested to Goldin and Callas back in chambers that they have
their own experts examine the prints so there would be no question
as to the reliability of the LAPD's new findings. When Goldin complained that the defense never had sufficient funds for such things,
Judge Young told Goldin and Callas that if they desired, he would
have the prints examined by an independent expert at county expense. Goldin and Callas declined the offer, saying they accepted the
accuracy of the LAPD's conclusions.

The fingerprint testimony, sometimes too technical even for trial
lawyers, had consumed one and a half days of court time.

An article in the L.A. *Times* the next morning was headlined:
"Prosecutor's Tenacity Saves Fingerprint Testimony." The article did
not apprise the readers of how a desperate, hardly inspired late night
thought was responsible for the "save."

When I arrived at the Hall of Justice the day after the fingerprint testimony, Mr. Palliko stopped me on the front steps. His face was flushed.

"Why are you doing this to Alan?" he demanded. "You know he's not guilty. Why are you doing this?"

His loyalty to his son was understandable. I answered him calmly. "Mr. Palliko, if you have any evidence whatsoever that shows Alan is innocent, tell me what it is, and I give you my word I'll present it from the witness stand this afternoon."

He waved me away and turned to my wife, Gail, who was with me that morning. "I'd like to know how your husband can look at himself in the mirror."

I was about to answer that when Sandra's mother, Harriet Bingham, walked up and interceded. "Leave Mr. Bugliosi alone, why don't you," she said. "He's just doing his job."

After an awkward moment of silence, Mr. Palliko turned and went up the courthouse steps. A sad smile on her face, Mrs. Bingham nodded to me, and slowly followed.

The history of Alan's and Sandra's acquaintanceship was one of written record. I called Mary Munn of the Automobile Club of Southern California's personnel department to testify to details of their employment at the company, an employment that dealt—and perhaps not coincidentally, considering the inspiration for Alan's and Sandra's crime had to come from somewhere—with insurance.

Over 1,800 people worked in the Auto Club's downtown headquarters, but Alan and Sandra, quite fatefully, had been assigned to the same small section of the Metro Unit from mid-1964 to early 1966—Alan, as a B.I. (bodily injury) investigator, and Sandra as a claims processing clerk. Munn also testified to their starting salaries of $490 (Alan) and $275 (Sandra) per month and to their respective salaries of $580 and $367 at the end of their employment.

The next witness I called, John St. John, is an old-fashioned cop. He is not the most articulate man in the world, which is perhaps one of the reasons he is able to relate to some of the street criminals he must deal with. In court, his extreme deference on the stand almost suggests he is slightly intimidated by people in the legal profession. Lawyers are often called "counselor," but I have heard only St. John address an attorney as "Mister Counselor."

St. John related the February 16, 1967 talk he had had with Alan down at the Auto Club, wherein Alan had admitted to dating Sandra five or six times the previous year (in January and February of 1966) during her separation from Henry, but had stated he had had no social contact with her since that time. Alan's claim was contradicted at the trial both by Katherine, who would later testify to the phone bills she had discovered in September of 1966, as well as by Sandra's apartment neighbors, who testified they saw Alan and Sandra together in August of 1966.

Mark Oberlin, the salesman at Pachmyr Gun Works, testified to having sold Sandra her Hi Standard .22 caliber Sentinel revolver. Although he could not remember the purchaser by face, both the purchase receipt and the copy of the police registration which he brought to court were adequate proof that it was Sandra who bought the gun.

Dewayne Wolfer, the LAPD firearms expert, followed gun salesman Oberlin to the stand and testified that although the gun which killed Henry Stockton had "probably" been manufactured by Hi Standard (the largest manufacturer of that particular type), it could have been a Harrington & Richardson, an Iver Johnson, or any one of several Spanish models.

On cross-examination, Goldin and Callas made hay of the fact that the fatal bullets *could* have been fired from a revolver that was not a Hi Standard.

Nov. 29, 1968

My Dear Kyle,

Well, mama's trial has started. It promises to be very long and drawn out. Now is the time for us to double our strength in ourselves and draw our circle tighter around us. The jury are the people who will decide whether mama is innocent or guilty. There are twelve of them. This is the law's way of assuring the accused a fair trial. After all of the evidence has been presented to these twelve people they go into a room together and talk over all that they have heard, and make up their minds as to what will be fair to all concerned. The courtroom looks like this.

(A sketch by Sandra was inserted.)

Grandma can explain the room in detail to you. Hey, you know what? I love you. You. I'm so proud of you. How are you doing in school? I sure miss you, darling. But knowing you're doing okay sure makes me happy.

God is with us.

Your mama

Vicky Stowe, Sandra's childhood and lifelong friend whom I called on the sixth day of testimony, was, although clearly sympathetic to Sandra's plight, both polite and responsive to my questioning. I was able to elicit from Mrs. Stowe the fact that Sandra's call and suggestion that she and Kyle visit her at Twentynine Palms had come somewhat out of the blue. Following her testimony concerning Sandra's tearful reaction to the news of Henry's death, I asked Mrs. Stowe what Sandra had done thereafter.

Mrs. Stowe replied: "After she came out of the bathroom I gave her a tranquilizer and we sat down for a few minutes. And then Sandra suggested we go ahead and take the kids to the stables and let them ride for a few minutes like we had planned."

Q. "When did you go to the stables?"

A. "Shortly after she received the phone call."

Q. "Well, was it twenty minutes later or three hours or—"

A. "More like a half hour to forty-five minutes."

Forty-five minutes after news of her husband's death Sandra had taken Kyle horseback riding—that fact alone, I believed, told the jury a good deal about Sandra Stockton.

On cross, Terry Callas sought elaboration of Sandra's supposed trauma that day.

Q. "Did you observe Sandra's facial expression while she was on the phone?"

A. "Yes."

Q. "Would you please relate what you saw?"

A. "She slumped against the refrigerator, and I thought she was going to faint. She turned very pale and began to shake. And she just closed her eyes."

Before I could recall Sergeant Joe Aguirre to the stand to testify to Sandra's statements and behavior during his first interview with her, I met up, just as I had anticipated, with strong objections from the defense on a key issue. Their argument was that on the Sunday that Sandra had arrived back in Los Angeles and was interrogated by Aguirre, he had not advised her of her constitutional rights, most importantly, her right to consult a lawyer and have him present during her interrogation, and her right to remain silent. And therefore, to introduce into evidence any statement she made to Aguirre would violate the U.S. Supreme Court's landmark decision in *Escobedo v. Illinois*. In very simplified form, *Escobedo* and a long line of other cases, including the famous case of *Miranda v. Arizona,* which expanded *Escobedo,* generally provide that if, at the time the police interrogate someone, the person is not considered by the police to be a suspect, the police are then only in the *investigatory* stage and they do not have to advise the person of his constitutional rights. Incriminating statements made by such a person can be used against him. If, however, the police consider the person to be a suspect, and there is "custodial" interrogation, (the person has been taken into custody, or has been otherwise deprived of his freedom of action in any significant way), then the *accusatory* stage has been reached. If the police do not then advise the person of his constitutional rights, any incriminating statement made by the person thereafter in response to police interrogation designed to elicit such a statement, even if it be a full confession, cannot be introduced into evidence. Contrary to the misconception of many lay people who believe that when a defendant was not advised of his rights the case against him is dismissed, only the statement is kept out of evidence. The case against the defendant proceeds, unless the remaining evidence against him is insufficient.

It is frequently difficult to determine when the police's investigatory stage passes that fine line into the accusatory stage, but I had no doubt that on that initial Sunday, Aguirre did not consider Sandra a suspect. Even in a police progress report written several weeks later, it was stated that the case had been transferred to Parker Center because "the investigation by the assigned investigating officers failed to locate any suspect or suspects." To determine Aguirre's state of mind during his first interview with Sandra, however, we had to question Aguirre in the judge's chambers, out of the presence of the jury. Upon the completion of that questioning, Judge Young ruled that the accusatory stage had not been reached that Sunday, and that Aguirre could testify before the jury.

Taking the stand, Aguirre testified to Sandra's steady demeanor only hours after learning of her husband's violent death, her asking down at the police station if she were going to be arrested, and her collapsing to the floor, exclaiming, "Oh, my God," when they started to take her fingerprints. Unusual conduct, I hoped the jury would infer, for someone who is innocent.

Concerning another of Sandra's statements, I asked to approach the bench.

MR. BUGLIOSI: "Sandra stated to Aguirre that an individual named Dick Scott gave her the gun, and she gave a description of

Dick Scott which fits Alan Palliko to a T. I don't think that portion of the statement is admissible because I think it would violate the *Aranda* rule. It would be an extrajudicial statement of one defendant indirectly implicating a codefendant, even though she doesn't identify the party as Alan Palliko."

Judge Young agreed. Outside the presence of the jury I carefully instructed Aguirre that in relating for the jury Sandra's claim that a Dick Scott had given her the .22 caliber revolver as a present, he was to make absolutely no mention of Sandra's description of Dick Scott. If Aguirre had, all of the jurors' eyes would certainly have turned to Alan, sitting several seats away from Sandra at the defense table.

The reasoning behind the decision in the 1965 California Supreme Court case of *People v. Aranda* (and later the U.S. Supreme Court decision of *Bruton v. United States,* which is applicable to all the states), is this: If a defendant is implicated by an out of court statement made by his codefendant, he is then, in effect, being accused by his codefendant. Every person on trial, however, has the constitutional right to confront and cross-examine his accuser in court. But since the codefendant cannot be forced to take the stand, where he does not voluntarily do so the accused defendant loses his opportunity to cross-examine.

In this case, at this stage of the trial, Sandra had not taken the stand nor was it known whether she would. Therefore, those portions of her out of court statements indirectly implicating Alan Palliko had to be deleted.

Aguirre related to the jury Sandra's story about Dick Scott, but without the physical description.

On cross-examination of Aguirre, it was Callas' turn to ask to approach the bench.

MR. CALLAS: "I gave a lot of thought last night to this question. I wanted a ruling before I asked it in front of the jury, Your Honor. My question for Aguirre is: Did you ask Sandra Stockton to submit to a lie detector test during the conversation you had with her? I offer to prove that Sandra said, 'Yes, I will submit to it.'

". . . I'm offering it to show that during this conversation she did not give evidence of any consciousness of guilt."

Any testimony at all, I responded, regarding lie detector tests is inadmissible in a court of law. Judge Young concurred without needing even a moment to weigh the decision. I pointed out to Terry that if that testimony were allowed, then I would have to be permitted to introduce the fact that two weeks later Sandra called up Guy and St. John to tell them she had decided to refuse a polygraph examination. That would have been far more damaging to the defense than her original agreement to take the test would have been helpful to them. The first time she was asked the question, I could have argued, Sandra had probably just been caught off guard.

I wanted to show that Alan and Sandra not only shared the insurance money, but that they did it surreptitiously and conspiratorially—in a manner which exhibited a consciousness of guilt.

First, I had to establish for the jury that the money Sandra shared with Alan did, in fact, come from Henry's insurance policies. Before delving into the dates of Alan's deposits, I called those witnesses who could shed some light on Sandra's finances: Stanley Hayes, assistant personnel manager at Sears, who testified to sending Sandra her $15,000 Metroplitan Life insurance check on February 14, 1967, two months after Henry's death; Glen Reed, operations officer at Security Pacific Bank (Downey branch) where Sandra did her banking, who gave the jury their initial insight as to just how secretively Sandra began operating after Henry's death.

Ledger books spread across his lap, Reed read off Sandra's financial transactions during those first few months after the murder: her deposit of $15,000 on February 16; her purchase of $3,000 worth of American Express traveler's checks on February 17 at the Lakewood branch where Sandra did *not* have an account; her $1,500 cash withdrawal a week later on February 24; and her $4,900 withdrawal two weeks after that, on March 7—$2,000 of it as a cashier's check, $2,900 in cash.

For what reason does one walk around with that kind of cash? The reason that I hoped was suggesting itself to the jury was—to make payoffs.

Robert Huntsinger, property damage examiner for Allstate, with whom Henry carried a homeowner's fire insurance policy, testified to his company's sending Sandra a little over $1,300 in January of 1968 for personal property loss resulting from the fire.

On cross, Terry Callas elicited the fact that the larger sum of money for the damage to the house itself, $2,997, had gone to the mortgagee, the Santa Barbara Savings and Loan Company, not to Sandra. When Thomas Nixon of Santa Barbara Savings and Loan took the stand a day later, Terry brought out the additional fact that there was no mortage redemption insurance on the home and that actually, because of foreclosure, Sandra wound up losing the $4,000 in equity Henry and she had put into the house.

I would later present evidence through Sergeant Guy that on the two occasions he interviewed Sandra, she told him she believed there *was* mortgage redemption insurance on the house and that the home would be free and clear because of Henry's death. In my closing argument, I would point out that what Sandra had *believed* at the time was the important fact.

The tension of the trial had, thus far, no apparent effect on Alan's style. While in the holding tank waiting to be returned to his cell, he saw Ruth Bailey, the court reporter, pass by with a cup of coffee. Bound to twenty other men by chains that jangled from his ankles, Alan moved to the front bars of the tank and, arching his eyebrows, asked, "That coffee for me?" Ruth blushed and continued walking.

"Nice shoes. Very pretty," Alan called after her.

December 4, 1968

My dear Kyle,

How did you like the thunder and lightning the other night? Wasn't it beautiful? The lights went out a second or two here. It was so black, you couldn't see your hand in front of your face. Then the lightning flashed and the whole dorm was lit up with the electric blue light of it. It was so pretty. It's been a long time since I've seen the lightning so clear and bright. It brought back memories of when I was a kid like you, and your aunts and I slept on the floor one hot summer night, and there was an electrical storm. This storm also brought back memories of the last time we shared thunder and lightning. Remember it? We watched it on the horizon, driving home from school. We could clearly see the streaks of the long wiggly lines of it as it flashed down from the black sky. And the thunder. Oh, how I love the sound of it as it rumbles and rolls across the sky, finally crashing right over your head. Such delicious chills it gives me. I thought of you snug in your bed. I saw you as if I was standing over you, watching you sleep. So clear. I love you. I'm so proud of your progress in school. Practically all I'll let grandma talk about on her visits is you. I'm so very, very proud of you.

How do you like the new home? You know, I was going to call today while in court and I was ready to dial when I realized I didn't know the new phone number. I'll have to wait until I see grandma again. Did grandma tell you I'm going to make you a sweater? Hey, when am I going to get your letter?

Oh yes, I am working in the kitchen at night. The girls want me to go to work in the beauty shop. I do everyone's hair anyway. I enjoy it though, and I think I would like the job.

Grandma's coming tomorrow. She brings you to me in so many, many ways. I feel your presence always, but it seems more tangible when she's here. You, me, her are a circle growing ever stronger. My heart is so full of you, it's hard to express. I'm sure you know how I long for your nearness, the sound of your voice. How I pray that someday maybe soon . . . I know our thoughts are the same on that. I must close now, my darling one. How I love you. Stay you. God is with us.

Your mama

5

PRACTICALLY EVERYONE IN Los Angeles, it seems, from Santa Monica to Pasadena, has a phone answering service. As if they were still at this country's frontier edge, Angelenos, curiously, are terribly concerned about not getting messages. Perhaps it is the transience of residence and employment—a missed call can be a missed job. For those in the city who are younger, the ones on the climb, the hired message taker lends a hint of status.

Back in Judge Young's chambers, I stated my intention to have Olive McCann, chief operator of the Glendale Telephone Answering Service, the one Alan employed, testify to the messages Alan was receiving from "Miss Walther" in the Spring of 1967, in particular the message of March 9, 1967: "Definite word on policy tomorrow." Introducing that March 9 message was vital, in that in the entire case against Alan and Sandra, it was the only piece of evidence showing a direct communication between them about insurance proceeds. Testimony concerning phone messages, however, gave rise to a hearsay problem.

When used in a legal sense, hearsay has a very specific meaning:

Hearsay is a statement made outside of court (i.e., not from the witness stand at the present proceeding) which is offered into evidence not merely to prove that the statement was made, but that the statement is true. If, for example, a witness intended to testify: "John told me he saw Gary rob the bank," John's statement would be inadmissible hearsay if it were offered to prove that Gary robbed the bank. On the other hand, if a witness testifies at a competency hearing over Grandpa's will: "Grandpa told me the sky was falling,"

Grandpa's statement would not be hearsay in that it would not be offered to prove that the sky was actually falling, but merely to prove that Grandpa made the statement.

Although almost all hearsay consists of oral or written statements, even conduct, if intended to be a substitute for words, (e.g., nodding one's head in answer to a question; pointing to a person for identification purposes), is a hearsay "statement."

It is commonly stated that hearsay is where a witness relates what some other person said, but an out of court statement by the witness himself can also be hearsay. An out of court writing of a witness, for instance, can be hearsay, and if certain requirements are not met under an exception to the hearsay rule called "past recollection recorded," the writing will not be admissible.

The hearsay "exceptions" are situations where the out of court statements carry a likelihood of trustworthiness, e.g., death-bed declarations, self-incriminating statements of a defendant (since people normally do not falsely incriminate themselves), etc. There are, in fact, so many exceptions to the hearsay rule (twenty-two), a number of legal scholars feel the tide is in the direction of eventually abolishing the rule, and like most European countries, allowing hearsay in, to be given whatever weight the jury feels it is entitled to.

The March 9, 1967 statement, "Definite word on policy tomorrow," technically was not hearsay inasmuch as I was not offering it to prove that there was, in fact, a *definite* word on Henry's National Life policy the next day, because as far as I knew, there was not. I was offering the statement merely to show it had been made. Given the LAPD's information that the call-back number Miss Walther left most often was an unpublished number belonging to Sandra, the irresistible inference was that not only were Sandra and Miss Walther one and the same person, but that the message about a "policy" pertained to Henry Stockton's policy.

Judge Young, nonetheless, ruled that the phone message *was* hearsay and hence inadmissible unless I could find an applicable exception to the rule.

I offered three, the most solid of which was the "admissions" exception, covering incriminating statements made by a defendant, which I maintained this surely was.

Goldin and Callas argued strenuously back in chambers that the message did not constitute an admission. Judge Young could only smile at them for this contention.

Goldin and Callas, however, had more objections to the introduction of the message. The strongest of them, and one which Judge Young felt had merit, was Goldin's contention that if the message were, in fact, an incriminating statement which fell within the admissions exception, it was one that implicated her codefendant and therefore was inadmissible under *Aranda,* which, unlike the hearsay rule, has few exceptions. I knew of one and cited it for Judge Young. It was the little known case of *People v. Gant.*

Gant was a lower appellate court case in California which held that for *Aranda* to make any sense, it should apply only to statements made by co-conspirators *after* the conspiracy had ended. Statements made by co-conspirators *during* the conspiracy and used by them to "further the object" of the conspiracy should be admissible. The pivotal question, then, was: at the time of the phone message, was the conspiracy still in existence or had it already ended? If the former, I could get the statement in. If the latter, I could not. It was as simple as that.

I gave Judge Young an argument I had tossed out a couple of nights earlier as a trial balloon to my criminal law class at a night law school where I taught one night a week. Although we were alleging there was a conspiracy to commit murder here, the murder was not committed just for its own sake. The *ultimate* object of the conspiracy was to secure the insurance proceeds from that murder. Even though the murder had been committed, until those proceeds were secured, the conspiracy was still in existence, and the *Gant* case would apply.

Judge Young listened, his forehead creased, and at last nodded in agreement. It was an important victory, but Goldin made one further objection to keep the damning phone message out of evidence. Dave spoke sharply: "The Court should require independent proof of the conspiracy before allowing this type of testimony in. All we have is Mr. Bugliosi's bald assumption that there is a conspiracy."

He added that the whole notion of conspiracy was "a figment of the prosecutorial fixation."

The genesis of Goldin's argument was an old common law dictum that you cannot convict a man out of his own mouth alone. From this has emerged the rule that before an incriminating statement made by a defendant can be introduced against him at a trial, the prosecution must first present evidence, independent of the statement, that a crime was committed. There have been cases where a defendant has fully confessed to a murder, but walked out of court because the prosecution was unable to present evidence that the victim died by criminal means (e.g., no gunshot or stab wounds, no poison in system, etc.).

Although I had not sought to indict Alan and Sandra on the separate and somewhat superfluous charge of *conspiracy* to commit murder, to invoke the all-important rule of vicarious liability (making Sandra equally responsible for Alan's act of murder), I nevertheless had to prove such a conspiracy did, in fact, exist.

The gist of Goldin's objection was to force me to prove a conspiracy existed, but without using the statements of the co-conspirators as proof. I cited cases to Judge Young which held that the rule requiring proof of the crime before introduction of incriminating statements did not apply to those statements which are uttered as a very part of the commission of the crime itself. As opposed to most crimes, whose perpetration invariably and often exclusively involves *conduct,* by the very nature of the crime of conspiracy, its formation and execution involve conduct *and statements* (i.e., communications between co-conspirators). To mechanically apply the rule to a crime such as conspiracy would in effect be to many times preclude the only possible proof that the conspiracy ever existed.

While tending to agree with my argument, out of an abundance of caution Judge Young nevertheless sustained Goldin's objection, ruling that I first must present additional, independent evidence that the *corpus delicti* (body or elements of the crime) of conspiracy existed before allowing in the phone message. The next day I put on an uninterrupted succession of witnesses who could offer testimony of Alan's and Sandra's conduct in Las Vegas, which was circumstantial evidence of a conspiracy.

Jerry Lanz, record coordinator for Western Airlines, was the first to take the stand. Lanz testified to the February 18, 1967 flight that "Mr. J. Pace" and "Mr. B. Johnson" had taken on Western Airlines. As I had requested, Lanz brought to court with him the ticket coupons which indicated the consecutive serial numbers of the two tickets.

Q. BY MR. BUGLIOSI: "Does the fact that the ticket agent wrote the name Mr. B. Johnson necessarily mean that Mr. B. Johnson, the person who actually took the flight to Las Vegas, was a male?"

A. "No, any passenger may present himself at our ticket counter and request tickets for the name of any other passenger and they will be prepared as the passenger requests."

On cross-examination, Goldin questioned the likelihood of a passenger flying under an assumed name of the opposite sex and not being detected.

Q. "If I came to the window and said, 'I'm *Mrs.* Goldin, I have a reservation,' would this seem strange to a Western Airline personnel?" Dave's sense of humor brought a slight smile to the faces of a few jurors.

A. "No."

Q. "No? I am not sure how to take that."

Callas, like Goldin, also believed that the false name would be caught, even if the passenger already had his (her) ticket and went directly to the boarding gate. Lanz, however, explained that commuter flights are something like cattle herding with little time for the attendant to do anything but tear out the coupons.

When I asked Hertz rental clerk Ellen Bendas about her having identified Alan and Sandra from photographs shown her by John St. John, Terry Callas immediately objected. His point, made at the bench, was that St. John had violated a ruling in several California and United States Supreme Court cases by showing Miss Bendas only two photographs, one of Alan and one of Sandra, rather than mingling their pictures with a number of others. It had not been, Callas argued, a very fair "line-up." Callas was right, and Judge Young sustained the objection.

I did not really need to make use of those photograph identifications anyway.

Q. BY MR. BUGLIOSI: "Directing your attention, Miss Bendas, to the gentleman seated fourth from your right at the table in front of you. Have you ever seen him before?"

A. "Yes, Alan J. Palliko. He's the person I rented the car to."

Q. "Directing your attention to the woman seated farthest from your right at the table in front of you. Have you ever seen her before?"

A. "Yes, she was the lady companion who showed up at the counter with Mr. Palliko at the time of the rental."

Following Bendas, I called the remainder of the Las Vegas witnesses: Edward Doumanni of the El Morocco, who identified Alan and Sandra as the two people who registered at the hotel under the names Jerry Pace and S. Stockton, listing, on the registration card, Pace's rented Mustang Fastback, Nevada License C–82541 (the same car Alan Palliko had rented that morning at Hertz); Lawrence Mushkin, to seeing Alan in Sandra's hotel room when he delivered a pair of shoes to her; Sal Bel Angelo, pit boss at the Thunderbird, to Alan's winning over a thousand dollars at blackjack on his first night, but losing all of it and more the very next evening, playing as much as $100 a hand.

A little bit of Vegas glittering from his fingers, Bel Angelo sculpted the air as he told of his seeing a blonde, who was "short and a little on the stout side," at the slot machines, the woman Alan said was his sister.

I asked the Court to direct Sandra to stand up. If other people thought of Sandra as stout, she apparently did not. Even that day in court she was wearing a miniskirt. A mixture of disgust and embarrassment on her face, she stood up as Judge Young directed.

MR. BEL ANGELO: "I didn't see her face, I saw her back at that time. Of course, there were no miniskirts then." Bel Angelo exhibited a mischievous grin to the gallery of spectators. "I can't swear to it. But she looks like she could have been the one."

Gerald Tassone, shift manager at the Thunderbird Hotel's casino, testified to his having seen Alan, when Alan returned to Las Vegas, drop "in the neighborhood of $2,000" on one evening-long play at the twenty-one tables.

When Goldin asked for and I agreed to a stipulation, which Goldin read for the jury, that the tall good-looking redhead who was with Alan on his second trip to Las Vegas was not Sandra, Sandra glowered at Alan, her crossed leg kicking a little beneath the defense table. I was told by several spectators that whenever testimony was given about any of Alan's willowy girlfriends, Sandra's leg invariably began to swing.

Sergeant Robert Smith, a handwriting expert in LAPD's "questioned document" unit, testified he had "no doubt whatsoever" that the Sandra Stockton who had filled out the booking slip on the night of her incarceration was the Sandra Stockton who had signed the traveler's checks (brought to court by an American Express representative), and that the Alan Palliko who had made out the writing and printing exemplars at the Central Jail was the same man who had signed "Alan J. Palliko" on the Hertz rental agreement and had printed "Jerry Pace" and "S. Stockton" on the El Morocco Hotel's registration card.

I mused to myself about all the deceptive endeavors Alan and Sandra had engaged in after they had essentially pulled off a murder without a hitch. So often, the means a criminal employs to conceal his crime are the precise means that reveal his culpability.

There is no escaping the tension in a trial in which the death penalty is being sought against the defendants. Like the oppresive heat before an electrical storm, an air of death—the horrible murders already committed and the possible consequences for the accused—settles on the courtroom.

During the thirteen week trial, I lost ten pounds. Sandra gained twenty-five. As the testimony came in, one piece of circumstantial evidence piling up on top of another, even Alan lost a certain edge of aloofness. He remained confident, laughing if anything humorous was said in the courtroom—certainly a contrast to Sandra's grim, unbroken silence—but even in Alan some of that cockiness was slowly draining. No more winks for Ruth Bailey, the court reporter.

The Stocktons, Henry's quiet retiring parents, chose to stay away from the trial. The Davises came every day. In the hallway I overheard a friend of theirs remark that unlike her husband Franklin, Ethel Davis was "out for Alan's blood."

In the course of the trial, working seven days a week, as I invariably do in a major trial, I had time to take Gail to exactly one movie. The occasions she glanced over at me, there was a tolerant smile on her face, as I spent a good part of the evening leaning out over the dim aisle light scribbling notes to myself. When I felt a hand on my shoulder midway through the mystery story which was showing that night, it was the person behind me wanting to know which newspaper I was the film critic for. Informing him I was not a critic, I added that I would be the last person to review a movie mystery.

The embarrassing truth of the matter is that although I enjoy them, unlike Gail, I can never figure them out.

After having heard the testimony thus far concerning Alan's and Sandra's conduct in Las Vegas, Judge Young finally allowed me to introduce the crucial phone message left for Alan by Miss Walther which the defense had been trying so vigorously to keep out.

Just two hours after Young's ruling, a representative from the telephone company arrived at the courthouse with the telephone records I had subpoenaed, and to my utter chagrin, I was informed that the phone number Miss Walther left most often with Alan's answering service, the one an LAPD Intelligence Division memo to Guy and St. John had stated was an unpublished number belonging to Sandra Stockton, was in actuality Alan's home number. That sudden revelation snatched from me, in one quick swipe, the only link I had connecting Sandra with Miss Walther, and thus, the extremely important evidence of the phone message.

I had to report to Judge Young that I no longer intended to introduce the March 9 phone message into evidence, and that the entire day we had spent in chambers arguing its admissibility had been nothing but a waste of the court's time. I apologized profusely, and Young, always a gentleman, accepted my apology with a gracious, almost bemused smile.

Miss Walther *was* Sandra Stockton, I was convinced of it. Alan owned two Walther guns, and in all of Guy's and St. John's investigation, they had not come across any friend or associate of Alan's by the name of Miss Walther. The name, as utilized for the answering service purposes, was, I was sure, an obvious fiction. There had to be some other way, I felt, to prove that Sandra Stockton was Miss Walther.

It was not long before I hit upon something solid and really rather elementary. The message left by Miss Walther on March 9 was: "Definite word on policy *tomorrow*." If Sandra were in fact Miss Walther, then surely, I reasoned, Sandra must have had some cause to *believe* she would receive a final word on the policy the next day. There was, it occurred to me, at least one way to go about proving that.

I phoned William Hodges, Downey branch manager for National Life, and requested to see all correspondence between his company and Sandra (and/or her lawyer at the time, Roy Marchetta). Hodges informed me that because a settlement had been reached, the file was "closed," which meant all papers were now held at National Life's Nashville, Tennessee headquarters. I asked that he get the file for me as quickly as possible.

Four days later, Hodges brought the copies of correspondence and related papers to my office. Examining them, I found the following: On March 8, 1967, one day before Miss Walther's message, a Mr. G.O. Lloyd, then manager of National Life's Downey office, had written a letter to Mr. F. Oakley Williams, supervisor of the life claims division in Nashville. In the letter, Lloyd stated he was being "besieged" by phone calls from Sandra Stockton and her attorney demanding payment on the policy, and that he (Lloyd) needed a reason to give them for the delay. Then, on March 9, the *same* day as the phone message, the files revealed that Roy Marchetta wrote a letter to Mr. Lloyd requesting Lloyd to expedite the matter "in view of Mrs. Stockton's *extremely bad* financial situation." It had been only three weeks earlier, I noted to myself, that Sandra had received $15,000 from Metropolitan Life. Where had all the money gone, one might have wondered.

Lastly, on March 10—the "tomorrow" alluded to in Miss Walther's message—a Mr. Moran, Life Claims Manager in the Nashville office, wrote Marchetta in response to his letter of the previous day, telling Marchetta that National Life was still in the process of determining its liability under the policy. Thus, although Sandra did not, on March 10, receive the *"definite* word" she had hoped for, she did receive some word a few days later when Mr. Moran's letter arrived. That Sandra expected her lawyer's letter of March 9 to reach Nashville in one day was, I felt, not completely unreasonable, and in fact, that is exactly what happened. Sandra's expectation of an immediate response (by telephone or telegram, presumably) from the insurance company the very same day, March 10, I could only attribute to a flush of anticipation on her part.

The files had produced a big payoff to my hunch. Shoving them into my briefcase, I returned to court.

Finally, after the long and tedious legal battle, Olive McCann of the Glendale Answering Service was permitted to take the stand and testify to the very incriminating March 9 phone message.

On cross, Goldin asked Olive McCann if Alan had not listed himself with the answering service as a "private investigator?" The answer was yes. It was Goldin's way of informing the jury that Alan not only worked for an insurance company, the Auto Club, but that he also moonlighted as a private investigator for an attorney, namely Roy Marchetta. The implication was that a man in Alan's field would quite normally be getting messages involving "policies."

After McCann, however, I put on William Hodges for his important testimony about the correspondence between Sandra, Marchetta, and National Life.

If the logical conclusion to be drawn were as obvious to the jury as it was to me, Miss Walther's message, "Definite word on policy tomorrow," had at last come home to roost—on the defense table just in front of Sandra Stockton.

Throughout the trial, there were of course the usual courtroom hangers-on looking for their front row seats—lonely, white-haired widows with brown bag lunches; retired, perpetually sour looking men with sunglasses. But in a greater number than those at this trial was a new, seldom seen type of spectator—young, smartly dressed housewives dropping by in their sports cars between a social set of tennis and lunch, fascinated by the story of revolving, jagged relationships among pretenders to their lifestyle.

Alan's parents had asked that the entire first row of the gallery be reserved for them. Their request, odd in that there were only two of them needing seats, was denied. Thereafter, they were the first ones into the courtroom almost every morning, and never seated themselves in any row but the first. Mrs. Palliko sat emotionlessly, chewing her gum from morning to afternoon. Mr. Palliko began making a habit of expressing his disapproval with some of my questions and a number of Judge Young's rulings by groaning. An intelligent man, Sid Palliko should have known better than to think his conduct was helping his son's case in the eyes of the jury one bit.

Having put on evidence of Sandra's financial activities in early 1967, I turned to the subject of Alan's finances during the same time period. Royce Straub, installment officer at Valley National Bank where Alan had had a checking account, testified to his having watched Alan on February 23, 1967, peel off and deposit $2,500 from a thick wad of cash which he put back into his pocket. February 23 was one week after Sandra had received her $15,000 check from Metropolitan Life.

On cross-examination, however, Dave Goldin was able to render that testimony almost harmless to Alan—at least for the time being.

Q. BY MR. GOLDIN: "During the lifetime of the account there were a number of large deposits made, is that correct?"

A. "I believe so, yes."

Q. "On December 28, 1966, there was also a $2,500 deposit. Is that right?"

A. "Yes.

Q. "And a little under $600 was deposited in March, 1967. Right?"

A. "Yes."

Q. "A little more than that in April?"

A. "Yes."

Q. "And $2,725 was deposited on August 4?"

A. "Right."

Q. "And $3,500 on September 15?"

A. "Yes."

MR. GOLDIN: "No further questions."

Goldin had made his point. Regardless of when Sandra was getting her various checks, Alan, like anyone, was making deposits and withdrawals on any number of occasions. Goldin was proving what every trial lawyer knows: being caught with a smoking gun takes some explaining; circumstantial evidence that is less glaring can require very little.

After Straub, I called one of the prosecution's most important witnesses: Katherine Drummond, a woman who, although she would not be permitted to testify to most of them, had amazingly survived no fewer than five separate plans for her murder (two hit and runs, San Diego, the beating, and the trip to the mountains).

A couple of weeks before the trial's commencement, Michael Brockington had phoned Katherine and suggested that as long as they would both be going to the courthouse as witnesses for the prosecution, they might at least make an effort to get on speaking terms with each other.

The two had lunch together, and Katherine found Michael to be nothing at all like his former friend and her former husband, Alan Palliko. Michael lent a sympathetic ear to the problems of Katherine's tender emotional state. The approaching trial was something of a trauma for Katherine, forcing her to relive the years of her life she had tried to put behind her. A friendship between Katherine and Michael blossomed, and by the time of the trial, they were driving down to the courthouse together.

When Alan saw the two of them walk into court together that first afternoon Katherine testified, his eyes flashed wide with stunned anger. His thick neck muscles corrugated and turning red, he fixed his stare first on Michael, then on Katherine. A number of times during the trial, Alan would stare at them for long moments, and both of them, I could see, grew anxious and fidgety under the gaze, always looking away from Alan. I worried that the implicit threat in Alan's face might get to them and do the job it intended to do.

I sought at this point in the trial to introduce Alan's crucial statement to Katherine which he made in mid-December of 1966: "I'm expecting a large sum of money after the first of the year." The defense objected to its admissibility. An exchange at the bench probably showed how much all of us were in need of temporary diversion from the constant, mentally straining battle over the complex points of law.

MR. BUGLIOSI: "He (Alan) wasn't referring to gambling wins, as I'm sure the defense is going to claim—because if you expect to *win* money you don't make a statement, 'I'm expecting a large sum of money after the first of the year.' That is just not the language I think a person would use. I am going to argue that."

THE COURT: "Unless you were Nick the Greek."

MR. BUGLIOSI: "Yes."

MR. GOLDIN: "Or think you are Nick the Greek."

THE COURT: "And the evidence seems to indicate that the defendant Palliko is not Nick the Greek."

MR. GOLDIN: "He thinks he is Nick the Greek."

MR. BUGLIOSI: "Right."

MR. CALLAS: "Incidentally, there is a difference of opinion whether Nick the Greek is a good gambler."

MR. BUGLIOSI: "Is there?"

THE COURT: "All right, let's get to the point."

Diversions aside, the defense argued that because Alan and Katherine were still married (although separated) at the time Alan made the statement, the rule of marital privilege precluded her being allowed to testify to such communications between them. My argument was that Alan had made almost exactly the same statement to Michael Brockington, and that a repetition of a statement to a third party legally constitutes a waiver of the marital privilege. I agreed with the defense that other statements Alan had later made to Katherine (e.g., "Don't ask" where the money came from; "It was a horrible thing I had to do."), but had not repeated to anyone else, should be protected by the privilege. Young concurred with my position, and Katherine was allowed to testify to Alan's "expecting a large sum of money" statement in mid-December. I also had Katherine testify to Alan's *conduct* (which, unlike words, is not protected by marital privilege) in the months following Henry's murder.

Q. "In December of 1966 and January and February of 1967, did Alan Palliko appear to be acting any differently than he normally acted?"

A. "He seemed very much on edge, nervous."

Q. "In late February of '67, did you go over to his apartment?"

A. "Yes, I did."

Q. "Did he appear to have any large sum of money inside the apartment?"

A. "Yes, sir. In an attaché case on a footstool in the living room."

Katherine told of how Alan gave her $200 that day in large denominations (she could not recall whether it was two hundreds or one hundred and two fifties), and that whenever he asked her out to dinner afterward his wallet appeared full of big bills. Having already heard that Sandra had received her first $15,000 of insurance money in late February, the jury could draw its own conclusions.

When I asked Katherine why she divorced Alan, her answer was a single name: "Sandra Stockton." She told of the phone bills she discovered upon returning from one of her trips to Michigan that revealed Alan's calls to Sandra at all odd hours of the day and night.

On cross, the usually placid and soft spoken Terry Callas jumped down Katherine's throat with accusatory questions about her own affair with the man in San Diego, implying that Sandra was not the reason for the failure of Alan's and Katherine's marriage. From the trial's outset, Callas was understandably protective, at times emotionally so, of his client Sandra Stockton—he was of course fighting for her life—but raising his voice as much as he did with Katherine was, I believe, a tactical error. Katherine is a very demure woman, and I doubt the jury sympathized with any of the aggressive cross-examination of her. Sitting prim and straight in the woolen suits she wore to court, her answers from the witness stand continued to be polite and sincere. Her manner, in fact, was so ingenuous—always "yes, sir" and "no, sir"—I often had to come back on redirect examination to give her an opportunity to fully explain herself. Some of her "yes, sirs" and "no, sirs" were tending to give the jury some incomplete impressions.

She admitted on Callas' questioning, for example, that she had once spent a weekend with the other man in San Diego. When Goldin asked her, however, if she had ever been intimate with any other men during her marriage to Alan, Katherine merely answered, "No, sir." I knew the reason for the answer was that the man in San Diego had been impotent. Not wanting the jury to think she was intentionally trying to hide something, I came back to ask her if she *would* have had sexual relations with the man if he had been able to. Her answer: "Yes, sir. I would have."

Q. BY MR. BUGLIOSI: "Was there any reason why you went out with another man?"

A. "A very, very personal reason that I would prefer not to have to say."

Q. "In very broad terms did it involve sex?"

A. "Yes."

Q. "Between you and Alan?"

A. "Yes, sir."

Callas, on re-cross, brought out the fact that adultery was not mentioned in Katherine's divorce action. Again Katherine looked like a liar for having said the reason for her divorce was Sandra Stockton. To bail her out once again, I elicited on redirect the fact that it was Alan who insisted that adultery not be listed as the grounds, and that there be no mention in the suit of the name, Sandra Stockton.

When I asked if there were other reasons for leaving Alan, Katherine's answer was a simple and sad comment on the marriage: "I was terrified of my husband."

Because he was not charged with them, the jury was not allowed to hear about the two hit-and-run incidents. Nor did they hear about Alan's having Katherine in the cross-hairs of his rifle sight in San Diego—a collateral matter whose prejudice to Alan in front of the jury would far outweigh its relevance.

Giving testimony was a painful ordeal for Katherine. She had once loved Alan and had come to realize that he had probably never, even if he had perhaps been trying in all of those six unrecoverable years, really loved her. Katherine told of Alan's having accompanied her back to Michigan at the time of her father's heart attack, and telling her: "When we were married I never once gave you a shoulder to lean on. I want to make up for that." As she recalled her believing and needing Alan then, when her father was critically ill, Katherine began to cry softly on the witness stand.

We took a several minute recess before continuing.

On cross-examination, Goldin whittled away at the prosecution's case. First, he was able to bring out the fact that Alan and Katherine had once gone to Las Vegas, that Alan had been a winner there, and that therefore February of '67 was not the first time she had seen him with big bills in his wallet. Katherine had testified earlier that she had "never" during their marriage seen Alan with hundred dollar bills. More importantly, to show that Alan's use of the name Jerry Pace in Las Vegas was not incriminating, Goldin asked if Alan had ever used the name Jerry Pace for making restaurant reservations and the like during the years they were married. Katherine's answer was yes, he had.

The reasoning behind one of Goldin's last lines of questioning had me momentarily confused.

Q. "Alan never caught you in bed with another man. Is that right?" Dave growled at Katherine.

A. "That's right."

Q. "And he didn't kill a man that he caught you in bed with?"

MR. BUGLIOSI: "Your Honor, this is a ridiculous question. I think Mr. Goldin is badgering this witness."

THE COURT: "I sustain the objection. I think you should rephrase that question, counsel."

Q. BY MR. GOLDIN: "There was never in the course of your marriage a time when Alan threw a man out the window and killed him because he had slept with you. Is that right?"

It was obvious to me now where Dave was going.

Katherine answered, no, Alan had never thrown any lover of hers out the window. Goldin later presented testimony about Alan's having told a number of people he had been dismissed from the police force for having thrown his wife's lover out the bedroom window. Goldin was laying the foundation that Alan was a storyteller, and that much of his bullslinging involved convincing others what a tough violent man he could be. The question Goldin was hoping the jurors would ask themselves was: can anyone believe anything said by a man who was, for all intents and purposes, a pathological liar? And if not, why then believe what he told Michael Brockington, namely that he had killed Henry Stockton?

After long perseverance, the police were finally able to track down Bernard Croucher, the former National Life Insurance agent who sold the Stocktons Henry's $20,000 double indemnity policy. He was living in Medford, Oregon, and that is where I reached him by phone.

Once again, an insurance agent collided with the prosecution's case, this time on the first murder.

Mr. Croucher confessed his memory of the sale was somewhat clouded after two years, but what he did recollect of the incident was this: Sandra had been tardy with the premium payment on her own $1,000 life policy, and thus it was Croucher who had sought *her* out in October of 1966, not the other way around. Croucher informed me in our long distance conversation that in his subsequent meeting with the couple, it was Henry, not Sandra, who had broached the subject of getting a new, substantial policy on his own life. Sandra, he recalled, had sat quietly by during the entire transaction.

That version of the insurance purchase obviously was in direct opposition to the prosecution's theory of the murder. A prosecutor's job, however, is not to hide whatever facts in a case might be damaging to his side. I called Terry Callas immediately, apprised him of the new information, and told him I had already made arrangements to fly Croucher down for the trial.

Croucher's prospective testimony was so damaging to the prosecution, I could not afford to automatically accept his version as the last word on the incident, especially in light of how much he had been hesitating on the phone over each of my questions, how unsure he seemed to be of his own memory. I phoned John Morrow, the attorney for National Life who negotiated the settlement with Sandra's lawyer, and asked him to check his own files for anything that might confirm or refute Bernard Croucher's recollections of the insurance purchase. Morrow found two very telling pieces of paper. One was a signed memo from Croucher indicating that it was Sandra, not Henry, who had asked about and pursued the subject of buying a new life policy for Henry. And secondly, Morrow had a copy of Henry's insurance application. On the back of it was a series of boxes of marketing information that the company had all of its agents fill out for office use. In the box marked "Instigator of Purchase" for Henry's policy, Croucher had checked off "Spouse."

I went back to Callas with the new information. Terry, needless to say, was no longer anxious to subpoena Mr. Croucher. For my part, I decided not to subpoena him either. The best I could do, after all, would be to impeach my own witness' present memory with the written statements he had made previously. Terry and I discussed the matter and agreed that the facts of the incident were inconclusive, and that Croucher's testimony would only add confusion as to what

212 : TILL DEATH US DO PART

had really transpired. A day after making Mr. Croucher's flight reservation for him, I called back to tell him he could unpack.

As we started the fourth week of trial, I called to the stand the prosecution's "star witness." Having been Alan's best friend, Michael Brockington was in a position to testify to nearly every misadventure of Alan's. A very significant portion of the prosecution's case against Alan and Sandra came down to Michael's credibility. In midtrial, Mel Belli, who kept in close contact with Callas by telephone during the week, and on weekends up in San Francisco, sent a private investigator to interview Michael's former wife at her home in the small northern California community of Hayward, seeking personal, hopefully damaging information against Michael. She refused to talk to him.

In court, the defense did everything they could to brand Michael a liar.

A problem for me was Michael's insurance adjuster manner of speech which, in a case such as ours, sounded contrived and rehearsed. In describing the car trip that Alan and he had taken to Santa Fe Springs, for example, Michael did not say merely that they "went," but rather that they "transitioned" from one freeway to another. It was not simply money he had seen Alan pick up, rather it was "United States currency." Knowing that kind of formality can alienate a jury, I made a point of informing the jurors during my closing argument that that stilted type of language was, quite frankly, almost a part of an insurance adjuster's breeding.

Although Alan's and Michael's relationship went back even further, the earliest time I asked Michael to trace it back to was early winter of 1966—the planning of the first New Year's Eve party at the Biltmore Hotel.

Q. "Did you ask Alan why he was throwing the party?"

A. "Yes, I did. His reply was that this was a coming-out party for him."

Q. "Did you ask him why he was willing to spend all the money for the party?"

A. "Yes. He said he could afford it because he was expecting a rather large sum of money after the first of the year."

Michael related how in January and February of 1967, Alan started to become "upset, quite upset" because of a delay in getting his money. I probed those first few months of 1967 at some length, for it was during that time that Alan and he had had a number of very significant conversations. When I began to ask Michael about Alan's comments concerning the maintenance of safe deposit boxes under fictitious names, Goldin objected. At the bench he told Judge Young, "The probative value here is nil and moot, and the prejudicial value is tremendous. The People's case is based solely on the proposition that Mr. Palliko is not a nice person and therefore they should find him guilty."

Judge Young showed Dave a sour and impatient expression.

THE COURT: "Unfortunately, Mr. Goldin, evidence in a criminal case sometimes *does* reflect badly on a defendant. Objection is overruled."

When I then went on to ask Michael about the phone conversations he overheard in which Alan kept referring to the caller as "Tiger," Callas objected to these conversations being allowed in, in that they cast suspicion on Sandra without any hard proof that the caller had really been Sandra. Judge Young permitted the conversation to come in, but only after he gave the jury a "limiting instruction" that the phone conversations were to be considered as evidence only against the defendant Alan Palliko, not Sandra Stockton.

Michael testified how it was clear to him the caller had been a woman because he knew Alan well enough to know his change of voice when a woman was on the other end.

MR. BROCKINGTON: "The first conversation, as I remember, Mr. Palliko spent a considerable amount of time quietly talking to the individual who was at the other end. And he was reassuring the caller to 'have a cool head,' in a sense, to be patient. He did make a statement that I remember wherein he stated that, 'It had been done,' or, 'It had been completed.'"

Other phrases from subsequent calls that Michael remembered were: "Calm down"—"Don't let the police rattle you"—"They can't prove anything"—"We have gone this far, don't blow the deal now."

MR. BROCKINGTON: "Continually throughout the conversations he would say, 'Yes, Tiger,' 'Look here, Tiger,' 'Okay, Tiger.' This was a continual reference to the caller."

Q. "During that same period of time, Mr. Brockington, between January and March of 1967, did you have any personal conversation with Mr. Palliko at his apartment with respect to the subject of murder?"

A. "Yes, sir, I did."

Q. "What did he say to you and what did you say to him?"

A. "Mr. Palliko asked my opinion of a problem that he posed to me, and he put it in so many words as to say: 'If two people had gotten together for the purpose of killing someone to obtain insurance money, and that if the person who was your partner, you became very doubtful about this person, or you worried about the person, that they were weak, would you kill this person?'"

Wondering how Sandra was taking this revelation of her partner's possible plans for her, I looked over my shoulder toward the defense table. Although her blue eyes were turning hard enough to cut diamond, she did not dare direct them at Alan in front of the jury.

I had almost forgotten I had a witness on the stand.

Q. "He posed this question to you as somewhat of a hypothetical?"

A. "Yes, he did."

Q. "I take it you answered in the negative?"

A. "I didn't answer."

I then asked Michael to relate the conversation he had with Alan that early evening in February around dusk, when Alan asked him to join him for a drink at the Marlindo Bowling Alley across the street from the Grand Duke. Callas had objected to the entire conversation on the ground that Palliko's statements implicated Sandra and therefore violated the *Aranda* rule. Judge Young overruled the objection, holding that actually, the statements did not implicate Sandra in any *preexisting conspiracy* to murder her husband. Young's ruling, of course, would preclude me from arguing to the jury, in my summation, that they did.

As always, Michael spoke unemotionally; he was all business up there on the stand.

Q. "Where were you inside the bowling alley at the time?"

A. "We were in the cocktail lounge, precisely we were at the west end."

Q. "You were speaking privately to Mr. Palliko?"

A. "That is correct."

Q. "What did Mr. Palliko say to you at the Marlindo Bowling Alley?"

A. "He asked me a question."

Q. "What did he ask you?"

A. "He asked me if I knew how he got all his money. And I said no. He then said, 'You might as well know all there is to know about me.'"

The courtroom grew terribly quiet.

"At that time Mr. Palliko told me—asked if I had remembered Sandra Stockton and I told him yes, that this was the person I had known from work. And he then told me that it was her husband that he himself had killed."

Q. "Did he elaborate on how he killed Sandra Stockton's husband?"

A. "He did not."

Q. "Did you ask him?"

A. "No."

Q. "Why didn't you ask him?"

A. "Shock."

Q. "Did you report this matter immediately to the police?"

A. "No, I did not."

Q. "Why not?"

A. "I didn't want to have my head blown off."

Q. "By whom?"

A. "By Mr. Palliko."

The threat, I knew, still hung over Michael. In his jail cell during the trial, Alan told the visiting Reverend Vigeveno, the man who had married Alan and Katherine: "One of these days Mike and Katy are going to pay for this."

I asked Michael on the stand if he ever saw Alan carrying a loaded gun, and he replied there was one gun in particular Alan often kept concealed in his waistband. It was Alan's favorite gun, a Walther PPK. That was the second context in which the jury heard the name Walther. It would not be the last.

I had now come to the paradoxical point in my direct examination of Brockington where I felt I had no choice but to elicit testimony that could very well discredit him as a witness and, in the process, the People's case in the murder of Henry Stockton. It was but a small slip of paper that had brought me to the dilemma:

Three days before he was scheduled to testify, Michael phoned me to say he had just received a rental bill for the safe deposit box Alan had taken out under Michael's name over a year earlier. A bill, Michael hooted, he was not about to pay. His memory was now jogged, Michael said, to recall that the trip to Santa Fe Springs, which he had previously told me occurred in late August, 1967, had actually, to be even more precise, taken place two to three days before he loaned his wallet to Alan to open up the safe deposit box. Because the rental bill revealed the date of that opening to be August 25, Michael now said with total certainty that the trip to Santa Fe Springs had occurred August 22 or 23.

As he spoke casually, it was clear to me Michael was unaware of the monumental problem he was handing me with this new bit of information—Roy Marchetta had not forwarded Sandra her proceeds from the National Life policy until August 29.

At the time of the Santa Fe Springs incident, then, where had Sandra gotten several thousand dollars to give Alan? Certainly not from the Metropolitan proceeds, which she had dissipated months earlier.

I asked Michael if he might not be confusing the sequence of the two incidents and the time lapse between them, i.e., if the trip had not, in fact, taken place at least a week *after* Alan opened up the safe deposit box (and thus *after* Sandra had received her National Life money), not before.

Prideful of his own insurance adjuster's ability to be precise, Michael would not budge. The trip took place *before* the lending of the wallet. There was "no doubt about it," he said. If the safe deposit box had been opened on August 25, as the bank records showed, then Alan, he said, had picked up the cash from the place where Sandra Stockton was working, absolutely no later than August 23.

Witnesses can be off in their testimony by several days, or under some circumstances, even weeks or months, and in the eyes of the jury this does not necessarily mean they are lying. They are simply demonstrating their fallibility as human beings. But when there is something such as a bank record as an exact base of reference, errors are far less explainable.

Unless I could find some explanation for what Brockington was telling me, I would be faced with the unpleasant probability that Brockington's testimony about Santa Fe Springs would lead the jury to either one of two conclusions: that the money Sandra gave Alan that August was not the insurance proceeds from Henry's death or, and this was even worse, that Brockington manufactured the whole Santa Fe Springs incident. If they believed this, then the jury would most likely believe that he had also concocted, as I knew the defense would obviously contend, the entire Marlindo Bowling Alley conversation.

But perhaps Michael was right about his dates, I thought. Had Alan, impatient with waiting for his cut of the insurance proceeds, pressured Sandra into borrowing his share from a third party? And it was *that* money she had given Alan in Santa Fe Springs?

I immediately called Guy and St. John and asked that they check the bank accounts of everyone related or close to Sandra to try to ascertain if anyone had withdrawn any large sums of money which might have been loaned to Sandra before August 25, or if there had been any unexplained transference or manipulation of funds. The investigation had to be done quickly, I said, and I asked that they put extra men on it if necessary. A week later, they reported back with the bad news: they had found nothing.

Whenever I know the defense is going to present evidence damaging to the prosecution, I try to introduce the evidence myself. That strategy tends to shave a few decibels off the defense's trumpets, and it conveys to the jury my willingness to see that all evidence, unfavorable to the prosecution as well as favorable, comes out—that I am not trying to suppress it back in judge's chambers or in open court.

Q. "Mr. Brockington, People's 36 for identification here (the safe deposit rental bill) indicates that the safe deposit box was opened August 25, 1967, and you have testified you feel that the Santa Fe Springs incident took place two or three days before you loaned Mr. Palliko your ID to open that box. Is that correct?"

A. "Yes, sir, this is correct."

On this one crucial point, Brockington would say from the stand he was "absolutely certain," that he "expressly remembered" the time sequence.

Goldin and Callas did little to hide the excited smiles they were exchanging at the defense table.

There being no doubt in my mind that Brockington was merely making a simple honest error, I proceeded to have him give his version of the trip. From the blown-up, police helicopter aerial photographs I had ordered, he pointed out the T-intersection Alan turned the car around in, the building he went behind (Allied Pacific Manufacturing Company—Sandra Stockton's place of employment at the time), etc. Sergeant Guy would later testify to Brockington's having directed him and Sergeant Henderson to this same spot.

The defense paid little attention to Brockington's geographical knowledge (which they could argue any half-sophisticated framer would have had) and, knowing Brockington would be buried on his dates when Roy Marchetta would later take the stand, they contented themselves with painting the lily by adducing other discrepancies in

Brockington's story. Had he not once told Marjorie Huebner that the city had been Covina, not Santa Fe Springs? (Marjorie told the police that Michael said it was Covina.) Michael replied no. Had he not, in addition, told Marjorie that the money was in an attaché case as opposed to a manila envelope? (Marjorie told this to the police, also.) No, Michael replied, Marjorie was confused about that as well. Had he not once told the police that the manila envelope was brown, but told the Grand Jury it was yellow? Michael answered that he, too, made human errors, but the fact of the matter was the envelope was yellow, and if he had ever said differently, he had misspoken.

Dave Goldin, pumped up by the dramatic turn of events concerning Santa Fe Springs, made it clear during the long and heated cross-examination on other subjects that followed, just whom he had in mind when, in his opening statement at the beginning of the trial, he said he believed the evidence would reveal the identity of the real murderer. Goldin grilled Michael on the interview he had had with the Burbank P.D., reading sizable portions of that transcript into the court record.

The tone of Goldin's questions was that the overall effect of the interview showed Michael had been evasive to the point of being suspect, and that he had turned on Alan only to cast suspicion away from himself for the murder of Judy Palliko.

Goldin went on to imply that Michael himself had both the means and the motive to commit, if not the first murder, at least the second one.

Q. "What kind of gun do you carry?"

A. "I own no guns."

Q. "Have you ever carried a gun?"

A. "I have owned guns, yes. I sold them in 1961."

Apparently with a defense witness ready to contradict Michael, Goldin asked if Michael had not once attended a birthday party and, while discussing guns with Judy at the party, remarked, "Myself, I like a small .25 caliber gun because it fits in the palm of your hand and no one can see it." Michael vigorously denied having ever made that statement. He did admit that once, at Alan's request, he carried one of Alan's guns in his car because he was transporting receipts from the bar.

Goldin felt that the less reference made to Alan's alleged *mea culpa* at the Marlindo the better, and by dealing with it lightly on cross-examination, he would convey to the jury his belief that the conversation was fabricated and entitled to little of the jury's consideration.

Q. BY MR. GOLDIN: "After Alan told you this, you didn't ask any questions?"

A. "No, I didn't."

Q. "You didn't say, 'Does Sandra know about what you did?'"

A. "I said nothing."

Q. "Or 'What did you do that for?'"

A. "Uh-uh. I said nothing."

Q. "And after that, you were the best man at his wedding; right?"

A. "Correct."

Q. "You never told anybody about it?"

A. "The police."

Q. "April 30, 1968?"

A. "Yes."

Q. "On April 23, 1968, you met with Agent McNulty of the FBI, did you not?"

A. "Yes, I did."

Q. "Didn't tell him about it?"

A. "No, I did not."

The subject Goldin pursued without let-up was Michael's subservient role to Alan, and the possibility of resentment because of it.

Q. "Did you bring a girl to the (New Year's Eve) party?"

A. "Yes, I did."

Q. "Who did you bring?"

A. "I brought an Alice McKinney."

Q. "That was Alan's date, wasn't it?"

A. "I think that he had asked Miss McKinney to go to the New Year's Eve party and Mr. Palliko went to the party with a Natalie Post."

Q. "He went with another girl and you ended up driving Alice McKinney. Right?"

A. "Right."

Q. "That kind of set a pattern, didn't it?"

And then later:

Q. "What was the nature of your work for Alan?"

A. "A bar manager."

Q. "That is the only work you ever did for Alan? It was a continuous period of running errands; isn't that right?"

A. "Uh-huh."

Q. "You'd get his cleaning?"

A. "Yes."

Q. "Do his shopping?"

A. "Partially. Sometimes."

Q. "Get his car washed?"

A. "Correct."

Q. "And you chauffeured his girls around?"

A. "On occasion."

Q. "During this period of time you really didn't go out with girls, did you?"

A. "Not frequently."

Q. "And the girls you did go out with were girls you met through Alan; isn't that right?"

A. "Not necessarily, no."

Michael's face was beginning to grow flushed.

Q. "Whenever you went out on dates, Alan would pick up the bill; isn't that right?"

A. "When I went with Mr. Palliko, correct."

Q. "He was in the limelight and you were the follower. Right?"

A. "No."

Q. "Didn't you feel that other people looked at you as his errand boy?"

A. "No."

Q. "Didn't Debbi Fox look at you as his errand boy?"

A. "No."

Goldin had not been oblivious to who walked into court during the trial with whom, either.

Q. "What is your present address?"

A. "1255 South Orange Street in Glendale."

Q. "And that is the same address as Katherine Drummond?"

A. "Correct."

Q. "You came to court together today?"

A. "Yes, sir, we rode down together."

Q. "And you pick her up every day you come to court and bring her. Right?"

A. "This is correct."

Michael explained that it was Alan, not he, who had suggested Michael move to that apartment building a year and a half earlier, but I doubt the explanation did much to mitigate Goldin's implications. The growing friendship between Michael and Katherine simply did not look good.

Goldin went on to the subject of Alan's accusing Michael of embezzlement from the Grand Duke Bar.

Q. "You went around making up stories about Alan after that; isn't that true?"

A. "I did not, no. It is not true."

Q. "You went around telling people he was a homosexual."

A. "No, sir."

As a matter of trial strategy, I try to make as few objections in a jury trial as possible. By constantly interrupting proceedings, one can only irritate the jury that must sit there in weary forebearance. Moreover, if the jury concludes from a prosecutor's objections that he is trying, by technicalities, to keep out relevant evidence, this has to hurt him in the eyes of the jury, and rightly so. On the last line of questioning, however, I simply had to approach the bench and ask Goldin to make an offer of proof before proceeding any further. Goldin assured Judge Young that he was asking the questions in good faith and that he would produce witnesses who could testify to Michael's alleged behind-the-back vilification of Alan.

If there had been any doubt that Goldin was gradually getting around to accusing Michael of Judy's murder, by the end of his initial cross-examination, he had made his intentions abundantly clear.

Q. "When Alan started getting involved with Judy that sort of aced you out, didn't it?"

A. "No, sir."

Q. "He didn't need you anymore as an errand boy; isn't that right?"

A. "I don't think I can logically answer that question."

Q. "Didn't you feel that your position with Alan was no longer going to be the same?"

A. "No."

Q. "Didn't you resent Judy?"

A. "No, I did not."

Q. "You and Judy didn't get along very well, did you?"

A. "We got along fine."

Q. "She didn't like you, did she?"

A. "She didn't tell me."

In the course of questioning Michael about his dating of Alan's ex-girlfriends, Goldin had made a tactical error. He brought up the dispute between Alan and Michael concerning Debbi Fox and implied that the dispute had essentially been over a love triangle. The real reason for the ill-feeling between the two men at that time had stemmed of course from Alan's expropriation of the $4,700 of insurance money from Debbi, not a love triangle. Alan was not emotionally attached to Debbi in the least by that time. Since the incident was unrelated to the charges against Alan, I would not normally have been able to probe the matter. Because Goldin had opened the lid of that Pandora's Box on cross-examination, however, I had the right to open the box the rest of the way on redirect.

I had Michael relate for the jury how Alan had Debbi cover her ears for a moment and then suggested to Michael that they dump her over the balcony and call it a suicide.

Dave Goldin almost knocked his briefcase off the table as he stormed to the bench.

MR. GOLDIN: "I move for a mistrial! This is so prejudicial at this point to bring in threats to other people—"

MR. BUGLIOSI: "Don't bring these subjects up on cross-examination, Dave. You're getting a very expensive lesson in the law here."

I gave Judge Young two reasons I felt the testimony was completely proper. One, I had the right to show the jury that Alan's and Michael's dispute over Debbi was not a love triangle. And secondly, because earlier in the trial Goldin had brought out the fact that Alan was constantly making large deposits to his bank account, I wanted the jury to know that every one of those deposits was explainable (in this case, the money coming from Debbi), that Alan had no mysterious source of income that would account for his deposits around the very same times Sandra received her insurance checks. Judge Young denied Goldin's motion for a mistrial in no uncertain terms.

THE COURT: "It is unfortunate, but you cannot open the box on cross-examination and then simply close it."

The testimony stood. (Debbi Fox would later take the stand and corroborate Michael's version of the insurance incident. Obviously protective of Alan, however—perhaps even in love with him still, though she was married to another—she denied having ever heard Alan use the names Tiger and Sandra in the phone conversation she had overheard and had later related to the police.)

It was for the end of Terry Callas' cross-examination of Brockington that he had saved *his* key question.

Q. "Mr. Brockington, when Alan Palliko told you he killed Henry Stockton, did he say Sandra was associated with him in any way in this?"

A. "No."

Sandra Stockton allowed herself a moment's hopeful look at the jury.

My headaches had only begun that week. I was told by a reliable source whose identity I cannot divulge that Alan Palliko, back in his jail cell, was privately admitting to the first murder, but categorically denying having killed his wife, Judy. An accused person making a denial is nothing new. When the denial, however, is coupled with an admission on a second charge—a charge of murder, no less—that is another story.

That evening I spent in my study, staring absently at law volumes on the shelves. The old Fifth Canon of Ethics of the American Bar Association reads: "The primary duty of a lawyer engaged in public prosecution is not to convict, but to see that justice is done."

Was it possible I was actually prosecuting the wrong man for Judy's murder? Moreover, were the jury to convict Alan, the difference between it being on one or two murder counts could also mean the difference between life imprisonment or death.

Bringing me a cup of coffee, Gail sat down across the desk from me.

"I had hoped you'd never be confronted with a situation like this, honey."

"I've always been down on DA's who throw the book at people without being sure," I said, tossing a paper clip at the wastebasket. "What happened, Buttons? Somewhere along the line, did I become one of those guys?"

6

WHAT ALAN WAS saying in private had me emotionally hamstrung and wavering in my belief that I could sincerely proceed with the prosecution on the second murder count. I decided there was only one possible course of action to try to resolve the matter. I called Dave Goldin at home over the weekend and told him I wanted to offer Alan the opportunity to take a polygraph examination. The questions on the test would involve only the second murder count, not the first. Because the results of lie detector tests cannot be introduced in court, Alan had nothing to lose. It was an open invitation for him to convince me and, in turn, my superiors in the District Attorney's office that he was innocent of his wife's murder. I had not yet begun to present evidence on the second murder charge, and I promised that if Alan passed the examination I would request that that charge be dropped. Dave said he would relay the message to Alan and get back to me before Monday morning's court session.

Dave called me at my office early Monday morning to tell me that Alan had refused my offer. I had my answer. There was only one reason Alan would have refused—having been a policeman and no doubt familiar with the usual accuracy of the polygraph when it is administered by a competent operator, he knew he could not "beat the box."

Several reasons occurred to me as to why Alan might have, while privately admitting to Henry's murder, still insisted to his confidant that he had not killed Judy. One was that he might have been able to admit to the murder of a man but not of a woman, let alone his own wife. Or perhaps with the distorted logic of an Alan Palliko, it was even possible for him to claim that he "did not kill Judy" merely because he had not been the one to actually pull the trigger.

In any event, I now had a restored confidence that I had been right all along about Alan's guilt in the second murder, and it was a tremendous relief. That Monday morning in court there was nothing new on Alan's confident face. He gave me a brief but polite smile and nodded a hello.

Knowing the defense intended to call attorney Roy Marchetta to testify to the critical date he sent Sandra her share of the National Life proceeds—August 29, 1967, a week *after* Michael Brockington claimed Alan picked up his money in Santa Fe Springs—I continued in my effort to shave decibels by calling him as my own witness. When he testified he sent Sandra her check for $17,677 on that August 29, after having deducted his legal fees, I doubted that more than a few jurors immediately grasped the enormous significance of the date, being inundated with so many dates and events as they were. I knew, however, that before the defense finished their final summations, each and every one of the jurors would be almost as familiar with August 29 as his own birthday.

About all I was able to elicit from Marchetta which was helpful to the prosecution was the fact of his longstanding relationship with Alan and his admission it was Alan who had referred Sandra to him. The implication I would proffer in my summation was that Alan felt it would be much less likely Sandra would ever think about turning state's evidence and testifying against him if she were represented by a friend of his.

Although the detectives, Guy and St. John, had done a thorough job of tracing Alan's and Sandra's funds back in February of '67 (when Sandra had received her first insurance check), surprisingly they had made absolutely no investigation of what Sandra had done with the money from National Life.

I had telephoned Glen Reed at Security First National in Downey and inquired about Sandra's account during the months of August and September, 1967. On the stand, Reed testified that on August 31, two days after Sandra had received her National Life money via the check from Roy Marchetta, she deposited the $17,677 check in her bank. She put $13,177 in her savings account, $1,000 in her checking account, and took away with her $3,500 in *cash*. Subsequent withdrawals were made as follows: $7,500 in cash September 8; $300 in cash September 15; and $5,377 in cash September 22.

With Brockington's Santa Fe Springs debacle still hanging over the prosecution's case, I proceeded to call two more witnesses on the first murder charge who could testify to Alan's financial activities in the fall of 1967, just after Sandra had received her money from National Life: Howard Koebrick, to Alan's having sought a loan from him during much of 1967, but to having told him in early September that he now had his own money and no longer needed the loan, and to Alan's, in fact, furnishing him with $5,000 to purchase the cashier's check payable to Alan for the phony loan; and Katherine Drummond, for her testimony that after having difficulty getting Alan to dole out even $25 every two weeks in lieu of a formal alimony agreement, Alan gave her close to $400 in money and gifts in late August and early September, 1967.

The most probable area of incriminating activity around the time Sandra received her National Life proceeds, however, was void. Other than Alan's September 15 deposit of $3,500 from the $5,000 cashier's check purchased by Howard Koebrick, there were no meaningful deposits or withdrawals from Alan's bank account during this period.

My last witness on the first murder was Mr. William Gardner, Henry's supervisor at Sears. His testimony was very brief, but it said a lot. Gardner poignantly described Henry as an "easygoing, hardworking fellow," a man so docile he never once in nine years of work had sharp words with anyone. Gardner's testimony showed the jury the great unlikelihood that anyone other than Alan and Sandra had any reason or motive to kill Henry Stockton.

The testimony on the first murder count concluded, Terry Callas asked Judge Young if Sandra could be excused from the courtroom during the trial on the second murder count. Callas did not want his client even in the jury's sight when the evidence, much of it quite ugly, began coming in against Alan for Judy's murder. I expressed my belief that the request, although unusual, had merit, but Young asked Callas to find points and authorities for such a decision. Terry could find none, and Young ruled that Sandra would have to remain seated at the defense table. As prescribed by law, however, Young did give the jury emphatic instructions that the evidence that was to follow in the trial was to be received only against Alan Palliko, and was to play no part in their deliberations on whether Sandra Stockton was guilty or not guilty of Henry's murder.

The evidence against Alan on the attempted murder charge took only two hours. I could have called in doctors and the arresting officers, but I did not deem even that necessary. Nothing could have been more convincing to the jury than Katherine's own testimony and the pictures taken of her at the hospital.

When Katherine retook the stand in that fifth week of the trial, there was little doubt she was telling the incident sincerely and just as she remembered it. Her voice quivered at times; her hands squeezed the armrests of the witness chair. Showing her the photographs taken at the hospital was a procedure I unfortunately had to go through in order to verify they were a "fair and accurate representation" of her. When I handed Katherine the pictures, her hand sprang to her mouth as she gasped, "Oh my . . ." She had to turn away, and a short recess was needed for her to recompose herself. The second time out I shuffled them before her eyes as quickly as I could, and Katherine merely nodded.

Some eight years later, in the writing of this book, I reviewed those pictures. At first I could not even clearly discern who the woman was. The entire face was swollen, the facial bone having been broken in three places. The head was lacerated; dried blood revealed where it had been dripping from the mouth and ears. Sickened, I remember putting the pictures down and searching for others, thinking I had mistakenly taken out the coroner's pictures of Judy Palliko. It was an easy mistake to have made.

In a soft, at times almost inaudible voice, Katherine testified to her returning home from her Eastern Star meeting on June 25, 1966, of stopping to pick Alan up a block from their apartment, and of his immediate attack upon her. The few times Katherine let go of the witness chair's armrests were to demonstrate the way Alan had pulled her across the VW's front seats and started to choke her.

MISS DRUMMOND: "Then he pulled me out of the car and my head hit the cement when I landed. And then he took my head and just beat it against the pavement, the back of my head."

Katherine looked over at Alan, but he did not return her glance.

"I tried screaming again and he started hitting me with his fists . . . in the head and in the face and in the chest. And then he got me up from the ground and tried to push me back in the car, and I was . . . I just knew if he got me in the car he'd kill me then for sure. And I grabbed hold of the top of the car and I held on for dear life.

"Then he took my head and just beat it against the car." Katherine threw her head to the side several times, against an imaginary car frame next to the witness stand. I could see an anger flowing into her cheeks as she demonstrated—and remembered. She testified that sometimes she still had pain on the left side of her head.

I asked if she was wearing her wedding ring the night of the beating.

A. "Yes, sir. It wasn't in those pictures. They had to cut it off."

Most important of all was Alan's own admission to Katherine when he came to see her in the hospital.

MISS DRUMMOND: "He said he was surprised I looked as well as I did, that he had hit me harder than he had ever hit any man in his life. He said that he was trying to kill me."

Dave Goldin, wisely, did not go after Katherine with any kind of aggressive cross-examination. About the only point he sought in his very brief questioning was that Alan had been under the influence of alcohol, the implication being that Alan therefore was not completely responsible for his actions. It was the only time in the trial that Katherine, always very proper, acquired a tart edge to her voice.

Q. "Did he tell you that he had been drinking?"

A. "Yes, he told me he had been drinking."

Q. "Could you tell he had been drinking?"

A. "Well, I really didn't stop to take notice of that while he was beating me, Mr. Goldin."

The sum of evidence on the attempted murder count concluded, Judge Young adjourned court early that afternoon for the ten-day Christmas recess.

It was impossible to enjoy the Christmas holidays. Brockington's testimony on the Santa Fe Springs incident was so damaging to his credibility, and therefore to our chances for a conviction on the first murder count, that it was beyond my power to stay away from the office over those holidays. It was the gravity of two murders that pulled me from bed to the deserted Hall of Justice every morning and did not release me until late every night. The telephone became a part of my body.

Brockington's testimony concerning the date of the Santa Fe Springs trip simply could not be left standing.

Since Brockington had mentioned the Santa Fe Springs trip to Marjorie Huebner, I wondered if he had not also mentioned it to Debbi Fox, with whom he had been much closer. I phoned Debbi over the Christmas recess and asked if Michael had ever told her about it. He had—the day it had occurred.

The crucial question I had for Debbi was when did her conversation with Michael take place? She told me it had to have been after August 29 (the date Sandra received her National Life Insurance proceeds) because August 29 was the day Alan and she broke up (although she had moved out of Alan's apartment two weeks earlier), and it was within a day or two after the break-up that she started dating Michael. Debbi was certain it was after August 29 that Michael told her about the trip to Santa Fe Springs for one very clear reason: before her August 29 break-up, she had never, except for the party where she had first met Michael, talked with Michael outside of Alan's presence.

A problem in court I could foresee was Debbi's credibility. She had already, for example, given three different dates for when she had moved in with Alan, (June 1, July 1, and the correct one, July 24), the two mistaken dates given in two separate police interviews. Debbi, I was sorry to discover, was what even Michael once described as "the original dumb blonde." With the exception of Michael and Katherine, Alan seemed to have made a habit of surrounding himself with people whom he could intellectually tower over—Del Cook, Debbi, Tod Glenn, and even Sandra being only the start of the list.

But allowing for Debbi's questionable astuteness, I still had reason to give weight to her memory of the Santa Fe Springs incident. Debbi was a helpless romantic, the kind of woman who would remember to her dying day the date she broke up with the man she loved and wanted to marry. She could not have been more certain that it was August 29. She even recalled accurately (I verified it later) what day of the week it was, a Tuesday.

Just because I believed Debbi about this one point, however, did not mean a jury would. She was not what could be termed an unimpeachable witness. To prove Michael Brockington wrong about his dates, I needed corroboration.

It has always been my practice to give long study to the trial transcript pages, where I often find the solution to a problem in a case. When court is in session, I have to stay late at the office until that day's transcripts have been typed, usually around 6:30, and then take them home to read. Over the Christmas recess in the Palliko-Stockton trial, however, I had the time I needed to study those pages even more carefully, and to reflect on what had already been said in court.

The portion of Michael Brockington's testimony that particularly caught my eye was his description of the day that Alan and he drove out to Santa Fe Springs. The weather, Michael had testified, was "extremely hot." The car's air conditioning, he said, had been "on maximum—at full capacity." I phoned Dave Correa, one of our DA investigators, and asked him to get me copies of Los Angeles' weather reports for August and September of 1967. The next morning, Correa delivered the climatological data sheets published by the U.S. Department of Commerce. On August 22 and 23, the temperature in L.A. had been eighty-five degrees. August 24 was eighty-eight degrees, August 25 was eighty-five degrees. Certainly that is warm, but not what most Angelenos would describe, especially in summer, as "extremely hot." On August 30, on the other hand, the mercury in L.A. had soared to one hundred degrees. August 31, it was one hundred and three degrees, and September 1, it was again one hundred degrees. Now that *is* "extremely hot."

I phoned Michael and asked him to elaborate on his description of the day for me. What exactly had he meant by "extremely hot?"

"Oh, a hundred degrees easy," he answered. I then informed him of my discovery, but it did not change his mind about the date of the trip. An awfully proud man, I thought, but one with integrity.

I had not conclusively solved the problem, but I at least was now armed with solid evidence that Brockington may have been making a good faith mistake on the dates. I continued to investigate the subject over that Christmas recess, and as I did so, matters, as Lewis Carroll once wrote, became "curiouser and curiouser."

Although detectives Guy and St. John had opened up the Bank of America safe deposit box which Alan had kept under Michael Brockington's name, and had found nothing significant in it, they had not checked the dates of entry into the box by Alan.

I drove over to the Sunset-Echo Park branch of the Bank of America and spoke with the operations officer, Mrs. Rose Owen. Although the actual contents placed into or taken out of a safe deposit box are never recorded, the *dates* on which the box is entered are.

The bank's records revealed that although a man purporting to be Michael Brockington opened up a deposit box on August 25, 1967, no entry was made in the box that day. It came as no shock to me that the first entry was made on September 1, that one-hundred-degree day in Los Angeles which just happened to be one day after Sandra had deposited her settlement money and had left her bank with $3,500 in cash. The two other dates that entries were made in the Bank of America safe deposit box were September 22 and October 5. September 22 was the date Sandra had withdrawn $5,377 in cash from her own bank account.

When Mrs. Owen showed me the safe deposit box application, I had to smile. On the line for mother's maiden name was written: "Walther."

The next day I walked over to the LAPD and showed a photostat of the application to Sergeant Robert Smith, the handwriting expert. I asked him to compare the writing of the names "Walther" and "Michael Brockington" with Alan Palliko's writing exemplar. There was no doubt in Sgt. Smith's mind. The writing was identical.

The Bank of America attendant who signed the entry cards was a Patricia Wasilewski. The attendant is the employee who always checks the safe deposit box number with the number on the key that the customer brings in, then goes back into the vault to open up the box for the customer. Miss Wasilewski was no longer working at the bank, but I had little trouble finding her at her new place of employment, United States Steel in Los Angeles.

Miss Wasilewski picked Alan out from a series of pictures I showed her, and stated that on one of his trips in she had watched him remove a packet of cash from the box. I asked how she could be so sure of Alan's face, so sure that he was the man claiming to be Michael Brockington. The answer was interesting, for it revealed Alan had once again done it to himself. She remembered Alan because he had been such a flirt with her.

When the court reconvened January 2, 1969, I informed Judge Young of my holiday recess discoveries and asked that the prosecution's case on Count I be allowed to be reopened. Young granted the request. Ironically (perhaps), Terry Callas, his client back in the thick of testimony, came down with a bad case of flu that afternoon, and we had to take an immediate recess again until the following Monday, January 6.

After my DA investigator, Dave Correa, testified to the climatological reports for the late August, early September, 1967 period he had researched, I called Debbi Fox to the stand. As centerfold Debbi purled her way up the aisle, one male spectator was heard to whisper, "Jesus." A smug grin on his face, Alan Palliko folded his arms across his chest. Sandra Stockton tugged her lips to the side in disgust.

Debbi reiterated for the jury what she had related to me over the holiday recess. Neither Goldin nor Callas was able to break down Debbi's reason for knowing the trip to Santa Fe Springs had taken place after August 29, but Goldin, as expected, had little trouble showing she was something less than reliable when it came to remembering dates in general.

After Debbi, I called: Rose Owen, to testify to the dates of entry into the safe deposit box; Patricia Wasilewski, who identified Alan as the man who entered the box on the subject dates, purporting to be Michael Brockington; and Sergeant Robert Smith for the handwriting comparison.

The Christmas recess investigation had reaped handsome dividends. Although I had had to impeach my own star witness' memory as to an important date in the process, I had, far more significantly, offered weighty evidence that the trip to Santa Fe Springs *had* taken place, that it had taken place only one or two days *after* Sandra had received her money from National Life, and that by Alan's subsequent, secretive handling of his share of the money, all that cash reeked of conspiracy.

Even as the trial was seven weeks old, and testimony on the first murder count nearly concluded, Burbank detectives were still out in the field continuing their investigation of the murder of Judy Palliko. Lieutenant Vandergrift and Detective Strickland had picked up scuttlebutt at the Grand Duke that one of Alan's former barmaids, a Paula Boudreau, had been telling friends of some incriminating statements Alan had made to her a week before Judy's murder. The morning of January 7, 1969, while I was in court questioning the final witnesses on the first murder, Vandergrift and Strickland were interviewing Mrs. Boudreau at her home in North Hollywood.

Paula Boudreau was extremely reluctant to speak with the detectives. When asked if she had not confided to several friends that a week before Judy's murder Alan had told her that within two weeks she would see how "short life could be," Mrs. Boudreau denied having ever said that to anyone. She did relate, however, how on the night of the murder she and her husband, Thomas, went to County General Hospital to see if they could be of some help to Alan. When they walked into the waiting room Alan was sitting there with his head in his hands. Alan took his hands away and looked up at them, Mrs. Boudreau told the detectives, and at that instant, she said, she felt sure Alan was involved. "His look gave him away," she told Vandergrift and Strickland.

It was just moments later, she added, that Alan had pounded the table and declared, "I know who did it!"

Although Paula Boudreau was clearly jittery throughout the interview, periodically interjecting that she had said all that she knew, Vandergrift and Strickland would not let up. Their persistence paid off. Mrs. Boudreau eventually admitted knowing a good deal more.

Alan, she said, asked her to write thank you cards for him to the friends who had sent condolences. The evening of Tuesday, April 30, 1967, ten days after Judy's murder, she went to the Grand Duchess to pick up a list from Alan of the people he wanted cards sent to. She arrived at the bar just after Alan had been arrested and taken down to the County Jail. While she was still at the bar, another barmaid, Janet Turnbull, received a call from Alan, who was apparently phoning from jail. Mrs. Boudreau stated she saw Janet, while talking on the phone, write ".22 caliber" on a notepad and circle it. After hanging up, Janet asked the bar manager, Pete Morris, to go with her to the Castillian Apartments, supposedly only to move the Jaguar off the street.

Paula Boudreau added that Judy had always seemed in love with Alan, but was also lonely in a way. She had never been given reason to think Judy was afraid of Alan.

At last, Mrs. Boudreau opened up all the way for Vandergrift and Strickland, but she demanded that the rest of what she had to say was to be "strictly off the record." She stated that a week before the murder she had been out with Alan, helping him look for and interview new barmaids. When they stopped for coffee, Alan made a pass at her which she simply ignored. Then, she said, not sure as to how he started the conversation, Alan began talking about gun collecting and people who hired others to kill for them. He drew three circles on a napkin and connected them with two lines, telling her that that was how people got caught. Then drawing two unconnected circles, one at the top of the napkin and one at the bottom, he stated that the way people got away with such things was to make sure there was no middle-person connection.

Mrs. Boudreau told the investigators she was afraid for her life and for the lives of her family, her young son in particular. Only a week earlier, while working tables at the Surfside Bar, she had been paid a visit by Alan's friend and employee, Gus Pilich. Pulling her aside, Pilich told her he had heard she was thinking of talking to the district attorney and testifying.

"I like you a lot, Paula. I'd hate to see you get hurt," Pilich had said, straight out of a late night movie.

Mrs. Boudreau now told Vandergrift and Strickland that Alan had said to her that within two weeks she would see how "cold and cruel" life could be, and that "some things just have to happen." By the end of her interview with the detectives, however, she became panicked that she had already said far too much, and out of the most transparent desperation, added that she interpreted Alan's statement to mean he was going to sell one of his bars soon, thus laying off several employees.

When Paula Boudreau saw Lieutenant Vandergrift still taking notes at their conversation's end, she just shook her head and said, "I won't repeat a word of this from the stand. No way."

January 10, 1969

Dear Kyle,

Grandma tells me I'll be getting a letter from you soon. Needless to say, I can hardly wait. Guess Grandma has been keeping you up to date on what's happening in court each day. This all seems to be taking so long, I know, but on the other hand we wouldn't want them to rush it, either. I wish I could tell you that when the trial is over I'll be home. But there is the possibility I won't. I know how hard that is to face, but face it we must. We must be able to face facts. I want you to be aware of the possibilities of the ways this could go. If mama does have to go away for even a longer period of time, you can bet I will do all I can to see you first before then. Like I did at the beginning of all this, remember?

My love is with you.

Your mama

7

AT EVERY RECESS, Judge Young, as is the custom, repeated an exact set of words for the jury: "Ladies and gentlemen, we will now take a recess with the admonition to not discuss this case among yourselves or with anyone else, nor to form or express any opinion on the case until it is submitted to you." Not to discuss a case until it is concluded is an important and certainly obeyable command; not to even begin to form a private opinion, however, is just not in the scheme of human nature. The second part of the judge's admonition, an attempt to hold back the wind with a fish net, brings a cynical yawn to the courtroom regulars.

As we started in on the evidence of the second murder charge, I obviously would have liked a glimpse at the jurors' inchoate thoughts about Count I of the indictment. There was little doubt in my mind that if the jury were not inclined to convict Alan and Sandra for Henry's murder, the count in which we had the greater amount of evidence, it was highly unlikely they would convict Alan for the murder of Judy.

The evidence surrounding Judy Palliko's murder was not just circumstantial, it was dismally circumstantial. There were no fingerprints, no murder weapon ever found, no eyewitnesses to place Alan at the scene, and, in fact, three witnesses who placed him elsewhere. Moreover, there was a respected insurance salesman, Jack Dodd, who maintained Alan had had to be badgered into taking a policy out on his wife's life, as well as a string of witnesses, friends of Alan's, who would give testimony on other points that would support Alan's claim of innocence. I did not doubt for an instant that many of them were committing perjury, but to prove to a jury that so many people lied can be a very difficult task. Destroying the credibility of a key witness certainly can sometimes help in destroying the credibility of the others, indeed the credibility of an entire defense, but the question is: how does one get even one of those witnesses to fall?

Unlike their fictional counterparts in novels and on the screen who cave in under the pressure of the third good question, real witnesses exhibit a remarkable doughtiness. When all but trapped, and at the brink of a public, courtroom humiliation, human beings seem to suddenly secrete a type of mental adrenalin that gets their minds working almost as speedily as Houdini's hands used to move in a trunk at the bottom of the Hudson. Textbooks on the art of cross-examination, wherein classic, courtroom cross-examinations compiled throughout the years are presented, reveal that even the most piercing cross-examination rarely, if ever, completely destroys a witness. At best, the witness is only hurt, not demolished.

Alan Palliko's life during the year and a half following Henry Stockton's murder was not impenetrable to scrutiny. It was as colorful and loud as a parade. Parties, sporty cars, expensive apartments, newly acquired businesses, evenings on the town—and all of it, like many a Southern California parade, in a hollow worship of the beautiful women who got to ride on top, at least for a while.

Many of my witnesses who testified on the first murder count were now recalled to the witness stand to give testimony on the second murder. When I recalled Debbi Fox to the stand, I had the feeling that while she was still a little protective of Alan, she was becoming progressively more willing to tell what she knew. Perhaps after being a spectator during part of the evidence on Count I, she was beginning to think Alan was, just maybe, not the syndicate-trapped, misunderstood man he had represented himself to be.

Debbi testified to the "plan" Alan had talked about in August of 1967, the plan which he said would take place the following March or April and would leave him either "rich or dead."

March or April, Alan had said. Judy Palliko was murdered April 20.

Q. BY MR. BUGLIOSI: "Did he mention the word 'newspapers' to you?"

A. "Well, jokingly he said, 'You might see me in the newspapers.'"

Q. "While you were living with Mr. Palliko, did you get the impression that he was concerned about money?"

A. "Yes."

Q. "How concerned?"

A. "Very concerned. He was always talking about it."

Q. "He seemed preoccupied with it?"

A. "Yes."

Q. "Did he indicate what he needed the money for?"

A. "He wanted to start a business . . . he said he would like to be set up for life."

When I asked Debbi about Alan's vague promises to marry her, she related his eventual discouragement of the idea and his telling her he was involved with the "wrong type of people," that it would be dangerous for anyone to be married to him.

Because attorneys cannot go into subjects on cross-examination that are not brought up on direct, Goldin asked Judge Young if he could make Debbi his own witness for a single important question. Young granted the request. Goldin's question concerned Alan's explanation to her as to why he had been dismissed from the LAPD. Debbi answered that Alan had found his wife in bed with another man and that he had, in the course of a fight, thrown the man out the window, killing him. In her naive, little girl voice she added, "But he wasn't accused because it was self-defense in some way or another."

With that, Goldin had managed to tie up the point he had initiated earlier in the trial, the point that was crucial to Alan's defense.

Alan was just a storyteller.

To demonstrate to the jury just how actively and singlemindedly Alan had pursued his plan to find a woman to marry, I called the three to whom Alan had proposed and were still alive to tell about it. My first such witness, Marjorie Huebner, testified to Alan's having proposed marriage to her after only their third date.

Marjorie is a gutsy woman, and at no time did she appear afraid of testifying against Alan. Her determination was no doubt bolstered by the suspicion that during all of that sweet talk, Alan had perhaps been assessing her, too, as an ideal victim.

As he did with Debbi, Goldin brought out, on cross-examination of Marjorie, Alan's phony story to her of having killed his wife's suitor. Goldin, no doubt, would also have liked to introduce through other witnesses the fact that Alan told them he had "nine hits" to

238 : *TILL DEATH US DO PART*

his credit. There was only one problem for Dave with that particular story, however—he had no way of proving Alan had not killed nine people.

Immediately after Marjorie, I recalled Katherine Drummond for her testimony that she too had received proposals of marriage from Alan during late 1967 and early 1968. Barbara Gutman would later testify that Alan had proposed to her once during this same period as well.

With Katherine, however, the proposals were many. As late as January, 1968, Alan popped the question one last time. That would have been approximately three weeks before he proposed to Judy Davis. Because Alan's and Katherine's divorce was final in early November, 1967, their conversations after that point were no longer protected by marital privilege. Katherine therefore was permitted to testify to Alan's having told her, after she turned down his last offer of marriage, that he was going to do something again he did not want to do, but that he was involved with the wrong type of people and she would probably be reading about him in the papers.

I could not help being struck by Alan Palliko's ability to objectify and disengage himself from the circumstances of his own life, to excuse what he was about to do as if he had no control over his actions, to talk about himself the way a mother might excuse a son who took a wrong turn in life. Just as he had insisted to Katherine that any prejudices or other distasteful values he held as an adult were his parents' doing, not his, he disclaimed responsibility for his own wrong acts, even the act of murder.

Not only was Alan going to do something, he had said, but he was going to do it *again*. Perhaps because they did not want to risk having that phrase repeated, Callas and Goldin chose not to cross-examine Katherine.

Out in the hallway at the next recess, Mrs. Davis, with tears flooding her eyes, clutched Katherine's arm.

"If someone had only told us. Maybe we could have done something to stop the marriage . . . kidnapped Judy . . . anything."

Suddenly, in the very middle of the trial, a piece of information significantly damaging to the defense on the second murder count found its way into my office. Katherine had apparently been talking to friends of hers, Steven and Jill Stone, about the case and about their mutual friend, Jack Dodd. Dodd had become a friend of the Stones' through Alan and Katherine and had, in fact, sold them their own family insurance. Steven Stone, a fire inspector for the city of Beverly Hills, and his wife, Jill, knew Dodd was going to testify that he had to virtually twist Alan's arm into taking out a policy on Judy, but the Stones had information of their own about that intended testimony.

During the summer of 1968, while Alan was in jail awaiting trial, Jack Dodd had visited the Stones and in the course of conversation had stated his intention of doing anything he could to help Alan. According to both Steven and Jill Stone, he told them he was well aware of Alan's hatred for blacks, and that he did not really like Alan, but he was determined to show Alan that a black man could be counted on as a friend when all others had deserted him. What did Dodd mean by this, I wondered. That he intended to commit perjury for Alan?

After interviewing the Stones myself, I immediately added their names to my list of witnesses.

Jack Dodd had a solid background. Having received his B.A. from UCLA, where he majored in psychology, he went on to do postgraduate work in psychology at Cal State, began but did not complete law school at Southwestern Law School, and eventually became a parole agent in the narcotics division for the state of California. Married and with two sons, he augmented his income by selling insurance part time for the Equitable Life Assurance Society. Dodd was highly respected, we had discovered, at both his insurance company and with the California Department of Corrections.

The only written statement of Dodd's with which I had to work was his memo to his superiors at Equitable. In it he stated: "Alan Palliko at no time solicited life insurance on Judy. Secondly, in my opinion, he would rather not have had her insured. Thirdly, from what I know about the man, I do not see him as capable of committing such a dastardly crime. Considering the fact that I am an Equitable underwriter, I am certainly concerned that the company not pay claims based on the acts of wrongdoers. I am also concerned that just claims be paid and that no client of mine become a victim of circumstances. Legally, regarding the criminal act involved, the courts will make a just decision. Although I am neither judge nor jury, I feel that Alan Palliko is innocent and will be exonerated of this charge."

And *my* feeling was that Jack Dodd was lying. The detectives, who had spoken with Dodd, felt even more strongly about this than I. Only after I had talked with the Stones had a reason been given me why he might lie.

Two days after my conversation with Steven and Jill Stone, I asked Michael Brockington to come to my office one last time to ascertain if there was any other possible information he possessed that could help us in our case against Alan and Sandra. He said there was nothing else, that he had told the police and me everything he knew. Casually, and not expecting an affirmative answer, I asked him if he knew anything about the insurance on Judy's life, mentioning to him how Dodd claimed he practically had to force Judy's policy on Alan. Michael pulled his head back and looked at me as though we were talking about two different cases.

"But that isn't at all the way the sale happened," he said. "I ought to know. I was there."

"You were *what?*" I said, tossing my pen on the desk. Both the police and I had simply assumed Michael knew nothing of the circumstances surrounding the insurance sale. I listened intently to his version of the incident. *But that isn't at all the way the sale happened,* had been an understatement. As he finished telling me about that night back in February, 1968, I already had the phone cradled on my shoulder. The court clerk was to add another name, Michael Brockington, to my list of witnesses on the second murder count. And there was another change needed as well. In the back of my mind a strategy was brewing. Before putting Brockington back on the stand, I first wanted Jack Dodd to irretrievably commit himself on the witness stand with his claim that no one, aside from Alan and Judy, was present during the insurance transaction. Dodd was already scheduled to testify for the defense. Wanting to control Dodd as a witness (i.e., not wanting to be limited on cross-examination to those matters brought up by the defense on direct), the next day I subpoenaed Dodd. Dodd was informed that he was needed in court earlier than anticipated—he was being called to the stand not by the defense, but by the prosecution.

Dave Goldin, knowing I intended to cross-examine Dodd, objected strongly to my being able to do so with my own witness. I argued to Judge Young that Dodd was a close friend of Alan's, that he had refused to give the police a written statement—in essence, that he was a hostile witness to the prosecution, and that under the California Evidence Code I therefore had the right to cross-examine him (i.e., ask leading, more aggressive questions) even though I had been the one to call him to the stand. Young concurred with me, and for three days, on and off, Jack Dodd sat on the stand while he and I went at it.

As old and venerable as the history of jurisprudence, cross-examination has been the principal weapon known to the law for separating truth from falsehood, actual knowledge from hearsay, fact from imagination and opinion; it is the best technique, as one legal scholar wrote, "for reducing exaggerated statements to their true dimensions." Professor John Henry Wigmore, acknowledged to be the foremost authority on the law of evidence, called cross-examination "beyond any doubt the greatest legal engine ever invented for the discovery of truth." Advocate-scholars like the famed trial lawyer, Jake Ehrlich, have bemoaned "the lost art of cross-examination."

Cross-examination takes on more importance than direct examination because juries listen to it more closely. First of all, they realize that unlike direct examination, there has been no dry-run in a lawyer's office, and secondly, they find it far more interesting because of its adversary nature.

As with all other facets of a trial, the keynote to successful cross-examination is thorough preparation. But a cross-examiner, to be effective, must also have the ability to deftly improvise. The trite legal caveat, "Never ask any witness a question unless you *know* what his answer is going to be," although valid for direct examination of one's own witness, is not always valid for cross-examination. Of necessity, cross-examination oftentimes is a trek through new terrain, and experience, caution, and instinct sometimes are one's only guide.

Cross-examination is frequently meant to be exactly that—*cross*. Yet so many trial lawyers grow timid in court and, without ever coming out from behind their tables, simply stand up, and except for occasional frowns on their faces do little more than have an amicable conversation with the witness. That is not my style. I believed Jack Dodd was fabricating the circumstances of the insurance sale, and as I saw it, the way Jack Dodd, a clean-cut and articulate professional man, fared on cross-examination would be one of the determining factors on whether Alan Palliko would be convicted or acquitted on the second murder.

Q. BY MR. BUGLIOSI: "Mr. Dodd, what is your present occupation?"

A. "Parole agent, State of California, narcotics, and also life underwriter, State of California contract, Equitable Life Assurance Society."

Q. "You work part time for Equitable Life Assurance?"

A. "I wouldn't say part time. It is also my occupation. I'm self-employed."

Dodd was quite poised on the stand, sitting with his legs neatly crossed, his clasped hands resting on his lap.

Q. "When did you first meet Alan Palliko?"

A. "Oh, about 1964, I believe. We were in law school together."

Q. "While you were going to law school with Alan you became fast friends with him; is that correct?"

A. "I wouldn't say fast friends. Over a period of time we became friends, yes."

Q. "You socialized with him?"

A. "Yes."

Q. "Attended the same social gatherings?"

A. "We attended the same gatherings, yes."

Q. "On Sunday mornings you and your wife frequently would go over to his residence or he and his wife would come over to your residence and have breakfast and political discussions; is that correct?"

A. "No, that's not correct. Sunday morning he would come to *my* house. *Sometimes* we had discussions, yes."

Even on a simple question, his adversary position against the prosecution had begun to creep into his voice.

Q. "Were you present when Alan married Judy Davis?"

A. "I wasn't present when he married her. I was at the reception, yes."

Q. "Were you one of the pallbearers at Judy's funeral?"

A. "Yes, I was."

Q. "Did you make the funeral arrangements?"

A. "No, I did not."

Q. "Did Alan ask you to?"

A. "Yes, he asked me to get him a mortuary, which is what I did."

Q. "Did Alan ever call you during the year 1968 and tell you that he wanted to purchase some insurance on himself?"

A. "Yes, he did."

Q. "You did not contact him?"

A. "No, although I had contacted Alan for several months prior to his calling me."

Q. "When in '68 did Alan contact you?"

A. "I don't recall the exact date. I believe it was in February."

Q. "Did you ever make an appointment with Alan for February 22, 1968, to finalize the insurance?"

A. "Yes, I did."

Q. "Where did you meet with Alan on February 22, 1968?"

A. "At his apartment in Burbank."

Q. "And Judy Davis was present, was she not?"

A. "Yes, she was."

Q. "Was it in the evening, or afternoon, morning or what?"

A. "In the evening. Late evening."

Q. "And did Alan agree to purchase a life insurance policy on himself?"

A. "Finally, yes. I believe it was a $20,000 policy previously written but turned down by him."

Q. "Was this an ordinary life policy with a cash surrender value or was it a term policy?"

A. "Twenty payment life policy, cash values, dividends."

Q. "Now, as I understand it, Mr. Dodd, you sold Alan a policy for $20,000, and then you say you asked Alan to take out some insurance on Judy and he said no. Is that correct?"

A. "That is correct."

Q. "And then you persisted. Is that correct?"

A. "Quite a bit, yes."

Jack Dodd's eyes followed me closely as I walked back and forth slowly behind the counsel table. As a counselor of parolees and seller of insurance, he possessed a practiced, steady gaze.

Q. "What type of policy did Alan finally agree to take out on Judy Davis?"

A. "He took out a $25,000 decreasing term insurance policy, which was, by the way, the minimum that I can write in that particular policy."

Q. "Did you advise Alan to take out an ordinary life policy on Judy?"

A. "Right."

Q. "But Alan settled on a decreasing term. Is that correct?"

A. "I guess you could say he settled on it, yes."

Q. "Decreasing term insurance has no cash surrender value, is that correct?"

A. "That is correct."

Q. "And the policy premiums are considerably lower than on ordinary life policies. Is that correct?"

A. "That is correct."

Q. "Did Alan indicate to you why he wanted ordinary life for himself, but he felt a term insurance policy was good for Judy?"

A. "No. In fact, Alan indicated to me he had no interest in getting insurance on Judy. I think he did it to get me off his back."

Q. "I see. Did he actually tell you he was doing it to get you off his back?"

A. "He said he was fed up. Almost lost his friendship over it."

I paused, and with our eyes dead center on each other's, let the faintest of smiles cross my face. Jack Dodd knew as well as I that we were not nearly finished exploring the consequential implications of his "friendship" with Alan.

Q. "What was the premium on Judy's policy?"

A. "I think—let's see—I think Judy was about twenty-two years old —it should have been about $17 or $18 a quarter. Every three months."

Q. "What about Alan's policy?"

A. "$60 a month."

Q. "So Alan's policy, then, was—oh—about ten times more expensive than Judy's; is that correct?"

Dodd glanced at Alan and then back at me. He folded his arms across his chest.

A. "Well, because of age and because of the kind of policy, it was much more expensive."

Q. "Did Alan convey to you the impression that he understood a little bit about insurance?" I understated the obvious.

A. "I think that Alan understood a little bit about insurance, yes."

Q. "If a person were interested in a long-range, lifetime insurance program, you wouldn't recommend term insurance, would you, Mr. Dodd?"

A. "I would never recommend term insurance unless a man just isn't going to buy. You sell him term insurance and you come back to convert it to permanent insurance later, if you can."

Q. "Is it a fair statement, Mr. Dodd, to say that term policies are normally for a specific need that exists only for a limited period of time?"

A. "No, I wouldn't say that. I would say that a term policy is basically for the man that cannot afford other kinds of insurance."

Q. "Well, for instance, if a person wanted to purchase insurance with a cash surrender value, he wouldn't get term; right?"

A. "No, he wouldn't."

Q. "And if he wanted to purchase insurance so there would be some type of endowment for his children, he wouldn't purchase term insurance; right?"

A. "Not necessarily. It depends upon the man, depends upon what he wants, how much he wants to spend."

Q. "But you certainly would never recommend that, would you?"

A. "No, I wouldn't."

Q. "Now, by a decreasing term policy, does this mean that the longer the policyholder lives the smaller the face amount on the policy becomes?"

A. "This is correct. Each year the face amount decreases."

Q. "So looking at it from a rather morbid point of view, Mr. Dodd, on a decreasing term policy, the longer the policyholder lives the less value that policy has to the beneficiary; is that correct?"

A. "That's correct."

Q. "Other than today, have you seen Alan Palliko since he was arrested?"

A. "Yes, I've visited him in the county jail."

I was not in any way finished with the subject of the insurance sale, but when you believe a witness is lying, bouncing back and forth between subjects is one good method of catching that witness in discrepancies within his testimony. The object is to stay one step ahead, to never allow him to settle in too comfortably in one line of thought, one line of rehearsed testimony. I was now circling the courtroom, firing questions rapidly at Dodd from all directions.

Q. "How often have you visited him in the county jail?"

A. "I would say no more than three, four times, maybe. I haven't had the time, otherwise I would have been there more."

Q. "You consider Alan a very close friend of yours; is that correct?" I asked once again, to impress on the jury the probability of bias in his continuing testimony.

A. "I think you could call him a good friend, yes."

Q. "On February 22, 1968, what time of day did your discussion commence with Alan on the purchase of insurance?"

A. "I don't have the exact time. It was in the evening, maybe 6:30 or 7:00 o'clock."

Q. "And when did it terminate?"

A. "Should have been around, I'd say, 10:30, 11:00 o'clock."

Q. "So you were there for about four hours?"

A. "Could have been, yes."

Q. "Do you recall Michael Brockington being present?"

A. "No, I don't. In fact, as far as I know, Mike was not present."
Jack Dodd had just made his first big mistake.

Q. "Mr. Dodd, do you personally like Alan Palliko?"

A. "Yes, I like Alan."

Q. "You are aware of the fact that Alan is anti-black, aren't you?"

A. "Yes, I am. I am aware of the fact that he was, at least," Dodd admitted, frowning.

Q. "To your knowledge, were you the only black with whom Alan associated socially?"

A. "No, it is not correct, to my knowledge."

Q. "He associated with other blacks socially?"

A. "He may have. I don't know."

Q. "To your knowledge, you were the only black, isn't that true?"

A. "This is correct," Dodd now answered.

Q. "Is it true that Alan led you to believe that he was very much anti-black?"

A. "I don't think he could have been 'very much' anti-black. He associated with me, came to my home and I went to his home. I saw him as a man."

Q. "Well, what leads you to believe he is anti-black at all then?"

A. "Views. Political views."

Q. "What did he tell you?"

MR. GOLDIN: "Objection. Irrelevant."

THE COURT: "Overruled."

A. "There are many, many things he told me that would lead me to believe he was anti-black. Political views, the candidates he was for. I would say the same things that many other whites say and do that lead one to believe that they are anti-black."

Q. "Do you know a Mr. and Mrs. Steven Stone?"

A. "Yes, I do."

Q. "Do you recall telling them in June of 1968 that you did not like Alan Palliko, but that you would prove to him that a black could be his friend?"

A. "No, I don't have to prove that to anyone. I never said that. No."

Dodd uncrossed his legs and quickly crossed them the other way.

Q. "You categorically deny telling Mr. and Mrs. Stone that?"

A. "Yes, I do."

I was on delicate ground, accusing this man of feeling a need to be a racial martyr, but it was exactly what I believed had happened. For the moment, I lowered my voice and changed the subject.

Q. "Mr. Dodd, why did you persist, as you claim, in trying to sell Alan insurance on Judy? What was the particular reason for that?"

A. "In the business you try to sell insurance where you can."

Q. "Including to friends, I take it."

A. "Yes. Even to a friend. In fact, they are the best clients if you work with them."

Q. "In other words, you use your friends. Is that correct?"

A. "No, you never use them."

Q. "I ask you again, then. Why did you want to sell insurance to Alan on Judy's life?"

A. "I wanted to sell insurance to Judy because wives' insurance in the insurance business is big business."

Q. "In other words, you use your friends. Is that correct?"

A. "No, I do not."

I walked up and stood right next to the witness stand.

Q. "What was your reason, then, for asking Alan to take out insurance on Judy?"

A. "Please quit screaming in my ear."

I was not screaming in Jack Dodd's ear. Judge Young, in fact, asked Dodd, as politely as possible, if he had an ear problem.

Q. "I will walk away if you will give me a truthful answer."

A. "I will do that."

Q. "For the fourth time, why did you persist, as you claim, in urging upon Alan that he take out insurance on Judy?"

A. "There is a thing in the insurance business called estate planning. In estate planning with corporations, or people in business, you write insurance on the wife because once two people have married, every other property they have at that point becomes community property. The estate part has to do with taxes."

Q. "But according to you, Alan kept saying, 'No. No. No. I refuse to take out insurance on Judy.' Right?"

A. "He didn't say, 'No. No. No.'"

Q. "What did he say?"

A. "He simply said he had no need for it; he didn't want it."

Q. "And you kept on persisting. Is that correct?"

A. "Until I convinced him that he needed it, yes."

Q. "Finally he broke down and said, 'Jack, you are a very persuasive individual. You talked me into it.' Is that what he told you?"

A. "No. He finally said, 'Write it up.'"

Q. "How many times did you have to ask Alan to take out insurance on Judy?"

A. "I don't recall how many times. Numerous times."

Q. "Ten or fifteen?"

A. "May have been."

Q. "Do you normally ask people ten or fifteen times when they keep saying no? Do you normally keep telling them what they should do?"

A. "Agents sometimes work on cases for years."

Q. "Wait awhile. This is one night, sir."

A. "Okay."

Q. "One night, sir . . . when you go out to a person's residence and they say they do not want to buy insurance, do you normally keep asking them ten or fifteen times?"

A. "If necessary, if you think you can make the sale, yes."

Q. "The fact of the matter is, Mr. Dodd, when you came there that night the sale of the policy on Judy's life had already been agreed upon, and you just put out the papers there for finalization. Isn't that true?"

A. "This is not true."

MR. GOLDIN: "May we approach the bench?"

I made it to the judge's bench to meet Goldin in four strides. I was angry. The interruption by Goldin was breaking the momentum of my questioning.

MR. GOLDIN (at the bench): "That is a question that better have been asked in good faith."

MR. BUGLIOSI: "It was. I'm putting on Brockington after this. Let's get on with the trial. It was asked in good faith. Does that satisfy you? Shall we get on with the trial?"

Before Judge Young even had a chance to comment, Goldin and I were stalking back to our tables like boxers to their respective corners. After a few more questions, I terminated my examination for the time being, knowing full well that Dodd would be on and off the stand for the next few days.

Many of Dave Goldin's questions of Dodd on cross-examination were aimed only at bringing out Jack Dodd's background, reasons the jury should find him believable. Goldin also asked at some length about Alan's condition the day after Judy's death.

Q. "Where did you first see Alan?"

A. "Well, I had been trying to contact him as soon as I heard the news, but was unsuccessful. Finally, I got a call from Alan, and he told me where he was and said that he needed someone to talk to. I went up to a friend's home, gave him the address, and stayed with him until about two, two-thirty in the morning."

Q. "How would you describe his condition?"

A. "Well, all I can say is that at that point he was a wreck. Physically and mentally."

Q. "Was he crying?"

A. "He was crying. Depressed. Kind of out of it, you might say."

Q. "Afterward did you go to the Coroner's for identification of the body?"

A. "Yes, Alan requested that I go with him, and I did."

Q. "Did anything happen with respect to going in to view the body?"

A. "Well, first of all I volunteered to go in. The Coroner said that I could identify the body, that Alan did not have to go in, but Alan chose to go in. When he went in he looked at it and started crying, and just stood there, so I pulled him out. I said, 'Let's go,' and we did."

Dodd testified that he and Alan went to a bar for a drink after viewing Judy's body and that Alan's crying continued at the bar.

On redirect, I asked:

Q. "Who was present at the Coroner's office when Alan started to weep?"

A. "We were in the viewing room alone, and as we walked out I believe there was an attendant standing outside the door."

Q. "Were tears still dripping down Alan's face when he walked past the attendant?"

A. "As far as I know they were. I know they were when we went over to the bar."

Q. "Were the tears making puddles on the ground?"

A. "No."

MR. GOLDIN: "Objection on the grounds it is argumentative and sarcastic."

THE COURT: "The question is asked and answered."

Q. "Do you know this gentleman right here, seated on my left, Detective Strickland from the Burbank Police Department?"

A. "Yes, I know Detective Strickland."

Q. "Do you recall his asking you to make a written statement concerning the circumstances surrounding the issuance of the insurance policy on Judy?"

A. "Yes, I do."

Q. "And do you recall telling him that you would not do so?"

A. "Yes, I did tell him that."

Q. "Why wouldn't you make a written statement, Mr. Dodd?"

A. "I got advice from an attorney. I think it is my constitutional right not to make a written statement to the police or anyone else out of court."

Dodd had long since lost his original confidence and poise on the stand. He now appeared nervous and very uncomfortable, which was precisely what I wanted. Juries watch a witness' demeanor very closely in determining whether or not the witness is telling the truth. This, in fact, is the reason that witness stands are always situated on the jury side of the courtroom.

Q. "You have given written statements to people before in your life, haven't you, Mr. Dodd?"

A. "Not that I recall. I gave one to Equitable, a pretty long one. There may be others. I don't recall. They were not matters involving things like this."

Q. "Well, you are just a witness in this case. Right?"

A. "Yes, I am."

Q. "Why did you go out and get an attorney?"

A. "Because this is a legal matter. It is a serious matter, and I wanted to know where I stood in terms of my rights."

Q. "Why did you ask Detective Strickland if you were a suspect in this case?"

A. "Why shouldn't I be, sir?"

Q. "That is a good question," I shot back, conveying to the jury my belief that Dodd *was* a suspect, at least in the sense of his covering up the insurance transaction for Alan, and therefore being an accessory after the fact.

Dodd paused for several moments.

A. "You have made several implications here," he finally blurted out, stung by my innuendo.

Q. "What constitutional right were you exercising in not making a written statement, the right against self-incrimination?" I fired on, becoming less oblique in my suggestion of complicity.

A. "It is a matter, I think, of things being distorted when they are written."

Q. "You feel there is a greater chance that what you say may be distorted when you write something down on paper than when you talk to someone? Surely you don't mean that, Mr. Dodd."

A. "I say I think you can take it and do anything you want to it. Sure you can distort it."

Q. "You have asked other people for written statements during your career, have you not?"

A. "Yes."

Q. "And they have made written statements for you, have they not?"

A. "I have never been involved in this kind of thing before, sir."

Q. "You have never been involved in a murder case?"

A. "In any kind of criminal activity, criminal charge."

Q. "What is your job now?"

A. "Parole agent, State of California."

Q. "A parole agent doesn't deal with criminal charges or criminal activity, anything like that?"

A. "They have nothing to do with me."

Q. "The criminals don't have anything to do with you?"

A. "I am not involved in the sense that I am involved in this situation. I wrote the policy. I didn't cause my parolees to get into difficulties. I wrote no policies, I had no relationship with them in that sense."

MR. BUGLIOSI: "Thank you. No further questions at this time."

As he stepped down off the stand, Dodd tugged at the shirt cuffs beneath his suit coat as if my assault on him had been physical. I glanced over at Alan. He was rolling a pin between his fingers.

I requested that Jack Dodd be directed to remain in the courtroom to hear Michael Brockington's testimony, which followed.

Q. BY MR. BUGLIOSI: "Mr. Brockington, you heard the testimony of Mr. Dodd?"

A. "Yes, I did."

Q. "You heard him testify that he doesn't recall your being present that evening?"

A. "Yes."

Q. "Were you present that evening, Mr. Brockington?"

A. "Yes, I was."

Q. "Any particular reason why you remember this date, February 22, 1968?"

A. "Yes, sir. February 22 is Washington's Birthday, which I had off, and during the day Mr. Palliko had asked me to take his 1968 Charger to a—I believe it is a Goodyear store located on the northwest corner of Colorado and Brand in the city of Glendale, for the purpose of having a set of Mag Wheels, Crager Mag Wheels, put on his Dodge Charger."

Michael Brockington's overly precise ways, which I had worried about earlier in the trial, were indeed inuring to our benefit now.

He went on: "Prior to leaving for this establishment, Mr. Palliko gave me a check. I believe he had filled in the signature and the date, and when the work on the car was completed I was to fill in the number of the check, the payee and the written amount of the check."

MR. BUGLIOSI: "Your Honor, I have here a check of Alan Palliko's dated February 22, 1968 for $161.70, payable to Goodyear. May it be marked People's next in order for identification."

THE COURT: "It may be marked People's Exhibit 66 for identification."

I showed Brockington the check, which he identified as the one Alan had made out that day. I had obtained a copy of it from the microfilm kept on file at the Goodyear store's bank.

Brockington continued: "When I arrived back at the apartment—I think after I handed Alan back the keys to the car—we went outside and looked at the wheels and then we came back inside. To the best of my recollection, it was sometime during this period of time that Mr. Dodd arrived.

"I believe Mr. Dodd was present when a conversation ensued on the telephone between Alan and someone at Goodyear due to the fact that a price had been prearranged between the people at the Goodyear store and Mr. Palliko, and to the best of my memory, it was around $135 or $140. However, this did not include what they call chrome lug nuts which they had had to make a special trip to get. Consequently, the total amount came to $161.70."

Brockington testified that while Dodd was present, Alan had had a screaming battle over the phone with the Goodyear people and had threatened to stop payment on his check. The check we had in court did, in fact, bear the bank-stamped words, "Stop payment."

Confirming his belief that Dodd and he were present at Alan's apartment at the same time, Brockington testified further: "What really sticks in my memory is that Mr. Dodd, I am almost positive of this, showed me a picture which was a family portrait of his wife and two children, two boys, and I remember that he told me his wife's name was Dianne. I am not positive, but I think that the picture itself was an eight-by-ten. That I am not positive of. But it was what you call a sepia tone print—toned in a brown toner. I can say that because for seven years I was a photographer."

Having established Michael Brockington's rather convincing memory of the evening, I proceeded to the important subject matter of that evening, the sale of Judy's life insurance. Michael repeated from the stand what he had told me in my office. The testimony was undoubtedly the most important offered by the prosecution on the second murder count. Michael testified that Alan had been quite adamant, almost paranoid, about getting the refund of his premium for his own original health policy which he had canceled, but that the only time consuming conversation about Judy's life policy concerned a disability waiver. Other than that, there had been no debating about Judy's policy whatsoever.

MR. BROCKINGTON: "I do not remember lengthy applications being filled out. It just appeared to me that—well, I know there was no pushing and there was no, 'You have to take this. You should take this. This is a good deal.' There was none of this. It was like this had been—everything had been agreed upon. It was just a matter of signing. After this we sat around for a while. We socialized."

Brockington testified that of the three or four hours that Jack Dodd remained at the apartment, no more than an hour "at the very outside" had been spent on business. I knew I had to be prepared for an argument by the defense that the insurance transaction and all of the alleged debating over it had occurred *before* Michael had returned from the Goodyear store.

Q. "Mr. Brockington, you indicated that you don't know for sure whether you or Dodd arrived at the Grismer Street apartment first, but you believe that he arrived after you; is that correct?"

A. "Correct."

Q. "In any event, were you present at the *commencement* of the discussion between Dodd and Mr. Palliko about Judy's insurance?"

A. "Yes, I was."

Q. "Why do you believe that you were present at the commencement of the discussion?"

A. "Because at the time, Mr. Dodd had a briefcase, or whatever he had his papers contained in, which was sitting on a chair near the bar —he and Alan and Judy and I were at the bar, which was in Alan's apartment. I was standing next to Mr. Dodd—and at one particular point Mr. Dodd took the papers out and put them on top of the bar and began talking to Mr. Palliko."

Q. "And the discussion about Judy's insurance commenced at that point?"

A. "Yes, sir."

Q. "Did you hear, at any time, Alan Palliko tell Mr. Dodd words to the effect, 'No, I do not need or want insurance on Judy'?"

A. "No."

Q. "Are you positive about this?"

A. "I am positive."

Q. "Did you hear any objection from Alan about taking out insurance on Judy? Any objection whatsoever?"

A. "No."

Head down, Alan scribbled and shoved notes to his lawyer.

The next morning I recalled Jack Dodd to the stand.

Q. "Mr. Dodd, you heard the testimony of Michael Brockington?"

A. "Yes, I did."

Q. "Is your memory now refreshed, sir, that Michael Brockington was present during the entire transaction?"

A. "No, this is not correct. He was present for a short period of time. I do recall showing him the photograph that I have."

Q. "So you do remember now that Michael Brockington was present that night; your memory is refreshed, is that right?"

A. "It is refreshed, yes, that he did come. He came by the apartment, yes."

Dodd's credibility had been hurt, seriously so.

Dodd went on to give his revised version of the evening in some detail: "I met Alan at the bar—at the time he and Michael were coming out of the bar. I followed them home in my car. Brockington came into the apartment, Alan gave him the car keys and he left. I know that Brockington did come back later. He gave Alan the receipt (from Goodyear), and at this point I remember the conversation that Alan had on the telephone where he became furious about the discrepancy in charges. At that point, Brockington left again. Now, *from the time that Brockington was gone until he came back,* if he came back, I did discuss insurance with Alan and Judy."

I almost felt like handing Dodd an umbrella, his attempts to walk between the raindrops were do desperate by this point.

Q. "So not only is your memory now refreshed, Mr. Dodd, that Brockington was there that night, but now you remember exactly everything that Brockington did that night?"

A. "Not exactly everything."

Q. "You claim to know exactly when he arrived and left, don't you?"

A. "I don't know exactly when he arrived."

Q. "Just about exactly, right?"

A. "About, yes."

Q. "Was that, in fact, an eight-by-ten photo you showed him?" I asked, changing my direction slightly, using Dodd to further bolster Brockington's already enhanced credibility.

A. "I believe it was, yes."

Q. "Is your wife's name Dianne?"

A. "Sure is."

Q. "Do you have two young boys?"

A. "Yes, I have."

Q. "And didn't Alan, in fact, ask you when he was going to get some money back on the canceled policy?"

A. "That's the first thing that Alan asked . . . and he made some nasty remark about the company, which he always does."

Q. "When Alan was talking to the people from Goodyear and he was furious, you and Judy were seated at the bar. Right?"

A. "That is correct."

Q. "And Mr. Brockington was standing next to you, is that correct?"

A. "I think that the entire time Brockington was there he was standing not next to me, but somewhat in the passway . . . between the kitchen and the living room."

Q. "Kind of out in the wings someplace? Really didn't know what was going on at all, did he, Mr. Dodd?" a shade of disbelief to my voice for the jury's ears.

A. "I'm sure he knew what was going on. Alan was screaming all over the place."

Having proven that Michael was, in fact, present that night, it was important that I also prove he was present during the discussion of insurance, which Dodd still vigorously denied.

Q. "Mr. Dodd, do you recall Mr. Brockington's testimony that you and Alan had a conversation about a disability waiver on Judy's policy?"

A. "I think he stated that, yes."

Q. "Did you and Alan talk about a disability waiver on that date?"

A. "No."

Q. "I show you what appears to be a photostatic copy of the application on Judy's policy, and direct your attention to Part I, Block number 4, to the words 'Disability premium waiver.' You'll notice that there is an X after it."

Dodd glanced briefly at the application.

A. "That is correct."

Standing next to him, I could see his jaw muscles working. His breathing was growing heavy and defiant.

Q. "What does that mean?" I asked, making my own voice progressively more calm and matter-of-fact.

A. "That means that the disability waiver premium is included in the policy."

Q. "Does that encompass an additional premium?"

A. "That is correct."

Q. "Why did you check off 'Disability Waiver' without a discussion?"

A. "Routinely in writing policies, again with clients who have confidence in you, you give them benefits that go along with the policy . . . you simply tell them what the policy costs and what it will provide and that's it—you get a check."

Q. "Do you mean you add provisions to the policy without even asking them if they want it? Even if it will cost them more money?"

A. "You don't have to ask. In many cases you *tell* the client what is best for him and he takes it."

Q. "But you just said you had *no* discussion with Alan Palliko about a disability premium waiver on Judy's policy."

A. "We did not discuss the disability premium waiver in *this* policy."

I looked at Jack Dodd, and just smiled.

When he resumed the stand yet a third day, he and the defense took a new tack. They claimed that, according to Dodd's appointment book, the appointment with Alan had been at 3:30 in the afternoon, not in the evening, and that the discussion of insurance had taken place *before* Brockington had returned from the Goodyear store.

Q. BY MR. BUGLIOSI: "You testified yesterday that you arrived in the evening on February 22, 1968. Is that right, sir?"

A. "That is correct."

Q. "But now you say you arrived at 3:30 P.M."

A. "I checked my appointment book. It was 3:30 in the afternoon, yes."

I asked to look at that appointment book.

Q. "Mr. Dodd, you'll notice the time, 3:30 P.M., has been gone over several times. Why did you go over the time, 3:30 P.M., several times, sir?"

A. "You may find that many times you go over the ink several times. As you note, there has been nothing written there except 3:30—so it's been traced over, yes, so?—it's still 3:30."

Q. "Why did you trace over it?"

A. "Again, I traced over it because I wanted to make it clear there. That is all. I wanted to be able to read it."

Q. "Do you have a problem with your eyesight, Mr. Dodd?"

A. "Sometimes from a distance, not close up, no, not in writing or reading, no."

Q. "So why did you want to make sure that you'd see this, then?"

A. "I traced over it. I can't give you any specific reason why I traced over it. I traced over it."

Q. "Directing your attention, Mr. Dodd, to the name 'Alan Palliko' opposite '3:30,' did you run out of ink after you wrote the word 'Alan'?"

A. "Well, that date, February 22, I had one appointment. Any appointment I have had with Palliko has been very lengthy. On that date I made only that one appointment."

Q. "The question, Mr. Dodd, is—and I will ask you for the second time—did you run out of ink after you wrote the word 'Alan,' A-l-a-n?"

A. "No, I did not."

Q. "Why did you change pens?"

A. "I didn't change pens."

Q. "Why did you use blue ink for the word 'Alan' and black ink for the word 'Palliko'?"

A. "I think you can look at that closer, sir, and you will find it is . . . oh, I see what you mean. That I can't answer."

Q. "It looks like you wrote the word Alan with one pen and then you pulled another pen out of your pocket and wrote the word Palliko, isn't that right?"

A. "That's right. I have no explanation for that whatsoever. None at all."

Q. "The letters A-l-a-n don't look like the blue pen was gasping its last breath, do they, Mr. Dodd?"

A. "No, no, they don't."

Wondering if Jack Dodd had not, perhaps, filled in that appointment notation just prior to testifying, I called the crime labs of both the LAPD and the L.A. Sheriff's Office over the noon recess, and was surprised to learn that there is no instrument by which one can determine even the approximate age of ink impressions. I phoned the FBI in Washington D.C. and was told essentially the same thing. Only the approximate age of *very* fresh or *very* old ink impressions can be determined and even then, not by scientific instruments, but simply by visual observation. I therefore had no place to go with my new possible suspicions.

Back in court in the afternoon I did, however, ask Dodd the following:

Q. "Do you ever make an appointment, sir, and then decide to cancel it and extend it to a later time or later date?"

A. "I have done that, yes."

Q. "So when you wrote 3:30 here, you could have given Alan a jingle thereafter and said, 'I can't make it at 3:30. I'll be there later in the evening.' Right?"

A. "I could have, yes."

Q. "When you testified yesterday that you went over to Alan Palliko's apartment in the evening, did you say evening because in your memory it was dark out?"

A. "As I recalled it at the time, it was the evening. I don't know whether it was dark out."

Q. "In any case, your notation says 3:30, but your memory is that it was in the evening. Is that correct?"

A. "This is correct."

MR. BUGLIOSI: "No further questions."

I could only hope that the jury felt as I did—that it was clear the discussion of insurance *had* taken place in the evening, not the afternoon, that Michael Brockington *had* been present during it, and most importantly, that Dodd did not talk Alan into taking out life insurance on Judy.

On recross, Goldin asked Dodd if he had told Steven and Jill Stone that he was going to do anything he could to help Alan and prove his friendship to him; Dodd denied it up and down.

MR. DODD: "Jill was convinced that Alan had killed Judy . . . and I wasn't really willing to listen to this, and I pointed out that she didn't know he was guilty, that she had convicted him already. Mr. Stone said very little. But Jill insisted Alan was no good. I agreed that there are some things about him that are no good. Then she pointed out to me that Alan had spoken to her and Mr. Stone about me, making derogatory remarks about blacks and what have you. I pointed out that Alan and I had had similar conversations, but that he had a right to his beliefs. I stated I would probably have to be a witness in this case and that I was going to get up here and tell it like it is. And I said, you know, if it helps Alan, okay, and if it hurts Alan, okay . . ."

When I called Steven and Jill Stone to the stand, their versions of that conversation were a good deal different than Jack Dodd's.

MRS. STONE: "Jack said that he knew Alan didn't like black people, and he knew that his relationship with Alan had been unusual. But it didn't make any difference to Jack. He said he really didn't care for Alan, but that he was going to prove to Alan that in this particular situation Alan was now in, he would be his friend when all others deserted him . . . that he would do anything he could to help Alan."

Mr. Stone's testimony was substantially the same.

MR. STONE: "We were sitting around the kitchen table having a cup of coffee, and Jack brought up this subject of Alan . . . and he said, 'Personally I feel that Alan hates my guts and I have no great love for Alan, either; however, I am going to do everything I can to help him in this situation and prove that even though all others seem to forsake him that a black can definitely be his friend and stand by him."

Q. BY MR. BUGLIOSI: "Is there any question in your mind about this?"

A. "None at all. Because the sequence of the words that he spoke: hate, guts, love and help came in that order. Jack was very concerned about this, and he said he did not believe Alan could have done this thing."

On his final questioning of Dodd, Dave Goldin tried desperately to rehabilitate Alan's "star witness." He even ventured as far afield of the issues at hand as to ask Dodd about his supposedly cordial relationship with Evelle Younger, the District Attorney. That rather irrelevant line of questioning, I believe, only made it clearer that even the defense recognized that although Dodd had not been destroyed, he had been badly hurt as a witness. His version of the insurance sale had been battered; his credibility concerning any issue at all, including Alan's alleged grief after Judy's death, was seriously in question.

By the time Jack Dodd left the stand for the last time, I was quite frankly baffled. His manner in a certain sense indicated he sincerely believed he was telling the truth. He continued to come to court on a number of occasions as a spectator, and whenever we passed in the hallway he could not have been more amiable. It was as if he believed that although we were on opposite sides, we were both making honest attempts to get at the truth.

Although I had felt at the beginning that he was openly lying, I began to consider that perhaps Jack Dodd's version of the insurance sale was not really a conscious piece of deceit, but rather a far more subliminal distortion of the facts. Just as Alan Palliko may have used his "friendship" with Jack to convince himself that he really was not a blind racist, a similar force may have been working on Dodd. Perhaps Jack Dodd could never really admit to himself that he felt a need to "prove" his race to the Alan Pallikos of the world, but by the tricks of the mind and memory, went ahead and did exactly that.

Michael Brockington had now become the prosecution's star witness not only on the first murder count but on the second as well. Lest the jury buy Goldin's mounting accusations that Michael had become just too convenient a witness because he, in fact, was framing Alan, I put Warren King (elevated since the beginning of the investigation from lieutenant to captain) on the stand for his testimony that Michael, when first questioned at the Burbank station, did everything he could to protect Alan.

In my own office, Michael expressed his feeling that, although he knew his testimony was damaging Alan, he personally did not believe

Alan had killed Judy. Even from the stand he said almost as much.

Q. BY MR. BUGLIOSI: "You believe that he loved Judy?"

A. "I don't think Alan is capable of love, as we know it, but in his own way, yes, Alan loved Judy."

8

THE BARMAID, SUSAN PETERS, who answered the call on the pay phone behind the bar just after Judy had left on the night of her murder, was prepared to testify that the caller was a woman. I gave considerable thought to the admissibility of that fact, and asked that all counsel meet with Judge Young in chambers to discuss the matter.

MR. BUGLIOSI: "I am going to urge upon the jury the good possibility that the person who called Alan was the killer. If the jury accepts that, this could conceivably hurt Sandra Stockton. So my point is this: I could instruct Susan Peters in advance not to blurt out that it was a woman. This would involve coaching a witness, but I feel it is necessary."

Terry Callas naturally agreed with my position, but Dave Goldin had a very good point in opposition to us.

MR. GOLDIN: "The District Attorney is going to go into the force of the injuries, the beating on the head. I think these are injuries that would have been more likely to have been caused by a man than a woman. If he is going to argue it was the killer who called, I want to point out to the jury that it was not the killer. That the caller was a woman."

Personally, I did not think the brutality of Judy's murder was beyond the power of a woman, but I had to admit to Judge Young that Dave Goldin was correct about the inequity of foreclosing his right to cross-examine Susan Peters on the gender of the caller.

Whichever way we proceeded, one of the defendants was going to have his (her) rights impaired, but my feeling remained that the prejudicial impact against Sandra was the greater of the two evils.

Judge Young sat on the problem for several days and finally ruled that the gender of the caller could not be disclosed to the jury. Dave, unhappy, had no choice but to accept the ruling and I, in the meantime, instructed Susan Peters to be extremely careful of her wording while on the stand. Even a small slip such as, *"She* asked to speak with Alan," could result in Terry Callas, on behalf of Sandra, demanding a mistrial.

Susan Peters, a small, brown-eyed woman in her mid-twenties, testified that the Grand Duchess Bar had been open for business for only two weeks prior to Judy's murder. During the first week, Alan had come in every other day, she said, but during the seven days leading up to the night of the murder, he had not been in at all. The place had been left in the hands of his manager, Gus Pilich.

If Alan had anticipated being accused of murdering Judy himself, he obviously knew that the Grand Duchess, at nine miles from the Castillian Apartments, would be a far more persuasive place for an alibi than the Burbank bar, which was only a matter of blocks from the Castillian.

Q. BY MR. BUGLIOSI: "How would you describe Alan's disposition the two weeks prior to April 20th?"

A. "He wasn't himself."

Q. "In what way was he different?"

A. "He was jumpy, nervous."

Q. "Much more so than usual?"

A. "Yes."

Peters, still Alan's friend and employee, added that she believed Alan's edginess was attributable to the poor business the new bar was doing. I would later argue to the jury that was an unlikely reason for Alan's frayed nerves. Any business is slow going at the beginning. Alan had already been through one such period when the Grand Duke in Burbank first opened. After six or eight weeks under Alan's new management that bar began to do fine, and by the time the new Grand Duchess opened in Sunland, the first bar was grossing $4,500 a month. A Dun & Bradstreet financial check on Alan, run by Detective Strickland, revealed that in February, 1968, only two months before Judy's death, Alan had liabilities of only $6,000 and assets of $30,000.

Mrs. Peters testified to the conversation with Judy on the night of the murder in which Judy told her she did not know what had been bothering Alan of late, but that she had been thinking of going back to live with her parents. She also admitted that after serving a few beers and talking with Judy for a while she heard Alan say to Judy, and quite firmly: "It's time for you to go now."

Alan walked Judy out to the car, and, per Susan Peters, was some "ten or fifteen minutes" in coming back into the bar. Alan had told the police that the only thing he could remember saying to Judy outside the bar was to tell her to get the Jaguar filled with gas on the way home. I wondered what else was discussed in the parking lot during the other "ten or fifteen minutes." Had Alan, wanting Judy to be vulnerable when she parked the car at home that night, given his wife some story about why the convertible's top should remain down that night? The Standard gas station attendant, who filled the Jaguar's gas tank on that chilly evening, would later testify to Judy's having been driving with a blanket across her knees and a scarf about her head.

If Alan did convince Judy to leave the convertible's top down that night, it was then logical for him to instruct Judy to park the car in the carport rather than on the street, as she so often did. The carport area gave cover—cover from rain and cover for a murderer lying in wait.

When we reached the point in Susan Peters' testimony concerning the phone call for Alan, the sex of the caller was scrupulously avoided, and all that the jury heard was that the call was short, lasting no more than two or three minutes. Peters went on to testify that after the call, Alan resumed a game of pool with the bar's bouncer, Gary Deaton, until approximately forty-five minutes later, when he received a second call (the one from Pete Morris relaying Mrs. Miller's message to call her at the Castillian).

MRS. PETERS: "He got the phone call and all I heard Alan say was, 'What happened? Where? Oh, my God. When?' And he had a very shocked look on his face."

On cross-examination, Dave Goldin worked in a piece of quite clever questioning concerning the first phone call.

Q. "Did Alan receive many calls at the bar?"

A. "Quite a few."

Q. "It wasn't uncommon for him to receive calls?"

A. "No."

Q. "Was there an ad being run for barmaids at the time?"

A. "Yes, there was. I believe there was."

With that one question, Dave had accomplished his objective. The fact that an ad for barmaids was being run in the paper at the time suggested that Alan would have been receiving a number of phone inquiries from women. Moreover, just by the fact that Susan Peters answered his question that an advertisement for bar*maids* was being run, and did not add, "but this call was from a man," the conclusion the jury might easily come to was that the call had, in fact, been from a woman. While obeying Judge Young's ruling about not asking about the sex of the caller, Dave had managed to get before the jury an inference of precisely what he had wanted.

In addition (and perhaps as a by-product that was unintentional), Goldin's implication that the caller was a woman who was answering the barmaid ad, if believed, eliminated the possibility of prejudice to Sandra.

Bar bouncer Gary Deaton's testimony about that Saturday night was virtually identical to that offered by Susan Peters. Gus Pilich, the Grand Duchess' manager, had given the police a similar version of the night. Alan thus had an airtight alibi for his whereabouts at the time of the murder.

Theresa Condi, the other barmaid and the one possible employee of Alan's who was present that night who could contradict Alan's alibi, had not resurfaced after disappearing from Los Angeles shortly after the murder. Three weeks before our trial ended, word came back to DA investigator Dave Correa that Miss Condi had been located by the Utah Sheriff's Office. She had checked into a motel in Utah, where she was living under an alias. All she would say under questioning was that several days after the murder she had received an anonymous warning to get out of L.A. The day after she related this to the Utah authorities, Theresa Condi disappeared a second time and was never heard from or located again.

For the jury's sake, whenever feasible I tried to maintain a sense of continuity by calling witnesses in the chronological sequence of the events about which they were to testify. Robert Jenner, the young Standard station attendant who gassed up Judy's Jaguar around 11:00 P.M. that night, testified that Judy was "talking quite a bit and smiling." She gave no indication she thought she was being followed, nor did Jenner see anyone following her.

Larry Beauregard, tenant at the Castillian, then testified to his hearing, two or three minutes before 11:30 P.M., the three rapid-fire shots: "I can't remember exactly if it was one, two, three or one, and then two, three, just with one slight delay."

In either case, his testimony about the gunshots was somewhat puzzling in that the police's only explanation for the two unexpended rounds of ammunition found at the scene was that the murderer had had to take the time to twice manually work the slide of a malfunctioning automatic, thereby ejecting two unfired cartridges. This would have caused two pauses. Beauregard, however, seemed sure of his memory.

John Miller, the Castillian's resident manager, testified to his finding, at 11:30 P.M., Judy in the Jaguar, its motor, lights, and radio still on.

MR. MILLER: "I wouldn't say she was conscious or unconscious. She was just in . . . well, it's . . . I really couldn't say. It's . . ." Mr. Miller swallowed thickly, obviously distressed at having to recall that night. "I think you would have to have a doctor to tell you that. I tried to talk to her but she . . . she couldn't tell me anything."

The first time John Miller saw Alan after Judy's death was early Sunday morning, around breakfast time.

Q. BY MR. BUGLIOSI: "Did you get any impression as to how he was taking it?"

A. "Well, when I first met him, Alan was outside. He had a cup of coffee and he was walking up and down the street, kind of shaking his head. When I started to talk to Alan, well . . . to me he just didn't seem like a man who just lost his wife."

Q. "Didn't act bereaved?"

A. "Other than he had his head bowed down, kind of half shaking it."

Miller stated that Alan asked him that morning if he had seen anyone suspicious the night before. Miller told him no. The next weekend Alan came to Miller, requesting to be moved to a different apartment in the building, and again Alan asked if Miller had seen anyone that Saturday night. A few days later, Alan asked the same question for a third time.

Q. BY MR. BUGLIOSI: "Had you been ambiguous at all, or had you told him clearly the first and second times that you did not see anyone?"

A. "I clearly told him I did not see anyone."

Q. "But he nonetheless asked you three times?"

A. "Yes, three times. I don't remember if he asked me any more."
I suspected the defense would argue at the trial's end that Alan
had merely been acting as a distraught husband, desperate for a lead.
My theory for his dogged, perhaps worried questioning was, of
course, a bit different.

After testimony from officer George Wood and inspector Robert
Wells as to the physical evidence at the scene of Judy's murder, Dr.
Holloway, who conducted the autopsy on Judy, testified to the cause
of death being cerebral concussion and hemorrhage due to skull fractures caused by the two gunshot wounds to the head. Autopsy pictures revealed the gunpowder tattooing around both wounds, indicating, as with the murder of Henry Stockton, that the muzzle of the gun
had been quite close to Judy's head when fired, almost at skin contact range. The multiple blunt force injuries to the head Holloway
cited merely as "other conditions."
I had Dr. Holloway draw an anatomical diagram on a blackboard
for the jury. He stated that the fatal bullets had taken a slightly front
to back and upward path.
With Judy seated in a low sports car, the killer would have had to
almost shoot from the hip for the bullets to have taken an upward
path. A more likely explanation, I thought, was that Judy had been
leaning over to reach the gun in her purse, thus putting her head at
an angle that would have made the bullet paths appear as they did.

Mrs. Miller testified to her having called Pete Morris at the Grand
Duke in Burbank and telling him that Alan's wife had been in an
"accident." She related how she subsequently learned that Judy had,
in fact, been shot and when she told this to Alan when he called her,
he had merely repeated the word: "Shot?"
Q. BY MR. BUGLIOSI: "Did he sound distraught in any way?"
A. "No. He was calm."
Q. "Mrs. Miller, do you consider yourself an enemy of Alan Palliko's?"
A. "No, of course not. I didn't even know him that well. He was
just a tenant."
MR. BUGLIOSI: "No further questions."
Following Mrs. Miller, James Warner, the L.A. Sheriff's Office
firearms expert, gave testimony about the murder weapon's probable
manufacturer, the caliber of bullets, etc. The fact that three out of the

five bullet casings were stamped "WW," Winchester's more recent insignia, would tie in later when the jury would hear Capt. Warren King's testimony that the partially empty box of .25 caliber cartridges found in Alan's apartment was of this newer "WW" vintage.

Perched nervously on the stand, Alan's former barmaid Paula Boudreau was in mortal fear of him and his friends, though she would not admit it in court. When I asked her about her conversation with Alan that she had related to Strickland and Vandergrift, I found that pinning Paula Boudreau down to a straight honest answer was like trying to rivet a nail into a custard pie.

Q. "About a week prior to Judy being shot, when you and Alan went out looking for girls to be barmaids, did you stop for coffee and have a conversation with Alan?"

A. "Yes."

Q. "Would you please tell the Judge and jury the substance of that conversation?"

A. "Well, could you be more specific?"

Q. "Apart from discussing barmaids, what did he say to you and what did you say to him?"

A. "Just conversation."

Q. "I am interested in what that conversation was."

A. "Well, it varied to a lot of things."

Glancing over at the jury, I saw forklift operator Wes Knudsen look at me with a sympathetic smile, as if for the first time in his life beginning to appreciate his own line of work.

Q. "Mrs. Boudreau, you understand that you are under oath?"

A. "Yes."

I finally got her to admit that the topic of guns and killing for hire "somehow" came up.

Q. "Who brought this subject up, Mrs. Boudreau?"

A. "Well . . ."

Not looking at me, Mrs. Boudreau moistened her lips as if about to answer, but then fell silent, as though hoping the question would simply go away.

Q. "Did *you* have any intention to pay someone to kill somebody for *you?*"

A. "Not hardly."

Q. "Isn't it true you told two officers that Alan Palliko started the conversation about killing for hire?"

A. "Somewhat."

Q. "Talk up, Mrs. Boudreau. Don't be afraid."

A. "In somewhat."

Q. "What did you say?"

A. "In somewhat, but just talk. *I* asked about it—it was just conversation."

Q. "*You* brought up the subject?"

A. "Umm—"

Q. "Do you know what I mean by 'brought up'? Who initiated the conversation about guns and a killing for hire? Who originated the conversation? Who started the conversation, Mrs. Boudreau?"

A. "I'd say I did."

Q. "Is that what you told Detective Strickland and Lieutenant Vandergrift?"

A. "Yes. I said I asked Alan how people got away with that type of thing—it was just conversation."

I had Mrs. Boudreau draw on a piece of paper and explain to the jury Alan's diagram on a napkin of how one gets away with a killing for hire. The diagram was hardly scientific, I thought to myself, but after an evening with his type of friends and a couple of stiff bourbons, Alan must have flopped into bed some nights feeling like a genius.

Q. "Did Alan Palliko tell you during the conversation that in a week or two you were going to see just how cold and cruel life could be?"

A. "No. He said within the next two weeks that something may happen that I might think was very cruel."

Q. "Did he add that some things just had to happen?"

A. "No."

Q. "You didn't tell Detective Strickland and Lieutenant Vandergrift that?"

A. "No."

Mrs. Boudreau reiterated from the witness stand what she had told the Burbank detectives—that she interpreted Alan's "cruel" statement as meaning he would have to close down one of the bars and fire the employees.

Q. "The night Alan called Janet Turnbull at the bar from jail, did you see Janet writing anything on a note pad?"

A. "Just scribbling writing."

Q. "What did you see her write down?"

A. "Nothing specifically that I would remember correctly. Something about a gun. But I don't know what kind."

Q. "Do you recall telling the police that you saw Janet write down '.22 caliber' (Henry was killed by a .22) and then put a circle around it?"

A. "No."

Q. "Do you know Gus Pilich?"

A. "Yes . . . yes, I do."

Q. "Did Gus Pilich come see you about a week ago at the Surfside Bar, where you work now, and tell you he didn't want to see you get hurt?"

A. "Just because he liked me and had known me for a long time."

Dave Goldin stormed to the bench, demanding a mistrial.

MR. GOLDIN: "What has happened now is that the District Attorney has been allowed to put on Gus Pilich indirectly, without calling him to testify, that if anyone testifies against Alan, harm will come to them."

MR. BUGLIOSI: "I am going to put Gus Pilich on next. He's in the back of the courtroom. He's a very close friend of Alan Palliko's and I am going to call him to the stand."

Judge Young denied the motion for a mistrial, but when I got back to the counsel table I discovered there was a quality trial lawyers would do quite well to possess—eyes in the back of their heads.

Q. "Mrs. Boudreau, do you see Gus Pilich in the courtroom right now?"

A. "No."

I turned and faced the rows of spectators.

MR. BUGLIOSI: "Is Gus Pilich in the courtroom?" There was no response. While we had been at the bench, Pilich had sneaked out. He remained in hiding for the duration of the trial.

After Paula Boudreau, I called Detective Strickland, who testified to each and every part of Boudreau's conversation with Alan which she had related to him but had denied in court. He told of her obvious fear of Alan.

"All Alan has to do is make one phone call from jail," Strickland quoted her statement to the police.

I then called Raymond Byrne, a fellow deputy district attorney who also happened to be a personal friend of Mrs. Boudreau and her husband. Byrne had visited their home only a week earlier, trying to coax Paula into testifying to all she knew.

MR. BYRNE: "She said she had an intense fear of both Alan Palliko and his associates. She named one particular person, a person by the name of Pilich."

I had little doubt that twelve intelligent jury members could add things up and realize exactly what had been going on backstage in Paula Boudreau's life.

Jason Simcoe and Donald Whalen had known each other since childhood, or as Whalen put it during his testimony: "We runned around together a little in Detroit." They wound up in the same child guidance center, and twelve years later would be caught for committing the armed robbery of Herman Siegel at his residence in Van Nuys. Although Alan's buying some of the property stolen in the robbery was irrelevant to the charges against him, and was not introduced at the trial, what was very relevant were the statements Alan had subsequently been foolish enough to make to these two men he had double-crossed.

Jay Simcoe, a compact fellow with a face as pale and pasty as prison food, and a small, telling scar to the side of his eye, testified not only to Alan's comment, "The police haven't found the gun yet and they never will, so I ain't worried," but also to another incriminating statement Alan had made to both Simcoe and Whalen. It was in October of 1968 that all three had met up in a holding tank at the Hall of Justice. Alan told them both at that time, according to Simcoe's testimony, "I hear they don't like snitches up at the state joint."

Goldin, as I knew he would, had a field day in attacking Simcoe's credibility. Simcoe, an ill-educated but not unintelligent man, had to walk a thin line between being vague enough about his own criminal history so as not to harm his own chances for an early parole, and yet trying to establish the honesty of his testimony about Alan.

Q. BY MR. GOLDIN: "Have you ever been convicted of a felony, Mr. Simcoe?"

A. "Obviously I have; I'm in the penitentiary."

Q. "The offense of which you are convicted, that involved pistol whipping somebody, didn't it?" Dave asked, knowing very well the circumstances of the Siegel robbery.

A. "I'm sorry, that wasn't part of my conviction. I was convicted of armed robbery."

Q. "Did the offense involve pistol whipping somebody?"

A. "I didn't plead guilty to that, sir."

Q. "Your memory has blacked out for those events. Is that right?"

A. "If I didn't plead guilty to it, it is, yeah."

Q. "Then it didn't exist?"

A. "Obviously it didn't."

Q. "And you, of course, are telling the truth under oath on the witness stand right now. Is that right?"

Alan, sitting up and smiling, was enjoying Simcoe's limbo dance.

Q. "It would never occur to you to take the stand and lie. Is that right?"

A. "Only if it was in my own behalf. Have to be awful high stakes."

Q. "How about the fact that you hate Alan; isn't that kind of a big stake?"

A. "No."

Q. "They can't punish you for perjury, can they? You are not afraid somebody might put you in jail if you tell a lie on the stand, are you?"

A. "I'm already in jail, pal," Simcoe replied, not without a touch of panache.

MR. GOLDIN: "No further questions."

I was glad Simcoe acknowledged that he had nothing to lose were he to lie about Alan. This type of candor could only help his credibility with the jury.

When Donald Whalen took the stand, he testified to Alan's "snitch" comment; that Alan told him, like Simcoe, that the police would never find the gun; and to Alan's having added that that was a "hole" for him to stand in. Whalen related further that while riding on the prisoner bus between the County Jail and the Hall of Justice he had asked Alan if he had really killed his wife. According to Whalen, Alan responded: "With two and a half murder counts over my head, you don't really expect me to answer that, do you?"

Alan had sneered, Whalen stated, that it would not matter if he squealed about selling Alan the stolen gun because, according to Alan, "it was a *Spanish* .25 that killed Judy."

Although I believed Simcoe and Whalen were telling the truth, I could not really have blamed the jurors if they had not believed a single word of two convicted felons who had reason to seek revenge against Alan. Their testimony was strongly corroborated, however, the very next day. Gary Booker, the bailiff in our trial, approached me with the information that he too had heard Alan make his warning about snitches. While he was leading a file of chained men, among them Alan and Donald Whalen, back to the holding tank several weeks earlier, Alan and Whalen had started to trade some belligerent comments. It was then that Booker heard Alan repeat his warning about snitches. Realizing that Whalen was going to testify in Alan's case, Booker instituted what is called a "keep away." Whalen was transferred to a different jail and kept out of contact with Alan.

Immediately after Booker testified to having heard Alan's warning, it was necessary to replace him as bailiff for the jury for the duration of the trial, since Booker had now become a witness for the prosecution. It is, after all, the jury bailiff who has more daily contact with the jury than any other officer of the court.

To further bolster Simcoe's and Whalen's credibility, I also called to the stand Simcoe's attorney, Paul Mostman, and Whalen's attorney, David Quan, for their testimony that no clemency or deal of any kind had ever been offered their clients for their cooperation in the case against Alan.

My purpose in calling Nick Tagli to the stand was for his testimony that Judy had stopped in at his restaurant (and according to what she told Nick, at *Alan's* request) around 11:15 on the Saturday night of the murder, and that Nick saw no one follow her when she left around ten minutes later. My theory of why Alan sent Judy to Nick's restaurant was graphically demonstrated for the jury when I had Detective Strickland bring photographs to court showing Strickland simulating a potential killer as he peered over the five-foot-two-inch lath fence of the Castillian Apartment's pool area (only twenty-four feet from carport 17), looking directly at the front door of Nick Tagli's Hearthside Inn at 2100 Glenoaks Boulevard across the three street (Grismer, Bonita, and Glenoaks) intersection.

Little did I know, however, when I first called Nick Tagli to the stand that Dave Goldin was about to suggest to the jury that if Michael Brockington was not Judy's murderer, then Nick Tagli was.

Goldin had obtained information, as had I, that assault with a deadly weapon charges were pending against the restaurateur. A fight had broken out in the Hearthside Inn some weeks prior to his testifying and Nick had allegedly reached for a gun and fired a shot. Goldin attempted to plant the seeds in the jurors' minds that a dangerous and armed man, namely Nick, was in the restaurant the night of Judy's murder. When he asked Nick in front of the jury if he was awaiting trial on an assault with a deadly weapon charge, I objected strongly. A lawyer can impeach a witness by asking about a felony *conviction* against him (as Goldin did in the case of Simcoe and Whalen), but he is not allowed to ask a witness about pending charges against him. Goldin was well aware of this basic rule of evidence, and Judge Young sustained my objection. The jury, however, even without Tagli's answer to Goldin's question, undoubtedly inferred that the criminal charges must have been pending against Tagli.

Goldin was not finished with this new stratagem of his. That same day in court, I called Captain Warren King to the stand for three specific areas of testimony: first, to a number of points concerning the Burbank P.D. interview with Michael Brockington (that Brockington was never considered a suspect in Judy's murder, that he was initially protecting Palliko, etc.); secondly, that Alan did not appear upset and that he kept avoiding King's eyes when he came to the station Sunday morning to accompany the police to the Davises' residence to inform them of their daughter's death; and finally, that Alan had admitted that Judy often parked on the street, and that King had measured the closest possible street space to be only fifteen feet from the Pallikos' apartment door, much closer than the carport (and therefore a more probable place to park if a space were available). This too played into my theory that Alan had given Judy a number of instructions that night which altered her routine and set her up for the murder.

On cross-examination, Goldin asked King if the area surrounding the Castillian Apartments and Nick Tagli's Hearthside Inn was not a high crime rate district. King answered no, that the area, in fact, had a particularly low crime rate. Goldin persisted by asking if there had not been several reported shootings over the past couple of years, and to that King answered yes.

Q. BY MR. GOLDIN: "Nick himself shot somebody in his bar, didn't he?"

MR. BUGLIOSI: "Your Honor, this man here knows that this is improper."

THE COURT: "Just a moment."

MR. BUGLIOSI: "And I want the jury to know that he knows—"

THE COURT: "Just a moment, Mr. Bugliosi."

MR. BUGLIOSI: "I am fed up with this nonsense."

THE COURT: "Just a moment, Mr. Bugliosi. Approach the bench, please. I won't tolerate outbreaks in court by counsel."

MR. BUGLIOSI: "I am fed up with this man's nonsense."

I knew I was risking a possible contempt citation with that last parting shot, but I wanted the jury to know just how improperly Goldin was conducting himself in this matter. At the bench, Judge Young warned me against making further comments against counsel in open court, and warned Goldin to cease asking obviously improper questions.

No more than ten minutes later Goldin did it again. He asked King if Nick had ever been a suspect in this case to which King answered no, never.

Q. "Judy stopped by Nick's bar just before going home. Isn't that right?"

A. "As far as what he told me, yes."

Q. "And there were other witnesses at the bar who said the same thing; isn't that correct?"

A. "Yes, sir."

Goldin, I had an inkling, was referring to one pathetic old barfly in particular, a woman by the name of Thelma Dewton who kept pestering the police with calls, trying to, in her words, "break the case wide open" for them.

Q. "And at least one of them said that she suspected Nick. Isn't that right?"

Dave Goldin was not only asking for blatant inadmissible hearsay, the hearsay was of the most serious nature imaginable—that of an out of court declarant who expressed the belief that someone, other than the defendant on trial, had committed the murder. Even if the declarant had been on the witness stand herself, this would be an inadmissible opinion. It was one of the most flagrantly improper questions I had ever heard in a courtroom.

MR. BUGLIOSI: "Your Honor, I again ask the Court—"

MR. GOLDIN: "If you have an objection—"

MR. BUGLIOSI: "My objection is to *you,* Mr. Goldin."

THE COURT: "Just a moment. Counsel, approach the bench."

The fight continued at the bench.

MR. BUGLIOSI: "Is there any way to stop Goldin? Is there any way to stop this man?"

MR. GOLDIN: "All you have to say to shut me up at any time is, 'I object.'"

MR. BUGLIOSI: "Oh, no."

MR. GOLDIN: "And I stop. I never finish the sentence—like you."

MR. BUGLIOSI: "No."

There was really nothing I could do at that point; Goldin's mission had been accomplished. Judge Young was upset with Goldin for what he had done, but was dismayed at me as well for my loss of temper. Young demanded that Goldin ask absolutely no more questions that called for obvious hearsay, and then reprimanded me for my 'objection is to you' comment. I did not need the reprimand. The instant the words had spilled out of me I knew I was wrong. The comment was unprofessional and disrespectful of a court of law. The next day, in open court, I made an apology to Dave Goldin and to the jury.

That Dave and I were able to resume our friendship after the trial was over, in fact have lunch together the day it ended, was nothing unusual in the practice of law. It is not that lawyers are feigning their hostility for the sake of the jury. The intensity of a trial is real. But as with professional football players, the mauling ends after the final whistle.

It came back to me four years later that in another case, while Dave was discussing a point of law at the bench, my name had come up and Dave had casually spoken of me in very favorable terms. The judge asked, "Didn't Bugliosi once object to you as a person?"

Dave, ever witty, just shrugged and said, "Yeah, but the objection was sustained."

It seemed every time I reinterviewed potential witnesses in my office they had something new and important to tell me that for various reasons they had failed to mention in previous interviews. Michael, in particular, kept my head spinning the entire trial. I joked with Gail that I was beginning to tense up every time I saw him in the doorway to my office.

The one witness, however, who more than any other sent the trial ricocheting off in a brand new direction, emerged almost at the end of the prosecution's case. The day I had been assigned the Palliko-Stockton trial I had read through the police reports and had come across a very brief, one paragraph interview of a Mr. Walter Wasson, a tenant at the Castillian Apartments. Wasson had stated to Officer George Wood that as he had pulled into the Castillian's alleyway at about 11:30 P.M. on the night of the murder, his headlights had picked up the figure of a man walking hurriedly out of the alleyway and onto Bonita Avenue. The man, wearing a light jacket, had paused and half turned his head toward Wasson's headlights before continuing up the street. Either his hair was white or he was wearing something white around his head. Wasson had not seen the face.

I had never discarded the possibility that the man Wasson had spotted could have been the murderer. But for all practical purposes, Wasson's observations shed virtually no light on our attempt to find Judy's killer, and the Burbank police had never contacted him again. The man he saw could have been anyone. I told Dave Goldin I did not plan to subpoena Wasson, and Goldin responded that if I did not, he would, not explaining to me, however, why he thought Wasson's testimony would be of much use to either side in the case. Knowing Goldin's sentiments, I went ahead and subpoenaed Wasson on my own.

When I arrived at my office at 8:30 the next morning, Mr. Wasson was already seated in a chair across from my desk, waiting for me. Walter Wasson, a man of about sixty, was a plain spoken, salt-of-the-earth worker, a lingering picture of an Americana I had last seen in my hometown of Hibbing. Dressed in his faded railroad jacket and coveralls, his old visor cap resting on his knee, he sat forward in his chair a bit nervously. He declined my offer of coffee and before I could ask a second question he said, "Y'know, a few days after you fellas last talked to me, I had just gotten home from work and my wife says to come watch the TV news because this case was on. Well, I'll tell you, Mr. Bugliosi, when I seen them walk this man Palliko into court I just about fell out of my chair. The same walk, I tell you. That funny kind'a shuffle. And the sloping shoulders, and that slow way he turns his head toward the camera. But the *walk*, never seen one like that before. I'll be darned, Mr. Bugliosi, if he ain't the man I seen that night!"

9

FOR NINE MONTHS I had been proceeding on the theory that Alan had arranged for someone else to murder his wife. The scraps of circumstantial evidence had not been easy to come by. Listening to Walter Wasson in my office that morning, I felt like a sailor who had worked patiently in setting his sails to collect whatever small southwesterly breeze he could get, only to find himself headed directly into the gusts of a nor'easter.

Walter Wasson's revelation presented me with considerably more of a problem than a solution, so much so that I seriously doubted whether I could put him on the stand and still secure a conviction against Alan on the second murder count. The problem was simply this: In my opening statement to the jury I had, precisely on the off-chance that a witness such as Walter Wasson might emerge before the trial's end, left open the door to eventually argue that Alan himself had killed Judy. Since giving that opening statement, however, and as the trial proceeded without any witness such as Wasson materializing, I had gradually settled rather firmly into a narrower stance, making it clear to the jury that the prosecution's decided theory was that Alan had had someone else murder Judy for him. By the time I began presenting evidence on this second murder count I was so convinced that this had been the true situation, I did not even attempt to impeach the alibi testimony of Alan's employees, who all placed Alan at the bar at the time of Judy's murder.

Juries are much less inclined to convict if the prosecutor himself seems unsure of the facts in the case. For me to put Wasson on the stand and thereby switch theories one week before I was about to rest my case would, it seemed, indicate I was floundering. I was afraid it would appear to the jury as if I were saying, "Well, I may have been all wrong about this thing on my first try, so let me trot out another theory you might like better."

When I related Wasson's statement to Goldin, he too immediately saw just how two-edged the sword was that had been presented me. The new evidence could conceivably help convict Alan of Judy's murder, but it could just as easily acquit him. Dave's usually guarded smile broadened to a full grin as he said, "If you don't call him to the stand, Vince, I'm not about to, either."

For an entire weekend I debated the question with myself and with Gail. There was no ethical problem in not calling Wasson to the stand; case law is clear that neither the defense nor the prosecution has the duty to call every witness who might have knowledge of certain facts to a crime. As a prosecutor, my only duty was to inform the defense of the existence of such a witness, as I had done. And *might have knowledge* was still an issue. Although I believed Wasson to be a sincere man, not someone who, for instance, had run to the media just wishing to capture the spotlight of publicity, he still could very well have been simply in error about his observations. Nonetheless, the night of the murder demanded reexamination.

Wondering if the police could have underestimated the time span between the shooting and when Alan returned Evelyn Miller's phone call, I decided to investigate this aspect first. Reviewing the prior testimony of relevant witnesses, I quickly zeroed in on Evelyn Miller's statement concerning her phone conversation with Alan: "And by that time the ambulance was just leaving."

I called Mrs. Miller and asked her how she knew the ambulance was leaving while she was on the phone talking to Alan. She told me that as she was informing Alan of what had happened to Judy, she could hear the siren of the departing ambulance. Phoning Burbank Community Hospital, I learned that the ambulance records revealed that the time of departure from the Castillian Apartments was 11:56 P.M.

From the several witnesses interviewed by the police who had heard gunshots, our estimated time of the shooting was somewhere between 11:27 and 11:28 P.M. Alan, therefore, had not just ten to fifteen minutes, as had been previously believed, but *twenty-eight* to *twenty-nine* minutes to have gotten back to the Grand Duchess and have his phone conversation with Evelyn Miller. This was a comfortably longer period of time than he would have needed to travel the distance. It had taken Detective Strickland only *twelve* minutes.

I issued a subpoena *duces tecum* for the CBS film clip of Alan that Wasson had seen on television. Viewing it, I saw that although Alan's hands were cuffed behind his back in the clip and his feet were not in the frame, the movements of his body from the very bottom of his calves up were clear, and that slouched, uniquely lumbering shuffle that many of Alan's acquaintances had always noticed was, as far as I was concerned, quite discernible.

To be surer of my position, however, I had Wasson sit in court as a spectator that Monday morning and observe Alan as he walked into the courtroom. At the first morning recess, Wasson informed me that there was no doubt in his mind—Alan was the man he had seen that night.

After dinner, I sat on a lawn chair out in the side yard, gazing down at the blue ribbon of light that crowned the savings and loan building in the valley. To throw a brand new theory at the jury on the basis of a single witness' account—observations that did not even include the defendant's face but rather a walk, albeit a unique walk—would clearly be a gamble. My decision was the most difficult one I had to make during the trial. Although I still believed Alan had someone else kill Judy for him, I could not rule out the possibility that Wasson was correct. In any event, I decided I should present all relevant evidence I had for the jury's consideration.

Having elected to put Wasson on the stand, I began pondering ways I could make the prosecution's case most palatable for the jury in my closing argument. The defense, I knew, would argue that the prosecution had invalidated its case by, if nothing else, offering inconsistent theories of the crime. The counter-argument I settled on was that my theories were not inconsistent; *both* pointed to Alan's guilt. If Wasson's testimony were true and accurate, then Alan killed Judy himself. If Wasson were in error, that error did not contradict the evidence that had gone before. I already knew the wording I would employ: the prosecution's theories were not inconsistent theories, they were *alternative* theories. Words, like footwork and feints to a boxer, determine whether a trial lawyer's blows will land or not. The nuances of their meanings and the contexts in which they are used can frequently alter the outcome of a trial.

When I walked into the courtroom the next morning, the greater part of me believed I had made sense of my position, while a smaller, incorrigible voice inside asked whether I had merely duped myself with my own penchant for wordplay.

Walter Wasson took the stand and testified to having pulled into the carport area two or three minutes before the Millers. I had a blown-up diagram of the streets and apartment complex wheeled into the courtroom, and had Wasson point out for the jury where he had seen the man come out of the driveway and then walk hurriedly up Bonita Avenue.

Q. BY MR. BUGLIOSI: "Did the headlights of your car pick him up at all?"

A. "Yes, as I swung, my headlights picked him up right here, and he hesitated just a minute right here and then he took off."

Q. "Did he look in your direction?"

A. "He looked in my direction, but I couldn't see his face because it was dark and I was about twenty to twenty-five feet from him, and to me it looked like he had something over his head. I mean it was white. Real white. It really stood out."

Q. "The whiteness extended from the top of his head down to his collar?"

A. "That's right."

Wasson described the man as about six feet tall (Alan was six feet, one and a half). "He took off real fast," Wasson testified, "and he had a funny walk. Not a limp, but like a shuffle." I asked Wasson to demonstrate, and although the old man gritted his teeth a bit with embarrassment, he got up and did an admirable job of it. When I asked about seeing Alan Palliko on television he repeated for the jury what he had told me: "When he come out I pretty near fell out of my chair. The shape of his shoulders and his walk was like the man I seen that night positively." Mr. Wasson took his oath seriously, and added: "Well now, I can't say it *was* him."

I then asked Judge Young to direct Alan to walk a distance in the courtroom for Wasson and the jury to observe, but to that Goldin objected strenuously. At the bench, he argued that no defendant could be compelled to give evidence against himself and that Alan was not about to "put on any demonstration or do a song and dance, or anything else that the District Attorney wants him to do."

I responded that the constitutional right against self-incrimination only covered verbal utterances, and that a walking demonstration was no different than a fingerprint exemplar, which, under current law, a defendant can be ordered to give. Judge Young tended to agree with me, but suggested we take a recess to research the case law on the subject. After that research, Young was firmly in agreement with me, and stated he would order Alan to show his walk to the jury. Until this point the jury had never seen Alan walk. Typical courtroom procedure is for the trial participants to be seated before the jury enters the box for each courtroom session.

Goldin still objected, stating: "Your Honor, the trial has been a tremendous strain for Mr. Palliko. The effect the trial has had on his mental condition is such that I feel I do not want to do anything or be a party to anything that might precipitate a break. I am very concerned about his stability at this point."

Goldin stated flatly that he would advise Alan to disobey the Court order. To that, Judge Young answered that he would then have no choice but to cite Goldin for contempt. Under that threat, Dave asked for one more night to research the law, and Young readily granted the request. The next morning, Goldin came back to court admitting he could find no authority for his position, and stated he would allow his client to perform the demonstration.

Alan Palliko's courtroom demonstration was a total sham. Walking in front of the jury box, he went at an excruciatingly slow pace, holding himself stiffly in an attempt to suppress his usual head-bobbing, lumbering movements. Even this best act of his, however, could not fully hide the unique shuffle of his feet.

I requested that Alan be ordered to walk again, but fast like the man hurrying away from the Castillian Apartments, and again I met up with Goldin's objections. Even Judge Young was disinclined to force Alan to give a second demonstration. I would not relent, however.

MR. BUGLIOSI (at the bench): "That was not Alan Palliko's walk. I have seen him walk many times. I am going to put on witnesses, if I have to, who will testify that that was not Alan Palliko's regular walk. This is a very crucial issue in the case. I want the jury to see Alan Palliko walk fast like the man was walking that night."

Judge Young just sighed. "All right, Mr. Bugliosi."

Alan was ordered to walk again, and he went ever so slightly faster. It was obvious I had pressed far enough, and I kept my dissatisfaction to myself. Walter Wasson resumed the stand and testified that Alan's walk in court was "practically the same that I seen. The only thing was that it was faster that night; you'd see more of that funny walk I explained."

Q. "Mr. Wasson, have you seen Mr. Palliko walk in court the last couple of days?"

A. "Yes, sir."

Q. "You are referring to observing him walk in court *other than* the walking he did right now?"

A. "That's right."

Q. "Is it your opinion that he has the same walk as the man you saw that night?"

A. "That's right."

Wasson added that the build was exactly the same and the way Alan had slowly arched his head toward the camera on the film clip was the way the man had turned his head toward Wasson's headlights the night of the murder.

On cross-examination, Goldin was able to partially impeach Wasson's testimony, not about his observations in court nor on the night of the murder, but on the subject of the news film. Wasson stated he believed Alan's arms were swinging freely in the film and that the camera had captured a "full body" shot. When the CBS film was later shown in court (only after a part with Sandra was, upon Callas' motion, spliced out), the jury, of course, saw that Alan's hands were cuffed and that his feet were not in the frame. Moreover, Goldin turned the tables on me by objecting that the film was being shown too *fast*. He even put the projectionist on the stand and elicited from him the fact that the projector speed control can vary a film's speed by up to 5 percent.

I called on Mrs. Davis, Judy's mother, to testify that Alan's walk in court was not his usual walk. She, too, got up to demonstrate, and I could only hope that the jury could discern in her and Wasson's demonstrations and in the film clip, those odd, give-away qualities of Alan's gait.

During one of the recesses, apartment manager John Miller, who as a spectator had heard Walter Wasson's testimony about the whiteness around the fleeing man's head, informed me that Alan had often kept a white towel around his neck when walking between his apartment and the Castillian's gym room. I had Miller repeat that information from the stand. The possibility I was raising was that Alan, hedging against the chance of being spotted by another tenant before Judy arrived home, dressed as if he were merely on his way to the gym room. In the eventuality of being seen waiting around the carport and pool area, he would then have had a nifty abort plan, and could have returned to the bar.

The day after I had presented this "alternative theory," Alan's father approached me once again, this time in the hallway. His deep, booming voice drew a crowd.

"This is all just for your own career, Bugliosi! Why don't you just admit that to everyone right now?"

I had once before calmly tried to explain to Sid Palliko that if he had any evidence in his possession which would tend to exonerate his son, I would present that evidence in court. This time I just shook my head and walked away. He grabbed the arm of Tom Martin, a reporter for the L.A. *Herald-Examiner*. "My son is a victim of this man's personal career. I'm giving you permission to quote me on that."

Tom Martin blinked absently at Sid Palliko a moment, and went back into the courtroom.

The remaining evidence I presented which was compatible with the theory that Alan killed Judy himself was: Detective Strickland's testimony that it had taken him only twelve minutes to drive from the Grand Duchess to the Castillian Apartments; a stipulation agreed to by the defense that the ambulance left the Castillian at 11:56 P.M.; and the testimony of Dave King and Ethel Davis.

King, the man who had sold Alan a .25 caliber automatic in July of 1967, testified that while he could not swear the gun had been a Colt, he would "bet a thousand dollars on it." Ethel Davis gave crucial testimony that in a telephone conversation with Alan on the evening of April 22, 1968, two nights after Judy's murder, Alan made several statements which I would later argue showed he had personal knowledge of the circumstances surrounding the murder: that Judy had put up quite a struggle; that she was pistol whipped; and that it was the first bullet that struck her in the breast. Goldin, conceding that neither the police nor the coroner had spoken to Alan of their speculations, would, in final summation, contend that Alan had learned these facts from the preliminary death certificate and, although Dave never produced any articles to support his position, possibly from newspapers as well.

To close the prosecution's case, I called the witness who was present the very moment Alan learned that Judy had died. Kathleen Egan, the registered nurse at County General Hospital, testified that although Alan seemed to be in disbelief when he was initially informed that Judy was not expected to live, he did not break down in any way when he was later told by the surgeon that Judy had expired. Goldin and I, through our respective questions, made it clear to the jury which of the two reactions we thought was the true Alan Palliko.

The prosecution had no further witnesses to call on the murder of Judy Palliko. I did not know that Dave Goldin had a strategy and two witnesses who, if believed, would virtually throw all suspicion away from Alan Palliko.

Wednesday, January 22, two months and four days after the trial began, the prosecution rested its case.

10

BOTH GOLDIN AND CALLAS made brief arguments to Judge Young under Section 1118.1 of the California Penal Code for a court-ordered acquittal because of insufficient evidence. The motion was denied, and the defense proceeded to present its own case to the jury.

Terry Callas presented a very short defense. Sometimes, short presentations by the defense signify a belief on their part that the most important aspects of their case have already been brought forth by their cross-examination of the witnesses for the prosecution. Still, I had to wonder about the wisdom of Callas' decision.

Callas elicited from Dave Correa, the DA investigator, the fact that none of the seven phone numbers Miss Walther had left with Alan's answering service belonged to Sandra. One was listed to the Auto Club, where Sandra no longer worked at that time, one was Alan's home number, three were public phone booths, and two belonged to other private residences.

On cross-examination, I brought out the fact that the two Los Angeles residents whose numbers had been used had stated, when Correa paid them visits, that they had never heard of a Miss Walther. As far as I was concerned, Callas had shown the jury little more than that Sandra had used her head enough to not link her own phone number with the name Miss Walther.

Both Tim Barnes, Sandra's brother-in-law, and Harriet Bingham, Sandra's mother, testified for the defense that Sandra had been very despondent over Henry's death. Callas prefaced his questions to Mrs.

Bingham by asking if she would lie to help her daughter and she answered with an admirable frankness: "Yes, I would."

After Callas finished examining Mrs. Bingham, he paused, slowly turning a few of his papers on the counsel table in front of him. The spectators, their coats and umbrellas across their laps on this rainy day, eyed Sandra. Anticipating the possibility that Sandra herself would take the few steps to the stand and attempt to explain the incriminating evidence that had mounted against her, I had, during the course of the trial, prepared twenty-two pages of cross-examining questions for her. The questions went for naught; Callas stood up and announced, "The defense rests, Your Honor."

Although many defendants who do not take the stand are still acquitted, I asked Callas out in the parking lot at the end of the day about his tactic of not putting Sandra on the stand, offering Terry my opinion that so often no sound in a courtroom is as loud as a defendant's silence. From the side of his mouth, Terry groused, "She's not quick enough for cross." He tossed his attaché case on the back seat of his car. "We have a much better shot at acquittal keeping her off the stand."

Dave Goldin came for a fight. The first string of witnesses he called to the stand gave testimony which, while technically relevant only to the second murder, applied equally well to the first murder count because it constituted a pointed attack on Michael Brockington's credibility.

A friend of Alan's and Judy's, Shirley Taylor, testified that while attending another friend's birthday party at a restaurant a month before Alan and Judy were married, Alan had stated he was thinking of buying Judy a .38 caliber handgun, and that it was then that Michael Brockington leaned over to Mrs. Taylor and made the comment, "Me, I prefer a .25. It's easier to conceal in the palm of your hand." The alleged statement had only been heard by Mrs. Taylor, whom I could not move one inch on cross-examination.

Dwight "Butch" Rolapp, Alan's car mechanic and friend, sporting muttonchop sideburns in court, testified that on January 10, 1968, Michael Brockington had brought his own car in to have a stereo tape deck installed, and that in the course of conversation, Michael vowed to someday cause Alan harm. Gesturing easily with smudged, meaty hands, Rolapp testified that Michael told him he had been wronged in business by Alan and that he was going to "get even with Alan at any cost." Michael also purportedly said that Alan was homosexual.

Rolapp's testimony struck me as blatant perjury. It was extremely unlikely that Michael would have made such comments to a man who was Alan's good friend, not his, knowing that the derogatory remarks and threats would get back to Alan. Furthermore, there was no other evidence that Alan's and Michael's relationship was on the rocks at the time of the supposed remarks. Michael continued working for Alan at the Grand Duke for two full months thereafter, and it was a month and a half after these alleged statements that Alan asked Michael to be the best man at his wedding.

But if Rolapp's testimony was perjurious, it did not surprise me. As the late Francis L. Wellman, a distinguished member of the New York bar, once observed: "Scarcely a trial is conducted in which perjury does not appear in a more or less flagrant form." Perjury is so common that prosecutors are not only not surprised by it, they expect it.

Essentially, there are two basic types of perjury at a criminal trial, the first being where the defendant who has committed a crime denies guilt under oath. This form of self-defense is obviously anticipated and almost invariably overlooked. If the defendant were not going to deny having committed the crime, he normally would have pled guilty and there would not have been any trial. In every case where a defendant has denied guilt from the witness stand and is subsequently convicted, the finding of guilt by the jury, by definition, is a concomitant finding that they believe the defendant committed perjury when he denied guilt under oath. Yet for the hundreds of thousands of defendants convicted every year throughout the land for various crimes, it is almost unheard of for there to follow, after their conviction, a prosecution against them (or members of their family who may have lied under oath on their behalf) for perjury.

The second type of perjury at a criminal trial is the kind that is not self-defensive in nature, one example of which occurring when a witness knowingly and falsely accuses an innocent party of a crime. This kind of perjury, if it can be proven, usually does result in a criminal prosecution.

Dwight Rolapp's claim that Michael vowed, "to get even with Alan at any cost" (the implication being that it was Michael who

had murdered Judy) approached, I believed, the second, far more serious category.

Q. BY MR. BUGLIOSI: "Mr. Rolapp, when did you first tell Alan
about this conversation you allegedly had with Mr. Brockington?"

A. "I believe I related part of it to him in jail."

Q. "You didn't feel any need before then to tell Alan that he might
be in trouble?"

A. "No, I didn't think there was going to be any trouble."

Q. "But you believed Michael Brockington when he told you he
was going to get even with Palliko at all costs. Is that right?"

A. "Right. But he could have meant he was going to smash him in
the mouth, for all I knew."

Q. "That is what the words—'I'm going to get even at all costs'—
means to you? Maybe a punch in the nose?"

A. "Not necessarily. It could have meant a number of things. Anything."

Q. "It could have meant that he wanted to kill Alan Palliko, isn't
that true?"

A. "It could have meant anything in my eyes."

Q. "Why didn't you tell Alan then?"

A. "It didn't seem like it was my place to involve myself in their argument," Rolapp answered rather lamely.

Rolapp also stated he did not tell Alan about Brockington's comments concerning his sexuality because to Rolapp, accusing a man of
homosexuality was of no more gravity than calling him an s.o.b. I
could only hope the jury found his entire testimony as patently ab-
surd as I did.

Rolapp's wife, Nora, who had recently gone to work at the Grand
Duke as a barmaid, testified that Michael had told her also that Alan
was homosexual, and that Judy was a lesbian. Her long black hair in
Indian pigtails, and wearing turquoise, quarter-moon earrings—like
an Arizona hitch-hiker with racy stories to tell—she testified further
that Michael told her of driving into the desert by himself to pick up
an envelope full of money for Alan. I did not believe her any more
than I believed her husband, and on cross-examination I did little to
bridle my sarcasm.

Q. BY MR. BUGLIOSI: "Did Brockington say that this desert was the
Sahara Desert?"

A. "He didn't say. He just said the desert."

Q. "Did he say whether the envelope was behind a rock?"

A. "No, he didn't."

Q. "He didn't say anything about Gila monsters being in the area, did he?"

MR. GOLDIN: "I'm going to object."

THE COURT: "Objection sustained."

Q. "Have you been visiting Alan up at the jail?"

A. "Yes, I have."

Q. "Pretty frequently?"

A. "Yes, I try and make it once a week."

Q. "Do you like Alan?"

A. "Very much so."

Q. "Alan Palliko is your boss now, isn't he?"

A. "In a manner of speaking."

Q. "In a manner of speaking?"

A. "Well—yes, he's my boss."

Q. "You want to continue working as a barmaid at the Grand Duke, don't you?"

A. "Well, yes."

MR. BUGLIOSI: "No further questions."

As Nora Rolapp stepped down off the witness stand, the high-heeled boots beneath her jeans clicking curtly on her way past me, a look of jowly disappointment was on Dave Goldin's face. He had never expected that Dwight and Nora Rolapp, by their testimony alone, would be able to return Alan to the Grand Duke, but he was hopeful they would at least give him a leg up in his effort to raise a reasonable doubt of Alan's guilt on both murders. It was obvious they had not done that.

But Dave now stood up, hands in his back pockets, his voice confident, and called the first of two witnesses whose surprise testimony he could not wait to spring on the crowded courtroom.

Daryl Lott, a hulking cost estimator at Northrop Aircraft, preceded his wife Denise to the stand. Both testified that they had visited Judy at Alan's and her apartment sometime between 11:00 P.M. and midnight the night before she was murdered, and that Judy had come to the door with a gun in her hand, concealed beneath the kimono she was wearing. When Mrs. Lott was on the stand, Goldin asked her if Judy told them why she had come to the door with a gun in her hand. The question called for pure hearsay, and I jumped to my feet and objected before an answer could be given.

Having heard the testimony thus far about Judy coming to the door holding a gun, I could only surmise that if Mrs. Lott were allowed to continue she was going to testify that Judy told them she was in fear of her life. Furthermore, it was obvious Mrs. Lott was going to say that the person Judy said she was in fear of was someone other than Alan. People simply do not walk around the house with loaded guns to protect themselves from people they have chosen to continue to live with.

There was little doubt in my mind that the Lotts' testimony was one hundred percent fabrication. It was just too pat. The very night before her murder, Judy supposedly declared a fear for her life at the hands of someone other than Alan. If it were true, why had the defense not already furnished me or the police with this fact so an investigation of this other suspect might have been initiated? Instead, all they were offering was hearsay—hearsay which, as Judy lay in her grave, could not be contradicted.

Judge Young stated that at first blush the proposed testimony appeared inadmissible, but that he would hold an evidentiary hearing outside the presence of the jury to determine exactly what Mr. and Mrs. Lott were intending to testify to. I asked that the courtroom be cleared of spectators as well, for I did not want to run the risk of the Lotts' story being later repeated by a spectator out in the hallway or in an elevator in the presence of a juror. Judge Young granted my request.

Daryl Lott took the stand and finished the story that his wife had begun. His testimony in the closed hearing was exactly what I had expected. The night before her murder, Judy supposedly told him and his wife that prior to her marriage to Alan, she had had a boyfriend back in New York City, and that this boyfriend had once chased her all over the city with a gun and had threatened to kill her if she ever took up with another man.

Judge Young ruled the intended testimony inadmissible hearsay.

My sense of victory, however, was not long-lived. As I began mulling the matter over during lunch, I realized I had been caught in a trap. The jury had already heard Denise Lott's testimony that Judy had come to the door with a gun. Although they had not heard the rest of the story due to my objection, the only logical inference for the jurors to now draw was that Denise Lott was prepared to testify that Judy was carrying the gun because she was in fear of her life at the hands of someone other than Alan Palliko. Even without the

Lotts' testimony as to this, Goldin had achieved precisely what he had intended to achieve. Moreover, by my objection, the jury would most likely believe that I, as the prosecutor, had invoked technical rules to suppress a significant piece of evidence that would have pointed to Alan's innocence. To be sure, the necessity of my objection had cast me in a bad light, and more importantly, a new doubt had now been injected into the case that could possibly lead to Alan's acquittal on the second murder count.

By the end of my lunch hour, I resolved to withdraw my objection and allow into evidence the totality of the Lotts' testimony, and take my chances on being able to impeach that testimony. There was very little time to gather rebutting evidence.

I immediately called Judy's mother, Ethel Davis, and learned that aside from Felix Zimmer (who was with the Davises at the time of Judy's murder), the only boyfriend of any significance whom Judy had had back in New York was the man by the name of Prescott Nelson. I asked Detective Strickland to contact the New York City Police Department and request that they find Nelson for us. The NYPD responded immediately. They located Nelson at his place of work on the floor of the New York Stock Exchange. Prescott Nelson was a respected broker in the city.

Nelson told me over the phone that while only his mother could testify to the fact that he was visiting her in upstate New York on the Saturday of the murder, his employers could verify he was at work on both the Friday preceding and the Monday following the murder. Certainly, a man's mother cannot be termed a disinterested alibi witness, but I felt the combination of her testimony and the sworn affidavits by Nelson's employers would yield a reasonably strong case that Prescott Nelson was not in California on April 20, 1968. I made arrangements to fly both Nelson and his mother out to L.A.

The next day I advised Goldin and Judge Young of my decision to withdraw the objection to the Lotts' hearsay testimony. When Goldin realized, however, that I could prove that the "boyfriend from New York" was highly unlikely to have committed the murder, he stated that he no longer wanted to offer the remainder of the Lotts' testimony.

I was furious. The prosecution had been trapped unfairly, and I launched into a tirade against Goldin to which he did not even respond. As we came out of chambers, the jury not being present, I continued my verbal attack upon him. Any first year law student

would have known that asking Mrs. Lott to relate what Judy allegedly told her was asking for inadmissible hearsay that was bound to
be objected to, I told Goldin.

Growing increasingly red in the face, Goldin suggested we return
to judge's chambers. There he backed down and stated he would recall the Lotts to the stand if I, in return, would allow another otherwise inadmissible piece of hearsay to come in. Goldin wanted the jury
to hear a statement by Mrs. Davis to Lieutenant Vandergrift that
Judy had told her the woman who had been staring in at her through
the apartment window a week before her murder was Alan's ex-wife,
Katherine.

I readily agreed to the deal. It was an unequal *quid pro quo* for
Goldin. Judy's sister Lisa was prepared to testify that despite what
her mother had once told the police, Judy had stated quite clearly to
both her and her mother that Alan had shown her pictures of Katherine, and that it was not she at the window. If Goldin were trying to
take suspicion away from Alan by fingering Katherine, I knew there
was no place for him to go with that theory. There was not a tad of
evidence that Katherine was jealous of Alan's second wife. It was
Katherine who had refused Alan's proposals of marriage, not vice
versa. All Katherine had wanted of Alan was to be left alone.

Before Daryl Lott retook the stand, I stood up before the jury and
stated: "Your Honor, as the record reflects, I previously objected to
the alleged conversation between Judy Palliko and the Lotts being received into evidence, and my objection was sustained. However, I
have reconsidered my position. I want the conversation to come in,
and hereby withdraw my objection." With that, Lott proceeded to tell
the jury of Judy's supposed fears of her old boyfriend from New
York.

I rose to cross-examine.

Books on cross-examination advocate never asking a witness
"why" he did something implausible, because this gives him free rein
to explain away his conduct. Normally, I do not follow this maxim of
cross-examination. Even if I do not ask "why," the lawyer who called
the witness, if alert, will do so on redirect. The witness has then often
had a court recess or perhaps overnight to think up the very best answer to the "why" question. I would much rather force the witness to
answer on cross, not giving him extra time to fabricate.

Although both lawyers can avoid asking the why question and, as
in some other situations, "save for final argument" the implications

of the witness' testimony, by that late point in the trial the witness' reason for his improbable act is a matter of competing speculations by the lawyers, not court record.

If I feel a witness is lying, a simple technique I frequently employ is to first elicit answers from him on preliminary matters, answers which, when totaled up, show he would be *expected* to take a certain *course of action*. The witness having committed himself by his answers, I then ask him what course he in fact took, and follow this up with the "why" question. If time after time a witness is unable to satisfactorily justify conduct of his which is incompatible with what would be expected of a reasonable person, the jury will usually conclude that his testimony is suspect.

I used this type of cross-examination extensively with Daryl Lott, starting in on the issue of whether he and his wife had even stopped at the Pallikos' apartment at all that night:

Q. "How did you happen to stop by Alan's and Judy's apartment around 11:00 P.M. Friday night, April 19, 1968, Mr. Lott?"

A. "I don't know. I do a lot of things on the spur of the moment. Just decided to stop in, say hello."

From the outset of my cross-examination, Lott was constantly readjusting his horn-rimmed glasses.

Q. "I understand you were a closer friend of Alan's than you were of Judy's, is that true?"

A. "Well, I knew Alan longer. Let's put it that way."

Q. "Is there any question in your mind that you were much closer to Alan than to Judy?"

A. "No. I was. You're right."

Q. "You had been to Alan's Grand Duke Bar on previous Friday nights, had you not?"

A. "Yes."

Q. "Did Alan normally close up the bar on these Friday nights?"

A. "Oh, yeah, I suppose he did. A lot of times he closes up the bar, yes."

Q. "About what time did Alan normally close the bar?"

A. "Two o'clock in the morning."

Q. "Did you think that this particular Friday night Alan would be home instead of at the Grand Duke?"

A. "I had no idea."

Q. "The Grand Duke is pretty close to their apartment, isn't it?"

A. "Sure is."

Q. "Would it have been out of your way to first stop at the Grand Duke?"

A. "I don't suppose so, no."

Q. "Did you first stop at the Grand Duke to see if Alan was there before you went to Judy's apartment?"

A. "No, I don't believe we did."

Q. "Any particular reason why you didn't, Mr. Lott?"

A. "Uh . . . no reason at all."

Fidgeting, Lott tried to push his glasses farther up the bridge of his nose, though they could go no higher.

Q. "So although you knew there was a strong possibility that Alan would not be home, you still decided to stop at his apartment unannounced; is that right?"

A. "That's right."

Q. "Did you knock on the apartment door, Mr. Lott?"

A. "Well, I believe I either knocked or pushed the bell. One or the other."

Q. "Did Judy say, 'Who's there?' "

A. "Yes, she called out, asked who it was."

Q. "And you identified yourself?"

A. "That's right."

Q. "And yet, even though she knew you, when she opened the door she was holding a gun in her hand?"

A. "Yes."

Q. "Didn't that frighten you?"

A. "No, it didn't. I suppose what happened was, she came to the door with the gun, and then, right after we identified ourselves, why, she just opened the door. She didn't go back and put the gun down before she opened the door."

Q. "To help Alan, you are making all of this up, aren't you, Mr. Lott?"

You ask a question like this not because you expect, as on TV, a confession from the witness that his testimony is fabricated, but because you want to underline in the jury's mind *your* belief that the witness is lying and because you want the jury to see the witness' demeanor while answering that question.

A. "No, this is the . . . this is the honest truth," Daryl Lott grumbled.

Q. "So Judy left this boyfriend from New York more than a year ago, but the night you came to the door, she was armed with a gun; right?"

A. "That's right."

Q. "And she led you to believe that she was in constant, everyday fear of this man killing her, is that correct?"

A. "Yes, she led me to believe that."

Q. "Then you learned that the very next day Judy was murdered?"

A. "Right."

Q. "And in your mind Alan Palliko was innocent; isn't that true?"

A. "Yes."

Q. "I take it the thought must have entered your mind that maybe this man from New York was the one who did it?"

A. "Yes, it did."

Q. "Did you ever contact the police in any way whatsoever, by phone, letter, or by going down to the station, and telling them what you knew?"

A. "No, I didn't tell the police."

Q. "Why not, sir?"

A. "Well, I believe I told Alan and I figured that was enough."

Q. "But you believed Alan was innocent and you knew he was being charged with murder. Didn't you want to help your friend Alan by telling the police that someone else probably murdered Judy?"

A. "That's why I'm testifying here right now."

Q. "You decided to wait until now, a year later, to tell your story. Is that right, sir?"

A. "No."

Q. "Why didn't you call the police then, Mr. Lott?"

A. "I don't know. I just didn't call them. I don't really know."

I saved my ultimate blow to Daryl Lott's credibility for last. Lott had been one of the defense witnesses from whom our investigator, Dave Correa, had been able to get a statement outside of court.

Q. "Have you ever heard of a man by the name of Dave Correa, Mr. Lott?"

A. "I don't believe so."

Q. "Did any man ever come to your residence on January 4, 1969, and identify himself as an investigator from the District Attorney's Office?"

A. "Oh, yes."

Q. "Okay. At some point in the conversation with Mr. Correa, you told him that on the night before the murder you visited Judy Palliko. Is that correct?"

A. "Yes, I did."

Q. "Did you tell Dave Correa, Mr. Lott, that Judy met you at the door with a gun?"

A. "I don't remember. I might have, I might not. I don't remember."

Q. "Do you recall Mr. Correa asking you if you had any idea at all who may have wanted to kill Judy? Do you remember his asking you that?"

A. "To be honest with you, I don't remember."

Daryl Lott's memory was suddenly a blank. I later called Dave Correa to the stand. Referring to the written notes he had taken during his interview with the Lotts, Correa testified that the Lotts had made no mention of Judy coming to the door with a gun or of her alleged fear of an old boyfriend. When asked directly if everything seemed all right with Judy the night before her murder, the Lotts had replied yes. They stated they had no idea of who would have wanted to kill Judy.

Goldin asked no questions of Correa. Dave reasoned there was little that could be said to explain the Lotts' failure to inform Correa of what they supposedly knew.

I asked very few questions of Mrs. Lott on cross-examination, hoping to convey to the jury my disgust with the Lotts and my refusal to waste any more of the court's time with their testimony. As it turned out, I did not even have to fly Prescott Nelson out to L.A. Denise Lott testified on redirect examination that the only description she remembered Judy giving of this old boyfriend from New York was that he was German. There was, of course, only one old boyfriend who fit that description—Felix Zimmer. I later called Felix to the stand, as well as Ethel and Lisa Davis, for their testimony that Felix Zimmer was with the Davis family at a Moose Lodge party in Glendale the entire evening of Judy's murder.

Having to live up to my end of the bargain, I did not object to Goldin's calling Lieutenant Vandergrift for the hearsay testimony that Mrs. Davis had quoted Judy as saying that the woman peeking through the window was Katherine. Ethel Davis later took the stand and denied having told Vandergrift that. Her own daughter Lisa subsequently gave testimony that seemed to be the most accurate explanation of the entire incident. Lieutenant Vandergrift, it appeared, had been almost as confused as Ethel Davis. Mrs. Davis, according to Lisa who had been present at the interview, told Vandergrift that Judy had said the woman was *not* Alan's ex-wife, Katherine, but that she (Mrs. Davis) still had suspicions at that time that it might have been Katherine. She simply had not had faith in Judy's ability to compare Katherine's pictures with the woman she had seen. Since Sandra was not charged with Judy's murder, what I could not allow Lisa to repeat from the stand was the description that Judy had given her of the woman who had been staring through the window at her just one week before her murder—"a short, stocky blonde."

11

GOLDIN CALLED SEVERAL witnesses to discredit the testimony of Simcoe and Whalen, one of whom was a detective sergeant for the Los Angeles Police Department. John Ide, the Van Nuys Division detective, testified that Alan called him a few days after Judy's death, complaining of a threatening call he had received from the then incarcerated Simcoe. Alan had told Sergeant Ide: "I've got enough problems without some punk yo-yo threatening me." Ide testified that Simcoe later confirmed the fact for him that he had called Alan, but denied having threatened him. Frankly, I myself doubted that Simcoe had phoned Alan just to shoot the breeze. To be sure, the testimony about Simcoe's alleged threats to Alan did little to enhance Simcoe's credibility as a witness for the prosecution.

Barmaid Susan Peters, a former girlfriend of Simcoe's before becoming one of Alan's employees, came back to the stand to testify that Simcoe told her he was going to have one of his friends outside of jail blow up the Grand Duke Bar, but that he would make sure someone would call her ahead of time, telling her when to clear out of the place.

Feeling it would be difficult for the jury to believe Alan could be responsible for Judy's murder if they felt he was genuinely grieved by her death, Goldin called a succession of witnesses to testify to their observations of Alan shortly after the murder. Ward Gullion, the businessman who sold Alan the second beer bar, insisted Alan was in "complete shock" the night after the murder. Susan Peters testified that everyone eventually knew not to bring up the subject of Judy's death, because anytime someone did, Alan broke down in tears. Pete

Morris added that the day after the murder, Alan was "beside himself, he didn't know what to do—he was looking terrible and very sad, and his eyes were red."

On cross-examination, I did get Morris to admit that he was still employed at Alan's Burbank bar, and that a week after the trial started, Alan's father had paid a large dental bill for him. The only concession Gullion would make on cross-examination was that he considered Alan "like a son."

To explain Alan's late November and mid-December, 1966, remarks about expecting money soon, Goldin called Sid Palliko, who testified to his loan of $3,000 to Alan on December 28, 1966.

Following Mr. Palliko, and as part of his rebuttal to Brockington, who had stated he heard Alan on the phone saying, "Calm down, Tiger, don't let the police rattle you," Goldin then called Tricia Rolapp, the ten-year-old daughter of Alan's car mechanic, who testified that "Tiger" was one of Alan's pet names for her and her sister. On cross, I had only one question for Tricia.

Q. "Did Alan ever tell you, honey, not to let the police rattle you?"

Tricia giggled. To a little girl the question, I am sure, must have seemed funny.

A. "No, he didn't."

MR. BUGLIOSI: "No further questions."

I had heard rumblings that Alan had been vacillating throughout the trial as to whether or not he would testify. In the event that he would take the stand, I had prepared thirty-five pages of cross-examination questions for him. But just as Callas had kept Sandra off the stand, Goldin, too, closed his defense without calling Alan to testify.

Dave confided to me that he was keeping Alan off the stand because, although at a certain personal level he found Alan immensely likable, under other circumstances (such as cross-examination) he was afraid the uglier side of Alan would dominate. "He's just too damn cocky," Dave told me. "An ex-cop still with a chip on his shoulder."

In the 1965 case of *Griffin v. California,* the U.S. Supreme Court forbade "either comment by the prosecution on the accused's silence or instructions by the court that such silence is evidence of guilt." It was, I felt, a thoroughly proper decision by the Court. For a prosecutor to insinuate in any way that a defendant's exercise of his Fifth

Amendment right against self-incrimination shows a consciousness of guilt is to in effect negate the entire benefit of that constitutional right.

The Rolapp girl was the last witness to be called to the stand, and Monday morning, February 3, the defense rested. The trial thus far had lasted eleven weeks; 109 prosecution and defense witnesses had testified. Coincidentally, the number of exhibits received into evidence was also 109. Before the final arguments by counsel, we had already consumed over 4,700 pages of court transcript. Judge Pierce Young observed that he had never seen a criminal trial so overflowing with delicate problems of admissibility and legal complexity. Back in chambers he chuckled, "Someone should write a book about this one."

Criminal procedure provides for the prosecution to make an opening argument (not to be confused with the opening *statement,* which is given at the beginning of a trial), followed by the defense's argument, which is then followed by the prosecution's closing argument (final summation). Because the People bear the burden of proof, they are given the "last word."

The body of evidence in the Palliko-Stockton trial had been considerable. Just as I had at the beginning of the trial, I once again reminded the jury to utilize the pads and pencils provided them to take detailed notes, which they did. My opening argument to the jury consumed two court days and 361 pages of court transcript. To hold a jury's attention for an hour can be difficult; to hold it for two days is genuine work. One has to employ drama, metaphor and, where appropriate, even humor.

I began by discussing in depth, sometimes with charts I had prepared, various points of law: deliberation, premeditation, malice aforethought, conspiracy, circumstantial evidence, and so on. Judge Young would later give the Court's formal instructions on the law, but instructions from the bench are always stated in that rather stilted, confusing legal jargon.

In trials where a defendant admits an unlawful killing, the only issue is the degree of homicide—i.e., first or second degree murder, voluntary or involuntary manslaughter. Malice, deliberation, premeditation, etc., are the contested issues. But here, I pointed out to the jury, even defense counsel would agree that regardless of who killed Henry Stockton and Judy Palliko, it was obvious the killings were deliberate, premeditated, and with malice aforethought—and therefore first degree murder.

The identity of the killer(s) and the existence or nonexistence of a criminal conspiracy were what this trial was all about.

I told the jury that although the term "conspiracy" sounds nebulous, it is really nothing more than a "partnership in crime." For there to be a conspiracy, I explained, only two elements need be present: first, an agreement between two or more people to commit a crime; and second, an act, any act, by one or more of the conspirators to help carry out that crime.

Moving to the heart of a conspiracy, the *agreement* element, I told the jury that from Alan's and Sandra's conduct and statements, the question they had to resolve was whether Alan and Sandra were "acting in concert, whether they had a meeting of the minds, a common purpose," or whether they were "at cross-purposes with each other and going in opposite directions."

I intended to put the evidence in this case under a "high-powered microscope," I added, evidence that, drawn into clear focus, would show the existence of a conspiracy to commit murder, and thereby make both Alan and Sandra responsible for the other's criminal conduct.

Painstakingly, I recapped and analyzed for the jury in my opening argument the testimony of each of the 109 prosecution and defense witnesses, not in the order in which they testified, but in the chronological order of *events* to which they testified. When citing particularly vital pieces of testimony, I reached for one of the many volumes of court transcript I had arranged at the counsel table, their relevant pages marked by snippets of paper. Reading directly from the transcript tends to carry a psychological weight of authority with the jury.

On a blackboard, I listed the dates and amounts of insurance payments to Sandra and the dates and amounts of her banking deposits and withdrawals. Side by side I put the dates and amounts of Alan's bank deposits and the dates of his safe deposit box entries. I reviewed each and every instance of known contact between Alan and Sandra over a period of two years. Facts, inferences, connections, conclusions. Motive, means, opportunity. Slowly, placing one speck of circumstantial evidence upon another, I reviewed the case until I had presented what I had thought was a recognizable, indeed unavoidable mosaic of guilt.

"Jurors are not expected to possess supernatural powers," I concluded my opening argument. "All that can be expected of you as reasonable men and women is to conscientiously evaluate the evidence, apply your logic, common sense, reasoning powers, and the law given to you by his Honor *to* that evidence, and thereby reach a just and fair verdict. That's all that can be expected of you."

All of the evidence, looked at in its *totality,* I told the jury, proved beyond all reasonable doubt that Alan and Sandra had conspired to murder Henry Stockton, that Alan had been the one who pulled the trigger and brutally murdered Henry, and that Alan, a year and a half later, had either engineered or personally committed the murder of his own wife. Alan and Sandra were guilty of murder, I said, and it was murder in the first degree.

For a protracted case of circumstantial evidence, where any number of inferences and arguments on both sides can always be made, Terry Callas' summation was disturbingly brief, approximately an hour and covering only thirty-eight pages of transcript.

Always speaking quietly—his was the soft sell—Callas said, almost defensively, "Don't be moved by the power and eloquence of Mr. Bugliosi. Look at the evidence." He maintained that his client was innocent of her husband's murder, that she had been a victim of circumstances. He drew attention to the testimony of Vicky Stowe, who had described Sandra as "pale and shaken, her eyes red from crying" upon learning of Henry's death. Callas argued that if Sergeant Aguirre had found Sandra "calm and unemotional" later on that Sunday afternoon, there had been good reason for Sandra's change in demeanor. Aguirre's interview with Sandra, Callas said, had been implicitly accusatory. First, the sergeant told her that Henry had died as a result of fire, then he implied that it might have been suicide and only at the end of the hour-long interview did he tell her that Henry had been shot five times. And it was then that Aguirre asked if Sandra would come down to the station for fingerprinting. Surely any woman, Callas argued, would be straightened up and pulled from a mood of grief by that kind of police interrogation.

Terry contended further that the insurance policy being found within arm's reach of Henry's body was an indication that the true killer had done what he could to make sure Sandra would have a lot of explaining to do. While conceding that Alan and Sandra did spend several days together in Las Vegas, the fact that Sandra "showered" that city with signed traveler's checks during the trip, Callas said, clearly showed a consciousness of innocence, not guilt. The plane ticket for "Mr. B. Johnson," he added, could not have belonged to Sandra. If she had wanted to use an alias, there was no reason she would not have picked a woman's name.

Callas turned to the blackboard where I had drawn the chart of Alan's and Sandra's banking transactions and offered a strong counterargument to my payoff theory. Conspirators, he said, split money neatly and cleanly, not in dribbles over a period of months. "Does it look like a payoff between co-conspirators?" he asked the jury. "Or does it look more like someone taking advantage of a source of money as the needs arise?" Callas' theory was that Alan, with an emotional hold on Sandra, had exploited Sandra's sudden new affluence.

By the end of his summation, Callas had made it abundantly clear that he wanted to put a distance in the jurors' minds between their thoughts about Sandra and their thoughts about Alan. He was arguing his own client's innocence, but definitely not her codefendant's. His last words, in fact, came close to implying that he believed Alan had engineered Henry's murder all on his own.

MR. CALLAS: "If you consider the evidence that has been presented against Sandra Stockton *only,* it is reasonable that you would return a verdict of not guilty. The only person who was using aliases was *Palliko*—not Sandra. There is nothing in the record of this case to show deceptive, fraudulent practices by Sandra. Nothing.

"Thank you very much."

Although Dave Goldin was clearly aware of the important facts and issues in the case, he still conveyed at times an air of unpreparedness. His papers strewn across the defense table, he rambled discursively during his final summation and apologized several times to the jury for the disarray of his notes.

His client was innocent of both murders, Goldin declared. As had Callas, Goldin argued that the prosecution's case was built solely on circumstantial evidence, and therefore the question of guilt should be compared to a chain, each and every linking fact in the prosecution's case necessary lest the chain be broken. There were many "missing links" in the People's case, Goldin asserted.

"When I look back at this kind of evidence," he said, "I can't conceive of a conviction being obtained on this kind of evidence."

Gaining speed in his summation, Goldin, also like Callas, put heavy emphasis on the instructions given a jury in cases of circumstantial evidence, particularly the one that stated that not only need the evidence be consistent with the theory of guilt to warrant a conviction, but it must be irreconcilable with "*any* other rational conclusion."

Goldin struck effectively at what had always been the heart of the problem for the prosecution throughout the investigation and trial of the Palliko-Stockton murders. Although the circumstantial evidence in the first murder count, Goldin conceded, pointed conceivably to a conspiracy between Alan and Sandra, did it not, he queried, also point to many other rational possibilities? Was it not possible that Sandra confided to Alan of hiring someone to kill her husband, to which Alan might have replied, "Baby, you just told the wrong guy," and thereafter blackmailed her for half of the insurance proceeds? Was it not just as likely that Alan, aware of Sandra's having come into money, simply extorted it, threatening harm to Sandra's son if he were not cut in for a share? If the jury were to believe Alan capable of murder, Goldin pointed out, surely they could view him capable of extortion. Was there anything so inconceivable, he asked, about Alan's simply being Sandra's gigolo? The possibilities were endless, Goldin said.

As to Alan's sudden affluence in 1967, Goldin observed of his client: "He borrows money, he gambles, he cons a little, promotes, hustles, he works at least one job at a time, sometimes three."

Time and again Dave properly reminded the jury that under the law, they could not convict unless they had been convinced of the defendant's guilt *beyond all reasonable doubt and to a moral certainty.* The prosecution, he said, had not met this burden of proof.

How can you send someone to the gas chamber or to prison for life, Goldin asked, when there is no direct evidence or even one piece of physical evidence to connect the defendant to the crime? (The testimony of the one "eyewitness" in the case was, in fact, circumstantial as opposed to direct evidence. Walter Wasson never testified he saw Alan Palliko, only someone with a physique and walk *like* Palliko's. Moreover, he only saw the man walking away from the general area of the murder, not committing the murder.)

Goldin argued that Alan's beating of Katherine did not constitute attempted murder because Alan had no specific intent to kill Katherine, a necessary element in the crime of attempted murder. While deploring the violence of his client's act, he asked the jury if it were reasonable that Katherine would have gone on living with Alan (and later seeing him after the divorce) if she herself had seriously believed Alan had intended to kill her. The hospital room admission, he said, was a matter of loose words, something Alan was known for. Had he really told Katherine, "I tried to kill you," or had he said something such as, "I was so angry I wanted to kill you?" Alan's words, Goldin contended, were not to be taken seriously.

As to the murder of Judy, Goldin asked: If, as the prosecution was alleging, Alan married Judy for the purpose of insuring her and then murdering her, why had Alan not chosen Debbi?

(It was a difficult question to answer. Perhaps an explanation, I thought to myself, was that Alan had sensed that, unlike Debbi, his other women, while attracted to many things about him, had not really approved of him as a human being. Even Judy had stormed out of the bar the day Alan celebrated Martin Luther King's assassination. Just maybe, Debbi's loyal nonjudgmental love for him had touched Alan and, by touching him, had saved her life.)

One could not believe Alan's big talk about dangerous "plans," Goldin continued. Alan was a storyteller. Dave told the jury that Alan's "hired killer" drawing of three circles and two lines was straight out of a Rod Steiger movie that Dave himself had seen.

The attack on my alternative theories was expected.

MR. GOLDIN: "And the District Attorney takes the principle—I'm proceeding on two theories: One theory is he was at the bar and you believe these witnesses who tell you he's at the bar, and he was nervous and edgy, and he sent her home, and he received a call ten minutes after that. And if you don't believe that, I want you to believe that he was there at the apartment walking out. Take your pick."

Growing more aggressive, Goldin charged me with having a "threatening manner" when cross-examining defense witnesses, and with making "deliberate misstatements" of the evidence in my opening argument. His most concerted attack, however, was not leveled at me alone, but rather at me and Michael Brockington together. He called Brockington my "Mr. Fill-in-the-Gap," a man who provided too many details on too many subjects to be believed.

Citing for the jury the instruction to be given by the judge that all unwritten, unrecorded admissions or confessions of a defendant should be viewed by the jury "with caution," Goldin characterized Alan's alleged confession to Brockington of having killed Henry Stockton as a complete fabrication of Brockington's "very active, weasel-wordy mind." And why had Brockington lied? To put the heat on Alan not only for the first murder but, more importantly, by implication, for the second murder as well. Dave Goldin came right out with it—he believed Michael Brockington murdered Judy Palliko.

Goldin harkened back to a critical point in the Burbank detectives' interview with Brockington. When King and Nylander sensed Brockington was lying about not knowing if Alan had fenced any stolen goods, the following exchanges occurred, exchanges Goldin read back to the jury:

KING: "The thing is, Mike, if you're not involved in the homicide, we want to be able to clear you . . . but if you did the favor and did his wife in, which we don't say you did, but *if* you did, your life isn't worth a plugged nickel."

BROCKINGTON: "Right."

KING: "Even if he knew you did it for him."

BROCKINGTON: "Right."

KING: "All we're saying, Mike, is this. We've got a young girl who was killed, brutally killed. We have our own ideas about it, but I don't want you to get caught in the middle of a trap because you know a lot of things."

BROCKINGTON: "Let's face it. If I'm going to get caught, then it's going to be one or the other. I mean if it's true, I mean he can't hurt us, I mean—"

KING: "I'm not saying you did it, Mike, but if you did the job for Alan, Alan is not above killing you."

BROCKINGTON: "Yeah."

"Let's face it. If I'm going to get caught, then it's going to be one or the other," Goldin repeated Brockington's words, a sneering smile on his face. The meaning was clear, Goldin argued. Brockington was referring to being caught for Judy's murder.

Goldin claimed that King had been, with these exchanges at the Burbank headquarters, openly accusing Brockington of Judy's murder, and that it was *only then* that Brockington began to incriminate Alan.

Dave Goldin, in his last few minutes of addressing the jury, observed: "If the police come down and say, 'Look, if you killed his wife . . .' you would say, 'What do you mean? Get off that kick. I didn't do it.' What ordinarily would you expect someone to say in a situation like that? But Brockington doesn't deny it. He says, 'Right.' Never a denial. Never *once* a denial!"

In my opening argument, I had challenged Goldin to fulfill his promise to the jury in his opening statement three months earlier that he would show by the trial's end who the real killer(s) had been.

"I said I had high hopes," Goldin responded in his summation, "that the evidence would show who really did kill Henry Stockton and Judy Palliko. Well, I can't say that I met that challenge. The evidence didn't show who committed either of these crimes, but as to Judy's murder, while we don't *know* who did it, I have my theory. The person who I think is most likely responsible is the person who the police first accused, and who *never* denied it."

Michael and Katherine were seated together at the back of the courtroom on the day of Goldin's final argument. When Dave finished and sat down, Michael folded his arms across his chest, his eyes sizzling with contempt.

"I can't even sue him for slander," he whispered to Katherine. "These lawyers have complete immunity in here."

After Goldin's final argument, I buttonholed a number of spectators out in the hallway and asked their opinions of how the verdict would go. Among the five spectators with whom I spoke, the sentiment was unanimous: although they believed Alan and Sandra had committed the first murder, they had serious questions as to whether Alan was involved in the second murder, and on both counts of the indictment, felt the verdict could go either way because the cases were so circumstantial. In a criminal trial, if just one out of twelve jurors votes *not guilty,* there is a "hung" jury and the entire case has to be retried.

The late, eminent trial lawyer Lloyd Paul Stryker, in his book *The Art of Advocacy,* observed: "The summation is the high point in the art of advocacy; it is the culmination of all of its many elements, the climax of the case."

I could not agree more. What leaves me nonplussed is that even a man the stature of Mr. Stryker, who defended Alger Hiss in his first perjury trial and was once a lecturer at Yale Law School, can go on in his book to advise lawyers: "If your *memory* has been well trained, you will *remember* the main parts of the evidence, and many expressions of the witnesses will stick there in verbatim form." Reliance on extemporaneous final summations is in fact recommended by most authors on the subject.

In my opinion, a summation must either be written out or put into a comprehensive outline. Unfortunately, the majority of trial lawyers, even many high-priced ones in major nationally publicized criminal trials, do neither, addressing the jury almost off the top of their head after scandalously little preparation. Far too often this results in their delivering arguments which are disjointed, at times difficult to understand and which, most injurious of all to their clients, omit a number of salient facts and inferences.

In a complex trial involving upwards of a hundred witnesses and thousands of pages of transcript, to discuss the highlights and nuances of the case, draw the necessary inferences, and in the most telling sequence, always seeking simplicity and clarity of expression, requires enormous *written* preparation. Once a lawyer begins to deliver his summation, there is no moment for pause or reflection. Without hesitation, the sentences must flow, sometimes for two hours at a time without even an interruption.

The one advantage, of course, of arguing extemporaneously is being able to talk to the jury, eye to eye, with the candor of spontaneity. If a trial lawyer, however, is willing to put in the hours, he can have such a grasp of his written or outlined argument that, like an actor on a stage whose lines flow naturally, he can deliver it to the jury giving the appearance of spontaneity.

For several months I had been aiming myself toward the moment of final summation in the Palliko-Stockton trial. I had stirred from bed in the middle of the night to jot down notes to myself, I had tested phrases aloud while driving on freeways. The actual writing of my argument had consumed well over one hundred hours of my time. Learning it to the point where I could powerfully *deliver* it, not read it, had taken additional weekends.

I arrived at the courthouse early on the morning I began my final summation. I even wore suspenders beneath my three-piece suit that day; my hands, like my mind, sometimes reach out for handles when I speak. Alone for a few minutes in judge's chambers, I did knee bends. Although it was warm that second week in February, at the risk of causing the jury and spectators some discomfort, I asked that the droning air conditioners be turned off. I wanted to be heard clearly. I was to speak for one and a half court days. After I finished, and while the jury was still deliberating, Judge Young would tell me my final argument was the finest he had heard in his years of sitting on the bench. I felt proud, but had to smile a little to myself.

Clarence Darrow gave the most dramatic summations ever heard in an American courtroom, yet lost the majority of his cases.

The following—quoted and paraphrased—are excerpts of my final summation in the Palliko-Stockton murder trial:

12

"YOUR HONOR, DEFENSE counsel, ladies and gentlemen of the jury.

"You know, as I was listening to my colleagues, Mr. Goldin and Mr. Callas, addressing you, I thought to myself that both of them went to the same law school I went to. So I happen to know that although they learned the law out at UCLA, they didn't learn how to be magicians. They didn't learn how to pull a rabbit out of the hat when there wasn't any rabbit in the hat.

"Based on the evidence in this case, their clients are as guilty as sin and there is nothing they can do about it. I have yet to meet the man," I said, tapping the counsel table stiffly with my forefinger, "who can convince twelve reasonable men and women that black is white and white is black.

"I wonder if any of you folks have read Victor Hugo's account of the octopus.

"He tells us of how it doesn't have any beak to defend itself like a bird, no claws like a lion, nor teeth like an alligator. But it does have what could be called an ink bag, and to protect itself when it is attacked it lets out a dark fluid from this bag, thus making all of the surrounding water dark and murky, enabling the octopus to escape into the darkness.

"Now I ask you folks, is there any similarity between that description of the ink bag of the octopus and the defense in this case? Has the defense shown you any real, valid, legitimate defense reasonably based on the evidence, or have they sought to employ the ink bag of the octopus and by making everything dark around them, escape into the darkness?

"I intend to clear up the water which defense counsel have sought to muddy, so that you folks can clearly see the evidence, the facts, the issues in this case, so that you are going to be able to behold the form of the retreating octopus and bring these two defendants back to face justice."

In discussing the term "beyond a reasonable doubt," defense counsel emphasize the word "beyond" as if the prosecution has to go beyond the horizon and to the ends of the earth to prove guilt.

Because of the confusing, misleading context in which it is used, I have developed a line of thought to explain the word "beyond" in this term. I point out to the jury that in *beyond a reasonable doubt,* "beyond" is a needless appendage which is not even used in its principal sense of "further," "more than." (If it were, the prosecution would have to prove there is *more than* a reasonable doubt of a defendant's guilt, when obviously, we have to prove just the opposite— that there is *less than* a reasonable doubt.) Instead, "beyond" is used in the sense of "to the exclusion of."

I argued: "The prosecution has the burden of proving the guilt of these two defendants *to the exclusion* of all reasonable doubt. With this in mind, we can completely eliminate the word 'beyond' from the term 'beyond a reasonable doubt' and come up with this: (Going to the blackboard and writing the words out for the jury) IF YOU DO NOT HAVE A REASONABLE DOUBT OF THE GUILT OF THESE TWO DEFENDANTS, CONVICT. IF YOU DO HAVE A REASONABLE DOUBT, ACQUIT. We have eliminated the word 'beyond' from the term 'beyond a reasonable doubt,' and we still have a very accurate definition and statement of the doctrine of reasonable doubt.

"As His Honor will instruct you, a reasonable doubt is not a mere possible doubt, because everything relating to human affairs and depending upon moral evidence is open to some *possible* or *imaginary* doubt. What is a reasonable doubt? It's a sound, sensible, logical doubt based on the evidence. Based on the evidence in this case, ladies and gentlemen, there is absolutely no reasonable doubt of the guilt of these two defendants."

My eyes on the jury box, I paced slowly behind Goldin's and Callas' chairs as I responded to their argument that a jury should demand more than just circumstantial evidence in order for them to convict:

"Common sense is going to tell you that there rarely are going to be eyewitnesses to a premeditated murder. When two people conspire to commit murder, that conspiracy is going to be hatched in the dark shadows. People who conspire to commit murder don't go down to Pershing Square and get on an orange crate and with a megaphone announce their plans to the world.

"Certainly, counsel aren't suggesting that if a man commits murder in the depth of night and there are no eyewitnesses, he's home free. It's not quite that easy, ladies and gentlemen. And when you come back into this courtroom with your verdict of guilty, you are going to tell these defendants," I said with a sudden, staccato loudness I was later told made Sandra flinch, *"It is not quite that easy!"*

Throughout the argument, I kept my tone of voice ever changing—sometimes asking rhetorical questions as softly as a divinity student, sometimes raising it to the pitch of a radical speechmaker. Only occasionally did I pause behind my counsel table for a glance at my notes.

"I think that counsels' problem is that they misconceive what circumstantial evidence is all about. Circumstantial evidence is not, as they claim, like a chain. You could have a chain extending the span of the Atlantic Ocean from Nova Scotia to Bordeaux, France, consisting of millions of links, and with one weak link that chain is broken.

"Circumstantial evidence, to the contrary, is like a rope. And each fact is a strand of that rope, and as the prosecution piles one fact upon another we add strands and we add strength to that rope. If one strand breaks—and I am not conceding for a moment that any strand has broken in this case—but if one strand does break, the rope is not broken. The strength of the rope is barely diminished. Why? Because there are so many other strands of almost steel-like strength that the rope is still more than strong enough to bind these two defendants to justice. That's what circumstantial evidence is all about."

In reply to both Goldin's and Callas' heavy emphasis on the instruction given in cases of circumstantial evidence, that for the defendants to be found guilty, not only must the proven circumstances be consistent with the theory of guilt, they must also be irreconcilable with any other rational conclusion, I turned that instruction around one hundred eighty degrees and asked the jury: "Would another *rational* conclusion be that the evidence in this case points toward the defendants' *innocence?* Would that be another rational conclusion?" Both Goldin and Callas had, for the most part, argued that Alan and Sandra could have been innocent and still exhibited the conduct which they did. The defense argument had not been, and could not have been, that Sandra's and Alan's conduct, such as transfer of monies, use of aliases, etc., was *affirmative* evidence of (i.e., pointing toward) innocence.

"Both counsel, during their arguments," I went on, "no more desired to look directly at the evidence in this case than one would have a desire to look directly into the noonday sun. The evidence was anathema to them, it was poison, it was unpalatable, and you really can't blame them, can you? If I were they and if you were they, we'd probably do the same thing, because when you look at the evidence in this case it points unerringly towards the guilt of Alan Palliko and Sandra Stockton.

"Mr. Goldin said whenever the prosecution needed some testimony in this case, they called on Michael Brockington to fill in the gaps. Why, of course. I am paying Brockington out of my pocket. Look how thin my wallet is."

I waved my wallet in the air a bit.

"Whenever I needed someone to help me, I called on Michael Brockington: 'Hey, Mike! The defense is hurting me. Can you make up a story to help, Mike? Can you get down here? I'll send a taxi for you.'"

Even Dave, I could see from the corner of my eye, was smiling a little.

"Mr. Goldin devoted almost fifty percent of his closing argument to attacking Michael Brockington and accusing him of murder, mind you. He also said that Brockington made many inconsistent statements on the witness stand and hence he is not a believable witness. Well, I don't think any normal human being could take that witness stand and answer several hundred questions pertaining to fifty or more events taking place over a period of two years without there being some minor discrepancies in his or her testimony.

"Goldin's theory is that if the prosecution doesn't call robots and computers to that witness stand, if we only call human beings, somehow or other Alan Palliko didn't pull the trigger on Henry Stockton. If Dave Goldin wants to play a game like that, ladies and gentlemen, let him play it by himself."

I looked over at Gail, who rarely misses my final summations. There was a wisp of a smile on her face. Having heard me practice my argument at home, she knew what was coming next.

"Recall Frank Borman—Colonel Frank Borman?" I asked the

jury. "He was the commander of the Apollo 8 flight that just recently circumnavigated the moon. On the first day of that flight, when Borman was sending transmissions back to Cape Kennedy, he referred to the Apollo 8 flight as the Gemini 8 flight, a flight he had participated in back in 1965.

"Now, just consider the monumental preparation that Frank Borman must have put into that Apollo 8 flight, and yet Frank Borman is sending back messages from Gemini 8. Can't you just hear Mr. Goldin in the control center down at Cape Kennedy when Borman would send any messages thereafter? 'We can't believe that man. His credibility has been destroyed. He is unreliable, and these photographs he's sending of the moon—how do we know they are not fake?' "

When Goldin, in his closing argument, had reread portions of Capt. Warren King's interview of Michael Brockington down at Burbank P.D. headquarters, a number of spectators had cast uneasy glances toward Michael as he sat at the back of the courtroom. Dave's accusation against Michael was a serious one.

The problem I had in rebutting Goldin's contention that Brockington had never once denied murdering Judy when the police interviewed him was major. Brockington, looking baffled himself on the witness stand, had been unable to explain the reason for his one word answers of "right" and "yeah" when the police suggested his life would not be "worth a plugged nickel" if he had killed Judy as a favor to Alan. Although it appeared from the flow of the interview that Michael had, with those answers, merely been following the logic of the detectives' questioning, I had been precluded from arguing that inference to the jury, in that inferences must be based only on evidence from the stand.

Picking up the transcript of the police interview with Michael and carrying it about the courtroom, I tried to show, however, that from the overall flavor of the interview, no incriminating inferences against Michael could be drawn.

"Goldin said that Brockington started talking about Alan only when Captain King accused him of murdering Judy.

"The statement Captain King made to Brockington, that is, if Brockington killed Judy as a favor to Alan, his life wouldn't be worth a plugged nickel, was *not* the statement that caused Michael Brockington to start talking about Alan Palliko." I pointed out that that statement by King came *after* Brockington had already started to tell what he knew about Palliko.

"In fact, the statement that caused Brockington to start telling what he knew about Alan was not an accusatory statement at all.

"Here's when Michael Brockington started telling the police about Alan Palliko—Question by Captain King: 'Here's the thing, Mike. Look. We don't want you to get involved and I know you don't want to get involved, *and we are not trying to involve you.* Obviously, we are concerned with one thing, and that is who killed Judy. If you are not involved in that, fine. But please don't lie to us about these other things because we just have too much information that you can't overlook.'

"When the police then assured him (albeit falsely) that the conversation would be off the record and the room was not bugged, it was at *that* point that Brockington started telling the truth about Alan Palliko. The accusatory statements about the plugged nickel, et cetera, came later on in the conversation.

"Dave Goldin didn't tell you folks that."

There is an element to human language called context; it is as odorless and invisible as ultraviolet light, and has just as searing an effect. Like any good lawyer, Dave Goldin knew how to use context to his advantage.

Responding to Goldin's most damaging contextual sleight of hand, I argued: "The context in which Brockington said, 'If I'm going to get caught, then it's going to be one or the other,' was this: Captain King said, 'All we are asking, Mike, is this—we have got a homicide, we have got a young girl who was killed, brutally killed, we don't know who did it. We'll be honest with you. We have our own ideas' (obviously *not* referring to Brockington, I argued to the jury). 'We have got our own ideas. But I don't want you to get caught in the middle of a trap *because you know a lot of things* (about Alan Palliko, obviously, I said to the jury).

"Brockington answers: 'Let's face it. If I'm going to get caught, then it's going to be one or the other.'

"When Brockington said, 'If I'm going to get caught,' it is clear from the context he didn't mean: if I'm going to get caught for the murder of Judy. He meant: if I'm going to get caught *because I know a lot of things* about Alan Palliko."

Caught by the police for not telling the truth, or caught by Alan for telling the truth.

"Yet Goldin interprets Brockington's statement to mean that he might get caught for the murder of Judy. The Burbank Police Department, experienced police detectives, didn't construe Brockington's statement that way. Goldin does. If the detectives had, it seems to me they would have arrested Brockington, or at least considered him a suspect, but, as Captain King testified, they didn't even do that."

I tossed the police transcript on the counsel table. "King testified that Brockington was trying to protect Palliko. If Brockington were out to save his neck and out to frame Alan Palliko, would he tell Captain King he did not think Alan Palliko murdered Judy? Does that make sense? Stop and think about it."

I emphasized to the jury that Michael would never have even related Alan's admission of having killed Henry Stockton to the police had the police themselves not brought that subject up, long into the interview. I reread the Q. and A.'s of the police interview for them:

Q. BY WARREN KING: "Now, let me ask you this question. Do you know Sandra Stockton?"

A. "If it's the same one who used to work at the Auto Club."

Q. "Right. Do you know her?"

A. "Oh, I worked with her for—it had to be the better part of three or four months while she was working down there."

Michael's answers were vague and general, I argued, not leading the police at all to what he knew about Alan's and Sandra's relationship. Michael once again was protecting Alan, and only after the police did not drop the subject did Michael finally relate Alan's admission of having killed Sandra's husband. Would these be the actions of a man out to frame Alan Palliko, I asked.

If Goldin sincerely thought Michael Brockington had been Judy's killer, why, I asked, had he called to the stand: the Lotts to testify to Judy's fear of the German boyfriend from New York; Lieutenant Vandergrift to testify Mrs. Davis had said it was Katherine staring at Judy through the window; Detective Strickland to testify to Alan's stated suspicion of Tod Glenn and Felix Zimmer; and Warren King for his testimony that the barfly Thelma Dewton thought Nick Tagli murdered Judy?

"I'll tell you what we have in this case against Michael Brockington," I observed. "Dave Goldin's finger. But unfortunately for Mr. Goldin, he can't detach that finger, mark it as an exhibit, and offer it into evidence. If he could, he probably would.

"And what about this confession of Alan's?" I asked. "Goldin made very light of it; he says the conversation never took place. He says that it is ridiculous to believe that Palliko would confess to Brockington that he murdered Henry Stockton. But is it ridiculous, ladies and gentlemen?

"To speculate on human motives can sometimes be a rather unprofitable undertaking. The subconscious motivations behind why people do things is very unclear. But the point is, it is very common for a suspect to confess to a crime. It has been said, as you know, that one reason a person confesses is that he wants to get it off his chest. It is a great relief.

"I think you can call on your own human experience. When we've done something that we're not particularly proud of, we feel a little better when we have told somebody about it, gotten it off our chest.

"Brockington was a close friend of Alan Palliko's. He was even the best man at Judy's and Alan's wedding. He worked for Alan. As Mr. Goldin categorized Brockington, he was an 'errand boy.' Brockington was the precise type of person in whom Alan Palliko would confide. Keep in mind also that Palliko had a propensity for confiding in many people other than Brockington about quite a few things he now regrets ever having talked about.

"Criminals make mistakes," I put it to the jury simply. "That's why they get caught."

Having addressed myself for over an hour to the credibility of my principal witness, Michael Brockington, I moved from the defensive to the offensive—to the hard, incriminating facts against the defendants. Rebutting the contention of the defense attorneys that guilt had not been proven beyond a reasonable doubt, I began with the People's case against Alan Joseph Palliko for the murder of Henry Stockton:

"We start out with the fact that Alan was seeing Sandra quite extensively in the year 1966. He was seen with her by Sandra's neighbors as late as August, '66 at her apartment on Stewart and Gray Road in Downey. Katherine testified Alan was calling Sandra's residence in August of '66 and Sandra's name was even mentioned on Alan's appointment pad as late as September of '66.

"I think it is a fair inference that Alan and Sandra were boyfriend-girfriend, that there was an emotional-physical relationship. They were having an affair.

"Mr. Goldin had a very interesting observation. He denied any romance between Alan and Sandra. He said Sandra 'wasn't Alan's type.' He didn't say Alan wasn't Sandra's type, he said Sandra wasn't Alan's type.

"If we assume that Sandra was not Alan's type, this *all the more* points to the fact that Palliko had to have had some reason other than love to romance Sandra. Some other reason, ladies and gentlemen.

"What other evidence do we have against Alan Palliko? We have Palliko's conversation with Officer St. John. We know Palliko lied to St. John because he tells St. John on February 16, 1967, that he hadn't seen Sandra since February of 1966, when we know he saw her throughout the summer of 1966. Why did Alan Palliko lie to Officer St. John in that conversation? Why was Palliko seeking to conceal his association with Sandra Stockton? I don't have to state the obvious—this false statement by Alan shows a consciousness of guilt on his part.

"And since Palliko knew on February 16 that St. John wanted to know about his association with Sandra, don't you think that if Palliko were innocent he would have told St. John, 'By the way, Officer, I thought you just might like to know that two days from now, she and I are going up to Las Vegas together under assumed names? I just thought you'd like to know that, Officer.' But he doesn't mention that trip to St. John."

I cited Katherine's testimony that in December of '66, the month of Henry Stockton's murder, and January and February of '67, the period shortly thereafter, Alan was very much on edge and nervous, much more so than usual.

"In mid-December of '66, Alan tells Katherine and Michael Brockington that he's expecting a large sum of money after the first of the year. Mr. Goldin says that Palliko was referring to the $3,000 he was going to get from his father, but it's obvious he was not.

"Alan Palliko received $3,000 from his father on December 28, 1966. *After* that, between January and mid-February of 1967, he tells Michael Brockington that the large sum of money had not come in yet, that there had been a delay.

"And there was a delay—in Sandra getting her Metropolitan Life Insurance proceeds. A delay of over two months."

I reminded the jury of Katherine's seeing Alan with a satchel full of currency in late February, 1967, around the very same time Sandra got her first $15,000. As I continued, getting caught up myself in the story of the crime, my voice grew progressively sharper.

"Right after Henry's murder, did Alan have anything to do with Sandra? No, not much. They stayed away from each other like the plague. He just referred her to his attorney—that's all. There are twenty-five thousand attorneys in this town, yet when Sandra went knocking on their doors, they all ran away from her. The only attorney in town she could find was Roy Marchetta—Alan Palliko's attorney."

I kept the story moving:

"New Year's Eve 1966, Alan throws an expensive party at the Biltmore. It was his 'coming out' party, he said. Alan expected to be in the chips soon.

"So what happened when Sandra recieved the first insurance proceeds on the sixteenth of February, 1967? Well, two days later, on the eighteenth, Alan and Sandra go to Las Vegas, Palliko using the name Jerry Pace, Sandra under the assumed name, Mr. B. Johnson.

"All right, what happened in Las Vegas?" I walked back to the counsel table and held up a packet of fifty American Express traveler's checks. I flipped through them with my thumb, letting the sound of the money coupons crackle through the courtroom. "They went through $3,000 in traveler's checks. Most of the checks were cashed at hotels, so it's a fair inference that Sandra turned over all or most of the money to Alan to gamble with.

"The only evidence there is in this case shows that Alan lost more than he won while he was in Las Vegas with Sandra. And when he returned to Las Vegas on February 21 for a three-day stay, he lost an additional $2,000. Yet when he returns to Los Angeles on February 23, he deposits $2,500 to his account, and he has a fistful of money he doesn't deposit. Where did Alan Palliko get all this money if it wasn't from Sandra?

"If Alan Palliko had won the $2,500 he deposited in his bank in Glendale on the twenty-third, is there any reason why the defense would not have wanted to subpoena that redhead, the good-looking redhead with the figure to match? That's the way she was described. Or Mr. and Mrs. Cavatelli? They were with Alan Palliko at the Thunderbird up in Las Vegas. Why didn't they take the stand and say, 'Yes, we were with Alan, and he won $2,500'?"

I tossed the checks back onto the table and, putting my hands in my pockets, began moving in a slow, casual circle about the defense's side of the courtroom.

"Then we have the very interesting telephone conversation sometime between January and March of '67 between Alan and the female caller, obviously Sandra, in which, among other things, Palliko tried to calm her down and told her that, 'it had been done,' and just to 'be patient.' 'Don't let the police department rattle you,' he told her. 'They can't prove anything. We have gone this far. Don't blow the deal now.'

"And, of course, we had that very interesting, chilling hypothetical Alan Palliko posed to Michael Brockington—which really wasn't much of a hypothetical at all, was it, ladies and gentlemen—in which it was clear Alan was referring to Sandra. By the nature of that hypothetical, it is apparent that Palliko was beginning to have doubts about Sandra. He thought maybe she was a little too weak as a partner. So it appears that Alan Palliko was contemplating murdering Sandra Stockton. When Sandra heard that evidence come from the witness stand, a couple of shivers must have gone up her spine. Why would Alan have doubts about Sandra, fearing that she might be weakening? Well, we have evidence of the way Sandra reacted the first time the police asked to take her fingerprints. She collapsed to the floor. 'Oh, my God,' she said, 'am I going to be arrested?' *That* is why Alan was having doubts about Sandra."

I glanced over at Sandra, and for what must have been the hundredth time in the trial, she looked away from me. Seeing her eyes fixed morosely on the floor, I wondered what she might be willing to give to reverse the exchange she had made of the men in her life.

"In late August, '67," I went on, "Sandra receives close to $18,000 on the second policy, and around the very same time, we have the Santa Fe Springs incident where Palliko picks up that large sum of cash from behind the Allied Machine Tools Building. It wasn't suspicious that Alan picked up money from behind that building, was it? He had to pick it up somewhere. The fact that it just happened to be behind a building where Sandra was working is just a coincidence. Things like that happen in life. After all, there aren't that many buildings in Los Angeles."

Having discussed the entire Santa Fe Springs episode in detail in my opening argument, I now merely pointed out that neither Goldin nor Callas made any effort in their arguments to dispute the Santa Fe Springs incident.

"Maybe your notes are better than mine. I don't recall any such closing argument by them. Apparently they conceded that the Santa Fe Springs incident did occur.

"Let's move on. As you recall, Sandra deposits her $17,677 check from National Life to her savings account on August 31 and withdraws $3,500, in *cash*. The very next day, September 1, Alan Palliko makes an entry into his safety deposit box at the Echo Park Branch of the Bank of America. Very next day. On September 8, Sandra withdraws $7,500 in cash. On September 14, which is six days later, Alan has $5,000 in cash which he gives to Howard Koebrick to buy that cashier's check, payable to Alan. Where did Palliko get the $5,000? Did he save it from his $580 a month salary at the Auto Club? It would just take him around ten years to save that amount of money.

"On September 22, 1967, Sandra withdraws $5,377 in cash. On the same day, Alan Palliko makes another entry into his safe deposit box at the Echo Park Branch of the Bank of America. Same day. Just a coincidence. These things don't mean anything."

I discussed the phony promissory note incident between Alan and Koebrick, and Alan's subsequent lie to Thomas Ritchie of the A.B.C.

"If that money had come from some legitimate source, like his earnings or his investments, I think he would have told Ritchie that. But he lies to Ritchie and engages in this fraudulent transaction with Koebrick.

"For a full year Alan is asking Koebrick for a loan, but once the money comes in from Sandra, he tells Koebrick, 'I don't need your money anymore. I've got my own.' "

Pointing at Alan, I asked: "If Palliko didn't get all the money in this case from Sandra, from whom did he get all the money he gambled with in Las Vegas when he was there with Sandra? And where did he get the $2,000 he lost when he returned to Las Vegas? Where did he get the $2,500 he deposited on his return? Where did he get the satchel full of currency that Katherine saw? Where did he get the $5,000 during the Howard Koebrick incident? Where did he get the money to lease all those expensive cars in 1967? Fifty-six hundred dollars in less than two years on leased cars! Where did he get all the money he was placing in that safe deposit box? If he got all of this money from sources other than Sandra, why didn't he subpoena witnesses who could testify to this?"

I turned away from Alan and back to the twelve jurors.

"Goldin argued, 'Well, Alan had a bar and this was a source of money for Alan.' But the sums of money I've just referred to were in

Palliko's possession *before* October 1, 1967, the day he opened up his first bar, the one in Burbank.

"Well, ladies and gentlemen of the jury," I drew toward the final, damning evidence against Alan on Count I, "by this stage of the game we knew who murdered Henry Stockton even without Alan telling us—we didn't need Alan to tell us at all, it was so obvious—but he did anyway. He confessed to Brockington in February of 1968 at the Marlindo Bowling Alley in Burbank. He told Michael Brockington in a weak moment that he was the one who killed Henry Stockton. There's no reason under the sun, the moon, the stars for Michael Brockington to lie about that.

"If all of this," I concluded my first day of summation, "isn't enough evidence that Alan Palliko murdered Henry Stockton, I don't know what in the world would be."

The next day Alan came to court looking almost a little shell-shocked. He had of course been hearing the evidence come in for three months, but like a man who has ignored the small daily symptoms of an illness, he seemed, on the morning the mirror was finally held up to him, dazed by how much it had all added up to. I did not see him utter a word that day, not even to his own attorney Dave Goldin.

On my second morning of summation, I started in on the People's case against Sandra Darcy Stockton:

"Mr. Callas contends there is insufficient evidence showing that Sandra was involved in the murder of her husband. My answer to Mr. Callas is that all of Sandra's conduct—all of it—points irresistibly to her guilt.

"First of all, although the $20,000 double indemnity policy was applied for on October 6, 1966, it wasn't issued until November 25, 1966, only sixteen days before Henry was murdered. Prior to November 25, 1966, Sandra had no way of knowing whether the policy would, in fact, be issued. So the murder takes place only sixteen days after Sandra learns for sure that she's the beneficiary on her husband's policy. The policy was applied for only six days after Sandra remarried Henry. And Henry already had $15,000 of insurance on him.

"I don't know, but for people of modest circumstances—they didn't even pay their property taxes the preceding year—it is kind of un-likely they would want to buy another $20,000 policy with a double indemnity clause. Of course, we don't know at whose insistence the policy was taken out. We don't know the circumstances surrounding the purchase of the policy. But we do know one thing: Sandra told Sergeant Guy that Henry Stockton would do anything she wanted him to do."

In regard to the Las Vegas trip, both Goldin and Callas had argued in their final summations that Mr. B. Johnson was not Sandra Stockton. After pointing out to the jury the two pieces of evidence that, when coupled, contradicted that claim—the consecutive serial numbers on the Western Airline tickets and the positive identification of Alan and Sandra together at Hertz only twenty minutes after the plane had landed—I remarked, "But to make Mr. Callas and Mr. Goldin happy, let's assume for the sake of argument that Sandra Stockton was not Mr. B. Johnson and see what we're left with. If Mr. B. Johnson is not Sandra Stockton, even though Alan Palliko and Sandra Stockton are in Los Angeles on February 17, 1967, and even though they were to spend the next three days in Las Vegas together, for some very, very curious reason, Sandra did not go to Las Vegas on the same flight as Alan Palliko.

"It seems to me that that is even *more* incriminating than if Sandra were Mr. B. Johnson. If Mr. B. Johnson is not Sandra Stockton, why didn't Sandra go to Las Vegas on the same plane as Alan? Why did she go up to Las Vegas by herself? I am just wondering at this time if defense counsel are starting to think maybe they should have left well enough alone and agreed with me that it appears Mr. B. Johnson was Sandra Stockton.

"Mr. Callas says that the fact Sandra showered her name all over Las Vegas in cashing these traveler's checks shows she wasn't acting deceptively.

"Number one, the only way she could have cashed those traveler's checks was to sign her name because she was the named purchaser. But number two, Sandra didn't have any reason to act deceptively up in Las Vegas. She didn't have any reason at all. Why? Because she was up in Las Vegas with Jerry Pace. So why should Sandra be acting deceptively? Everyone knows that Jerry Pace didn't kill Henry Stockton. Alan Palliko did.

"The only problem for Sandra is that the prosecution proved that Jerry Pace and Alan Palliko put on the same pair of shoes every morning.

"Next item: the .22 caliber Hi Standard revolver Sandra purchased. There is an excellent chance that revolver was the murder weapon. We haven't proven it conclusively, and I wouldn't purport to tell you we have. But there is an excellent chance that it is the murder weapon. We know from the testimony of DeWayne Wolfer that the murder weapon was a .22 caliber revolver.

"The weapon Sandra purchased was a .22 caliber as opposed to a .38 or a .45, et cetera. And it was a revolver as opposed to an automatic or some other type of gun. Furthermore, based on Deputy Wolfer's testimony, chances are, if we are going to talk about percentages, it was a Hi Standard.

"Also, Sandra's story about the purchase of that revolver is highly suspicious. She said that a man whom she dated named Dick Scott gave her the money to purchase the revolver, yet when the police asked her where they could find this Dick Scott, she had no idea where they could find him. She couldn't give them any information whatsoever: 'I don't know where he works. Don't know where he lives. Can't help you at all.'

"What about the most basic question of all: did Sandra have a motive for killing Henry Stockton?

"Well, although she didn't manage to get her hands on quite all of it, she stood to receive a total of approximately $75,000 from the death of her husband.

"And Sandra's love obviously was not for Henry Stockton. She was involved in what must have been a physical and emotional relationship with Alan. Alan and Sandra were going together right up to the time that Sandra remarried Henry, and then again, shortly after Henry was murdered. At least from an emotional standpoint, Sandra Stockton had no motive for Henry to keep on living. From an emotional standpoint, the motive ran in the opposite direction.

"Most important of all, we know Alan Palliko murdered Henry Stockton. He even confessed to it. So you have got to ask yourselves this question back in the jury room: what conceivable reason would Alan Palliko have had to murder Henry Stockton if there wasn't something in it for him?

"No reason in the world. He had to have been assured, *in advance,* that there was something in it for him. And that means a conspiracy with Sandra Stockton to murder Henry for the insurance proceeds.

"You might be saying to yourself: well, it's true that what the DA is saying makes a lot of sense, but we'd better look at Sandra Stockton's conduct just to make double sure that it's consistent with guilt, not innocence. So let's look at her conduct, conduct which Mr. Callas says was consistent with innocence.

"We start out with Sandra's trip to Twentynine Palms. Could it be any clearer that Sandra made a deliberate attempt to set up an alibi for herself? Sandra hadn't seen Vicky Stowe or heard from her for a year and a half. I guess we're supposed to believe it's just another coincidence that on the weekend that Henry was murdered, Sandra just had this irresistible urge to visit Vicky. She called Vicky December 2, which was just one week after the $20,000 double indemnity policy on Henry was issued. She arrives at 10:00 P.M. on December 9. Thirty hours after she arrives in Twentynine Palms, Henry Stockton is murdered.

"These aren't coincidences at all. The defense only wants you to *believe* that they are coincidences.

"I say that as Sandra was driving her car across the desert that Friday evening in December of 1966, she thought she was driving away from the murder, but unbeknownst to Sandra, she was putting on affirmative evidence for the prosecution.

"Mr. Callas said if we look at Vicky Stowe's testimony about how Sandra took the news of Henry's death, this will show Sandra's innocence. Well, let's take a look at Vicky Stowe's testimony. It couldn't possibly be more helpful to the prosecution and harmful to Sandra Stockton. When Sandra learned of her husband's death, she showed almost a complete lack of bereavement. Oh, she cried a little bit, she became pale, somewhat faint. But this was probably because of the sudden realization of how horrible a thing she had been a party to.

"Vicky testified that Sandra went into the bathroom and just a few minutes later when she came out, she had already stopped crying. Vicky said she got the impression that Sandra was keeping her emotions within herself. Vicky was being kind of generous with Sandra. Thirty-five to forty minutes later, Sandra takes her son horseback riding, and Vicky said that by this time Sandra had already collected herself. And this is the testimony which Mr. Callas thinks is helpful to his client, Sandra."

I looked from one juror to the next, my voice incredulous as I turned the matter over in my own mind: "Unbelievable. Unbelievable. Can you imagine that, folks? Sandra has just learned that not only is her husband dead, but that he has been shot to death, and instead of frantically racing back to Los Angeles, she has enough composure to take her son horseback riding! Sandra's incredibly steelhearted conduct in staying in Twentynine Palms for two hours before she came back to Los Angeles, and her taking her son horseback riding, couldn't possibly have been more indicative of guilt."

I paused to clarify a seemingly small but indeed important point: "The prosecution isn't claiming that Sandra Stockton hated her poor husband, Henry. We are not claiming that at all. The evidence only shows that Sandra had no love for Henry.

"After Sandra returns to Los Angeles," I continued, "and just a few hours after she has learned that Henry had been murdered, she talks to Sergeant Aguirre. Aguirre testified Sandra was very calm, not emotionally upset at all.

"Mr. Callas tried to explain Sandra's demeanor on the ground that Aguirre was firing policemen's questions at her.

"But does Sandra tell Aguirre, 'Officer, give me a break. My husband has just been murdered. Can't we put this conversation off until tomorrow,' or anything like that? Does she cry? Does she exhibit any of the normal emotions that an innocent person would exhibit when she had just learned her husband has been murdered? Nothing. Absolutely nothing. Why? Because what happened to Henry is exactly what Sandra had planned.

"Then we have Vicky Stowe's volunteering to Sergeant Aguirre the statement, 'I'm Sandra's alibi.' Aguirre just comes up to Vicky and asks, 'Are you Vicky Stowe?' That's all. And she blurts out, 'Yes, I'm Sandra's alibi.'

"Now, I'm not claiming Vicky is a part of any unholy triumvirate to murder Henry Stockton, nor is it likely that Sandra told Vicky that she conspired with some man back in Los Angeles named Alan Palliko to murder Henry Stockton. But what *is* very likely is that Sandra said something to this effect to Vicky: 'Henry has been murdered. Well, at least you're my alibi. Right?'

"Stowe's statement to Aguirre, under the circumstances, was highly unusual. The word 'alibi,' in legal contemplation, doesn't have any unfavorable connotation at all. It simply means that at the time of the alleged crime the defendant was somewhere else. But to the person out on the street, when one uses the word alibi, it has the flavor of an excuse. 'Oh, you're guilty. That's just an alibi. Why don't you admit it?'

"Vicky's volunteering that statement to Sergeant Aguirre, and her use of the word 'alibi,' strongly suggests that it was Sandra who planted that idea in her mind.

"Here's Henry Stockton, ladies and gentlemen." I held up a photo of Henry lying dead on the front lawn of his home. "Three bullets in the brain causing massive internal hemorrhage, and two in the chest. Sandra's husband. A dead man. Sandra gets an initial $15,000 from the murder of Henry Stockton, and where does the first $3,000 go? Places like the Thunderbird, the Stardust, the Desert Inn. In three days, Sandra and Alan go through $3,000. A thousand dollars a day in Las Vegas.

"Am I drawing an unreasonable inference to say that if Sandra had loved Henry and if she had had nothing to do with Henry's death, that being in Las Vegas two months after his murder, having a ball, would have been the very last thing she would have done?

"Mr. Callas said that even assuming Sandra gave Alan the money, the manner in which Sandra paid Alan didn't look like a payoff because the money was paid in dribbles. He used the word 'dribbles.'

"Within three weeks after Sandra received that first $15,000, she withdraws $7,900 in cash. All of the evidence points to the fact that a substantial percentage of that money went to Alan Palliko. This, remember, does not even include the $3,000 in traveler's checks. Again, within three weeks after Sandra received the $17,700 from National Life sent to her on August 29, '67, she withdraws $16,377 in cash, and all of that, or a substantial percentage thereof, went to whom? No one else but Alan Palliko. A total of $24,277. Close to $25,000 in cash withdrawn by Sandra within six weeks after she received the proceeds under both policies. Yet Mr. Callas said the money was paid out in dribbles.

"Now note carefully, that if Sandra had given Alan money a year or even several months after she had received the insurance proceeds, then the argument could be made—it might be a fragile argument, but the argument could be made—that the payments to Alan were completely unrelated to the murder of Henry Stockton. But here, her payments to Alan in both cases were in very close proximity to the time she received the insurance money. In fact, almost immediately after. The fact that she paid Alan all that money right after she received it shows what? That she owed Alan Palliko a debt. And what was that debt? What was that preexisting obligation?

"If these payments were not a payoff, why did Sandra feel it necessary to employ such a clandestine, surreptitious method in giving Alan the money, such as in the Santa Fe Springs incident? If the payments to Alan were aboveboard, why didn't she write Alan Palliko out a check? Payee: Alan Joseph Palliko. No. All cash, ladies and gentlemen. All cash."

Terry Callas, I could see, was emphatically shaking his head to himself. Although lawyers will, in many cases, take on clients they believe are guilty since guilty people, too, deserve their day in court, Terry, I sensed, believed from the very outset that Sandra was innocent, that she had been naively trapped and manipulated by the calculating mind of Alan Palliko.

"If this cash went to someone other than Alan Palliko," I asked, "why didn't the defense subpoena people to testify to something like this: 'My name is Jane Higgins. I loaned Sandra $3,000. She gave me the $3,000 back in cash on such and such a date.' Why didn't they subpoena these people? I've never heard of a defendant walking to the gas chamber making a comment such as: 'Well, I know a lot of witnesses and a lot of evidence that could clear me, but the prosecution has the legal burden of proof, so I'm not going to say boo.'"

While the defense, I pointed out, has no burden to prove innocence, it does have the same power of subpoena as the prosecution. In this case, I went on, when the defense wanted to prove a point, they called witnesses to the stand—thirty-four of them—the distinct inference being that when they did not call witnesses to prove a point, the witnesses did not exist.

In detail, I reviewed the March 9 phone message from Miss Walther, pointing out the almost inescapable conclusion that Miss Walther was, in truth, Sandra.

"So here we have one conspirator, Sandra Stockton, telling her co-conspirator, Alan Palliko, on March 9, 'Definite word on policy tomorrow.' A clear communication between conspirators baring, for everyone to see, the conspiracy to commit murder for insurance proceeds.

"If Sandra is not Miss Walther, why didn't the defense subpoena the real Miss Walther to take that witness stand and say: 'Yes, it was I who sent Alan all these messages, and the message on March 9 pertained to a certain policy and transaction'?

"They couldn't subpoena Miss Walther because there *is* no Miss Walther.

"I say to Mr. Callas that the reason he doesn't see any evidence in this case against Sandra is because he does not want to look. And if I were he, I wouldn't want to look either.

"By Sandra's conduct and her actions she shouted out for all the world to hear: 'I conspired to murder my husband!'

"I don't know whether she's sorry now or not. I don't know. But you cannot unring a bell."

Telling the jury that not only had we proven Alan's and Sandra's guilt beyond all reasonable doubt, which was our only burden, we had proven their guilt beyond *all* doubt, I said: "With respect to this first murder, ladies and gentlemen, the evidence is clear that somewhere in the dark shadows of this city, Alan Palliko and Sandra Stockton agreed that Henry Stockton's only value as a human being was a specific sum of money. The evidence that came from this witness stand under oath during this long, long trial focused a very bright, penetrating spotlight on those dark shadows, and what we saw was the chilling, ugly, sinister head of a conspiracy, whose participants, Alan Palliko and Sandra Stockton, sought to cover their eyes and scurry off into the sanctuary of other dark places.

"But our system of law is predicated on the concept of justice, which means that when you commit a crime like this, you should be punished.

"Ladies and gentlemen of the jury, I think we have beheld the form of the retreating octopus. We have brought these two defendants back to face justice."

My rebuttal was brief, only ten minutes, to Goldin's claim that Alan's attack on Katherine did not constitute attempted murder. Goldin's one valid question, I believed, had been why Katherine would have continued to have contact with Alan for over a year if she herself had thought the assault had been a serious attempt on her life. My answer was simply Katherine's own words from the witness stand: "It was wiser to remain Alan's friend than his enemy."

After the noon hour recess, I commenced my final summation on the second murder count, reminding the jury that it was separate and distinct from the first murder. Under the law I was prohibited, and properly so, from arguing, for instance, the unlikelihood that Alan out of mere coincidence would have been intimately involved in the circumstances of the two murders. Judge Young would later instruct the jury: "You must decide each count separately on the evidence and the law applicable to it, uninfluenced by your decision as to any other count."

Dave Goldin, in his own closing argument, had planted no fewer than half a dozen thought provoking doubts as to Alan Palliko's guilt in the murder of his wife. They were the small, nagging kind of doubts that flourish in the areas where evidence is thin and contradictions swirl in the void; they were the small doubts which, back in a jury room, grow into larger ones that soon can overrun a prosecution's entire case. Every point he made had to be solidly rebutted. A prosecutor, like a gardener who might grow lazy in his weeding late in the day, is kidding himself if he ever thinks: 'Well, I got most of 'em.'

"When a man is innocent of a crime," I began, "chances are there isn't going to be anything whatsoever pointing toward his guilt. Chances are there will be nothing. Now and then, because of the very nature of life and the unaccountability of certain things, maybe one thing, maybe two things, maybe even three things, may peculiarly point toward his guilt even though he's innocent. But with Alan Palliko on this second murder, how could he possibly be innocent when everything, virtually everything, points toward his guilt?

"Mr. Goldin argued that Jack Dodd testified he had to talk Alan into taking out the insurance, and this is inconsistent with the prosecution's theory. And Mr. Dodd's testimony, he says, is believable.

"Let me start off by saying one thing: even if Jack Dodd had to talk Alan Palliko into taking out insurance on Judy, this would not necessarily mean that Alan did not murder Judy for insurance proceeds. Alan could have had good intentions initially, and then later on decided to murder Judy for the insurance. Or the motive for the murder—and I concede this only as a very, very slight possibility—may not have been insurance proceeds. Could have been a sick mind, or hatred. Susan Peters, for instance, told us that on the night Judy was shot, Judy told her that two weeks before, she was thinking about going home to her mother. I just wonder how Alan took that news.

"There is another possibility. Palliko may have led Dodd into believing that he didn't want the insurance and, thus, hoodwinked Jack Dodd.

"But I don't believe this, ladies and gentlemen. It is a possibility, but I don't believe it.

"The evidence indicates that Jack Dodd took that witness stand and did not tell you folks the truth, and I say that for several reasons. He started out by telling you that he was alone with Alan and Judy

332 : TILL DEATH US DO PART

on the evening of February 22, 1968. Now, Judy is not here with us so it was rather easy for Dodd to say, 'I talked Alan into taking out insurance on Judy.' If Judy were here, for all we know she would have taken that witness stand and shouted out, 'Jack Dodd is a liar!'

"Michael Brockington took the stand, and his memory of what took place that night is so clear that Dodd knew he couldn't possibly deny Brockington's presence on that night. So the crafty but unruffled Jack Dodd retook the witness stand and testified, 'Well, I made a mistake. Michael Brockington was present.' "

I told the jury that Jack Dodd's flip-flops on the witness stand in this and other matters reminded me of a story people tell about a civil case years ago.

"The plaintiff," I recalled, "sued his neighbor, alleging that while he was walking along the sidewalk outside his home, the neighbor's dog had run out and bitten him. The neighbor filed an answer to the complaint in which he set forth three contentions: number one, he said, 'My dog was chained to the house and the chain does not extend out to the sidewalk, so there was no way for my dog to bite the plaintiff'; number two, 'Even if my dog did bite the plaintiff, my dog is old and has no teeth, so he couldn't possibly have hurt the plaintiff'; and number three, 'I don't even *own* a dog.'

"This is Jack Dodd," I told the jury, whose laughter cleared some of the tension that had been building up over these final, straining hours.

"Brockington," I continued, "testified that Jack Dodd put absolutely no pressure on Alan Palliko to take out insurance on Judy, that Alan wasn't reluctant at all. He got the impression that everything had already been agreed upon in advance, before Jack Dodd had arrived.

"Dodd's entire testimony about the insurance transaction with Alan simply did not have the ring of truth to it. It just didn't have that ring.

"If Alan Palliko were a close friend of Jack Dodd's and Palliko said, 'No, I don't want any insurance on Judy,' would Jack Dodd have persisted, as he claims, ten or fifteen times? Literally begging Alan? I don't think so. When your friend says 'no,' do you persist ten or fifteen times, ladies and gentlemen? Well, it is possible, I suppose. Especially if the agent felt that the friend could not get by without the insurance, that it was absolutely necessary, and for the friend's own sake the agent just refused to take a no answer. That's a possibility. I can conceive of it. But why did Jack Dodd feel it was absolutely necessary that Alan insure Judy? Particularly when Alan wasn't even married to Judy yet?

"Isn't it so very obvious that the reason Jack Dodd's testimony didn't ring true is because it didn't happen the way Jack Dodd said it happened?

"We have the testimony of Mr. and Mrs. Stone. Very interesting testimony. Mr. Goldin, in his argument, said that the Stones testified that Dodd merely told them he was Alan's friend and that he would stand by him like a friend. The Stones testified to a little bit more than that, didn't they, folks? You remember. You took notes.

"Dodd told them that Alan hated blacks and he said he didn't particularly care for Alan either, but that he was going to prove to Alan —that's the word he used—he was going to *prove* to Alan that even though all others were deserting him, a black man would be his friend, and that he would do everything he could to help Alan Palliko in the situation he was in.

"Now, there was no indication of any bad blood or ill feeling between the Stones and Jack Dodd. No reason for them to falsify their testimony.

"I'll tell you why the language that Jack Dodd used with the Stones was highly suspicious. If Alan had asked Jack Dodd to be a character witness for him, that is, to take that witness stand and say, 'Yes, Alan's a nice guy, he's not a violent man,' then the language that Jack Dodd used about proving friendship and helping out would have made sense, because you cannot force a person to be a character witness for yourself. A person has the right to refuse to be a character witness.

"But Jack Dodd sold Palliko that policy. Whether he was a friend of Alan Palliko's or an enemy was completely immaterial. He was a party to a relevant transaction, and he *had* to testify about it. He had no choice. 'Proving his friendship' and 'helping Alan out' simply aren't applicable to this type of situation.

"Take a look at Jack Dodd's conduct. All he did was sell a lousy insurance policy. That's all the man did. And he admitted on the stand that the Burbank Police Department did not accuse him or imply in any way that he was involved. He admitted that. Yet he testified that he had apprehensions when he spoke to Detective Strickland, and he asked whether he was a suspect in Judy Palliko's murder. Can you imagine that? He thought he might be a suspect.

Why would he have such thoughts? Jack Dodd was acting like a man who was very worried about something.

"Now, you might say, 'Well, Jack Dodd is just a layman and when the police come up and talk to a layman, the layman thinks maybe the police are talking to him because he's a suspect.'

"I don't believe that, ladies and gentlemen. I don't believe any insurance agent would think he's a suspect in a murder case just because he had sold an insurance policy. Insurance agents sell policies, they don't sell apples. And there is nothing suspicious about selling a policy. But Jack Dodd, for some reason, has fears.

"Furthermore, Jack Dodd is not really just a layman. He's a parole officer for the State of California. He makes arrests himself. He knows that when the police come out to interview a person, that doesn't mean the person is a suspect. All the police are doing is seeking information.

"Jack Dodd even refused to make a written statement for the police. He goes out and consults attorneys. He testified, 'I have the constitutional right not to make a written statement.' Well, I have heard suspects say that. But an insurance agent? Highly bizarre. Incredible testimony by Jack Dodd.

"I say this: the untruthful testimony of Jack Dodd's is itself affirmative evidence of Alan Palliko's guilt."

As the afternoon wore on, I made a conscious effort to avoid walking near the windows while roaming the courtroom as I spoke. I had worked hard to garner the jury's total concentration, and did not need to remind them there were more pleasant places we all would have preferred to have been on a mid-February day that was warm and surprisingly so clear one could, even from the Hall of Justice, see the snowy peaks of Mt. Baldy.

"Mr. Goldin says that Alan Palliko showed sorrow over the loss of Judy, so this means he never had anything to do with her murder.

"Really? Did Alan Palliko show sorrow over the death of Judy? Who testified that Alan Palliko showed sorrow? Very close, personal friends of his, some of whom are still economically dependent upon Alan Palliko. Alan still owns that bar on San Fernando Road in Burbank. Pete Morris still works for him. Nora Rolapp still works for him. Janet Turnbull still works for him. These are the people who said Alan was just completely broken up. Couldn't even talk. Just crushed.

"What about the people who weren't enemies *or* friends of Alan

Palliko? Mrs. Miller testified that Alan took the news of Judy's being shot very calmly. Mr. Miller, who had a conversation with Alan several hours after Judy died, testified, 'I got the impression that Alan was not a person who had just lost his wife. I got that impression.' The nurse at General Hospital, Kathleen Egan, who was present when one of the surgeons informed Alan of Judy's death, testified that Alan took the news very matter-of-factly. No emotion one way or the other. Nothing.

"Captain King said Palliko appeared calm several hours after Judy's death, and the only time he put his head down was when their eyes met.

"Mr. Goldin says that these people are the type to whom no reaction would ordinarily be expressed because of the very fact that they weren't close friends of Alan Palliko. I contend that people normally respond to tragedy the moment it strikes and they don't care where they are.

"Well, you might say to yourself, maybe Alan Palliko is not a normal person. Maybe his emotional makeup is such that he would not cry or break down in front of people whom he didn't know. Let's assume that. I still say this: even though he didn't cry, even though he didn't physically break down, wouldn't there have been *something?* Wouldn't there have been *something* in his eyes, his face, his expression, his voice, that would have communicated to other human beings that he was hurt, that he was grief-stricken? You can communicate the very deepest human emotions—love, hate, fear—with just one glance, one glance. You call on your own human experiences when you go into that jury room. You don't have to leave your own experiences here in the courtroom. You can take them back with you to that jury room.

"Mr. Goldin's basic contention is that the evidence is insufficient to prove Alan is guilty of Judy's murder. Let's see if that's true."

I started in by citing the plan Alan had told Debbi would take place the following March or April, the plan which would leave him either rich or dead, and that she'd be reading about him in the newspapers.

"Well, there was a plan in April of '68, a plan to murder Judy Palliko. If Alan were not prosecuted and convicted for Judy's murder, he would be rich, at least to the tune of $25,000. Not an insubstantial sum of money, is it, folks? Many people sweat and toil all their lifetime and don't end up with that kind of money.

"Whenever you plan to murder someone there *is* always the possibility that you yourself might end up dead, and Debbi Fox, as well as many other people, *has* been reading about Alan Palliko in the newspapers.

"Mr. Goldin says, well, if the plan was to marry a woman, insure her, and then murder her to collect the insurance proceeds, why didn't he do this to Debbi Fox?

"The prosecution is not alleging that Alan Palliko wanted to murder every woman with whom he ever came into contact. Not every woman, but the fact remains that Alan Palliko indiscriminately asked four women to marry him in less than half a year. He asked Marjorie Huebner to marry him in September of '67, Barbara Gutman in late December, 1967, Katherine Drummond in November and December of '67 and January of '68, and Judy Davis in February of '68.

"From the evidence you heard in this case, is Alan Palliko the type of individual who would fall in love *four* times within a half year with different women? True, Alan tried to make out with every good looking female who walked by, but that's not the same thing as falling in love four times within a half a year and wanting to get married. Even the average man is not going to have amorous propensities like that. But certainly not Alan Palliko.

"Now, if he wasn't in love with these four women he wanted to marry, then why did he want to marry them? Why this virtual crusade to find some woman to marry? The answer appears to be for money. Alan Palliko had such a quenchless passion for money he insured Judy before they were even married."

I reminded the jury of Alan's statement to Katherine after she turned down his proposal of marriage for the last time.

"What did Alan Palliko mean," I asked the jury, "when he told Katherine in January, 1968, just a couple of months before Judy was murdered, 'I'm going to do something *again* that I don't want to do' and that she, too, would be reading about him in the newspapers? What was Alan Palliko referring to?

"And, boy, talk about morbidity," I said, shaking my head. "That policy on Judy. Judy Palliko, twenty-two years of age, in the springtime of her life, and she has a decreasing term policy on her—the longer she lived, the less monetary value she had to Alan Palliko. Really morbid.

"Alan wasted very little time becoming the beneficiary on that pol-

icy. March 20, twenty-six days after the policy was purchased, he became the beneficiary, and one month later, Judy was dead.

"I ask you, ladies and gentlemen: who stood to profit from Judy's
death? Only one person on the face of this earth—Alan Palliko.

"Just one week before Judy was murdered, Alan told Mrs. Boudreau, 'Within two weeks, something is going to happen which you
will think is very cruel.' There is no reason to disbelieve Mrs. Boudreau. She was as close-lipped as she could possibly be when she
came up to the witness stand. That woman was in fear up there, and
you know it.

"If Palliko wasn't referring to the impending murder of Judy Palliko, what in the world was he talking about? Was he talking about
the fact that an American soldier might be killed in Vietnam within
two weeks? Or that some poor child in Biafra might die from starva-
tion within two weeks? What was Alan Palliko talking about if he
wasn't talking about the impending murder of Judy Palliko?

"Dave Goldin says Alan and Judy grooved together; they were a
team. Why would Alan murder someone who was meant for him?

"But were they meant for each other? Two weeks before Judy was
murdered, she was planning to go home to her mother."

Leaning against the jury box, I looked across the courtroom at
Alan. "Let's discuss the manner and the means, ladies and gentlemen, in which Palliko decided that Judy, his wife, should die."

Starting with the primary theory of the prosecution's case, that
Alan had someone kill Judy for him, I began by discussing several of
the incriminating circumstances and incidents leading up to the
murder: the diagram Alan drew for Mrs. Boudreau ("It appears
Palliko thought he was going to successfully remove himself from all
suspicion of guilt for his wife's murder," I told the jury); barmaid
Susan Peters admitting that Alan had been much edgier than usual
the week before the murder; and, both Peters' and bar bouncer Gary
Deaton's concession that Alan had not been into the Grand Duchess
all that week.

"Palliko was there that Saturday night, though," I noted for the
jury, "attempting, I would submit, to set up an alibi for himself.
Around 10:30 P.M. on Saturday night, Alan Palliko sent Judy home.
She didn't say to Alan, 'I think I'll go home now,' nor did Alan say to
her, 'Well, Judy, it's getting kind of late, maybe you should go now,'
or, 'Don't you think it would be a good idea if you went home now?'
No, there was no language like that. Alan was giving her instruc-

tions: 'It's time for you to go now.' That's what he told her: 'It's time for you to go now.'

"Susan Peters testified that Alan and Judy left the bar at that time. Five minutes after he returned to the bar, Alan Palliko got a very short phone call. If that phone call was from someone other than the killer, again why didn't the defense subpoena the party who called? It may have been some guy who called Alan and said, 'Alan, I've got two free tickets to a Lakers game. I thought you might want to go, Alan.' Maybe that was what the phone call was all about. But then again, maybe the phone call was from the killer.

"Perhaps the very most important thing, circumstantially, that proves the phone call was from the killer is this: the apartment manager testified that the murder scene is a well-lighted area, even at 11:30 P.M. This is a 54-unit apartment building. At 11:30 P.M. on a Saturday night, I think it is reasonable to assume that cars were pulling in and out of that carport with a certain amount of regularity. The killer couldn't very well have waited for Judy for hours—oh, he could have, but it wouldn't have been very wise for him, because he would have been detected. His presence would have been suspicious. He had to know almost exactly *when* Judy was going to arrive at the Castillian Apartments, the *type of car* she was going to be driving, and exactly *where* she was going to park that car, so he could commence his lying in wait within minutes before Judy arrived.

"You will recall that this is the first day that Judy had ever driven that yellow, *convertible* Jaguar. First day. This is very significant. You'll also recall that Palliko told Captain King that he and Judy never parked in the same place. Sometimes they'd park in carport number 17. Sometimes they'd park on Bonita Ave. Sometimes they'd park on Grismer Street, which was even closer to their apartment than the carport. It would have been very simple for Alan, in sending Judy home, to say, 'Judy, it's a new car, the top is down, it's going to be a damp night. Park in the carport, honey, rather than out in the street.'

"Almost of necessity, the killer had to be waiting for Judy, and waiting in the immediate vicinity of carport 17. If he were anywhere else in that large carport area, it would have taken him time to walk or run to reach Judy, and in that brief interlude, Judy would at least have had an opportunity to turn off the ignition or the radio or the lights. But she never had a chance to do any of those three things. She was hit the moment she arrived at carport 17.

"Now, I want you to ask yourselves this question back in the jury room: who else knew *when* Judy was going to arrive at the Castillian Apartments, exactly *where* she was going to park, and even though it was the very first day she had the Jaguar, the *type of car* she was going to be driving, except Alan Palliko? Please ask yourselves that question back in the jury room.

"Even assuming that Alan was not the killer, the killer had to receive this information from someone, and if he did not get it from Alan Palliko, from whom did he get it? Who else had knowledge of *all three* of these things except Alan Palliko?"

It was assuring to see all twelve jurors, even at this late stage of argument, still concentrating so dutifully on the many inferences to be considered that only rarely did they turn their heads when the courtroom door opened or the clerk's phone rang.

Reminding the jury of the perfect view the killer would have had of Nick Tagli's Hearthside Inn from the Castillian pool area, and Tagli's testimony that when Judy stopped in only minutes before her murder she told him Alan had sent her to assure him they would be in Monday to pay for their wedding reception, I observed:

"The bill hadn't been paid since March 1st, yet on this late evening, April 20, Judy just happens to drop by at Alan Palliko's instance. Palliko, I contend, sent Judy to Tagli's so the killer could watch her from that pool area and poise himself for her arrival at carport 17.

"Here's a very interesting point—you can accept it for whatever it's worth. Mr. Goldin argued that when Mrs. Miller told Alan that Judy had been shot and was badly hurt and in an ambulance on her way to the hospital, it was the most natural thing in the world for Alan to be calm and cool. As an ex-police officer, he had been trained to act calmly under stress.

"All right. How is it, then, ladies and gentlemen, that in the conversation before that, when Alan hears from Pete Morris that Judy had only been in an accident—which is far less serious than being shot and badly hurt and on the way to the hospital—according to Susan Peters' testimony, Alan was shocked, visibly shaken, and said, 'Oh, my God!'? Yet five minutes later when he receives the far worse news that Judy had been shot and was badly hurt, he's very calm, very collected. All he says is, 'Shot. What happened? I'll be right down.'

"Could the answer be that the news Alan got from Mrs. Miller was

not the worst news for Alan Palliko; the news he got from Pete
Morris was the worst news? If Alan Palliko had someone murder
Judy for him, when he learned from Morris that Judy had only been
in an 'accident' and he wasn't told anything else, can you imagine the
thoughts that went through Alan Palliko's mind? 'Oh, my God! What
could have happened? What could have gone wrong? Why was I only
told she was in an accident? Why wasn't I told she was shot dead?
Judy probably saw him. Oh, God, I've had it.' "

I moved on to the second of the prosecution's theories—that Alan
himself had killed Judy. Responding to Goldin's criticism that this
theory was inconsistent with the prosecution's primary theory, I
pointed out to the jury that in the most important sense my "alternative theory" was not inconsistent because both theories pointed to
Alan's guilt.

"We know that Alan Palliko is a violent man. And whoever did
this to this poor girl," I said, holding up the coroner's photographs of
Judy for as brief a moment as possible, "was a very, *very* violent
man, or violent woman."

One of the middle-aged men on the jury, turning his head away,
took in a deep breath and—I could not blame him—spied the picture
only from the corner of his eye.

"We have the testimony—only from Alan's barmaid and his
bouncer, mind you—that at the time of the murder Alan was at his
bar in Sunland. Alan probably was at his bar that Saturday night, but
this doesn't necessarily mean that he was at the bar at the time Judy
was murdered.

"Susan Peters and Gary Deaton testified that Alan left the bar for
ten or fifteen minutes with Judy. Being friends of Alan's, it would be
the simplest thing in the world for them to say ten or fifteen minutes
when it was actually forty or forty-five minutes. Then again, maybe it
was much longer than ten or fifteen minutes and they just made a
mistake, an honest mistake.

"And don't forget they never saw Alan with Judy outside the bar.
Judy could have left immediately after Alan and she walked out of
the bar, and Alan could have left immediately thereafter in his own
car, taking a different route.

"Alan told Judy to stop for gas on the way home. That took time.
Alan also sent Judy to Nick Tagli's Hearthside Inn on the way home.
That took time. Palliko could have very easily reached the Castillian
before Judy."

I was heading now toward a major weakness in my case, but one that I was well aware of. I am always concerned when defense counsel, in their own closing arguments, miss some of the more conspicuous weaknesses in the prosecution's case. Just because the defense attorney does not point out the weakness does not mean the jury will not see it. And if they do, I had better have an explanation to offer. In his closing argument, however, a prosecutor is only permitted to rebut points directly or indirectly raised by the defense in *their* argument. To set up my own straw man, then, I try to find some hook in defense counsel's argument which will permit me to discuss the issue.

One such issue in this case was that if Alan murdered Judy himself, would he have really picked his own apartment house, where he could have been easily recognized, as the locus for the murder? I thought Dave Goldin would surely have asked that question, but he did not. I felt sure, however, that at least one person on the jury would ask it back in the jury room. Although Goldin never pointed out this improbability in the prosecution's case, he had discussed the physical set-up at the Castillian Apartments' carport area, and I took that topic as my opportunity to raise this important question and answer it myself.

"Palliko knew," I told the jury, "that if he were ever accused of killing Judy himself, he could always say, 'Well, why would I kill my wife at my own apartment house? It would be stupid of me.' Knowing he could make this statement which at first blush seems persuasive, if he murdered Judy himself this might have been the *precise reason* he murdered her where he did."

The most important testimony on the second, alternative theory was, of course, that of Walter Wasson. Dave had done quite a job on the old man in his own closing argument. It required rebuttal.

"Mr. Goldin criticizes Wasson for not recalling that Palliko was in handcuffs when Wasson saw Alan on television, and for testifying he could see Palliko's whole body on TV when he really couldn't. He also criticized Wasson during the trial because Wasson could not articulately describe Alan Palliko's walk. You remember: 'The Palliko shuffle,' Mr. Goldin called it.

"Whether Wasson," I countered, "can remember now, a year later, if Palliko had handcuffs on in the film clip, and whether his whole body could be seen, is of little significance. The important thing is that when he saw Palliko on television, a silent bell rang and, in his own words, he almost fell out of that chair. And Mr. Wasson's ability or inability to describe the way Alan Palliko walked is also ir-relevant. I don't care if he took that witness stand and said that, to him, Alan Palliko's walk looks like an alligator doing the polka. It wouldn't have made any difference whatsoever. It is the impression he received which is important.

"Animals can't talk at all, yet an animal can recognize a face, a walk, or a gesture. Under Mr. Goldin's reasoning, if a man has been eating steak all his life, and you ask him how a steak tastes and he can't describe it with words, that means he has never eaten a steak. When a person sees something, whether a face, a body, or anything, an impression is left and registered in one's mind. When Wasson saw Alan Palliko on TV he said, 'That's the man.'

"Recall that Wasson saw the man walk away from the murder scene on April 20, 1968, and the TV clip of Alan was on May 2, 1968, only twelve days later. The impression that Wasson had re-ceived was still fresh in his mind. Wasson also testified he saw Palliko walk here in court several times in addition to the demonstration Alan Palliko put on for you folks, and said he's never seen a man walk like Alan Palliko. Mrs. Davis testified that once you have seen Alan walk, you can never forget it. I think you have to concede that Alan Palliko does have an unusual walk.

"I am sure that even though Palliko has a very unusual walk, somewhere there must be a man who walks quite similarly to Alan Palliko. Where the coincidence comes in is that a man who walks like Alan Palliko would just happen to be at the scene of the murder of Alan Palliko's wife and, in addition to that, acting suspiciously. And the further coincidence is that this man who walks like Alan Palliko is, according to Wasson, around the same height as Alan, has the same physique, has sloped shoulders like Alan Palliko, and has the same distinctive way of turning his head slowly.

"And remember this," I stressed, pointing to the spot where Alan had walked for the jury, "you saw Palliko demonstrate his walk here in court, and you saw Palliko on television walking. There shouldn't be any doubt in your mind that Alan Palliko made a deliberate effort here in court to take away the distinctive characteristics of his walk. Judge Young told him to walk fast, but Alan did not do so. His walk in court was a very slow walk and he held himself straight up. In the television clip, you saw that his shoulders were sloped forward, his head was forward, and he was swaying back and forth. That was not the walk you saw here in court, ladies and gentlemen.

"Ask yourself this question back in the jury room: if Palliko knew that he wasn't the man whom Wasson saw, why did he change his walk here in court? *Why?*

"Wasson testified further that the man he saw either had pure white hair or was wearing something pure white on his head. He said, however, that the man was not elderly, but appeared to be rather young, and that the man was walking briskly. If he were a young man, chances are it was not white hair extending down to his collar. Chances are it was something white the man was wearing on top of his head."

Recalling to the jury Mr. Miller's testimony that Alan Palliko frequently walked around the carport area on his way to the apartments' gymnasium with a white towel around his neck, I suggested my theory of Alan's using a towel as part of an abort plan were he to have been seen by any tenants before Judy arrived.

Addressing myself to the central issue of whether Alan physically had enough time to commit the murder and get back to the Grand Duchess to return Mrs. Miller's call when he did, I pointed out how Alan had twenty-eight to twenty-nine minutes to travel a distance that took Detective Strickland only twelve minutes, via either the freeway or city streets.

Having concluded my argument on the prosecution's alternative theory, I went on: "Alan's conduct before and on the night of the murder, I think, are alone enough to convince you beyond a reasonable doubt of his guilt. But even after the murder, Palliko continued to show his guilt by his own statements."

I first referred to Alan's rather curious conduct in asking Mr. Miller three times if he had seen anyone leaving the scene of the crime even though Miller had responded with an unequivocal "no" on each occasion. And then there were Alan's statements to Judy's mother showing his knowledge of the circumstances of the murder.

"Mr. Goldin said that Alan had received information about the murder from other sources before he spoke to Mrs. Davis. The only information he could have received was from that preliminary death certificate at the Coroner's office. From that, he could have known that Judy died from gunshot wounds and multiple wounds to the head caused by a blunt instrument. Of course, he could have also inferred, even if he were innocent, that the murder weapon was a .25 caliber gun because Detective Strickland picked up a .25 caliber gun from Alan's apartment several hours after the murder. But Alan had knowledge of other things which cannot be explained away.

"Mrs. Davis asked Alan Palliko whether Judy was pistol-whipped and Alan said, 'Yes.' Now, the police don't know what that blunt instrument was. It could have been the butt of a gun. It could have been a tire iron. It could have been anything. But when Mrs. Davis asks, 'Was my daughter pistol-whipped, Alan?' Alan answers, 'Yes.'

"Alan also told Mrs. Davis that the first shot went into Judy's breast. Where did Alan Palliko get this information about the sequence of the bullets? The police don't know the sequence. The Coroner doesn't know. But Alan Palliko knows."

In rebutting Goldin's contention that convicts Simcoe and Whalen had falsified their testimony against Alan, I zeroed in on a key word that had been used in the trial: "Perhaps the best evidence we have that Whalen and Simcoe told you people the truth, ironically came from the lips of Alan Palliko, and I will tell you why. Palliko told both of them, 'I hear they don't like snitches up at the joint.' We know he told at least Whalen that. Gary Booker, the bailiff, overheard it and testified to it. Now you ask yourself what the word *snitch* means. When you snitch on a party, does that mean you're lying about him, or does it mean you're telling the truth and the truth will be harmful to him?

"For example, Whalen and Simcoe themselves accused Alan of 'snitching' on them about the robbery. Was Alan telling the truth? Yes, Alan was telling the truth. Whalen and Simcoe pleaded guilty to that robbery. If Palliko felt that Whalen and Simcoe were lying about *his* case, why didn't Palliko say something to them like, 'I hear they don't like liars up at the joint,' or, 'Why are you trying to frame me?' —something to that effect? No. Alan Palliko says, 'I hear they don't like *snitches* up at the joint.' This is the word that Alan Palliko used."

One of the jurors, an older woman in the back row, I could see was nodding just slightly to herself. It was the only indication I had from anyone on the jury that the testimony of Simcoe and Whalen would be given any weight at all back in the jury room.

I pressed on:

"Simcoe testified that in May or June of 1968, he had a conversation with Alan in which he told Alan he heard there had been thirty-three witnesses at the Grand Jury hearing against him on the murder charges. Palliko replied he had nothing to worry about because they 'hadn't found the gun and they never would.'

"And what did Palliko tell Whalen? That Judy was murdered with a .25 caliber Spanish. Where did Palliko get this information? The firearms expert, Mr. Warner, doesn't know. He said it was either a .25 caliber Colt automatic *or* a .25 caliber Spanish imitation of a Colt. But Alan Palliko doesn't state it in the disjunctive. He says it was a .25 caliber Spanish gun. Period.

"Alan also told Whalen that he had a 'hole' to stand in, referring to a loophole, according to Whalen. Is that the remark of a man who had nothing to do with his wife's murder?

"Whalen's and Simcoe's testimony had the ring of truth to it for this simple reason: if they had wanted to frame Alan Palliko, it would have been the simplest thing in the world for them to take that witness stand and say, 'Yes, Alan Palliko confessed to me. He told me he killed his wife.' Couldn't they easily have done that, ladies and gentlemen? But Whalen testified: 'No, Alan didn't admit the killing.' That sounds like Whalen is telling the truth."

In drawing toward a close, I set my sights on ferreting out the true intention of the defense. I called to the jury's attention the fact that during the course of the trial and closing arguments, Dave Goldin had tried to put the hat of guilt on no fewer than five people other than Alan Palliko. By either direct accusation or innuendo, he had tried to lead the jury to believe not merely that his own client was innocent, but that Judy Palliko's true murderer was: first, Michael Brockington, then Nick Tagli, then Judy's former boyfriend, Felix Zimmer, then Tod Glenn, and finally, even Katherine Drummond. It was a defense of diversion, the octopus' inkbag.

"Mr. Goldin said he wasn't trying to put the hat on anyone. And I say that Goldin's objective was to put the hat on every breathing body he could find," I told the jury. "Unfortunately for Mr. Goldin, the hat only fits one person, and it fits him perfectly. He is sitting here in this courtroom. He goes by the name of Alan Palliko, aka Jerry Pace.

"A few more minutes, ladies and gentlemen of the jury, and you will get rid of me. In summary, I will say this: if Alan Palliko didn't conspire with Sandra Stockton to murder Henry Stockton, then Alan Palliko and Sandra Stockton have been the victims of the most perfect, sophisticated frame-up ever conceived. And I will also say that if they were the victims of a frame-up, Alan Palliko and Sandra

Stockton certainly gave their 101 percent cooperation to the person framing them, didn't they? They really acted out their roles in a convincing fashion. Alan Palliko and Sandra Stockton could just as well have had a sign on their backs stating in bold, glaring letters," I said, my voice reverberating throughout the courtroom: " 'We murdered Henry Stockton!'

"Of course, folks, there was no frame-up in this case by some phantom, unidentified killer. Who hated Henry Stockton enough to place a deadly revolver against his head, fire three shots into his brain, two into his chest, and then set his house on fire? Henry Stockton, a stock clerk at Sears. An easygoing, quiet man, who, even according to Sandra, would do anything anyone wanted him to do. A man who apparently led a simple uncomplicated life. A man who liked to sit in front of the TV set in his modest home and enjoy his beer. Who would hate Henry Stockton that much? Apparently no one. If hatred were not the motive, then who stood to profit from the death of Henry Stockton? Again, only two people on the face of this earth: Alan Palliko and Sandra Stockton.

"Mr. Callas and Mr. Goldin may be hoping for miracles, but I tell them that twelve reasonable men and women chosen from this community heard the evidence in this case, and they are going to base their verdict, not on a Perry Mason script, but on the cold, hard ugly facts that came from this witness stand under oath. Erle Stanley Gardner, the man who created the Perry Mason series, isn't here to help Dave Goldin or Terry Callas. There's not one tiny grain of evidence, not one microscopic speck of evidence that anyone had any reason to murder Henry Stockton except these two defendants.

"With respect to Judy's murder, can there be any reasonable doubt in any of your minds that Alan Palliko was responsible for that murder? We don't know whether Judy was murdered by Alan's hand or by Alan's hired hand. But one thing is clear: Alan Palliko's hands are bathed with Judy's blood."

Discussing the credibility of the witnesses, both prosecution and defense, I observed, "I don't believe any human being always tells the truth." But what of the probability of the various witnesses in this case telling the truth, I asked.

"Several of the prosecution witnesses, among them Katherine Drummond and Michael Brockington, are in fear of their lives at the hands of Alan Palliko. Being in fear of their lives, the very last thing they would do is take the witness stand and lie about Alan Palliko.

But the truth, ladies and gentlemen, is extremely difficult to smother and suppress. The truth has a way about it of seeping to the surface. It is the chemistry of truth. And these people had the courage to take that witness stand and testify to the truth.

"Did the witnesses who testified for Alan Palliko have any reason at all to lie and take liberties with the truth? Assume that a member of your family or a close friend were drowning in the ocean. Wouldn't you do everything in your power to try to help save that individual? Isn't Alan Palliko now being surrounded by an engulfing ocean of legal trouble? And isn't it very likely that his friends are trying to help Alan now, just as they would try to help him if he were drowning in the ocean?

"You are twelve reasonable men and women. The prosecution's case literally overflowed with circumstantial evidence against these two defendants. Based on the evidence that came from that witness stand, we've proven the guilt of these two defendants beyond all reasonable doubt."

Lowering my voice, I concluded: "I turn you over to your good common sense in evaluating the testimony and the evidence that you heard in this case. The police did their job in gathering the evidence. I did my job in presenting the evidence. Now you are the last link in the chain of justice.

"I respectfully ask that you come back into this courtroom after your deliberations and say: 'We the Jury in the above-entitled action find the defendants Alan Palliko and Sandra Stockton guilty of murder in Count No. I of the Indictment, and we find it to be murder in the first degree. And we further find Alan Palliko to be guilty of first degree murder in Count No. II of the Indictment and attempted murder in Count No. III.'"

My summation at an end, I thanked the jury for their patience and attention throughout the long and complex trial. As I walked behind the defense table back to my seat, Alan looked up at me with a rented smile and said, "You're incredible, Vince. You almost had *me* believing it."

I had concluded my final argument at 4:00 P.M., Thursday, February 13. I felt I had scraped loose every last particle of evidence, inference, and conclusion that had been accumulated over a year and a half of police investigation and months of personal preparation; I had tried to scour the prosecution's case until I simply could make it shine no brighter. Going home that night, I felt that whichever way the verdict were to now go, the People of California had had their day in court.

Young adjourned the trial until 9:00 A.M. the next morning, at which time he instructed the jury on the laws they were to follow during their deliberations. Certainly, no society can hone its system of justice to absolute perfection, but with that in mind, I must pause here to make a few observations about several of those instructions which come from the bench.

There are two principal legal concepts dealing with the defendant's guilt or innocence in a criminal trial: the presumption of innocence and the requirement that guilt must be proven beyond a reasonable doubt. With respect to the first, legal presumptions are based on the rationale of probability. Under certain situations, experience has shown that when fact A is present, the presence of fact B is so probable that fact B should be presumed to exist unless and until an adverse party disproves it—e.g., a letter correctly addressed and properly mailed is presumed to have been received in the ordinary course of mail.

When, however, we apply this underlying basis for a legal presumption to the presumption of innocence, the presumption, I contend, should fall. Statistics show it is ridiculous to presume that when the average defendant is arrested, charged with a crime, and brought to trial, he is usually innocent. But obviously, the converse presumption that a defendant is presumed to be guilty would be far worse and, indeed, intolerable. Our system, for readily apparent reasons, is infinitely superior to those in nations, mostly totalitarian, which presume an arrested person is guilty and place the burden on the accused to prove his innocence.

The solution would seem to be to simply eliminate the presumption of innocence instruction to the jury, keeping those two necessary corollaries of the presumption of innocence which do have enormous merit—first, the fact that the defendant has been arrested for and charged with the crime is no evidence of his guilt and should not be used against him; and secondly and more importantly, under our system of justice the prosecution has the burden of proving guilt. The defendant has no burden to prove his innocence.

It is one thing to say that the defendant does not have to prove his innocence, and that in the absence of affirmative proof of guilt he is entitled to a not guilty verdict. To say, however, that he is legally presumed to be innocent when he has just been brought to court in handcuffs, is nothing more than hollow rhetoric. One day a defendant is going to stand up in court and tell the judge, "Your Honor, if I am legally presumed to be innocent, why have I been arrested for this crime, why has a criminal complaint been filed against me, and why am I now here in court being tried?"

Notwithstanding that the presumption of innocence was misconceived at birth and has led a questionable legal life, ironically, this presumption gives rise to the most important doctrine in the criminal law, the commandment that a defendant can be convicted of a crime only if his guilt has been proven *beyond a reasonable doubt*.

Although legal scholars have openly confessed that the term "beyond a reasonable doubt" does not lend itself to a good definition and the attempt to define it only confuses further, one all-important principle, although damaging to the prosecution, is implicit in the term—namely, that a jury does not have to believe in a defendant's innocence in order to return a verdict of not guilty. Even their belief in his guilt, if only a moderately held one, should result in a not guilty verdict. To convict, their belief in his guilt has to be beyond a reasonable doubt.

In every federal court in this country the judge properly instructs the jury that to convict the defendant, they must conclude that his guilt has been proven beyond a reasonable doubt. But unbelievably, in the very same instruction (#11.06 of the Federal Criminal Jury Instructions), and as if he were merely stating the same thing in a different way, he tells the jurors: "You are here *to determine the guilt or innocence of the accused.*" This added instruction simply does not belong under existing law. Yet even the U.S. Supreme Court, in case after case (e.g., *Jackson v. Denno,* "There must be a new trial on guilt or innocence"), continues to loosely and erroneously define the jury's function in a criminal trial. Needless to say, far less insightful state, county, and municipal courts throughout the land make this same mistake.

While a defendant's guilt or innocence obviously is the most important *moral* issue at every criminal trial, and could not possibly be more legally relevant (since if a jury believes a defendant is innocent, the verdict has to be not guilty), the *ultimate legal* issue for the jury to determine is not the defendant's guilt or innocence. It is whether or not the prosecution has met its legal burden of proving guilt beyond a reasonable doubt. These two issues are *not* the same.

Stated another way: to say one is "guilty" is to say he committed the crime; to say one is "innocent" is to say he did not commit the crime. In American criminal jurisprudence, however, the legal term "Not Guilty" is not totally synonymous with innocence. "Not Guilty" is a legal finding by the jury that the prosecution has not met its burden of proof. A "Not Guilty" verdict based on the insufficiency of the evidence can result from one of two states of mind on the part of the jury: that they believe the defendant is innocent and did not commit the crime; or, although they do not believe he is innocent and *tend* to believe that he did commit the crime, the prosecution's case was not sufficiently strong to convince them of his guilt beyond a reasonable doubt.

As long as the terms "Not Guilty" and "Innocent" are used interchangeably in courts of law, thousands of defendants throughout the nation will continue to be tried before juries who are misinstructed on the most fundamental issue at a criminal trial.

Under present law, although this instruction is never given, the defendant is entitled to have the judge tell the jury that *innocent* and *not guilty* are not synonymous, and they do not have to believe the defendant is innocent to return a verdict of not guilty.

The jury in the Palliko-Stockton trial commenced deliberations at 10:32 A.M. Friday morning, February 14. At 4:30 P.M. they concluded for the day and were taken to the Holiday Inn for the evening. To insulate them from news on the case, they were not permitted to listen to the radio, watch TV, or read any newspapers. They resumed deliberations on Saturday morning at the hotel and continued throughout the day.

Sunday, February 16, the jury had off.

On Monday, the jury returned from the hotel to the Hall of Justice at 9:00 A.M. and began another day of deliberations. Just before 5:00 that afternoon, as I relaxed on the office cot listening to Maynard Ferguson on my portable record player, the phone rang. It was the court clerk, Ronald Johnson. The jury had buzzed three times; three buzzes meant a verdict. After calling Gail to tell her to hold dinner for a bit, I bounded up the stairway to the eighth floor. The hallway was jammed with spectators the courtroom could not hold.

At 5:45 P.M. Alan and Sandra were led in through a side entrance. Both looked confident.

Judge Young took the bench and asked: "Ladies and gentlemen of the jury, have you reached your verdicts as to all three counts?"

MR. HOLDBROOK (the foreman): "Yes, Your Honor, we have."

Bill Holdbrook handed the folded sheets of paper to the bailiff, who in turn handed them to Judge Young. Young looked at them and then passed them on to his clerk, Ronald Johnson. The courtroom was utterly still. A number of trial lawyers I know become so tense at the reading of the verdict, the most suspenseful moment at any trial, they send an associate or office clerk to hear them in their stead. Ruth Bailey, the court reporter, would say later that her hands were shaking as she listened for what she was to take down.

THE CLERK: "Superior Court of the State of California for the County of Los Angeles. The People of the State of California, Plaintiff, versus Alan Joseph Palliko and Sandra Darcy Stockton, Defendants, Case No. A-232749, Department No. 110.

"We the jury in the above-entitled action, find the defendant Alan Joseph Palliko, *guilty* of murder, a violation of Section 187 of the Penal Code, a felony, as charged in Count I of the Indictment, and find it to be murder of the first degree. This seventeenth day of February, 1969. Bill M. Holdbrook, Foreman."

A faint smile came to Alan's face. The clerk read the verdict against Sandra and it, too, was *guilty*. Nothing moved in Sandra's expression; she sat dazed. I looked over toward the jurors and nodded, conveying my appreciation for a just verdict.

Counts II and III were read. Alan was found *guilty* of Judy's murder and *guilty* of attempting to murder Katherine.

Unlike his reaction to the verdict on Henry's murder, Alan sat bolt upright at hearing the verdict on Judy's. He stared at the jurors. Incredulous, he shook his head.

Judge Young recessed the case until 9:00 A.M., February 19, for the commencement of the penalty trial. Sandra and Terry Callas left the courtroom immediately, refusing to grant interviews. As Sandra passed through the crowd, a woman spat on her. A deputy sheriff hustled the stranger away. Out in the hallway, Sandra's mother and sister Pat, their arms around each other, collapsed against a wall, sobbing. The father, Ted Bingham, struck a TV cameraman who was attempting to force an interview with the women.

My own comments to the press were brief, a couple of sentences. The verdicts, I said, had been based on the facts presented during the trial. I picked up my briefcase and left for home. The only people I wanted to be with at that moment were Gail and my children.

Alan, I saw later on the news at home, spoke to the radio, TV, and newspaper reporters in soft, measured words. He said that life without Judy was not worth living anyway. He hoped to receive the death penalty.

13

IT WAS UP to the jury to say whether Alan and Sandra should live or die. During the penalty trial the jurors were allowed to consider not only all of the circumstances surrounding the crimes, but also each defendant's background and history, and any facts in "aggravation" (presented by the prosecution, such as other crimes committed by the defendant) or "mitigation" (presented by the defense, such as extenuating circumstances). The final penalty was then left to the jury to be decided according to their own "judgment, conscience, and absolute discretion."

Judge Young ordered that everyone coming into the courtroom throughout our penalty trial be searched for weapons. The order resulted from a request by the Sheriff's Office, which is responsible for courtroom security.

The possibility of Alan Palliko's attempting suicide with a weapon brought to him in court was thought by some to be a real one. The Saturday after his conviction, a front-page interview with him in the L.A. *Herald-Examiner* appeared, in which Alan stated: "I'm innocent of both of these crimes, but I want my attorney to ask the jurors for the death penalty. I don't have a latent desire to die, but I can't think of anything more fatal than death in stages through imprisonment. Judy and I grooved together," he went on. "The impact of the jury's verdict that I am guilty was second only to Judy's death."

The idea of requesting one's own death sentence, Alan stated, had evolved from discussions he had had with fellow inmate Ronald Gibbons. A former Los Angeles deputy district attorney, Gibbons had been convicted of murdering his wife and her lover and, upon his

own plea to the jury, received a death sentence which was later commuted to life imprisonment by Superior Court Judge Kathleen
Parker. (While judges almost always follow the verdict of a jury, it is
by law within their discretion to reduce a verdict of death to life
imprisonment.)

Attempted suicide by Alan was not the only possibility in the opinion of Judge Young and the Sheriff's Office; escape was another one.
During the latter weeks of the guilt trial, some rather disreputable
looking characters with roaming eyes, friends of Alan's from the bar,
had been seen hanging around outside our courtroom, Department
110.

The woman deputy sheriff in charge of Sandra's transportation to
and from the courthouse complained of the increasing difficulty of
rousing Sandra from her jail bed each morning. The progressively
greater need for sleep was only one facet of Sandra's seeming withdrawal. With every passing day her cell was more heavily stockpiled
with candy bars and science fiction paperbacks. Except for the continued weight gain, however, Sandra's appearance did not change
after the convictions. She still came to court neatly dressed, her dyed
blond hair always carefully in place.

Alan's appearance during the penalty trial did alter, and radically.
Instead of his expensively handsome suits and ties, he wore loose
hanging sweaters. He stopped shaving. No more winks and smiles for
the young female spectators. Now he was sullen and more openly aggressive. "Just take that badge off one time," he told the bailiff, "and
we'll get down to it, you and me."

The most significant piece of evidence I intended to offer against
Sandra during the penalty trial was her admission to her former boyfriend Lonnie Rademacher of having involved herself in another
man's attempt to kill his wife—to, in her words, "just get away with
something." The admission to Lonnie Rademacher, I felt, revealed
Sandra's shockingly flip attitude about taking another human being's
life.

On the morning I intended to call Rademacher to the stand, I
spoke with him in my office. Lonnie told me of his continued fond-
ness, perhaps better described as compassion, for Sandra and his
great reluctance to testify against her. During the noon recess that
day, Lonnie skipped, leaving his car abandoned in the police parking

lot. For the week of the penalty trial he remained in hiding, not showing up at his apartment or at work.

What I was left with were the witnesses who could testify to Sandra's continued relationship with Alan long after Henry's death. My aim was to show that not only had Sandra shown no remorse for conspiring with Alan Palliko to murder her husband, but that she had maintained a close friendship with him until the very day of her arrest. I had not been allowed to present this evidence at the guilt trial for the very proper reason that showing Sandra's involvement with Alan around the time of Judy's murder could have easily led the jury to the inference that Sandra had played some part in that murder.

Castillian Apartments manager John Miller, one of the first witnesses in the penalty trial, testified to Alan's having introduced Sandra to him in early 1968 as his "fiancée." This was some fourteen months after Henry's murder. It was only two weeks later that Alan had introduced Judy as his wife to the understandably confused apartment manager. I have often wondered whether Alan during that time period might have been considering making Sandra, instead of Judy, his next insured spouse and victim. Even after Sandra had participated in the exact same plan against Henry, it is not inconceivable that Alan could have sweet-talked naive Sandra right into her own similar death.

Judy's mother gave testimony of having seen Sandra speaking animatedly with Alan at Alan's and Judy's wedding reception at Nick Tagli's Hearthside Inn on March 1, 1968, and of having overheard Sandra's comment when Judy had reached up to kiss her husband of three hours on the cheek: "Oh no, why did you have to go and do that?"

Throughout March and April, 1968, Sandra and Alan had maintained steady contact with each other by phone. I called Robert Krahl of General Telephone and Jewell Jones, a supervisor at Pacific Telephone, to the stand. They read off the dates of the calls for the jury: on March 15, 1968, a phone call was placed from Alan's apartment to the number listed to Sandra's sister Tracy (with whom Sandra was then living); on March 23, April 3, 5, 7, and 9, phone calls were placed to that same number from Alan's Burbank bar; calls were made *from* that number to Alan's Burbank bar on April 4 and 9; and on April 22, a call was made from Sandra's private number at her sister's residence to Alan's apartment. The jury also heard about the two most interesting calls, those on April 20 (from Alan's apartment to Tracy's number at 5:22 P.M., and from Alan's apartment to Sandra's private number at 5:24 P.M.), but since Sandra was never charged with Judy's murder, in my closing argument during the penalty trial I was not permitted to comment on the fact that those two conversations on April 20 took place only six hours before Judy's murder. Any inferences the jury might draw would have to be on their own.

Phillip Weatherwax, tenant at the Castillian, identified Sandra as the woman he saw coming out of Alan's apartment on the afternoon of April 22, the day after Judy's death. Mrs. Eunice Taplin, a neighbor of Judy's parents', testified to having seen Alan walk into the Mispagel-Beaver Mortuary along with two women and another man on the evening of April 23, when Judy lay in state. One of the women, Mrs. Taplin testified, was Sandra Stockton. She remembered Sandra because Sandra had stayed seated out in the foyer and had smiled so pleasantly at her when Mrs. Taplin passed by.

Lastly, Captain Warren King testified to his having found Sandra's name scattered throughout Alan's appointment book, which had been observed during the first search of Alan's apartment, and to an appointment with Sandra appearing on a sheet of Alan's personalized memo pad which had been torn off and thrown in the wastebasket. The date on the sheet, "4/28," was two days before Alan and Sandra were arrested. The other words written along the side of that sheet, "Gun Shop. Pasadena. Carbine clips, ammo. Enforcer stock," Judge Young ruled inadmissible in that they appeared highly prejudicial to Sandra while the prosecution could not state with certainty their meaning or context.

Although there was evidence of Alan's involvement in a number of scams and illicit dealings, the only crime of his I could prove and sought to introduce in the penalty trial was his swindling of $5,000 from barber Del Cook. After I spoke with the rugged open-shirted man who always seemed as if he had just been roused out of a fire in the middle of the night, I was more than a shade hesitant to put him on the stand. Cookie had a way of giving colorful but unrelated answers to the questions asked him and, as evidenced by his rather jumbled interviews with the police, his reliability was a matter for speculation.

When John St. John asked Cook about Alan's New Year's Eve party at the Biltmore, a bash that all others had agreed had been attended by no fewer than seventy people, Cookie guessed the number in attendance to be "about ten." Cookie went on in that interview to talk about the meeting at Alan's apartment to discuss the phony loan deal that would allow Cook to conceal $5,000 from his wife Gloria during their divorce proceedings. Cook dwelled on how Alan was outside throwing a ten-inch, silver handled knife over and over again into the curbside grass when Cook arrived. St. John was finally able to direct Cookie back to the subject of the phony loan, but even then Cook rambled on hopelessly.

Q. "What was the conversation about at this time?"

A. "Alan asked me in for a drink and I said, 'Gee, you got a nice place here, Alan.' And he says, 'What do you think of that couch over there?' And I said, 'That is pretty . . .' "

On and on Del Cook went while St. John and Guy muddled their way patiently through fifty-one pages of questions and answers. I was hardly looking forward to calling Cookie to the stand, but unfortunately he was the only one who could testify fully to the swindle. Alan had been careful enough to see to that.

Cook came to court in his usual skin-tight pants. His wife Gloria, who had decided not to leave Cookie, accompanied him.

My efforts to get Cook's story from him went as painfully as I had suspected.

Q. "Directing your attention to Alan Palliko, who is seated at the counsel table in the red sweater, do you know him?"

A. "Very much I do."

I had Cook tell the jury a little bit of how he had come to trust Alan and consider him a friend.

Q. "Did you tell Mr. Palliko about your marital problems?"

A. "Just about everything. He was a very nice fellow at that time. Very congenial, very helpful."

Q. "Was your wife trying to get everything that you owned?"

A. "Everything. If she could get it. She's here. Ask her. Right over there."

Laughter rolled through the courtroom as Cookie pointed over at his wife accusingly. Even Alan, relentlessly somber by this point in the trial, could not suppress a chuckle. Sitting perfectly still at the back of the courtroom, Gloria Cook, garbed totally in white—hat, dress, shoes and fur—just stared at her husband, her features frosting up in silence.

Cook went on to testify to Alan's suggestion of the false promissory note.

MR. COOK: "I was taking tranquilizers. I wanted to reconciliate with my wife. Then I called the bar, the Grand Duck Bar."

Q. "The Grand Duke Bar?"

A. "The Grand Duke Bar. I was very shook up, and Alan said, 'Listen, dry your tears. Throw some water on your face.' Believe me, I was pretty shook up. If you ever went through this before?"

Q. "I haven't, sir."

A. "I hope you don't."

Q. "I hope so, too, Mr. Cook," I smiled. "What happened next?"

Cook went on to tell how he sold his $6,400 worth of stock and, with $5,000 of it in cash, went to meet Alan in a lounge.

MR. COOK: "I usually eat down there every morning—sometimes hot cakes. I said, 'Hi,' to the girl, and she said, 'Hi, Cookie.' Alan and me, we just walked in like we owned the joint and sat at the bar and ordered Scotch and soda—no, wait, Scotch and water."

Q. "Did you give Alan the $5,000 in cash, Mr. Cook?"

A. "I took it out and he counted it right out like this below the bar, and he said, 'Beautiful.' I said, 'Well, wait a minute. Where's the notes?' He said, 'Look, baby, you're pushing me too fast.'"

Cook rose part way out of the witness chair, looking at Alan. "Am I right, Baby?"

Q. "Wait awhile, Mr. Cook. You can't talk to anyone in the courtroom except me."

THE COURT: "Mr. Cook, please try to listen to the questions counsel asks you, and answer those questions only."

MR. COOK: "I will."

Cook related for the jury the subsequent conversation at the barber shop and Alan's offer to kill Cook's wife in lieu of giving back the money. Cook testified that Alan's parting words were: "It's better that I have the $5,000 than Gloria. And don't mess with me, Cookie. Remember, you've got a daughter."

For corroboration of Cook's version of the story, I later called to the stand a friend of Cook's, Jack Holcombe, who had been in the barber shop at the time and had listened through the shop's open window to that sidewalk conversation.

Dave Goldin, in trying to clarify some of the more confusing points in Cookie's testimony, asked questions as simply as he could. Cook, not unaware of the periodic chortling in the courtroom, had the following short, rather sad exchange with Dave.

MR. COOK: "You are trying to make fun of me."

MR. GOLDIN: "I wouldn't do that, sir."

MR. COOK: "Don't."

My purpose in bringing Del Cook to court had hardly been to entertain the spectators but, indeed, to show how Alan had reached the point of offering his murderous services as if homicide were almost a lark to him, an offhand gesture for patching up friendships.

The incident between Cook and Alan revealed another, less lethal but equally calloused side of Alan Palliko as well. Del Cook, in a sense, was a comical, good-natured fellow. But in any deeper analysis he was, of course, a man to be pitied. To Alan, however, Cookie had been a kind of pet fool, a friend to keep around and engage in conversation while others were present, but to wink about when his head was turned. Taking Del Cook's last $5,000 had been about as difficult as taking a food dish away from a two-day-old puppy. I had wanted the jury to know the extent of Alan Palliko's contributions to this society.

After the testimony of Jack Holcombe, I rested the People's case.

As per Alan's request, Dave Goldin called no witnesses for the defense.

Terry Callas called only one. Tracy Bingham, Sandra's sister, testified that Sandra had been living with her and sharing the $120 apartment rent from June of 1967, seven months after Henry's murder, until the time of her arrest, the implication being that Sandra did not thirst for the fast high life after Henry's death and was loath to spend the insurance money that resulted from his murder. Tracy could not, however, testify that her sister, aside from the modest apartment, had otherwise been living a completely frugal existence. At the time of Sandra's arrest, she had been without a job, apparently not in need of work, and yet had just purchased a new Mustang.

Although capital punishment is inferentially sanctioned in three clauses of the Fifth Amendment to the United States Constitution, the strongest argument for it, I feel, is deterrence—that it may save lives of innocent people in our society. If we can accept the premise that punishment is a deterrent to unlawful conduct, it would seem to necessarily follow that the greater the punishment, the greater the deterrent. Statistics do show that the death penalty is not a deterrent when it is simply on the books but rarely, if ever, carried out (the usual situation in the United States the last fifteen years). When capital punishment is carried out, however, there is substantial evidence it does deter *some* people. Los Angeles law enforcement, for example, has many tape-recorded statements from defendants who, without even being asked, volunteered the fact that they were about to kill someone (e.g., the robbery victim), but decided not to when they thought of the gas chamber.

There is statistical evidence as well that the death penalty is a deterrent. In the state of California, for instance, between 1953 and 1963, there were nine to twelve executions per year. During that time, the rate of willful homicide remained relatively static. Between 1963 and the present, there has been only one execution, and the rate has risen 67 percent. To be sure, there are many factors which have an effect on homicide rates, but to suggest that the absence of capital punishment had nothing whatsoever to do with so dramatic a rise, is, I feel, untenable.

The moral basis for capital punishment, I believe, is that it is a form of self-defense. If no individual can be criticized for killing in self-defense, should a society be termed barbaric for attempting to defend the individuals who comprise it? Rather than being, as many people argue, a negation of life, the death penalty is a reaffirmation of the sanctity of life.

Despite all of these arguments, which I believe have merit, it may be that life imprisonment *without* the possibility of parole would be an equal deterrent and more compatible with the progressive society in which we live. But in the absence of life imprisonment without the possibility of parole, I feel we should retain the death penalty.

At any rate, in 1961, the California Supreme Court, in the case of *People v. Love,* ruled that prosecutors could argue only retribution, not deterrence, to a jury.

In the penalty trial, as in the guilt trial, the prosecution gives an opening argument which is then followed by the defense's closing argument. If, however, the prosecution chooses in the penalty trial to rebut the defense's closing argument, the defense is then allowed a surrebuttal. Under either circumstance, then, in California the defense is the last to address the jury.

This procedure of allowing the defense the final word was determined by the 1967 California Supreme Court in the case of *People v. Bandhauer.* It was a just decision. First of all, in the penalty trial, the People do not bear the burden of proof as they do in the guilt trial. More importantly, by the time the trial reaches the penalty phase the defendant is fighting for his or her *life.* I have always felt deeply about the defense's right to the last word in the penalty trial, and even before the 1967 California Supreme Court decision, I regularly waived final argument.

Closing arguments in the Palliko-Stockton penalty trial took place on Monday morning, February 24. My address to the jury, in which I asked them to return verdicts of death against both Alan and Sandra, consumed approximately one hour.

"I do not have to tell you, ladies and gentlemen of the jury," I began, "that you are facing an extremely solemn, serious decision—namely, whether these two defendants should receive life imprisonment or the death penalty. Unfortunately, you are going to have to make that decision all by yourselves. I can't offer you any assistance, defense counsel can't help you, even His Honor cannot help you. You are going to be back there all by yourselves.

"If anyone thinks I enjoy asking for the death penalty," I continued, "they have another thought coming. It is much easier for me when I am assigned to a noncapital case where my office is not seeking the death penalty. Much easier."

I told the jury that the law shows no preference for the death penalty over life imprisonment and that it would be unfair to the defendants to begin their deliberations in the jury room with a predisposition towards death.

"I would recommend that you start out neutral," I said. "Look for reasons why these two defendants should receive life imprisonment, look for reasons why they should forfeit their lives to the State, and settle upon that which you feel is the most persuasive."

I went on to discuss why I believed the evidence in this case did warrant the death penalty. The murders of Henry and Judy, I observed, were nothing less than "planned executions." Neither victim had had a chance. And could there have been a baser motive for these executions than Alan's and Sandra's—money? If this case did not call for the imposition of the death penalty, what type of case would, I asked the jury.

On the issue of aggravation, I asked: "Why did Alan Palliko have to fire five shots into the body of Henry Stockton? Three in the head, two in the chest. Were five shots necessary, ladies and gentlemen? Can you imagine the way Henry Stockton's body must have quaked and convulsed as it absorbed the full shock and impact of each bullet?"

Human beings, I said, could be reduced to targets in Alan Palliko's mind. Dartboards.

I looked directly at Alan, who without expression returned my gaze. "Why five times, Alan Palliko?" I asked.

"Henry Stockton deserved to live. He had every right in the world to live. But Alan Palliko stood next to him with a cold, loaded revolver in his hand and ordained like God himself that Henry Stockton would die."

The murder of Judy had been even more savage.

"As if two shots in the head were not enough, we had the indescribably horrible blows to the head with a blunt instrument. How any man can do that to his young, beautiful wife or have anyone else do it is almost beyond human comprehension.

"I don't think Alan Palliko realizes that most human beings pray at night that they will live to a ripe old age and die a normal, peaceful death. The thought of being shot in the head and murdered is such a horrendous thought most human beings dare not even think about it.

"People who are ninety years of age hang on desperately to life with a youthful passion. Animals fight desperately for life. Henry Stockton and Judy Palliko, if they had had it, would have given Alan Palliko the world if he would have just let them live.

"I don't think Alan Palliko realizes that Henry Stockton's and Judy Palliko's parents will die a thousand times throughout the rest of their lives each time they think of how their children were so brutally killed. Don't you think that Henry Stockton's parents are going to remember him as a baby they protected, and don't you think they are going to see the fright and horror on Henry's face when he knew he was about to be shot to death?"

Alan Palliko, I pointed out, had not had the upbringing we associate with murder and crime. He was not the product of poverty and violence; he did not come from a broken home. His life had been resplendent with opportunity.

"He is a bright man," I told the jury. "Apparently he is personable. He had a lot of friends. But somewhere in Alan Palliko's life—we hate to even think why or when—somewhere in Alan Palliko's life he decided that to kill a human being was like taking a drink of water.

What could cause a human being to reach a state where he places absolutely no value on human life other than money? This is beyond me—just beyond me. It is a terrifying thought."

I did not speak at any great length about Sandra, but enough to remind the jury that this woman had had all the time she needed to consider what she was doing. She could have called Alan, even from Twentynine Palms, to tell him that she just could not go through with it.

"Or did she call Henry and say, 'Henry, you will never speak to me again and I won't blame you. But, honey, I have been involved with a man named Alan Palliko and he's going to come by later tonight to murder you. He and I are in on it. I'm sorry. Save your life. Get out of the house. He's probably on his way over right now. Please save your life.'

"Did Sandra do that, ladies and gentlemen? No. How do we know? Because here's a photograph of Henry Stockton." I did not hold the autopsy picture up, but only pointed to it on the counsel table.

Sandra, I told the jury, had probably thought of Henry as an oaf, a clod. But oafs deserve to live too.

"She's not only equally as guilty as Alan, she is in many respects more guilty. Henry was her husband, the father of her son." Did Sandra even care, I asked, that Kyle would grow up without a father?

Only four women had ever been executed in the history of the state of California. Sandra Darcy Stockton, I felt, was as coldhearted a murderer as any of them.

I concluded with a thought I most sincerely believed: if and when the jury brought back verdicts of death against Alan and Sandra, not even the defendants, not honestly, could believe the decision was unfair.

Dave Goldin seemed to be wavering about whether or not to plead for Alan's life. In the *Herald-Examiner* interview with Alan before the penalty trial began, there had been a single quote from Goldin: "My intention now is to honor my client's request." (i.e., ask for the death penalty)

Dave appeared to be having doubts, however, which he expressed to me, as to whether an attorney was not morally bound to plead for a client's life no matter what that client's stated desires were. A day before the closing arguments in the penalty trial, Dave told Judge

Young he was thinking of bringing a knife to court and cutting Alan's flesh to symbolically demonstrate for the jury what it was to shed another man's blood, be it in the name of the State or otherwise. Young informed Dave quite flatly that he would allow no such demonstration to take place in his courtroom.

The morning of closing arguments, as we sat in chambers discussing procedure, Dave had a few pages of notes and a stack of books and articles with him, all of them written by opponents of capital punishment.

Once in the courtroom, however, as Dave sat looking terribly troubled next to his stoic, unshaven client, he announced with a heavy, burdened voice: "Waive argument, Your Honor."

Terry Callas did address the jury, briefly and effectively. "This is the most difficult moment of my professional career," he began. "It is hard to know what to say when there is so much at stake.

"My plea for Sandra's life is not based upon any specialized skill or knowledge that I may have learned in law school. We are not now dealing with a legal question. I make my plea just as another human being.

"I think I should level with you at the outset," he went on, his voice quiet, drained, "and tell you that I am and have been for some time opposed to capital punishment. You ought to know that about me."

In discussing the circumstances of the crime, Callas stated: "The most important fact in this case is that Sandra can be rehabilitated. I think that based on the evidence, the conclusion is inescapable that free of Palliko, Sandra would lead an uneventful life."

Sandra had had no prior record, Terry went on to say, no history at all of having sought out trouble. "Sandra went along with Palliko," he said, "either out of love or from some kind of Svengalian influence of his. I think that in some ways it is quite clear that her relationship to one man demolished her life."

By the time Terry drew to the end of his address his voice was breaking. "I beg you," he said. "I implore you. Don't pronounce the definitive judgment on Sandra."

When Terry sat down there were tears in his eyes.

It was obvious that he was taking the fate of his client very personally, and I was impressed. So many lawyers do not.

The jury retired to deliberate at 2:30 P.M. that afternoon. Under the charge of a Deputy Sheriff O'Carey, they were taken to their hotel for the night. At 8:30 A.M. the next morning, they returned to the Hall of Justice to resume deliberations. At 3:07 P.M. that day, February 25, a Tuesday, they had reached their verdict.

The courtroom was as crowded as it had been for the reading of the verdict at the end of the guilt trial. On both murder counts, the jury returned a verdict of death against Alan. As the decisions were read he appeared totally impassive, his hands clasped calmly in front of him. For Sandra, the jury had decided on life imprisonment. Upon hearing the verdict, Sandra broke down into sobs.

As was the right of the defense, Dave Goldin requested that the jurors be polled individually. All were asked if that had been their correct verdicts on all three counts. Bill Holdbrook, foreman of the jury, would later say how difficult it had been for many of the jurors to look straight at condemned Alan Palliko and say that simple word, "yes." The experience had defined for them the chasm between favoring the death penalty at a cocktail party debate, and returning into a courtroom with a verdict of death. Months after the trial, several would still have wakeful nights.

Her tears quickly dried, Sandra rose from her chair after the polling of the jurors, and with her chin thrown high, strutted out of court. Alan lumbered from the courtroom, massaging his wrists as if he had merely been lifting weights.

When I passed through the doorway of Department 110, my job as prosecutor in the case of People of the State of California v. Alan J. Palliko and Sandra D. Stockton was over.

On March 30, one month after the trial, a quarter pound stick of dynamite was placed in the locker of carport 17 at the Castillian Apartments, the locker that had belonged to Alan and Judy. No note was left indicating who left the dynamite, nor the reason for the act.

Two days later, April 1, Sandra appeared before Judge Young for formal sentencing. It was the same morning the L.A. *Times* carried a lengthy article about Sandra, headlined: "Diet That Made Woman Slender May Have Made Her a Killer."

Irrespective of the punishment decided upon by a jury, a probation report (containing among other things a summary of the convicted defendant's personal history) is routinely prepared for the judge's consideration in determining sentence. Ironically, a Mrs. Grace Shepherd, a member of the probation office which had prepared Sandra's probation report for Judge Young, had twenty years earlier been the leader of Sandra's Brownie troop, a time when all who knew Sandra described her as a "chubby, giggly little girl."

"I would like to state," Judge Young said at the sentencing, "that this Court feels no compassion for this defendant. Any compassion or sympathy which I might feel, and which I am confident the jury felt in this case, is to the family of the defendant."

Young pronounced the sentence of life imprisonment, and the following morning Sandra was taken to the California Institute for Women at Frontera, where the "cells" are pleasant cottages, the lawns manicured, and the wait on the tennis courts usually short—a place commonly referred to as a college campus with barbed wire around it. Under California law, life imprisonment for first degree murder carries with it the possibility of parole after only seven years. Convicted first-degree murderers in California serve, on an average, ten and one half years.

The day of Sandra's sentencing, April 1, was Alan's birthday. He was thirty-two years old. Patrons of the Grand Duke, who continued to proclaim his innocence, brought him a birthday card which they held up for him to see against the glass wall of the inmate visiting room. It read: "Happy Birthday, Crazy-Mad Killer." Alan laughed, and in the future he referred to himself by that name whenever he called his friends from jail.

Alan's professed desire for the death penalty now that Judy was gone lasted no longer than a beer-chugging fraternity man's somberness after a lost football game. April 1 was the day Alan would make his first of three escape attempts.

Informants told jailhouse security that Alan had fashioned a knife from a toothbrush and razor blade and was planning on taking an infirmary nurse as his hostage. When Alan stepped off the elevator at the infirmary, a dozen guards were standing around the hallway. Alan asked to go back to his cell. The alleged knife was never found.

April 4, Michael Brockington and Katherine Drummond were married. The only witnesses for the discreetly quiet ceremony were Franklin and Ethel Davis, with whom they had become friends during the trial.

Alan made plans for his second escape attempt in mid-April. He managed to have a contact on the outside hide a steel cutting chemi-

cal (in all likelihood, hydrofluoric acid) in the platen of Alan's typewriter that was sent out for repairs. According to a fellow inmate
who was later interviewed, however, Alan tested the chemical on
kitchen utensils and found the fumes too strong to avoid detection.
He ended up flushing the acid compound down the toilet.

By the time Alan made his third attempt, he was considered the
number one security risk among the thirty-six hundred inmates at the
Los Angeles County Jail. In this third plan he teamed with two other
inmates, one of whom was Gregory Powell, a man who had been
convicted of the execution style slaying in a farm field of Los Angeles
police officer Ian Campbell, and whose crime later became publicized
through Joseph Wambaugh's book, *The Onion Field*. On April 26,
Alan, Powell, and a third cohort used a wrench to unfasten the grid
over the one window in the County Jail's dayroom. Other inmates
helped shield their activity from guards who passed by the doorway
of the dayroom. Once again, however, the Sheriff's Office had been
tipped off to the escape plan, and a deputy sheriff, hidden in the
dayroom's air vent, watched the three convicts' every move. That
evening after the room had been cleared, security guards found a
hacksaw and file taped to the inside of the window grid. And thus
ended escape attempt number three.

Alan was formally sentenced on May 1. A.L. Wirin, distinguished
head of the ACLU in Los Angeles, filed an amicus curiae (friend of
the court) brief and orally argued to Judge Young that the death
penalty was violative of the Eighth Amendment's prohibition against
cruel and unusual punishment. Without comment, Judge Young
thanked Mr. Wirin for his argument to the court.

Alan had refused to cooperate with the probation officers; the report given Judge Young had been compiled without even the benefit
of an interview with Alan.

"I must say," Judge Young began, "that I find the defendant to be
something of an enigma. Unlike so many defendants who pass
through this court, he is certainly not an illiterate person, he is not
from a deprived background, and he is not the product of a broken
home. He is apparently a person of considerable magnetism, attractive to both men and women.

"Now, etched against this background is the enormity of the
crimes of which this defendant has been convicted. Really cruel and

deliberate destruction of two lives, two lives of very young people, who had a considerable amount to live for."

As Judge Young spoke, Alan, at age thirty-two still like an incorrigible kid in the principal's office, sat slouched, the ankles of his outstretched legs crossed, his arms folded across his chest. He wore a black sweater that day. He now had a goatee.

"I find that the verdict of the jury was not contrary to the law and the evidence," Young stated, "and therefore I decline to exercise my discretion to reduce this penalty."

Judge Young, who had never before had to pronounce a death sentence, was clearly shaken by the weight of his decision, a decision, he said, "which more probably belongs to the Creator than to man." Never looking up from his papers on the bench, he directed Alan to rise for formal sentencing and commanded the Sheriff to deliver Alan to San Quentin for execution by lethal gas. Listening, Alan did not take his eyes from the floor, and thus this severest of moments passed without either man looking at the other. When Young finished, he stepped down from the bench immediately and walked quickly back to his chambers.

At 5:00 A.M. the next morning, Alan's arms and legs shackled, four guards accompanied him and one other convicted murderer on the bus that took them to the dreary, one-hundred-year-old warehouse of a prison that sits on a projection of rock jutting into San Francisco Bay.

Two weeks after his arrival at San Quentin, Alan drew up his own petition for pro per status; he was once again requesting to be his own lawyer. The request was granted. Alan's subsequent motion for a new trial, and all appeals ultimately made by Alan and Sandra to have their convictions reversed by the appellate courts, were denied.

Jerry Cohen of the Los Angeles *Times* interviewed Alan on September 26, 1969, while Alan was on death row. Still wearing his new goatee along with a drooping Mandarin mustache, and chain-smoking cigarettes he rolled from his own pouch of tobacco, Alan spoke philosophically and with some insight about his own life. He told Cohen of how he wore hats in Los Angeles like a New Yorker and led other people to think he was associated with the syndicate because it built up his ego. He also spoke of his transformation during the early '60s from being a Kennedy supporter to becoming a member of the John Birch Society, and his subsequent disenchantment with the Society.

"Birchers are people who gain stature," he said, "by standing on someone else's back. Generally, people who are prejudiced are trying to sublimate a deficiency of their own," he admitted freely and articulately. When asked to describe his own emotional make-up, a puzzled midge of a smile came to Alan Palliko's face: "Sometimes I break up like a baby, sometimes I'm stone cold to people."

Alan broached the subject himself of his own wife's murder. "I didn't kill Judy," he repeated several times. "Would I have *really* killed her in my own carport?" he asked. "And after having provided her myself with a loaded gun?"

When Cohen asked whom he then suspected, Alan replied, "Someone trying to hurt me by killing someone close to me."

"Like who?"

The answer came low and calm. "Michael Brockington. If he hated me as much as to say the things he said about me, he was capable of it."

When the guards called an end to the visit, and as they led Alan from the dayroom, he turned back to the *Times* reporter from the doorway and said for a third time, quietly: "What I said was true. I didn't kill Judy."

When Cohen later interviewed Alan's parents, he found them still convinced of Alan's innocence. Sid Palliko related the time he had visited Alan at the County Jail and had brought along an attaché case he had found at the Grand Duke. Embossed on the case was "J. Palliko." Alan's middle name was Joseph. Alan, Mr. Palliko said, broke down when he saw the case. It had belonged to the other "J," Judy.

During the following difficult years, Kyle Stockton was raised by Henry's parents. On a day Kyle carried on about a toy his grandparents could not afford to buy him, Mrs. Stockton, trying to pass on what sense she had been able to make of the tragic past, told the child, "Your mother is exactly where she is because she wanted everything right now. So let's be satisfied with what we have."

In June of 1972, the U.S. Supreme Court ruled that the death penalty, as then being carried out by the states, was unconstitutional. They made their ruling retroactive, and Alan's sentence of death, along with the death sentences of every person on death row throughout the land, was irreversibly commuted to life imprisonment. Alan was eventually transferred from San Quentin to Soledad, where he is presently serving his time. His request for parole in 1975 was denied.

Sandra was paroled on April 29, 1976, after serving seven years in prison. She moved to Sacramento with her fourteen-year-old son, Kyle, where she took a job in a cannery. Parole officers reported she worked seven days a week in order to save money for college. At the time of this book's writing, Sandra is in her second quarter at the University of California at Santa Barbara.

Michael and Katherine are happily married and residing in Glendale, California.

A number of people who followed the Palliko-Stockton case believe that Alan had nothing to do with Judy's death. There are those who still suspect Michael Brockington, while others feel it was some hoodlum enemy of Alan's, trying to get even. Many believe it was Sandra, perhaps deeply resentful of Alan's having discarded her husbandless after he got his share of Henry's insurance, who decided to exact revenge by killing whomever Alan eventually married. For these observers of the case, Judy Palliko's murder remains a mystery.

I differ. I believe that Alan's statement to Cohen, "*I didn't kill Judy,*" is technically correct. I always did believe, and still do, that Alan engineered that killing, which was carried out by another. For me, the disturbing question that has never been answered is: who pulled the trigger? After the trial, jury foreman Bill Holdbrook informed me that six of the jury members believed Alan had been the one, while the other half of the jury believed Alan had someone else do it for him. What leaves me terribly unsettled is that if Alan did not actually commit that murder himself, then the person who did murder Judy Palliko is walking the streets today, perhaps even lounging by a pool under California's pampering sunshine. But if there is such a person, for him the warmth and relaxation must be pierced by an occasional chill, for he or she has to know there is only one crime in this country for which there is no statute of limitations—the crime of murder.

T